Constitutional Odyssey
Can Canadians Become a Sovereign People?

Third Edition

Constitutional Odyssey is a definitive account of the politics of making and changing Canada's constitution from Confederation to the present day. In this classic work, Peter H. Russell frames his analysis around two contrasting constitutional philosophies – Edmund Burke's conception of the constitution as a set of laws and practices incrementally adapting to changing needs and societal differences, and John Locke's ideal of a constitution as a single document expressing the will of a sovereign people as to how they are to be governed.

The first and second editions of *Constitutional Odyssey*, published in 1992 and 1993 respectively, were widely praised for their ability to inform public debate. This third edition brings the book up to date, with a new chapter on constitutional politics since the defeat of the Charlottetown Accord in 1993. Among the topics Russell addresses are the 1995 Quebec Referendum and its fallout, the Agreement on Internal Trade, the Social Union Framework Agreement, progress in the establishment of Aboriginal self-government, and electoral reform. Comprehensive and eminently readable, *Constitutional Odyssey* continues to be an invaluable guide to Canadian constitutional politics.

PETER H. RUSSELL is University Professor Emeritus in the Department of Political Science at the University of Toronto.

PETER H. RUSSELL

CONSTITUTIONAL ODYSSEY

Can Canadians Become a Sovereign People?

Third Edition

UNIVERSITY OF TORONTO PRESS
Toronto Buffalo London

© University of Toronto Press 2004
Toronto Buffalo London
Printed in the U.S.A.

Reprinted 2009, 2010, 2012, 2014

ISBN 978-0-8020-3936-1 (cloth)
ISBN 978-0-8020-3777-0 (paper)

∞

Printed on acid-free paper

National Library of Canada Cataloguing in Publication

Russell, Peter H.
    Constitutional odyssey : can Canadians become a sovereign people? /
Peter H. Russell. – 3rd ed.

Includes bibliographical references and index.
ISBN 978-0–8020-3936-1 (bound). – ISBN 978-0-8020-3777-0 (pbk.)

1. Canada – Constitutional history.   2. Canada – Constitutional law –
Amendments.   3. Canada – Politics and government.   I. Title.

JL65 1992 R88 2004   342.71′039   C2004-902107-9

University of Toronto Press acknowledges the financial assistance to
its publishing program of the Canada Council for the Arts and the
Ontario Arts Council.

University of Toronto Press acknowledges the financial support for
its publishing activities of the Government of Canada through the
Book Publishing Industry Development Program (BPIDP).

Contents

Preface to the Third Edition

The second edition of *Constitutional Odyssey* was written shortly after the failure of the Charlottetown Accord to win the approval of Canadians. That event, as I explained in the preface, showed that Canadians, through a national referendum, could exercise their constitutional sovereignty in a negative way, but suggested that they were far from being able to act as a sovereign people in a positive way and reach agreement on their ideal constitution. In the conclusion I expressed the hope that it would be a long time before Canadians were put to such a test again. It seems that my wish has come true!

I decided that I would only do a third edition if either of two situations occurred. One would be a sovereignist triumph in Quebec forcing yet another round – Round Six – of mega constitutional politics in which the whole future of the Canadian federation would be at issue. The other circumstance would be a decline of support for the Quebec sovereignists' project to the point where they officially abandoned it or lost power in Quebec. When Jean Charest's Liberals defeated Bernard Laundry's PQ government in April 2003, in my view the second condition had been met, and the time had come to add another chapter to *Odyssey*.

The new chapter 12 is an account of Canada's constitutional politics over the decade since the Charlottetown Accord. It falls into two distinct parts. The first part covers the constitutional crisis that came to a crescendo in the Quebec referendum of October 1995 and the judicial and legislative fallout from that event. Of course, had 31,000 Quebecers voted 'yes' rather than 'no,' I would have started work on the third edition then. Instead, I can now write a chapter whose second part describes Canada's return to constitutional normalcy, a condition in which the unity of the country and restructuring its constitution are not the dominant issues in Canadian political life, and constitutional change occurs in quiet, incremental ways. I consider this a good-news story.

Canadians became so accustomed to the mega constitutional game – the great Lockean project of democratically contracting together to adopt a Constitution – that it is difficult for them to realize that in these quieter constitutional times since the Meech Lake and Charlottetown Accord debacles the country's constitutional system has been changing and developing. But these constitutional changes and adjustments have been occurring, as they did through Canada's first century, in the evolutionary, piecemeal way that Edmund Burke thought proper for an organic constitution. The question for this generation of Canadians is whether they can revert to being the people of Burke rather than aspiring to be the people of Locke. I hope they can.

In reaching this conclusion, I must admit to having gone through a personal odyssey as I engaged as a scholar and as a participant in a generation of Constitutional politics. I began, as did so many of my contemporaries, full of optimism about renewing the Canadian Constitution in some grand, highly democratic Lockean way, and in the process ensuring the survival of our federal union. But constitution making on such a grandiose scale in a country like ours, with its deep differences of identity and national aspiration, turned out to be quite beyond us. At times the very effort at constitutional renewal did more to divide than to unite us. Still, it might be argued that, had the effort not been made, the federation would have broken up or been held together by force. The conflicting views about who we Canadians are and who we might be are still there, but the evidence is strong that the country can survive and function effectively despite these differences, so long as we don't try to overcome them by constitutional reform.

Preface to the Second Edition

The first edition of this book was completed at the end of February 1992, just as Canada's fifth round of mega constitutional politics was approaching its final phase. By then it was reasonably clear that if Canada's political leaders negotiated an agreement on constitutional change, their accord would be submitted in some kind of referendum to the Canadian people. Rather than wait for the referendum, I thought it might be useful to have an overview of Canada's constitutional odyssey available during the referendum.

This second edition of *Constitutional Odyssey* adds a new chapter on the negotiations that produced the Charlottetown Accord and on the referendum of 26 October 1992 that resulted in the rejection of that accord. It also has a new conclusion reflecting on these recent events. Other than the new chapter and the conclusion, the book is essentially the same as the first edition.

As the new conclusion explains, Canada's constitutional odyssey is not over. Nor has a clear answer been given to the question posed by the book's subtitle: Can Canadians Become a Sovereign People? The people of Canada have established that major changes in their constitution, to be legitimate, must have their direct approval. In that sense the people have established their constitutional sovereignty and exercised it in a negative way. Whether they can exercise their sovereignty in a positive way by agreeing, in all their deep diversity, on the kind of people they are remains to be seen.

In any event, it is this author's earnest wish that the people of Canada will not soon be put to this test and that, for a few years at least, nothing too serious will happen in the constitutional arena to make a third edition of this book necessary.

Preface to the First Edition

The underlying idea of this book was born twenty years ago when I was teaching a university course on the American and Canadian constitutions. I covered the Canadian material while a colleague, Walter Berns, presented the American side. We attended classes together, each listening to and commenting on the other's account of his country's constitutional experience. One day after I had been going on for some time about Canada's constitutional debate, Walter turned to me and said, 'Peter, you Canadians have not yet constituted yourselves a people.' I have been brooding about Berns's remark ever since.

As the years rolled by and Canada's constitutional debate went on and on and on, with rising levels of intensity, I had to concede that Berns was right. The debate has continued so long without resolution because Canadians have never squarely faced the question whether they share enough in common to form a single people consenting to a common constitution. The Meech Lake débâcle demonstrated that the Canadian people must be the ultimate proprietors, the sovereign of their Constitution. The point of the constitutional debate that follows is to see whether they can become a single, sovereign people.

I made that question the theme of my Presidential Address to the Canadian Political Science Association in June 1991. Ian Montagnes, editor-in-chief at the University of Toronto Press, encouraged me to expand the address into a book. I am grateful to him for this suggestion. Writing the book has got the Constitution out of my system – for a while. Is it utterly utopian to hope that it might be of some help in enabling my fellow citizens to do the same?

I wish to thank the many colleagues who have written on the Canadian Constitution before me. One worthwhile product of Canada's constitutional soap opera is a rich constitutional literature. In writing this book I have stolen from that literature, shamelessly. I hope I have not abused what I have stolen. I am indebted, more directly, to one contributor to that literature, my colleague Stefan Dupré, for his thoughtful comments on the manuscript. Passages that strike the readers as particularly foolish or perverse are probably those in which I resisted his sage advice. I would also like to acknowledge the valuable help I received from Eric Breton and Stephen Johnson, who at different stages served as research assistants on the project. I have learned much from both of them. At the University of Toronto Press, I am most thankful for Ian Montagnes's constant encouragement, which literally kept me going, and Rosemary Shipton's intelligent and expert editing.

Finally, I dedicate this book to my wife, Sue. Above all, I thank her for the unremitting love and good cheer she gave despite her own illness. My fervent hope is that both she and my country will enjoy better health in the days ahead.

CONSTITUTIONAL ODYSSEY

1   The Question of Our Time

Perhaps the most haunting lines in Canada's history were written in 1858: 'It will be observed that the basis of Confederation now proposed differs from that of the United States in several important particulars. It does not profess to be derived from the people but would be the constitution provided by the imperial parliament, thus remedying any defect.'[1] These words are from a letter signed by three Fathers of Confederation, George-Etienne Cartier, Alexander Galt, and John Ross. The letter was addressed to Sir Edward Bulwer-Lytton, the British colonial secretary. The future Dominion of Canada then consisted of a string of British colonies from the Atlantic westward: Newfoundland, Prince Edward Island, Nova Scotia, New Brunswick, the United Province of Canada – Canada East (Quebec) and Canada West (Ontario), Rupert's Land, British Columbia, and Vancouver Island. The writers hoped through their letter to interest the imperial authorities in a federal union of British North America. Cartier, Galt, and Ross could think of no better way of beginning their campaign than by distancing their constitutional proposal from the Constitution of the American federal republic and, above all, by disavowing the heretical idea that a constitution should be derived from the people.

Contrast the words of this mid-Victorian Canadian letter with those contained in a letter written on 15 January 1990: 'The constitution belongs to the *people* of Canada – the ultimate source of sovereignty in the nation.'[2] The author of these words was Clyde Wells, premier of Newfoundland, in a letter to Jack Pickersgill and Robert Stanfield, two staunch supporters of the Meech Lake Accord. Wells attacked not only the substance of the accord but also the process through which it had been reached. That process was illegitimate, he argued, because it denied the sovereignty of the Canadian people.

Between the two passages quoted lies much more than the gulf of years. The two quotations express profoundly different views of what makes a constitution and the régime based on it legitimate. For the mid-Victorian Canadian constitutionalists, legitimacy derives from the sovereign Parliament of the empire. For Clyde Wells, a modern Canadian constitutionalist, legitimacy derives from the people. Both spoke for the great mass of their contemporaries and both evoked the spirit of their times – at least so far as non-aboriginal people are concerned.

Canadians at the time of Confederation would not have appreciated this exception. For the Europeans who fashioned the Canadian Confederation, the aboriginal peoples were subjects on whom sovereignty could be imposed, not people with whom one formed a political community. The extent to which Canadians today recognize the right of aboriginal peoples to a constitution based on their consent is a measure of the ideological distance we have travelled since 1867.[3]

How and when the ideological transition from imperial to popular sovereignty took place is not easy to ascertain. Some see the insertion of a Charter of Rights in the Canadian Constitution in 1982 as the key turning point. This change, as Alan Cairns has put it, means that Canada's constitution is now regarded much more as a 'citizens' constitution' than a 'governments' constitution,'[4] though the roots of this change in the basic assumptions of Canadian constitutionalism can be traced far back in Canadian history. Notions of popular sovereignty were as integral to the Canadian nationalist spirit that worked for and welcomed Canada's independence from Great Britain as they were to the provincial rights movement that rooted the claims of provincial legislatures in the sovereignty of the people they represented. The principle of self-determination that animated Quebec nationalism after the 1960s and, more recently, the constitutional politics of aboriginal peoples are further manifestations of Canada's shift to a more populist form of constitutionalism.

My concern is not with the details of the change in Canadian constitutionalism but with the simple fact that this fundamental change has taken place. Although the process of change was evolutionary, the results are revolutionary. We Canadians, who for so long could be characterized as moderate, phlegmatic, and deferential to authority, have become constitutional democrats.[5] The idea that a constitution to be legitimate must be derived from the people – a dreadful heresy to our founding fathers – has become constitutional orthodoxy for most Canadians. Indeed, it may be the only constitutional ideal on which there is popular consensus in Canada.

We might celebrate this accord were it not for one crucial blemish when the principle is applied to the Canadian context. Not all Canadians have consented to form a single people in which a majority or some special majority have, to use John Locke's phrase, 'a right to set and conclude the rest.'[6] In this sense Canadians have not yet constituted themselves a sovereign people. So deep are their current differences on fundamental questions of political justice and collective identity that Canadians may now be incapable of acting together as a sovereign people.

That is why the popular consensus on democratic constitutionalism is not shared by some of Canada's leading politicians, especially those committed to maintaining Canadian unity. Aware of the discordant notes registered by the Canadian body politic, these leaders try to cling to the traditional, elitist style of constitutional politics. Such a style is referred to by political scientists as 'consociational democracy.'[7] This top-down form of democracy is thought to be most appropriate for a deeply divided society that can only be held together through accommodations reached by leaders who speak effectively for their respective segments of the community. If ordinary citizens become directly involved and take constitutional matters into their own hands, the argument goes, then the political community will fly apart.

Whatever can be said for the capacity of consociational democracy and its classical mechanism – the first ministers' meeting – to manage conflict, the conditions required for the success of this mode of constitutional politics are no longer present. Not only has the new creed of popular sovereignty at the level of principle replaced traditional elitist theories but, on the personal level, the political leaders in Canada today, especially at the federal level, have lost the respect of the people. The most significant finding of the Citizens' Forum of 1990–1 is that its participants 'have lost faith in both the political process and political leadership.'[8] The genie is clearly out of the bottle, and it is most unlikely that this generation of political leaders can put it back. The demand of the Canadian people to be directly involved in the making of their constitution cannot be resisted.

Thoroughgoing democrats should be cheered by this circumstance. They might well say it is about time Canadians had a genuine social contract with a constitution based squarely on the will of the people. The difficulty with this kind of democratic rhetoric is that it is deceptively simplistic. It glosses over the basic and troublesome question: 'Who are the people whose will is to count?' Those who say that Canada's constitution should be determined simply by a majority of the Canadian people must explain how those like the Québécois or the aboriginal nations came to be bound by the will of this majority. If a constitution derives its legitimacy from the consent of the people, then those who share a constitution must first agree to be a people. There is no evidence that either the Québécois or the aboriginal nations have agreed to be part of a Canadian people sharing a constitution determined by simple majority rule. By the same token, there is no evidence that the aboriginal and English minorities in Quebec have agreed to be part of a Quebec people whose constitutional destiny lies in the hands of a majority of the people in that province.

As people on other continents at other times have learned before us, the ideal of self-determination is as challenging as it is alluring. It involves reaching agreement on the 'self' that is to be constitutionally autonomous. When constitutional legitimacy comes to rest on the sovereignty of the people, the threshold question becomes just who these people are who are capable of sharing a common constitution based on their mutual consent. It is precisely this question that now confronts Canadians as they struggle to find out whether they can constitute themselves a single self-governing people. That is why the question of this book and of our time is: 'Can Canadians become a sovereign people?'

2   The Sovereignty of the People

The term 'popular sovereignty' does not describe where political power actually resides. In political communities of any scale, all the people or even a majority of the people can never be the effective political sovereign. Popular sovereignty is a theory of political obligation which holds that political authority is legitimate and ought to be accepted only if it is derived from the people. In modern times the people have replaced the gods as the highest source of political authority.

In societies where popular sovereignty is the prevailing political theory, the people can be said to be the moral sovereign if not the political, coercive, or legal sovereign.[1] The people in such societies do not actually or directly control the main levers of power. They may not themselves hold the highest legal power to change the constitution, but government institutions are thought to derive their authority from the people. In the United States, for example, a criminal case is referred to as the People v. John Doe. In Canada, in contrast, the traditional citation is the Queen v. John Doe.

In the course of history, highly elitist régimes have invoked the doctrine of popular sovereignty to justify their rule. This was surely the case in seventeenth-century England, when the parliamentary party justified resistance to Charles I by pitting popular sovereignty against the divine right of kings. The followers of Cromwell were too religiously devout to deny the sovereignty of God but they contended that God authorizes government through the people and thus sets the people above their governors. Popular sovereignty in this context, far from being the rallying cry of the great body of the English people, was a rhetorical device used by one section of the English ruling class to win popular support in its struggle against the royalists. It was, as Edmund S. Morgan has so neatly put it, 'a question of some of the few enlisting the many against the rest of the few.'[2]

Although the English monarchy was restored after the Cromwellian revolution, Charles II's claim to rule by divine right was successfully resisted by the Whigs. In their struggle to exclude Charles II's Catholic brother, James, from the throne, the Whigs revived the doctrine of the sovereignty of the people. But the Whig brand of popular sovereignty was a moderate one which viewed the ancient constitution of King, Lords, and Commons as embodying the will of the English people. When the Whigs prevailed in the Glorious Revolution of 1688, they vested legal sovereignty not in a written constitution ratified by the people but in Parliament itself, the institution constituted by the three traditional estates of the realm.

The great philosopher of the Glorious Revolution was John Locke. For Locke, government was legitimate only so long as it respected the conditions on which the people, the governed, consented to its authority. Locke's central idea found a more appropriate expression in America than in England. The pervasive political theory first of state constitution making and then of the new American republic conceived of a constitution as a compact or contract drawn up by the people setting out the terms on which they are to be governed. The core of this idea is manifest in the opening words of the American Constitution: 'We the people of the United States, in order to establish a more perfect Union ... do ordain and establish ...'

If you look behind the actual events that produced the American Constitution, it soon becomes evident there was plenty of fiction in the notion of the 'the people as a constituent power.' The conventions that drafted and ratified these state and national constitutions excluded large elements of the population. Indeed, the American people as a constituent body capable of intentional agency had to be invented by the American founding fathers. But the point is that the invention worked. It produced a coherent and popular foundation myth, a myth that gained credibility after a civil war and the democratic evolution of the country.

Crucial to this Lockean, American form of constitutionalism is the perception of the written constitution as a comprehensive statement of the basic principles of government and the rights of the people. The Constitution (and the capital C is essential) expresses the will of the founding people as to the terms on which they wish to form a political community with a common government. A statement by Louis Henkin, a contemporary American constitutionalist, succinctly captures the essence of this brand of constitutionalism: 'The social compact – the constitution – by which the people establish the institutions of government also articulates the limitations on government, notably those designed to assure respect for individual rights. That constitution, its limitations on government, and its safeguards for individual rights are law, supreme law, binding on the people and the people's representatives and superior to the laws of any parliament or the orders of any executive.'[3] The constitution as supreme law, representing the enduring will of the founding people, must be more difficult to change than ordinary legislation. Amendments to it must be by a democratic process approaching the degree of consensus required to produce the original.

The American constitutional style has been the most pervasive form of constitutionalism in the modern world. Indeed, the basic form of the American Constitution, together with its underlying political theory, is comparable in its global influence to that of Roman law many centuries ago.[4] It has been a particularly relevant and attractive model for societies making new, democratic beginnings after revolution, world war, or the withdrawal of empire. The idea of the constitution as a social covenant drawn up and ratified by the people is evident, for instance, in the founding of Australia in 1901 by British settlers just three decades after Canada's confederation. Although the Australian Constitution, like Canada's, was formally enacted by the British Parliament, it was first ratified by the Australian people through a referendum. In Australia there was never any doubt that the legitimacy of the Constitution depended on popular consent.[5]

The American constitutional model, influential though it has been, has not been without historical rivals. Indeed, at the time the United States and France were embarking on their experiments with constitutions as democratic social contracts, English constitutional theorists were unimpressed. In 1792 Arthur Young referred with contempt to the French revolutionaries' notion of a constitution 'which they use as if a constitution was a pudding to be made by a recipe.'[6] For the English, a constitution was the product of an organic development. This conception of a constitution was well expressed by Henry Bolingbroke in 1733 when he wrote: 'By constitution we mean, whenever we speak with propriety and exactness, that assemblage of laws, institutions and customs, derived from certain fixed principles of reason, directed to certain fixed objects of public good, that compose the general system, according to which the community hath agreed to be governed.'[7]

A constitution so conceived – an organic constitution – far from being a single document drawn up at a particular point in time, is the collection of laws, institutions, and political practices that have survived the test of time and are found to be useful by a people. In organic polities, as Daniel Elazar observes, 'constitution-making and constitutional change come in bits and pieces.'[8] The means of consent are implicit and informal.

The political philosopher *par excellence* of the organic constitution was the Anglo-Irish theorist and statesman Edmund Burke, who wrote a century after Locke. Burke did not share the Age of Enlightenment's optimism about the capacity of each rational individual to discern fundamental political truths. 'The individual is foolish, but the species is wise.'[9] Instead of abstract natural rights, Burke believed in the real rights and obligations which grow out of the social conventions and understandings that hold society together. For Burke, the social contract which formed the foundation of society was not between individuals here and now but from one generation to another, each handing on to the next the product of its collective wisdom. The Burkean notion of an organic constitution has little appeal to those who, unlike the English, have not enjoyed a long and relatively uninterrupted constitutional history. But it was certainly congenial to the Canadian Fathers of Confederation who, though organizing a new country, did not for a moment conceive of themselves as authoring a brand new constitution. Donald Creighton captured the spirit of their constitutionalism beautifully:

They were mid-Victorian British colonials who had grown up in a political system which they valued, and which they had not the slightest intention of trying to change by revolution. For them the favourite myths of the Enlightenment did not possess an even quaintly antiquarian interest ... They would have been sceptical about both the utility and the validity of abstract notions such as the social contract and inalienable rights of man ...

God, not government, these British Americans believed, could alone effect the regeneration of mankind. But government, within the limits of the humanly possible, must unquestionably be sovereign.[10]

The Fathers of Confederation were not particularly given to political philosophy, but if they had been asked to name a philosophical patron saint it would surely have been Edmund Burke, not John Locke.

The attitude of Canada's constitution-makers of a century ago does not resonate well with the current generation of constitutional activists. Canadians now are basically Lockean, not Burkean, in their constitutional aspirations. It would have been a miracle if Canada had been immune to the global appeal of the American model. A generation of constitutional wrangling has removed any reverence for the historic constitution. Ironically, having become one of the world's oldest constitutional democracies largely on Burkean terms, Canadians must now find out whether they are capable of re-establishing their country on the basis of a Lockean social contract.

3 Confederation

There was scarcely a whisper of popular sovereignty in Canada's Confederation movement. This was because the leading politicians in British North America at the time of Confederation were thoroughly counter-revolutionary in their political orientation. Earlier, the ideologies of both the American and French revolutions had found significant followings in Britain's northern colonies. Papineau's Patriotes in Lower Canada and Mackenzie's rebels in Upper Canada were stirred by more radical conceptions of democracy.[1] But the rebellions of the 1830s were totally crushed. By the 1860s the constitutional theories associated with the rebellions were in total eclipse. The political elites who put Confederation together were happy colonials. Their basic constitutional assumptions were those of Burke and the Whig constitutional settlement of 1689 rather than of Locke and the American Constitution.

That is not to say that Confederation was imposed on the British North Americans in a totally undemocratic matter. The imperial legislation, the British North America Act, 1867 (BNA Act), that legally created the Dominion of Canada was, in effect, Canada's fifth constitution. The three constitutions immediately preceding the BNA Act established essential elements of liberal democracy, but the BNA Act was the first in which the novel and creative elements were designed by the colonists themselves, not their imperial masters.

When New France became a British possession following the Peace of Paris, its first constitution took the form of the Royal Proclamation of October 1763 and subsequent instructions to the British governor. The Proclamation 'detached the old western territories of Canada, including the Ohio, from Canadian jurisdiction, and made them into a separate "Indian territory."[2] While the Proclamation referred vaguely to the possibility of establishing 'general assemblies' in the future, Governor Murray's instructions made it clear that, for Quebec, with a population made up almost entirely of Roman Catholic French Canadiens, a representative assembly was 'impracticable for the present.'[3] Murray would govern with the assistance of an advisory council from which Roman Catholics were excluded. Far from advising respect for the culture of the conquered people, Murray's instructions commanded him to erect Protestant schools and maintain Protestant ministers 'to the end that the Church of England may be established both in principle and practice, and that the said inhabitants may by degrees be induced to embrace the protestant religion and their children be brought up in the principles of it.'[4]

That particular objective, forced assimilation, was dropped from the second British constitution for Canada, the Quebec Act of 1774. The Quebec Act granted the French Canadians religious freedom and the use of their traditional civil law. This measure was motivated more by imperial strategy, as a means of containing the revolution building in the American colonies, than by a conversion of the British rulers to liberal principles of toleration. Nonetheless, this recognition of two basic elements of the Canadiens' 'old national rights,'[5] Catholicism and French civil law, was the foundation of a régime of cultural coexistence for the British and French in Canada. Some historians would go further and contend that the Quebec Act, by granting the liberty of non-English peoples to be themselves, established a fundamental principle for the British Commonwealth to come.[6]

But the Quebec Act did not establish representative institutions. That step was not taken until Canada received its third British-made constitution, the Constitutional Act of 1791. The Constitutional Act divided Quebec into two separate colonies: in the west, Upper Canada, the future Ontario, with an English-speaking, Loyalist majority; and in the east, Lower Canada, the future Quebec, with a French-speaking majority. The purpose of this division, the colonial secretary of the time explained, was to reduce 'dissensions and animosities' among two 'classes of men, differing in their prejudices, and perhaps in their interests.'[7] Elected legislative assemblies, based on a wider franchise than then existed in England, were established for both Upper and Lower Canada.

In acquiring representative institutions, the two Canadas were catching up to the Maritime colonies, where the dominance of British settlers had prompted the earlier establishment of British institutions. The first elected legislative body in what was to become British North America assembled in Nova Scotia in 1758. When Prince Edward Island in 1769 and New Brunswick in 1784 were carved out of Nova Scotia, they too were granted elected lower houses. But these elected legislatures were only a halfway step to representative government: executive power remained vested in a British governor advised by an executive council of his own choosing. The governors drew their advisers not from the leading politicians in the legislative assemblies but from the social upper crust, which in Lower Canada meant the urban English-speaking majority and in Upper Canada the Tory Family Compact. It was the tensions generated by this combination of quasi-aristocratic and democratic elements that gave rise to the 1837 rebellions.

The British response to the rebellions was the occasion of the fourth Canadian constitution. Again, the creative initiative in constitution making was imperial, in the person of Lord Durham. Durham, an English liberal, was appointed governor general of all British North America (except Newfoundland) and instructed to analyse the causes of the rebellions in the Canadas and to recommend measures 'conducive to the permanent establishment of an improved system of government in Her Majesty's North American possessions.'[8] Durham spent only five months in British North America, but the report that resulted from his trip was the basis of a new constitutional order for the non-Maritime colonies. Lord Durham's report contained two central recommendations: to reunite Lower and Upper Canada and to make the government of the united colony responsive in all local matters to the majority in the elected assembly. The first of Durhams's recommendations was accomplished in 1840, when the British Parliament passed the Act of Union creating the United Province of Canada with a single legislature. In the elected lower house of this legislature, the two old provinces, now Canada East and Canada West, would have equal representation regardless of their population. The long-term objective of legislative union was the assimilation of the Québécois into the culture of the emerging English-Canadian majority. 'I entertain no doubts,' Durham wrote, 'as to the national character which must be given to lower Canada; it must be that of the British Empire; that great race which must, in the lapse of no long period of time, be predominant over the whole of the North American continent.'[9] There was no place for the liberal principle of cultural diversity in this constitutional plan.

Durham's second recommendation, for a more democratic form of government responsible to the majority in the elected branch of Parliament, was achieved not through a formal constitutional text but in a manner more typical of British constitutionalism: in a change in instructions given by the imperial government to its governors in British North America. Henceforth the governor was to choose as his advisers (in effect, his cabinet) a group of politicians who could command the confidence of the elected Legislative Assembly. The change was first implemented in Nova Scotia in February 1848 when Governor Harvey invited James Uniacke, a leader of the reformers who had won the recent election, to form a one-party cabinet.[10] A month later, Lord Elgin gave effect to the same principle in the United Province of Canada when he asked Louis LaFontaine and Robert Baldwin to form a ministry following their election victory and the defeat of the previous government on a vote-of-confidence motion.

In this way the principle of responsible government, the democratic core of British parliamentary government, entered Canada's constitutional system. Under this principle the executive power of government legally is vested in the Crown or the Crown's representative, the governor general or lieutenant-governor. The political rule or constitutional convention, however, is that the Crown does not act on its own initiative but on the advice (direction) of ministers who have the support of a majority in the elected house. Constitutional conventions are difficult to comprehend for those who think of a constitution as a formal legal document, yet conventions – accepted rules governing the proper use of legal powers – have always been a crucial element in both the British and the Canadian constitutional systems.[11] Their efficacy obviously depends on a high degree of consensus and trust in the political community.

Although responsible government is the essential democratic principle in parliamentary/cabinet government, it lends itself to a highly centralized, executive-dominated form of democracy. By requiring that the executive be directed by leaders of the majority in the legislature, it fuses executive and legislative power. In the mid nineteenth century, when political parties were in their infancy and party discipline in the legislature was loose, the system's potential for centralizing power in the hands of a few party leaders was not apparent. That tendency is all too obvious to Canadian citizens today.

In practice, the United Province of Canada did not conform to the constitutional plan Lord Durham had ordained for Canada. The French Canadians made it clear they had the collective strength and will to resist assimilation. Although the Act of Union had implied a unilingual English state, bilingualism soon became a fact of parliamentary life and, in 1849, the governor general announced that French had the same status as English. Despite Durham's intentions in establishing a single legislature, Canada East and Canada West functioned as culturally distinct provinces – the one predominantly French and Catholic, the other mainly English and Protestant. The legislature, as John A. Macdonald explained, was conducted on a quasi-federal basis: 'in matters affecting Upper Canada solely, members from that section claimed and generally exercised the right of exclusive legislation, while members from Lower Canada legislated in matters affecting only their own section.'[12] The trouble with this system of double majorities is that it produced constant political instability as neither of the emerging political parties could sustain for long an overall majority.

Many forces and motives coalesced to produce Confederation. Not the least of these were the economic withdrawal of one empire, the British, and the military threat of another, the American. Powerful economic incentives such as western expansion, the removal of customs barriers, and a broader basis for raising capital also played their part. But aside from these geopolitical and economic factors, the proximate cause of Confederation, the source of political energy that moved politicians to be constitutionally restless and creative, was the utter frustration of the leading Canadian politicians with the union system of government. In this sense, Confederation was first and foremost a political, not an economic project.

By the early 1860s Canadian politics had reached a point of deadlock between two sectional alliances: the alliance of John A. Macdonald's Conservatives and George-Etienne Cartier's *Bleus*, with a clear majority in Canada East, was almost evenly matched by the combination of George Brown's Reformers, a growing force in Canada West, and Antoine Dorion's anticlerical *Rouges* in Canada East. English Canadians who had readily accepted equality for the two sections of Canada at the beginning of the union period, when Canada East was considerably larger than Canada West, began to embrace a different principle of political justice once the population ratios were reversed. When Canada West's population came to surpass Canada East's in the 1850s, Brown's cause of 'rep by pop' (representation by population) became increasingly popular with English Canadians and increasingly threatening to French Canadians, who, though still a majority in the eastern section of the province, were now just a third of the Canadian population. Anyone who contemplates a binational, double majority system as the solution to Canada's present discontents should consider the frustrations and animosities generated by such a scheme during the union period.

Much ink has been spilled on whether Confederation was a compact. The compact theory, as we shall see, developed after Confederation.[13] Provincial premiers would base their claim that the Constitution could not be changed without their consent on the argument that Confederation was a contract or treaty between the founding provinces. Defenders of Quebec's right to a constitutional veto would argue that Confederation was based on a compact between the English and the French, Canada's 'two founding peoples.' Historians have had no difficulty in showing that, in a strict legal sense, Confederation could not have been a contract because, in 1867, neither the original provinces nor their people had sovereign legal power. That power rested entirely with the imperial Parliament. But this debunking of the compact theory tends to miss the point that Confederation was based on a political agreement – a deal – first between English and French political elites in the Canadas and then between those Canadians and their Maritime counterparts.

The first stage of this deal occurred in June 1864 when George Brown and his Upper Canadian Clear Grits agreed to participate in a coalition government with their bitter opponents, John A. Macdonald, George-Etienne Cartier, and their Liberal-Conservative followers.[14] Since March 1864 Brown had chaired a parliamentary committee examining various approaches to constitutional reform. This committee, not unlike the Special Joint Committee of the Senate and the House of Commons on a Renewed Canada established in the Canadian Parliament in September 1991,[15] had at best lukewarm support from the various parties. Macdonald, Cartier, and Galt, as well as some of the Reform leaders, voted against its establishment. Nonetheless, the committee completed its work and, on 14 June 1864, reported that a federal system (for the two Canadas or for all of British North America) was strongly favoured as the solution to Canada's constitutional impasse. A few hours later the Macdonald-Taché coalition was defeated on a vote of confidence. Instead of forcing a dissolution of Parliament and yet another election, Brown, together with some other key Upper Canadian Reformers – to the total amazement of the political pundits of the day – agreed to join Macdonald and Cartier in a Great Coalition solely for the purpose of achieving a constitutional solution along the lines recommended by Brown's committee.

The Great Coalition represented something much more significant than a temporary agreement to set aside partisan differences. At its core was a recognition that if English Canadians and French Canadians were to continue to share a single state, the English majority could control the general or common government so long as the French were a majority in a province with exclusive jurisdiction over those matters essential to their distinct culture. This constitutional agreement was indeed a compromise. For many English Canadians (certainly for John A. Macdonald), federalism was an American abomination, a clear second choice to a unitary state. Not many English Canadians were committed to the long-term survival of French Canadians as a distinct collectivity. On the other side, many French Canadians, including the *rouge* leaders, saw the proposed federation as a sell-out, the latest in a long line of attempts to bring about the 'annihilation of the French race in Canada.'[16] Nonetheless, acceptance of a federal solution was the only possible basis on which leaders from the two sections of Canada could work together on a constitutional accord.

Brown's committee left open the question whether a federation of the two Canadas or of British North America as a whole should be the priority. Brown himself was so anxious to obtain justice for Upper Canada that he preferred the smaller project, since it would be easier to attain. But Macdonald and the Conservatives in the coalition had their eyes set on the larger vision and insisted that it be immediately pursued. An opportunity to do just that was at hand – a forthcoming conference of Maritime leaders to discuss Maritime union. And so the stage was set for the second part of the Confederation deal when Lord Monck, the Canadian governor general, on 30 June 1864 wrote to the lieutenant-governors or administrators of the Maritime provinces asking permission for a delegation from Canada to attend the conference on Maritime union.

Constitutional politics in the Maritimes had been moving in advance of events in Canada. On 28 March 1864 the Legislative Assembly of Nova Scotia adopted Charles Tupper's motion to appoint up to five delegates to meet with representatives of New Brunswick and Prince Edward Island 'for the purpose of arranging a preliminary plan for the union of the three provinces under one government and legislature.'[17] In April, similar motions were passed by the New Brunswick and Prince Edward Island assemblies. The idea of holding a conference on Maritime union did not arise from a ground swell of public opinion. As Creighton summarized the situation, 'It had been strongly resisted in one province, and accepted without any enthusiasm and with a good deal of sceptical indifference in the other two.'[18] Its most enthusiastic supporters were a few business-oriented politicians, who thought it would improve the prospects of an intercolonial rail link, and some imperial officials, who hoped it might be the first step to a larger union of the North American colonies.

Confederation would probably not have occurred without the pushing and prodding of the British Colonial Office and its field officers, the colonial governors. At this stage in the evolution of the British Empire, imperial policy-makers had come to the sensible conclusion that Britain's interests in the North American hemisphere could be more efficiently secured if its scattered colonies were brought together in a more self-reliant political union. Even though the imperial government possessed a full and uncontested legal sovereignty over the colonies, it was no longer willing to use this power in a coercive manner. The Duke of Newcastle, colonial secretary during these critical years, articulated the constitutional convention of the day: 'The initiative in all important internal changes in the colonies must lie with the colonists themselves.'[19] The colonial governors could encourage and throw the formidable weight of their office behind politicians whose ideas were in line with imperial policy; they could manipulate, but they would not dictate. Still, without the coaching, prodding, and fixing of imperial officials, Confederation would probably not have occurred. In the constitutional politics of our own time, for better or for worse, there is really no legitimate counterpart of this imperial steering force.

Through the summer of 1864 the eight members of the Canadian coalition cabinet hammered out a plan for a federal union of British North America. This was the plan they would present at the conference on Maritime union, scheduled for Charlottetown in September. As it turned out, this plan contained the basic elements of the constitution of the new Canada that would come into existence three years hence.

In designing the constitution for a new federation, the Canadian ministers were not starting from scratch. Schemes for uniting the central and Atlantic colonies had been floating around for years. Cartier and Galt, two of the authors of the 1858 letter quoted in chapter 1, were in the coalition cabinet. Not surprisingly, the plan worked out by the cabinet bore a close resemblance to the proposals set out in the letter.

While the politicians were debating and drafting behind the closed doors of the cabinet room, the numerous and lively newspapers of the day carried on a spirited constitutional debate.[20]

Among newspapers generally supportive of federation, the fundamental question concerned the division of powers. Today's Canadians will say, Was it not always so? The politicians then, like those of today, were not above using newspaper opinion to bolster their position in constitutional bargaining. Thus, we find George Brown's *Globe* insisting that in the federal system being planned, 'the local governments shall be delegated governments and ... the "sovereign" power shall be vested in the general or federal government.'[21] On the other hand, *La Minerve* was typical of French-Canadian *bleu* papers supporting Cartier and Taché in claiming that under the new federal arrangements, 'Il [le Bas-Canada] aura son gouvernement particulier dont l'autorité s'étendra à tous les objets qui suivent le cours ordinaire des affaires, intéressant de la vie, la liberté et la prosperité des citoyens ... il sera maître chez lui en tout ce qui regarde son économie sociale, civile et religieuse.'[22]

At this crucial stage in constitution making, the coalition cabinet members were not prepared to disclose how they were balancing these conflicting outlooks on the structure of the new federation. They did not want to risk a public row over the details of their constitutional plan. Elite accommodation, the mechanism of consociational democracy, was the order of the day.

At the public level, an attempt was made to forge stronger social links between Canadians and Maritimers. At the very time that the coalition cabinet was hammering out its proposals in the Quebec cabinet room, a delegation of about a hundred Canadians – politicians, journalists, and interested citizens – was travelling through New Brunswick and Nova Scotia. With D'Arcy McGee as their chief troubadour, the Canadians served as Confederation missionaries, mixing with Maritimers at scores of picnics, dinners, and oratorical concerts. They did not debate the constitutional details of the Confederation scheme but endeavoured to kindle Maritimers' interest in becoming part of a larger political community. In this, they clearly had some success. When the *Queen Victoria* sailed into Charlottetown's harbour on 1 September 1864 with eight members of the Canadian Coalition cabinet on board, Maritime interest in the approaching constitutional conference was beginning to match Canada's.

As an instrument for constitution making, the Charlottetown Conference was somewhere between a first ministers' meeting and a constituent assembly of the kind proposed by populist critics in the post-Meech era. This was not a conference of ordinary citizens. All the delegates were politicians – indeed, most were experienced politicians. Included in their ranks were the first ministers or leaders of the largest party and, with the one exception of the Lower Canadian *Rouges*, 'the principal leaders on both sides of politics.'[23] That indeed was a key to success: co-opting political opponents into the negotiating process reduced the political vulnerability of the constitutional proposals that emerged from the conference.

At this stage in their negotiations, the twenty-three delegates (five each from New Brunswick, Nova Scotia, and Prince Edward Island, plus the eight Canadians) did not expose their deliberations to public scrutiny. For five days they met behind the closed doors of Prince Edward Island's Legislative Council chamber. From the outset the Canadians dominated the conference. Brown, Cartier, Macdonald, and the other coalition ministers laid out their plan for a federal union during the first four days. The plan had three basic elements: first, a division of legislative powers that reversed the American system, with the residual power (those powers not explicitly mentioned) assigned to the general (central) legislature; second, a two-chamber federal parliament, with an elected lower house based on rep by pop and an appointed upper house based on sectional (regional) equality, where Canada's two sections and the Maritimes each counted as a section; and, third, a central government that would take over the debts and some of the assets of the provinces.

By the fifth and final day of the Charlottetown Conference it was clear that the second part of the Confederation deal was nearly consummated. While the Maritimers had not accepted all the details of the Canadians' scheme, they did agree to set aside the Maritime union project and to make a federal union of British North America their constitutional priority. On 10 September 1864, three days after the close of the conference, the delegates assembled again in Halifax, where they decided to hold another conference in October at Quebec. At this next meeting they would focus

on the confederation of British North America, and invite a delegation from Newfoundland.

The Quebec Conference was structured along the same lines as
the meeting at Charlottetown. Again the delegations included both
government and opposition leaders. An exception was Newfoundland, whose two delegates, F.B.T. Carter and Ambrose Shea, were
not government members – a fact that did not help the prospects
of confederation in Newfoundland. The delegations varied in size:
Nova Scotia had five members, New Brunswick and Prince Edward
Island each had seven, and the Canadians were now represented
by all twelve members of the coalition cabinet. Each delegation
had a vote, except for Canada, which had two. So, in principle, the
Atlantic colonies could outvote the Canadians two to one. The
thirty-three politicians squeezed into the reading room of Quebec's
Legislative Council, where once again the entire discussion took
place behind closed doors.

In that stuffy chamber in Quebec City over a two-week period in
October 1864, details of the new Canadian federation's Constitution were worked out in the form of seventy-two resolutions. The
Quebec Resolutions cover nearly all of what was to be contained
in the BNA Act. Little was added or changed in the subsequent
negotiations and enactment in London.

Most of the constitutional debate at Quebec – and indeed in
Canada ever since – concerned the federal aspects of the Constitution. Here is where the British North Americans had to be creative.
They were departing from Britain's unitary system and, with the
United States in the throes of civil war, the only federal system
they knew, the American, seemed thoroughly flawed. Their earlier
decision to give the residual power to the central rather the local
legislatures aimed at reversing what many regarded as the most
dangerously decentralizing feature of the American Constitution.
At Quebec they now spelled out in detailed lists the 'exclusive'
legislative powers of both the provinces and the new Canadian
Parliament. This may well have muddied the waters, for even
though the list of federal legislative powers was simply to be illus-
trative of the federal Parliaments's power 'to make Laws for the
Peace, Order, and good Government of Canada, in relation to all
Matters not coming within the Classes of Subjects ... assigned

exclusively to the Legislatures of the Provinces,' the listed powers would come under judicial interpretation to overshadow the general power. Among the explicit federal powers were many of what were then considered the main functions of government: defence, criminal law, trade and commerce, banking, currency, shipping, and interprovincial transportation. But the legislative powers assigned exclusively to the provinces were by no means negligible. They included 'Property and Civil Rights in the Province,' a phrase meant to cover the components of Quebec's civil law (most of the private, commercial, and family law), as well as education, hospitals, and other social welfare activities. The provinces were also given ownership of their lands and natural resources. Two areas, agriculture and immigration, were designated as concurrent fields of legislation, with federal law prevailing in the event of a conflict.

Other features of the structure gave the new federal government a paramount role. Under the fiscal arrangements, the federal government would have access to all modes of taxation while the provinces were confined to 'direct taxation,' licence fees, and royalties. The provinces could not levy customs and excise duties, which at the time constituted 83 per cent of the colonies' revenues.[24] The constitution-makers never conceived of direct taxes on personal and corporate income becoming the milch cow of public finance. The fiscal dependency of the provinces was underlined by building in a complex set of federal subsidies 'in full settlement of all future demands on Canada' – words that should make the Fathers of Confederation blush a little in their graves.

The judicial system was also federally dominated. The key courts for the new federation would be the existing superior, district, and county courts of the provinces, but the judges of these courts would be appointed, paid, and subject to removal by the federal government and Parliament. As for a supreme court, the colonial politicians were happy to carry on with the highest court in the empire, the Judicial Committee of the Privy Council, as Canada's final court of appeal, but if and when a general court of appeal was established for Canada, it would be created by the federal Parliament.

Considerably more contentious was the importation of an element of imperial structure into the federal plan. Just as the British government appointed the Canadian governor general, the federal government would appoint the provincial lieutenant-governors. The lieutenant-governor (in parallel with the governor general's power over federal legislation) could reserve legislation passed by provincial legislatures for consideration by the federal government. Further, just as the British government retained the power to disallow (veto) legislation passed by the federal Parliament, the federal government could disallow provincial legislation. The federal powers of reservation and disallowance were surely the sharpest deviation from the federal principle of government. Their inclusion in the Constitution is a clear indication that many of the constitutional architects, and none more than John A. Macdonald, preferred unitary to federal government.

The point of federal structure that proved most troublesome and took the most time to resolve was the federal Senate. Prince Edward Island and the United Province of Canada had recently shifted from the British tradition of an appointed upper house to an elected second chamber. Some delegates now pressed for a Senate that was directly elected or, as the American Senate then was, elected by the provincial legislatures. The balance of power within all the delegations lay with those who favoured the British parliamentary structure, and the Senate provided for in the Quebec Resolutions was a body appointed for life by the federal government, with full legislative powers except for the introduction of money bills. Even more contentious was the distribution of Senate seats among the provinces. With Newfoundland at the table, the Atlantic delegates now argued that their four provinces should have thirty-two senators – six more than Ontario's and Quebec's twenty-four. In the end, the principle of sectional equality was maintained by a resolution giving twenty-four each to Ontario, Quebec, and the three Maritime provinces (ten each for New Brunswick and Nova Scotia, and four for Prince Edward Island), with a vague promise of 'additional representatives' for Newfoundland.[25] The need for Senate reform was built into the very foundations of Confederation.

While the Constitution drafted at Quebec covered the new federal system in detail, it was relatively silent on other matters that have become of great importance to Canadian constitutionalists. The Fathers of Confederation expressed absolutely no interest in a bill of abstract natural rights. They were prepared, however, to afford constitutional protection to rights or interests that experience had shown were necessary for the peaceable coexistence of two distinct cultural communities. First, the English were assured of the right to use their language in the legislative and judicial institutions of Quebec, where they would be a minority, and the French were given a reciprocal right to use their language in the federal legislature and courts.[26] Second, the denominational schools of the Protestant minority in Quebec and the Catholic minority in Ontario would continue to function on the basis already provided for in law.[27] These two provisions for minority rights were not the only manifestations of cultural dualism in the new Constitution. Another dimension of dualism was the differential treatment of Quebec. Quebec, with its distinctive civil law, was exempt from a clause that envisaged the common law provinces eventually permitting the federal Parliament to take over their jurisdiction over property and civil rights.[28] Special provisions also governed the qualifications of Quebec judges and the appointment of Quebec senators.[29] Quebec, however, was not the only province to have differential treatment. New Brunswick received a special subsidy over and beyond those provided for the other provinces.[30] The Fathers of Confederation were not strict believers in the principle of provincial equality.

The constitution drafters saw no need to spell out the vital democratic principle that government be directed by ministers who have the confidence of the elected branch of the legislature. Formally, all executive power in both levels of government would 'be vested in the Queen' – a system that has persisted to the present day.[31] The principle of responsible government would continue to depend on unwritten constitutional convention. The only hint of responsible government in the final constitutional text is the reference in the preamble to the BNA Act to a 'Constitution similar in Principle to that of the United Kingdom.'[32]

Aside from some minor changes which each level of government could make on its own, the new Constitution was totally silent on the question of amendment. This void was to be expected. As we saw in the opening paragraph of this book, the Fathers of Confederation assumed throughout that Canada's Constitution would take the form of an imperial statute and, as such, would be formally amended by the British Parliament. Philosophically, this arrangement did not trouble them, nor did they see it as posing any practical problems. Canada's founding fathers suffered even more than the usual hubris that afflicts constitution-makers. As John A. Macdonald was later to explain to Canada's Legislative Assembly, the constitutional drafting was so thorough and detailed that 'we have avoided all conflict of jurisdiction and authority.'[33] Again, posthumous blushes are in order.

With the signing of the Quebec Resolutions on 27 October 1864, substantive constitution making was nearly complete. There were still, however, important political and legal steps to be taken before the Constitution could be put into effect. The seventieth resolution stated that 'the sanction of the imperial and local parliaments shall be sought for the Union of the Provinces on the principles adopted by the Conference.'[34] Enactment of the Constitution by the imperial Parliament was the essential, final legal step. Approval by the colonial legislatures was a political, not a legal imperative. Still, for politicians living under the constraints of responsible government, it was important to secure legislative support for their constitutional plan.

For some commentators of the day, approval by the legislature was not a strong enough measure of popular support. While there were no calls for a referendum or a directly elected constituent assembly, a number of newspapers in Canada West and New Brunswick insisted that sweeping constitutional changes should not be made until they had been tested in a general election.[35] The leading politicians in Canada, including Reform leader George Brown, brushed these demands aside: 'A general election on such an issue, they argued, would be nothing more or less than a plebiscite; and a plebiscite was a dreadful republican heresy, French or American in origin, which would violate all the principles of parliamentary government, without the slightest beneficial result.'[36]

The seventy-two resolutions were debated in both houses of the Canadian legislature. The debate extended over a period of six weeks, from early February to mid March 1865. It was, by any standard, a brilliant debate – by far the best record of the hopes, dreams, and fears of those who supported and those who opposed Confederation. (It is a measure of Canadians' lack of interest in their constitutional roots that the only published edition of these debates has been out of print for many years.)[37] In the end, the supporters of Confederation carried the day, but only after withstanding searing criticism of flaws and inconsistencies in the constitutional plan, especially from the *Rouges* who, as French Canadians, viewed support of the scheme as amounting to treason. The Quebec Resolutions (like the Meech Lake Accord many years later) was a carefully negotiated package deal, so no amendments were allowed. The overall majority in favour of the resolutions was 91 to 33,[38] but support was much stronger among members from Canada West, who favoured Confederation 56 to 6, as compared with members from Canada East, who voted 37 to 25 in favour. Among French-Canadian members the vote was even closer, with 27 for and 21 opposed – a clear majority, but hardly a ringing endorsement from the French component of the political elite.

New Brunswick was the only colony in which Confederation was submitted to the people in an election. Indeed, New Brunswickers went to the polls twice to decide contests between confederates and anti-confederates. In each case it was New Brunswick's mercurial lieutenant-governor, Arthur Gordon, not the politicians, who forced the appeal to the people. Gordon did not like the confederation plan because it did not go far enough in giving absolute paramountcy to the federal government. He threatened to dismiss the pro-Confederation administration headed by Samuel Tilley and appoint other ministers, unless Tilley agreed to hold an election before submitting the Quebec Resolutions to the legislature. Tilley agreed to a dissolution. In the ensuing election, which was conducted at the very time the Canadian legislature was debating Confederation, Tilley and his confederate colleagues were defeated, winning only eleven of forty-one seats. Just over a year later, Gordon, now under strict instructions from the Colonial Office to have Confederation submitted to the legislature, forced the resignation of anti-confederate ministers and dissolved the legislature. This time, the case for a stronger British North American union was bolstered by the massing of Fenians along New Brunswick's border, and the confederates triumphed, taking all but eight of the forty-one seats. Even so, the Quebec Resolutions, although approved by New Brunswick's appointed Legislative Council, were never submitted to its elected assembly.

While Confederation was limping to victory in New Brunswick, it was being pushed off the political agenda in the two island colonies, Prince Edward Island and Newfoundland. On the last day of March 1865 Prince Edward Island's Legislative Assembly, by a vote of 23 to 5, passed a motion rejecting the Quebec Resolutions. The motion had been moved by the premier, J.C. Pope, who had not attended the Quebec Conference.[39] Earlier in that same month, Newfoundland's Legislative Assembly adopted Premier Hugh Hoyles's motion to postpone a decision on Confederation until after the next general election. Although many of the pro-confederation politicians were returned in the election held later in the year, they were considerably outnumbered by those who were opposed or doubtful.[40] Despite considerable pressure from the Colonial Office and the St John's newspapers, Newfoundland's coalition government was not prepared to proceed with Confederation.

In Newfoundland and Prince Edward Island, the politics of Confederation were worked out in a relatively democratic fashion – albeit with a negative outcome. This was not so in Nova Scotia, where opposition to Confederation was, if anything, more intense and articulate than in either of the island colonies. Opposition in Nova Scotia was not to the general idea of a British North American union. Indeed, for that idea, with particular emphasis on the *British* nature of such a union, there was considerable support. Criticism focused on the Quebec Resolutions and especially on the alleged weaknesses of any system of federal government.[41] The anti-confederates found an eminent spokesman in Joseph Howe, a former premier and major force in Nova Scotian politics for over thirty years, who at the time of Confederation was serving as an imperial fisheries officer. Criticism of the Quebec Resolutions dominated a lengthy legislative debate in the Nova Scotia legislature in the early spring of 1865. But the premier, Charles Tupper, was able to avoid a direct test of the Confederation scheme by seeking approval only for Maritime union. A year later, when the

Confederation issue was forced by the opposition, with imperial connivance, he managed to corral enough support to win approval not for the Quebec Resolutions but for sending delegates 'to arrange with the imperial government a scheme of union which will effectually ensure just provision for the rights and interests of this Province.'[42]

The Quebec Resolutions were never approved by the Nova Scotia legislature. Indeed, the first time Nova Scotians had an opportunity to give a popular verdict on Confederation they left no doubt about where they stood. In September 1867 in the first Canadian general election, the anti-confederates took eighteen out of nineteen Nova Scotia seats and, in the provincial election, thirty-six out of thirty-eight seats in the Nova Scotia assembly. By then, however, Confederation was a fait accompli.

The implication of Tupper's motion that a new basis for British North American union could be negotiated from scratch had no basis in reality. Macdonald, Cartier, and the other members of the Canadian coalition had no intention of touching their delicate constitutional compromise. If there was any suggestion that the Quebec Resolutions were open to significant amendment, French Canada, in Creighton's words, 'would undoubtedly rise in violent protest.'[43] At the same time, the Canadian politicians did not dare admit publicly that the Quebec scheme was a sealed compact for fear of undermining the cause of Confederation in the Maritimes, which in both Nova Scotia and New Brunswick depended on the credibility of negotiating a different basis for union. The lack of consensus within the Confederation movement was therefore papered over by the political elites.

In December 1866 sixteen of these leaders (six from the Canadas, five each from New Brunswick and Nova Scotia) met for the third Confederation conference in a London hotel room close by the Westminster Parliament. The object of this meeting was not to renegotiate the Quebec Resolutions but to consider some minor modifications and tidying up of loose ends. The only change in the division of powers was to give the federal Parliament, rather than the provinces, jurisdiction over 'Sea Coast and Inland Fisheries.' The Maritime provinces gained a modest increase in their per capita subsidies. Religious minorities in all the provinces were given the right to appeal to the federal government against provincial laws affecting their denominational school rights. A final push by Ontario reformers for an elected Senate was of no avail. The only change made in the structure of the federal upper house was to provide for the appointment of extra senators to break a deadlock between the two houses – a constitutional provision that most Canadians did not realize existed until it was used for the first time in 1990.[44]

With the conclusion of the London conference, the constitution was entirely in imperial hands. Only one further significant change was made – the formal name of the new country. The Fathers of Confederation had favoured the title Kingdom of Canada, but left the final choice to Queen Victoria. It was the Americans who effectively vetoed the monarchical title of kingdom. In their ignorance of the principles of constitutional monarchy they objected to the founding of anything so blatantly non-republican on their border. The Queen then chose the British Americans' second choice: Dominion of Canada. Although this title held out the expansive promise of the Seventy-second Psalm's 'He shall have dominion also from sea to sea,' it struck the British prime minister, Lord Derby, as 'rather absurd.'[45]

In February 1867 the Canadian Constitution, in the form of the British North America Act, was introduced in the House of Lords by the colonial secretary, Lord Carnarvon. The attention of British politicians at the time was fastened on a major development in Britain's constitutional politics, the Second Reform Bill. There was a desultory debate as a handful of Canadian politicians watched the BNA Act go through the two Houses of Parliament. The most vigorous attack came from the few parliamentarians moved by Joseph Howe's petition (supposedly bearing thirty thousand signatures) to postpone further action on the Canadian Constitution until it had been submitted to the people of Nova Scotia in the approaching general election. On 8 March 1867 the BNA Act passed third reading in the House of Commons. It received royal assent on 29 March and was proclaimed in effect on 1 July 1867.

The Dominion of Canada was born, but the constitutional process that brought it into existence provided a thin and uncertain foundation for the birth of a people. True, elected politicians played the leading role in putting the Constitution together, but they were elected on a restricted franchise that excluded unpropertied males and all women.[46] Further, the dominant members, both English and French, showed not the slightest intention of submitting their constitutional handiwork to the people. At the elite level, the process of Confederation produced a wide-based and practical, though not philosophical accord; at the popular level, however, it did not produce a political community with a clear sense of itself. In the language of political science, Canada in 1867 'must be viewed essentially as a political unit that had become amalgamated without necessarily achieving integration.'[47]

For the aboriginal peoples affected by Confederation, the new Constitution was entirely an imperial imposition. There was no thought among the constitution-makers of consulting with the native peoples living on the territory encompassed by the BNA Act, nor did any of the legislative bodies that dealt with the Constitution represent these peoples. The Royal Proclamation of 1763, British North America's first constitution, enacted that the native peoples 'should not be molested or disturbed' on their hunting grounds in the territory reserved to them until the Crown purchased 'their' lands by a treaty of cession. This fundamental aboriginal right was recognized in the subsequent treaties between the British Crown and the aboriginal nations. Although the Royal Proclamation continued as part of Canadian law, the rights it recognized were not explicitly included in the BNA Act.[48] In the 1867 constitution, 'Indians, and Lands reserved for the Indians' were mentioned only as a subject of federal jurisdiction.[49] Aboriginal peoples were treated as subjects, not citizens, of the new dominion.

Not even among the small cadre of politicians who pushed through the Confederation plan was there a clear and common conception of the new nation they were building. As Eugene Forsey was tireless in pointing out, they all recognized they were establishing a new nation-state.[50] Their Constitution provided for the completion of a continental state stretching from Newfoundland to British Columbia,[51] and the lure of performing in this larger political arena was part of their shared vision. But while the Fathers of Confederation thought of themselves as nation-builders, they did not share a common vision of the essential nature of the nation they were building. A few like Cartier espoused the idea, daring in that day, of forming a new 'political nationality' based on deep 'racial' diversity – a society in which 'British and French Canadians alike could appreciate and understand their position relative to each other ... placed like great families beside each other.'[52] As we have seen, there were marks of this dualistic view of Canada in the new Constitution. But there were just as many Fathers of Confederation, especially in English Canada, who did not share Cartier's ideal of a culturally pluralist nation and who still harboured Lord Durham's dream of building a British North American nation. These Fathers of Confederation could empathize with George Brown, who, writing to his wife at the end of the Quebec Conference, exclaimed: 'Is it not wonderful? French Canadianism entirely extinguished!'[53]

In 1867 there was no need to agree on the fundamental nature of the new Canadian nation because the final custodian of its Constitution was not the Canadian political community but the imperial Parliament. Imperial stewardship of Canada's constitutional politics made it relatively easy to inaugurate Confederation. A new country could be founded without having to risk finding out if its politically active citizens agreed to the principles on which its Constitution was to be based. But if this was a gift, it was a tainted gift. The Confederation compromise was sheltered from the strain of a full public review in all sections of the country, but at the cost of not forming a political community with a clear sense of its constituent and controlling elements. Thus, at Canada's founding, its people were not sovereign, and there was not even a sense that a constituent sovereign people would have to be invented.

4   Provincial Rights

The great conceit of constitution-makers is to believe that the words they put in the constitution can with certainty and precision control a country's future. The great conceit of those who apply a written constitution is to believe that their interpretation captures perfectly the founders' intentions. Those who write constitutions are rarely single-minded in their long-term aspirations. They harbour conflicting hopes and fears about the constitution's evolution. The language of the constitution is inescapably general and latent with ambiguous possibilities. Written constitutions can establish the broad grooves in which a nation-state develops. But what happens within those grooves – the constitutional tilt favoured by history – is determined not by the constitutional text but by the political forces and events that shape the country's subsequent history.

Canada's constitutional development in the decades immediately following Confederation is a monument to the truth of these propositions. Although a majority of the Fathers of Confederation favoured a highly centralized federation, it soon became apparent that their aspirations would not be fulfilled. Instead, the most effective constitutional force in the new federation was the provincial rights movement. Far from moving towards a unitary state, Canada, by the end of the nineteenth century, had become a thoroughly federal country.

One might have expected the stiffest challenge to Macdonald's centralism to have come from Nova Scotia or Quebec. Nova Scotians, as we have seen, voted against Confederation in the provincial and federal elections of 1867. Immediately following Confederation a significant secessionist movement was developing in the province.[1] In 1868 Joseph Howe led a delegation to London seeking a repeal of the union. Nova Scotian opposition to Confederation, however, was not based on a desire for stronger provincial powers. In the end, Nova Scotian separatism was quelled by persuading Howe to join the federal cabinet and by offering Nova Scotia better terms, not through a constitutional amendment but by bringing its debt allowance into line with New Brunswick's.

From the very beginning, the Province of Quebec, in the words of A.I. Silver, 'was seen as the geographical and political expression of the French-Canadian nationality, as a French-Catholic province and the French-Canadian homeland.'[2] It was not just the *rouge* opponents of Confederation who championed the cause of provincial autonomy and resisted federal interference in provincial affairs. The *Bleus* had promoted Confederation in Quebec largely on the grounds that it would give the French majority in Quebec exclusive control over matters basic to their culture. A *bleu* paper in 1872, for example, claimed that 'as Conservatives we must be in favour of provincial rights and against centralization.'[3]

It was not Quebec but Ontario that spearheaded the provincial rights movement. Ontario would seem the least likely province to play this role. After all, support for Confederation had been stronger in Ontario than in any other province. With the largest and fastest-growing population, Ontario was expected to be able to dominate national politics. Why at this formative stage in the federation's history should its provincial government be in the vanguard of the provincial rights movement?

The answer is to be found in the pattern of partisan politics that developed soon after Confederation and has endured ever since. Even before Confederation, the Great Coalition of Conservatives and Reformers had broken up. The first federal government after Confederation was headed by the Conservative leader John A. Macdonald. As Ontario Reformers and Quebec Liberals began to organize a competing national party, they naturally took up the provincial cause. In the words of Christopher Armstrong, 'If Macdonald's Conservatives were the party of centralism, then its opponents would become the party of localism and provincialism, recruiting the anti-Confederates of the Maritimes to the Reform cause.'[4]

The Conservatives dominated the first thirty years of federal politics, holding office in Ottawa for all but four of those years. During that same period the Liberals were having their greatest success at the provincial level. Nowhere was this more true than in Ontario, where Oliver Mowat's Liberals won six successive elections between 1875 and 1896. While Mowat found Liberal allies in other provincial capitals, notably Quebec's Honoré Mercier, he was in office the longest and built the strongest record of provincial rights advocacy. Mowat's championing of this cause is remarkable in that he began his professional career as a junior in John A. Macdonald's law office, was a Father of Confederation, and had moved the Quebec Resolutions setting forth the division of powers between the two levels of government.[5]

The pattern of politics in which one party dominates at the federal level while its main opposition gathers strength in the provincial capitals has been repeated several times in Canadian history. For a long stretch of the twentieth century the Liberals dominated the federal scene while the Conservatives and other opposition parties won in the provinces. The reverse has been developing since the Mulroney Conservatives came to power in Ottawa in 1984. The fact that the largest national parties have gone through long periods in which their experience in government has been concentrated at the provincial level has done much to make provincial rights a cause that transcends partisan politics.

Although this phenomenon is one that stems from the fluctuating fortunes of partisan politics, it is closely tied to the Canadian system of parliamentary government. Responsible government, as we noted in chapter 3, tends to concentrate power in the hands of the prime minister and the cabinet. After Confederation it soon became apparent that this concentration of power would occur in the provincial capitals as well as in Ottawa. In Canada, provincial premiers emerged as the strongest political opponents to the federal prime minister. State governors in the United States, hemmed in by an elaborate system of checks and balances, are political pygmies compared with provincial premiers who perform as political giants on the national stage. Canadians, without any conscious design, found their liberal check and balance not *within* the national or provincial capitals but in the rivalry and tensions *between* those capitals.

The success of the provincial rights movement cannot be attributed to weak governments at the national level in Canada's formative years. Quite to the contrary, federal administrations presided over by John A. Macdonald, who was prime minister of Canada for nineteen of the country's first twenty-four years, were strong nation-building governments not at all shy about asserting federal power. Under Macdonald's leadership, Canada's 'manifest destiny' of becoming a continental nation-state was quickly fulfilled. In 1869 the Hudson's Bay Company's territories covering the prairies and the far north were purchased and added to Canada. A year later, following military suppression of the Métis led by Louis Riel, the Province of Manitoba was carved out of the North-West Territories. In 1871 Canada was extended to the Pacific, when British Columbia became a province on terms agreeable to its colonial government. Prince Edward Island became the seventh province, agreeing to join Confederation in 1873. To this expanding national territory Macdonald's Conservatives applied a National Policy, completing the transcontinental rail link, erecting tariff walls to protect manufacturing, and stimulating immigration to populate the west and provide a market for the protected industries.[6]

Important as the achievements of Macdonald's governments were in building the material conditions of nationhood, they contributed little to a Canadian sense of political community. Nor did they translate into constitutional gains for the federal government. The Conservatives' economic nationalism, as Reg Whitaker has observed, relied 'on elites and on their exclusively economic motives.'[7] It did not have much emotional appeal at the mass level. Government in far-away Ottawa had difficulty competing with provincial governments for the allegiance of citizens in the new provinces. During these years it was the provinces, not Ottawa, that seized and held the initiative in constitutional politics.

The first objective of the provincial rights movement was to resist and overcome a hierarchical version of Canadian federalism in which the provinces were to be treated as a subordinate or junior level of government. An early focal point of resistance was the office of provincial lieutenant-governor. From a Macdonald centralist perspective, the lieutenant-governors were essentially agents of the federal government in provincial capitals. In the 1870s, however, Ontario, under Mowat's leadership, began to insist that lieutenant-governors had full Crown powers in matters of provincial jurisdiction and that they exercised these powers on the advice of provincial ministers. Not surprisingly, the issue first arose over a question of patronage – the power to make lawyers queen's counsels.[8] Implicit in the provincial claim was an assertion of the provinces' constitutional equality with the federal government.

No element of the Constitution was potentially more threatening to provincial autonomy than the federal powers of reservation and disallowance. These powers derived from an imperial rather than a federal structure. Under the reservation power, the lieutenant-governor of a province could refuse to sign a bill that had passed through the provincial legislature and could reserve it for consideration by the federal cabinet. If, within a year, the lieutenant-governor was not instructed to give royal assent, the bill would die. Disallowance was simply a veto power under which the federal government could render null and void any provincial law within a year of its passage by the provincial legislature. These federal powers mirrored powers of reservation and disallowance over federal legislation that the imperial government retained and that were also written into the BNA Act.[9] The only difference was that the British government had two years rather than one to decide whether to block Canadian legislation.

The powers of reservation and disallowance are classic examples of how a shift in political sentiment and principle can render formal legal powers unusable. Well before Confederation, the British government had greatly reduced the use of its imperial powers of control over the British North American legislatures. Soon after Confederation these powers fell into desuetude. In the first decade a few Canadian bills were reserved, but royal assent was always granted and there were no reservations after 1878. Only one Canadian act was disallowed, in 1873, and the act in question was clearly unconstitutional.[10] At imperial conferences in the late 1920s declarations were made that these imperial powers would never be used and that steps would be taken to remove them from Canada's Constitution. Although the latter step was never taken, no one really cares that the powers remain formally in the Constitution because there is a clear political understanding – a constitutional convention – on both the British and Canadian sides that the powers are completely inoperative.[11] This convention of desuetude was established because use of the imperial powers was incompatible with the principle of Canadian self-government, a principle which, at least in matters of domestic policy, was so firmly in place by the 1870s that breach of it would have had the gravest political consequences.

A similar process occurred with respect to the federal government's powers of reservation and disallowance. Over time, the principle of provincial autonomy – self-government in those areas constitutionally assigned to the provincial legislatures – became so strongly held in the Canadian political system that the federal powers of reservation and disallowance, though remaining in the Constitution, became politically unusable. This did not happen all at once. It occurred only because the idea that the provinces are not subordinate to but coordinate with the federal government became the politically dominant conception of Canadian federalism.

At first federal governments – not only Macdonald's but the Liberals too when they were in power in the 1870s – made extensive use of the powers of reservation and disallowance.[12] Macdonald's first administration withheld assent on sixteen of twenty-four provincial bills reserved by lieutenant-governors. Between 1867 and 1896, sixty-five provincial acts were disallowed by the federal government. Although the powers continued to be used, they came under increasing attack from the provinces, and from no province more than Ontario. Even when, as was most often the case, the rationale for using these powers was the federal government's view that the legislation was outside the province's jurisdiction, provincial rights advocates were inclined to argue that questions concerning the division of powers should be settled in the courts, not by the federal cabinet. When the Macdonald government in 1881 disallowed Ontario's Rivers and Streams Act primarily to protect the interests of a prominent Conservative, Mowat decided to fight back. He promptly had the legislation re-enacted. After being disallowed and re-enacted three more times, the legislation was allowed to stand. The courts had the final say when the Judicial Committee of the Privy Council upheld the provincial law in 1884.[13]

Abolition of the federal disallowance power topped the list of constitutional proposals emanating from the Interprovincial Conference of 1887. The conference was called by Honoré Mercier, premier of Quebec, who had come to power largely on the strength of Quebec's resentment of the use of federal power in the hanging of Louis Riel. Macdonald and the Conservative premiers of British Columbia and Prince Edward Island declined Mercier's invitation. Delegates from the Liberal governments of the four original provinces and from Manitoba's Conservative administration, 'angered by repeated disallowances of their railway legislation,'[14] met for a week under Mowat's chaimanship behind closed doors. The twenty-two resolutions that they unanimously endorsed amounted to a frontal attack on the centralist conception of Confederation. Besides calling for the abolition of federal disallowance and an increase in federal subsidies, the conference proposed that half of the federal Senate be chosen by the provinces. Once these proposals had been approved by the provincial legislatures, they were to be submitted to London for enactment as constitutional amendments by the imperial Parliament.

In the end, nothing concrete came of these proposals. Only the lower houses of New Brunswick and Nova Scotia sent them on to London. The imperial authorities refused to act without having heard from the federal government or the other provinces.[15] Nonetheless, the 1887 conference is a significant landmark in Canada's constitutional politics, for it clearly demonstrated that the constitutional initiative had passed to the provinces. Strong centralist voices could still be heard, not least John A. Macdonald's, but the centralist view was losing its ascendancy in both French and English Canada.

During the first thirty years of Confederation, the provinces made their most tangible constitutional gains not through the process of formal constitutional amendment but through litigation in the courts. Their judicial victories were achieved in London before the Judicial Committee of the Privy Council. The Supreme Court of Canada had been created by the federal Parliament in 1875, but it was supreme in name only. Although the Liberal government which had sponsored the Supreme Court Act aimed at making the court Canada's highest tribunal, the Conservative opposition and the Colonial Office were able to thwart this objective.[16] The right of appeal to the highest court in the British Empire, the Judicial Committee of the Privy Council, was retained in Canada until 1949.

Retaining the Judicial Committee as Canada's highest court had significant consequences for the development of the Canadian Constitution. In the 1870s when the practice of bringing constitutional challenges against legislation in the courts was just beginning, the newly created Supreme Court of Canada decided a few cases very much in the federal government's favour. In Severn v. The Queen, decided in 1878, the Supreme Court found an Ontario law licensing brewers unconstitutional or *ultra vires*, outside the powers of the provincial legislature.[17] The Supreme Court judges gave the widest possible interpretation of the federal Parliament's exclusive power to make laws in relation to 'the Regulation of Trade and Commerce,' and supported this judgment by arguing that the Constitution's framers wished to avoid the 'evils' of states rights that had plagued the American federation. A year later in Lenoir v. Ritchie, the Supreme Court firmly rejected provincial pretensions to Crown prerogative by denying provincial governments the power to appoint queen's counsel. [18]

It did not take long for the English law lords who manned the Judicial Committee of the Privy Council to reverse the Supreme Court's approach to the Constitution. By the 1880s a steady stream of constitutional cases was being taken on appeal to London. The fact that so many constitutional questions were coming before the courts gives the lie to the pretension of the Fathers of Confederation to have settled all questions of jurisdiction.

One of the Judicial Committee's earliest decisions, Citizens Insurance Co. v. Parsons,[19] is a good example of the kind of issue that arose and the kind of outcome that obtained in the Judicial Committee. Section 91(2) of the BNA Act gave the federal Parliament exclusive jurisdiction over 'the Regulation of Trade and Commerce.' Section 92(13) gave the provincial legislatures exclusive jurisdiction over 'Property and Civil Rights in the Province.' At issue in the Parsons case was whether an Ontario statute regulating fire insurance contracts was within provincial powers. Such a law would seem clearly to be a regulation of trade and commerce and a regulation affecting property and civil rights in Ontario. Under which power did the Ontario legislation fall? The Judicial Committee reasoned that unless some limits were attached to trade and commerce and to property and civil rights, such broadly phrased powers would contradict each other. In this case they chose to put limits on the federal trade and commerce power, ruling that it applied to interprovincial and international commerce and to trade 'affecting the whole Dominion,' but not to the regulation of an industry within a province. Thus the Ontario act was upheld as a law relating to property and civil rights.

Between 1880 and 1896 the Judicial Committee decided eighteen cases involving twenty issues relating to the division of powers. Fifteen of these issues (75 per cent) it decided in favour of the provinces. What is even more important, as Murray Greenwood has observed, is that in these decisions the committee reversed 'every major centralist doctine of the [Supreme] Court.'[20] No area of policy making was as hotly contested as the consumption of alcohol. At first, the Judicial Committee appeared to favour federal power by upholding the Canada Temperance Act, a federal law providing a nationwide system whereby towns and cities could opt for local prohibition.[21] However, in subsequent decisions it ruled that only the provinces could provide for the licensing of taverns and retail liquor outlets in areas that did not opt for prohibition.[22] Finally, in 1896, the Judicial Committee upheld an Ontario local prohibition scheme. It was in this case that the imperial court called for a restrained interpretation of the federal Parliament's general or residual power to make laws for the 'Peace, Order, and good Government of Canada.' That power should be confined 'to such matters as are unquestionably of Canadian interest and importance,' and must not encroach on any of the subjects assigned exclusively to the provinces. 'To attach any other construction of the general power which, in supplement of its enumerated powers, is conferred upon the Parliament of Canada, would,' wrote Lord Watson, 'not only be contrary to the intendment of the Act, but would practically destroy the autonomy of the provinces.'[23]

The Judicial Committee went beyond the details of the division of powers to articulate a conception of federalism which would have been anathema to John A. Macdonald. The key judgment came in 1892 in the Maritime Bank case and involved that touchiest of constitutional questions – sovereign Crown powers.[24] At issue was New Brunswick's use of the Crown's prerogative to claim priority over other creditors seeking to recover funds from the liquidators of an insolvent bank. In upholding the province's right to use this power, Lord Watson set down the following thesis about the purpose of the BNA Act:

> The object of the Act was neither to weld the provinces into one, nor to subordinate provincial governments to a central authority, but to create a federal government in which they should all be represented, entrusted with the exclusive administration of affairs in which they had a common interest, each province retaining its independence and autonomy.

So much for John A. Macdonald's view that 'the true principle of a Confederation lay in giving to the General Government all the principles and powers of sovereignty.'[25] For the tribunal which had the final say in interpreting the Canadian Constitution, the provinces were not a subordinate level of government. The federal and provincial governments were coordinate levels of government, each autonomous within the spheres allotted to them by the Constitution.

The theory espoused by the Judicial Committee of the Privy Council is often called the theory of 'classical federalism.'[26] There can be no doubt that Macdonald and many of Canada's constitutional founders did not think of the country they were building as a classic federation. Some of the Fathers of Confederation, however, especially Quebec leaders like Cartier and Taché, were apprehensive of the centralist view and hoped that the provinces would be autonomous in the areas of law making reserved for them. The Quebec supporters of Confederation realized they could not retain their political support if they portrayed Confederation publicly in centralist terms. The political coalition that put Confederation together never came to a clear and explicit accord on federal theory.[27] What the Judicial Committee did was to give official legal sanction to a theory of federalism congenial to those who, at the time of Confederation and afterwards, could not accept centralism.

The impact of the Judicial Committee's constitutional decisions demonstrates a fundamental feature of constitutional development which is still, at most, only dimly understood by the Canadian public. In countries with written constitutions stipulating the powers of government and the rights of citizens, and in which the constitution is taken seriously, judges will play an important role in enforcing the constitution. The process through which judges play that role is called 'judicial review.' In performing the function of judicial review, judges review the acts of the executive and legislature and rule null and void those that do not conform with the constitution. Through these determinations, especially those of the highest court, the meaning of the constitution's general terms is fleshed out. This process of judicial review has been so important in the United States that it is said that 'the constitution is what the judges say it is.'[28]

The Fathers of Confederation did not discuss judicial review. Although some of them were aware of the important role the Supreme Court was playing in the United States, they did not see that there would be an immediate need for a Canadian Supreme Court.[29] Their constitutionalism was much more British than American, and hence more attuned to an unwritten constitution. They were accustomed to having the Judicial Committee of the Privy Council, as the highest imperial court, review colonial laws for their conformity with imperial law. Since the Canadian Constitution took the form of an act of the imperial Parliament, it was logical that this mechanism of imperial judicial control would apply to the BNA Act. For enforcing the rules of federalism internally, within Canada, it is evident that the Fathers of Confederation looked more to the federal executive using its powers of reservation and disallowance than to the judiciary. Also, it was to the federal executive, not the judiciary, that the BNA Act directed minorities to appeal if they believed a province had infringed their constitutional right to denominational schools.[30]

Federal government enforcement of the Constitution made sense, of course, so long as Canadian federalism was viewed primarily as a hierarchical, quasi-imperial structure in which the provinces were a junior level of government. From this perspective, the objective of constitutional enforcement was to keep the provinces from exceeding their powers. John A. Macdonald never contemplated that Canadian courts would find federal laws unconstitutional.[31] Once, however, the hierarchical view of federalism began to be eclipsed by the theory of classical federalism and dual sovereignty, it was much more logical for a judicial tribunal independent of both levels of government to exercise the primary responsibility for applying the Constitution.

Judicial review in Canada could not be justified in the same way as it was in the United States. There it was possible to justify judicial review on the grounds that in vetoing laws passed by popular majorities, the judiciary was giving effect to the enduring will of the American people as expressed in the Constitution.[32] Given the imperial and undemocratic foundations of the Canadian Constitution, this justification could hardly be advanced in Canada. Nonetheless, the Judicial Committee's constitutional interpretation could not have made the impact it did had it not coincided with powerful political forces in Canada. By the late nineteenth century, Canada had moved too far away from colonialism towards self-government to have complied with the rulings of an imperial tribunal that were out of line with political opinion in the country. The federal election of 1896 demonstrated that in Canada's national politics, the tide was running in favour of provincial rights and a balanced view of Canadian federalism.

The 1896 election was won by the Liberals led by Wilfrid Laurier. The Liberals and Laurier were to remain in power for the next fifteen years. Laurier's political success stemmed in part from his championing of provincial rights. This support occurred in a most ironic setting – the Manitoba Schools crisis.[33] In the 1896 election, Laurier, a French Catholic from Quebec, opposed the Conservative government's threat to force Manitoba to restore the denominational schools of that province's Roman Catholic minority.

In 1890, Manitoba, which by that time had developed into a largely English Protestant province, passed legislation reducing the rights of the French Catholic minority.[34] One law made English Manitoba's official language, ignoring the clause in Manitoba's terms of union guaranteeing the use of English and French in the province's courts and legislature.[35] Nearly a century would pass before this statute would be effectively challenged in the courts.[36]

The other statute replaced a dual system of Roman Catholic and Protestant schools in existence since 1871 with a system of secular public schools to be supported by all taxpayers, including parents of children attending the Roman Catholic schools. This legislation was immediately challenged on the grounds that it violated another clause in Manitoba's terms of union guaranteeing denominational school rights held 'by law or practice' at the time of union.[37] Although the challenge was initially successful in the Supreme Court of Canada, it failed in the Judicial Committee of the Privy Council.[38] Nevertheless, in a subsequent decision, the Judicial Committee ruled that Manitoba's Catholics could, under another section of the constitutional guarantee, appeal to the federal cabinet to introduce remedial legislation forcing Manitoba to restore their school rights.[39] A few months before the 1896 election, the Conservatives, now led by Charles Tupper, agreed to submit a remedial bill to Parliament. This was the bill that Laurier successfully opposed in the ensuing election campaign.

It was not the substance of that bill which Laurier and the Liberals opposed. They were strongly committed to the restoration of Catholic school rights in Manitoba. In national politics the Laurier Liberals provided the main resistance to a growing movement within English Canada led by D'Alton McCarthy, president of the Ontario Conservative Association, calling for a Canada free of papism and rejecting 'the *nationaliste* thesis that the French were a permanent and equal element in Canada.'[40] Still, Laurier, who drew his strongest political support from Quebec, remained as committed to provincial rights as to minority cultural rights. Instead of federal coercion of a province, Laurier proposed the 'sunnier ways' of negotiating an accommodation with the provincial government. In the end, it was Laurier's 'sunnier ways' and his respect for provincial rights that prevailed politically.[41]

The success of the provincial rights movement did not mean that in terms either of governmental power or of citizens' allegiance the provincial political realm had come to surpass the federal. Laurier, after all, was a national leader whose government would pursue important initiatives in domestic and international politics. Indeed, Laurier and other Quebec leaders, by supporting the rights of French Catholics outside Quebec, were encouraging

Quebecers, in the words of A.I. Silver, to look beyond 'the still-special home of Quebec' and see that 'all Canada should yet be a country for French-Canadians.'[42] Since the 1890s there have been shifts back and forth in the balance of power between the two levels of government, but there has always been a balance; neither level has been able to dominate the other. Canada's citizens have been thoroughly schizophrenic in their loyalties, maintaining strong associations with their provincial governments as well as the federal government. In this sense Canada, despite the ambiguities and contradictions in its Constitution, became, as Donald Smiley put it, 'in the most elemental way a federal country.'[43]

One measure of how ingrained the balanced view of federalism has become is the fate of those imperial powers of reservation and disallowance which the federal government held over the provinces. They are still in the Constitution, but they are simply not used any more. Disallowance has not been used since 1943. The last time a lieutenant-governor reserved a provincial bill was 1961, and then his action was totally repudiated by the federal prime minister, John Diefenbaker, as violating the basic principles of Canadian federalism.[44] When the Parti Québécois came to power in Quebec in the 1970s and enacted Bill 101, the Charter of the French Language, the Trudeau government in Ottawa, which bitterly opposed this legislation, did not ever indicate that it would disallow it. And again in 1988, when Quebec adopted Bill 178 to overcome a Supreme Court ruling and restore a unilingual French sign policy, although Prime Minister Mulroney and opinion leaders throughout English Canada denounced the legislation, neither government nor opposition leaders called for disallowance of the legislation. By the 1980s political parties and leaders of all persuasions, like Laurier and the Liberals a century earlier, would not protect minority rights at the cost of violating provincial rights.

The sovereignty at issue in the struggle for provincial rights was not the sovereignty of the people but the sovereignty of governments and legislatures. The sovereignty claimed and won for provincial legislatures and governments within their allotted sphere of jurisdiction was primarily a top-down kind of sovereignty.[45] Canadian constitutional politics continued to be highly elitist, with federal and provincial leaders contending against each other in intergovernmental meetings and the courts. Still, traces of a more democratic constitutionalism were beginning to appear in the rhetoric, if not the reality, of the constitutional process.

Robert Vipond has shown how exponents of provincial rights defended the sovereignty of provincial 'parliaments' against federal intrusions by emphasizing the right to self-government of local electorates. Provincial leaders attacking federal intervention in provincial affairs appealed to the same principles of self-government as earlier colonial politicians had invoked in objecting to imperial intervention in internal colonial affairs. The exercise of the federal powers of disallowance and reservation was portrayed as 'autocratic and tyrannical' whereas, according to Liberal leader Edward Blake, to support provincial autonomy was to sustain 'the educating and glorious attributes which belong to self-government, to a government of the people, by the people, for the people.'[46] Although the provincial leaders were still too British, too wedded to the notion of parliamentary sovereignty, to talk about the people as sovereign in the constituent American sense, they were edging closer to this conception of popular sovereignty when they referred to the rights of provincial legislatures as powers entrusted to them by the people.[47]

Out of this rhetoric and the political success of its authors was born the myth of Confederation as a compact entered into by sovereign provincial communities. According to the compact theory, the provinces as the founding, constituent units of the federation retained the right to alter the terms of their original union.[48] This was the theory promulgated by Honoré Mercier and the other provincial premiers who attended the 1887 Interprovincial Conference: 'the conference represented all of the original parties to the compact of 1864, and the partners should now assess the state of their joint enterprise.'[49] Not surprisingly, the theory found its most articulate spokesmen in Quebec, where the notion of the province as a founding community could be infused with a sense of ethnic nationalism.

What is meant in referring to the compact theory as a 'myth' is that its validity depends not on its historical accuracy but on its capacity to serve as a set of 'beliefs and notions that men hold, that they live by or live for.'[50] Confederation, as we have seen, did involve a two-stage agreement, first between English- and French-Canadian politicians and then between Canadian and Maritime politicians. Leading participants in the agreement, including John A. Macdonald and George-Etienne Cartier, as well as some of the imperial authorities, frequently referred to the Quebec Resolutions as a treaty or pact. But it is not clear that when they used this terminology they had the same thing in mind. It is most unlikely that when John A. Macdonald talked of a treaty he meant that the parties to the agreement exercised and retained sovereign political authority.

From a strictly legal point of view, the founding colonies in 1867, as colonies, did not have sovereign powers to retain. They did not formally sign or give legal authority to the Constitution. Further, given the elitist quality of the process and the failure, indeed the disinclination, to seek a clear popular mandate for the Confederation deal, it is a total fabrication to maintain that the peoples of the founding provinces had covenanted together to produce the Canadian federal union. This fabrication flies in the face of the top-down process whereby new provinces were added – especially the two provinces carved out of the North-West Territories in 1905. As Arthur Lower observed, 'there was not the slightest vestige of a "compact" in the Acts of Parliament that created the provinces of Alberta and Saskatchewan in 1905.'[51]

Nor was the compact theory strictly followed in constitutional practice. If the Canadian Constitution was a compact or treaty among the provinces, then no changes should have been made to it without the consent of all the provinces. Formally constitutional changes, as amendments to the BNA Act, were enacted by the British Parliament, but that body would act only on a request from Canada. During the period that the compact theory was gathering force, however, several amendments were made to the BNA Act at the request of the federal government and Parliament without consulting the provinces or seeking their consent. While none of these amendments directly affected the powers of the provinces, two of them related to the structure of the federation: one empowered the federal Parliament to create new provinces and the other provided for the representation of territories in the federal Parliament.[52] Prior to the 1907 amendment,[53] which revised the subsidies paid to the provinces, Laurier did hold a federal-provincial conference and eight of the nine provinces (British Columbia held out for better terms) agreed to the federal proposal. But the provinces were not consulted on the 1915 amendment that redefined the divisions of the Senate, forming a new section out of the four western provinces.[54]

Even though the compact theory was not consistently observed in the constitutional amendment process, it had become a powerful constitutional ideal by the turn of the century. Provincial rights and the compact theory had, as Ramsay Cook put it, 'attained a position close to motherhood in the scale of Canadian political values. It would be difficult to find a prominent politician who was not willing to pay lip-service to the principle of provincial rights and its theoretical underpinning, the compact theory.'[55] As a constitutional doctrine, the compact theory may have contained ambiguities and lacked precision, but its strength as a political value in Canada meant that the Canadian political community that was forming would be complex and deeply pluralist. Canada would take its place in the world as an interventionist state and its nation-wide activities would take on increasing significance in the lives of its citizens, but the provinces would nonetheless endure as strong constituent elements of the Canadian community.

The ambiguities of the compact theory were intensified by the coexistence of two competing versions of the compact: a compact of founding provinces and a compact of founding peoples.[56] The latter contended that Canada was founded on the basis of a covenant between English Canadians and French Canadiens. In the final analysis, the making of Canada in 1867 was 'the free association of two peoples, enjoying equal rights in all matters.'[57] These were the words of Henri Bourassa, the theory's most eloquent spokesman and founder of the great Montreal newspaper *Le Devoir* in 1910. Again, the significance of this theory in Canada's constitutional politics rests not on its historical accuracy but on its potency as a political myth. It is easy to show that neither in law nor in politics was the BNA Act a formal agreement between the French and English people of British North America. Nonetheless, that

constitutional settlement depended, as we have seen, on English-
and French-Canadian leaders agreeing to a federal structure with
a province in which the French Canadians would remain a majority. For many English Canadians, assent to this agreement was only
grudgingly given; for French Canadians it represented liberation
from Lord Durham's scheme to assimilate them into a unicultural
English political community, the triumph of their cultural survival
– and, indeed for many, of national survival. The expectations on
the French side flowing from that agreement gave rise to the
theory that Confederation was based on a compact between two
founding peoples.[58]

As originally espoused by Bourassa and other French Canadians,
the two founding peoples theory was applied to all of Canada.
Indeed, it was advanced as the theoretical underpinning for a pan-
Canadian nationalism that viewed all Canada in dualist terms. Its
exponents defended the rights of the French minorities outside
Quebec and of the English minority in Quebec. In this sense, it
may have provided 'moral support for minimizing the consequences of the compact of provinces' and of provincial rights.[59] At
the same time, this dualist view of Canada always retained a special
place for the province of Quebec. As the homeland of one of the
founding peoples, it had the right to be secure against intrusions
into its culture by the general government answerable to an English-speaking majority.

Lurking within these rival compact theories were deep-seated
differences on the nature of Canada as a political community. The
idea that Quebec has a special place in Confederation as the only
province in which one of the founding peoples forms the majority
would collide with the doctrine of provincial equality. More fundamentally, the idea of a Canada based on the English and the
French as its two founding peoples would be challenged at the end
of the twentieth century by Canadians who were neither British
nor French in their cultural background and by the aboriginal
peoples.

So long as Canadians were not interested in taking custody of
their Constitution into their own hands, this conflict over the nature of Canada as a political community was of no great political
importance. It was bound, however, to become salient once that

condition changed. The time arrived in 1926, when the Balfour Declaration declared Canada and the other self-governing dominions to be 'autonomous Communities' within the British Commonwealth.[60] Canada's political leaders then faced the challenge of arranging for Canada to become constitutionally self-governing.

5 An Autonomous Community

The Balfour Declaration was issued at the conclusion of the Imperial Conference of 1926. It recognized the political independence of the self-governing members of the British Commonwealth – Australia, Canada, Eire, New Zealand, and South Africa. The declaration described the mutual relation of these countries and Great Britain in the following terms: 'They are autonomous Communities within the British Empire, equal in status, in no way subordinate one to another in any aspect of their domestic or external affairs, though united by a common allegiance to the Crown, and freely associated as members of the British Commonwealth of Nations.'[1] The Balfour Declaration was not a formal legal document. It expressed a political understanding reached by the prime ministers of the countries concerned. In effect it recorded a constitutional convention. It would remain for the Statute of Westminster in 1931 to dissolve the formal legal subordination of the self-governing dominions to the imperial Parliament. By then Canadians would discover that while Britain was willing to terminate its formal custody of Canada's Constitution, Canada was not yet prepared to take its Constitution into its own hands.

Canada attained political autonomy within the empire through a gradual process, without any major struggle with or resistance from the imperial authorities. The whole process was a quintessential example of the British organic style of constitutional evolution. Soon after Confederation it was clear that Britain would not interfere in Canada's internal affairs. The British government retained its formal legal powers of disallowance and reservation over federal legislation but, by the 1870s, use of these powers was governed by the convention of non-interference in internal affairs, and these powers were simply no longer used.

Canada's external affairs were another matter. The BNA Act did not empower either level of government in Canada to conduct foreign relations. The only explicit mention of external affairs in Canada's Constitution (then and now) is section 132, which gives the federal government and Parliament whatever powers are needed to perform Canada's obligations under British Empire treaties. Despite the absence of any explicit authorization, Canada gradually, step by step, took control of its foreign affairs. The process began in 1870 with the inclusion of John A. Macdonald in the imperial delegation that negotiated the Treaty of Washington with the United States, grew through the appointment of ambassadors and the establishment of a Department of External Affairs, and culminated in the Chanak Incident in 1922, when Mackenzie King's government refused Britain's request for Canadian military support in defending British interests in the Near East.[2]

Achieving independence from Great Britain was not, for Canada, a unifying process. The fact that it was an evolutionary, not a revolutionary development, without dramatic confrontations, robbed the process of the unifying sense of nationalism so often accompanying decolonization. In fact, as the process in its latter stages played itself out in Canada's domestic politics, it had some distinctly disunifying effects. The conflict between nationalists and imperialists in Canadian politics was not over dominion autonomy itself. By the twentieth century, the spirit of self-government was too advanced on all sides for there to be any significant support in Canada for remaining under British rule. The key issue was whether Canada, as it gained autonomy, would remain closely aligned with Britain and the empire.[3] Quebec hostility to Canada's participation in the Boer War and to conscription in World War I demonstrated how foreign ventures at Britain's side could endanger national unity. Many English Canadians continued to see Canada as primarily a British North American nation. As Canada gained formal nationhood, it was increasingly clear that this vision of the country was incompatible with the sense of nationalism stirring not only Quebec but newer communities in English-speaking Canada as well.

Differences within Canada among its governing elites, not differences between Canada and Great Britain, prevented Canada from assuming the full autonomy proclaimed in the Balfour Declaration. As 'an autonomous community,' Canada, logically, should have assumed full responsibility for amending its Constitution. Great Britain was more than willing to hand over custody of Canada's Constitution to Canada. The question was: To whom or what in Canada should custody be given? Which people or legislature or combination of peoples and legislatures should be constitutionally sovereign in Canada? That was a question for Canadians to answer, and it was a question that Canada's political leaders quickly indicated they were not prepared to answer.

Federal and provincial leaders met for the first time to deal with this question at a conference called by the federal government in November 1927. The format of this conference tells us much about the constitutional assumptions that prevailed not only at that time but for a long time to come. The fact that the federal government would not act on the question of Canada's constitutional sovereignty without full consultation with the provincial governments shows that the Government of Canada did not feel it had full authority to speak for the majority of Canadians. The provincial governments were accepted as essential constituent elements of the 'autonomous community.' Further, it was governments, federal and provincial, not the people of the constituent units, that had the primary responsibility for the Constitution. The 1927 Dominion-Provincial Conference, like so many more to come, was a closed, elitist affair. The nomenclature would change (to federal-provincial conferences), but the methods of consociational democracy – closed-door bargaining by federal and provincial leaders – would remain the prevailing mode of constitutional politics. And, for many years, most Canadians would not complain.

At the 1927 conference, Ernest Lapointe, the federal minister of justice and Mackenzie King's Quebec lieutenant, proposed a formula for amending the Constitution in Canada. Amendments would be enacted by the federal Parliament but, in the event of 'ordinary amendments,' only after obtaining the consent of a majority of the provinces. For 'fundamental amendments' involving 'such questions as provincial rights, the rights of minorities, or rights generally affecting race, language and creed,' the unanimous consent of the provinces would be required.[4] There was no agreement to accept this formula. The official *Précis* of the conference discussions laconically reported an absence of any sense of urgency about being able to amend the Constitution in Canada and that, indeed, many felt 'there was no widespread demand for such a change.' Fears were expressed that submitting proposals to the provinces would 'stir up local party strife' and even, God forbid, 'arouse sentiment and feeling.' Concern was expressed that, despite the amount of provincial consent required under the Lapointe formula, 'amendments might become too easy to secure.'[5] Some provinces still trusted London more than Ottawa with custody of their rights.

Canadian representatives at the Imperial Conference of 1929, held to settle the legal implications of dominion autonomy, reported that Canada's Constitution, the British North America Act, would continue to be amended by the British Parliament and, therefore, must be explicitly omitted from legislation being drafted to give the dominions full legal autonomy. When the conference report was considered in the Canadian House of Commons, the Conservatives, then in opposition and championing provincial rights as national opposition parties are wont to do, insisted that no action be taken on the wording of imperial legislation without full consultation with the provinces. A few months later, this position was bolstered by Howard Ferguson, the Conservative premier of Ontario, who submitted to the newly elected Conservative prime minister, R.B. Bennett, a lengthy, formal memorandum setting out the theory that Confederation was a compact among the provinces and that no constitutional changes could be made without the provinces' consent.

Bennett acted accordingly. Before submitting a proposal to the House of Commons requesting a special Canada clause in the pending imperial legislation giving the dominions legal autonomy, he called a federal-provincial conference in April 1931. At this conference the provinces gave their unanimous approval to the wording of a clause to be inserted in this Statute of Westminster. That wording was accepted by the Canadian Parliament and by the Parliament of the United Kingdom when it enacted the statute in

December 1931. Section 7 exempted Canada's Constitution, the BNA Act, from the full legal autonomy otherwise extended to Canada as a self-governing dominion. Canada would still have to go to Britain for formal amendment of its Constitution. Canadian political leaders could only agree that the autonomous community of Canada was not yet ready to take custody of its highest law, the Constitution.

Canada's Constitution remained formally in British hands – unpatriated – until 1982. For more than a generation Canada's political leaders struggled, sporadically, with the definition of an acceptable formula for amending the Constitution in Canada. Federal and provincial first ministers and justice ministers attended conferences to discuss this subject in 1935, 1950, and the early 1960s. The more they met, the more complicated the proposals became. These meetings produced a world-class group of experts on constitutional amending formulas for federal states. They did not, however, produce an agreement on the right formula for Canada.

While this failure to reach an agreement on an amending formula may have been frustrating to the politicians and lawyers who worked on the problem, it was not a source of great frustration for the Canadian people. Constitutional politics throughout this period was a relatively low-key affair. There was no sense anywhere that the country needed a new Constitution or that national unity was at issue. Failure to patriate was more of an embarrassment than a practical inconvenience. By international standards, constitutional amendments under an unpatriated constitution were not difficult to obtain. Between 1930 and 1964, Canada's Constitution was amended nine times, considerably more often than were the fully patriated constitutions of Australia or the United States.[6] Still, so long as it was necessary to traipse over to England to have its Constitution amended, Canada appeared to be less than a fully mature member of the international community.

More seriously, failure to patriate meant that Canadians had not yet been able to agree on the locus of constitutional sovereignty in the nation they were endeavouring to build. In this sense, the Canadian nation-building project was profoundly incomplete. Only a few intellectual worry-warts were much concerned, however, and a small coterie of federal and provincial technicians was left at the edge of national politics to burrow away on the seemingly eternal puzzle of the amending formula. All would change dramatically in 1964 when the project of constitutionally completing the Canadian nation collided directly with another nation-building project based on Quebec, and constitutional politics began to spill out of closed conferences to the people.

After 1964 the patriation question became entangled with a much broader constitutional agenda and a much more intense form of constitutional politics. The patriation issue became even more difficult to resolve and, from the perspective of Canadian unity, more dangerous. Looking back, some may wish that the British had been more hard-boiled when Canada's constitutional politics were relatively low key and, in the 1920s, simply cast Canada adrift, forcing the autonomous community to take full responsibility for its own Constitution. By so doing, Britain would have forced Canada into what in constitutional jargon is called constitutional 'autochthony' – a constitution drawn from the land itself.[7] But the British placed too much value on legal continuity to perform such an incautious act, and Canada continued to lean on the legal crutch of imperial sovereignty.

Canadians who today call for a democratic constitutional settlement should thank Britain for its caution. If the British had forced Canada to patriate its Constitution in the 1920s or 1930s, it is most doubtful that the resulting constitutional settlement would have approximated a Lockean-type social contract – a constitution made by a sovereign people. The style of constitutional politics remained thoroughly and complacently elitist. Occasionally someone would be brash enough to propose that the people, through a referendum process, might play a role in the amending process, but such ideas were quickly squelched as thoroughly un-Canadian. Even as liberally minded a Canadian as Frank Underhill poured cold water on such proposals. The ordinary voter, in his view, was incompetent to understand the intricacies of constitutional change.[8] Parliamentary sovereignty remained the dominant constitutional paradigm.

Canadian democracy was still at an underdeveloped stage. The participation of women in politics had just begun.[9] As late as 1928 the Supreme Court of Canada, in a decision subsequently reversed by the Judicial Committee of the Privy Council, had ruled that for constitutional purposes women did not qualify as 'persons' and therefore could not be appointed to the Canadian Senate.[10] Full female suffrage was not complete until 1940, when women were enfranchised in Quebec. Racist laws discriminating against black Canadians and Canadians of oriental background were still in force.[11] The aboriginal peoples, discarded as military allies and economic partners, were now in a position of colonial subjection to the white settlers. Indians could become citizens only by giving up their Indian status. As J.R. Miller summarizes federal policy at this time, 'Ottawa still aimed at the peaceful elimination of Indians as a legal and social fact.'[12] At the time Canada became 'an autonomous community,' the adult persons resident in this community were scarcely in a position to act as a sovereign people. Far too many of them were excluded from the constitutional process for that to have been a possibility.

In the 1940s there was one short, sharp departure from the traditional elitist mode of constitutional politics – the process whereby Newfoundland decided to join the Canadian federation. In 1946 the people of Newfoundland and Labrador elected a national convention to decide on their constitutional future. For a year the convention debated the major constitutional options: a return to full responsible government, which had been abandoned in 1933 when a bankrupt Newfoundland was put under the rule of a British commission; a continuation of commission government; or Confederation with Canada.[13] In June 1948 these three options were put to the people in a referendum. Responsible government edged out Confederation (45 per cent to 41 per cent), with commission government being roundly rejected. A month later, in a second referendum, Newfoundlanders voted on the two preferred alternatives. This time Confederation prevailed, narrowly, over a simple return to responsible government, 52 per cent to 48 per cent.

When the time came to review Newfoundland's constitutional status after World War II, there seems to have been no doubt on the part of either the British or the Newfoundlanders about the appropriateness of a highly democratic constitutional process. The

Newfoundlanders were treated as a sovereign people who could determine their constitutional destiny by majority vote. The process used was in line with the democratic forms of constitution making followed in West Germany and Italy to establish democratic constitutions after the war and which were soon to be used in the process of decolonization in the Indian subcontinent and parts of Africa.

But these procedures of popular participation were not employed in taking the steps needed to implement the will of Newfoundland's majority and make Newfoundland and Labrador the tenth province of Canada. Newfoundland's terms of union with Canada were negotiated in Ottawa in the fall of 1948 by a Newfoundland delegation and representatives of the federal government. There was never any suggestion that these terms of union should be submitted for approval to the Canadian people. Instead, they were approved by an act of the Canadian Parliament, followed by the usual procedure of addresses from both Houses requesting the necessary enactment by the United Kingdom Parliament. This resolution was passed by a Liberal majority overriding an amendment moved by George Drew, leader of the Conservative opposition, that the provinces should be consulted. In March 1949 the British Parliament passed the amendment to the BNA Act joining Newfoundland to Canada.

It was not only the constitutional process that continued in a traditional mode. In substance, too, the Constitution at this time was still not treated as a great charter of fundamental law. Canadian constitutionalism remained more Burkean than Lockean. When the first major effort got under way in 1935 and 1936 to work out a method of amending the Constitution, the political and legal elites involved in the process immediately began cutting up the BNA Act into various segments, each subject to a different amending process. Some elements that pertained strictly to the federal government were to be amendable by the federal Parliament alone. Others that concerned one or more but not all of the provinces could be amended by the federal Parliament and the legislatures of the provinces concerned. Sections of the Constitution affecting all the provinces and the structure of the federation would require the agreement of the federal Parliament and some special majority of provincial legislatures (an early suggestion was two-thirds of the provinces representing at least 55 per cent of the total population of Canada). A few sections concerning what were referred to as 'fundamental' matters (the list usually included the monarchy, the guarantee to small provinces of a minimum number of seats in the House of Commons, denominational education, and minority language rights) would be deeply entrenched by requiring the agreement of the federal Parliament and all the provincial legislatures.

This business of chopping up the Constitution into different categories, each subject to a different amending rule, is the approach that prevailed in every effort to work out an all-Canadian amending formula. The amending rules adopted when Canada's Constitution was finally patriated in 1982 (see chapter 8) are faithful to this approach. It has produced an amending formula much more complex than the systems in most other constitutional democracies, and one not easily understood by the ordinary citizen.

Until well into the 1960s, public interest in the amending formula was minimal. Debate over its arcane intricacies was left largely to lawyer-politicians participating in intergovernmental conferences. Their deliberations seemed highly legalistic and technical – which sections of the Constitution to put in which amending rule box. Nonetheless, underlying these exchanges, major differences were emerging about the fundamental nature of Canada as a political community, differences that would become more difficult to resolve when the debate was engaged at a more popular level.

The provincial rights ideal was alive and well. It had survived the 1930s, when provinces were going bankrupt and it was evident that only a strong central government could deal effectively with the economic and social consequences of a worldwide depression. The insistence that provincial governments have a fundamental share of Canadian sovereignty was reflected in all the amending formula proposals. As a minimum, there was broad agreement that changes in the basic structure of the federation and the division of powers must not be made without the consent of a substantial majority of the provinces. Some provinces went further. Here Ontario, throughout the 1930s, was in the vanguard, insisting that the most important provincial powers and the amending system itself not be altered without the consent of the federal Parliament and of all the provincial legislatures.[14]

A rising tide of political sentiment ran in the opposite direction. From the mid 1930s through to the end of the 1950s the centralist perspective was the dynamic, initiating force in Canadian constitutional politics. Centralism was never stronger than during this quarter-century. Initially it was the Canadian federation's demonstrated incapacity to grapple with the enormous dislocations caused by the Depression that moved national political elites of all political persuasions to look for a constitutional restructuring that would give the central government the powers needed to deal with problems of this magnitude. That indeed was the rationale for establishing the federal Royal Commission on Dominion-Provincial Relations (Rowell-Sirois Commission) in 1937. Subsequently, the nationalism engendered by Canada's participation in World War II and strong popular support for postwar reconstruction added further momentum to the centralist trend.

The most enduring feature of this tendency was the attraction of centralism to the Canadian left. Those who favoured government intervention to overcome the inequities and inadequacies of capitalism articulated the most coherent and potentially popular case for a strong national government. Whereas centralism in the nineteenth century was primarily a Conservative cause, by the mid twentieth century its most ardent advocates were on the left of politics and, above all, in the social democratic party founded in the 1930s – the Co-operative Commonwealth Federation (CCF) and its successor, the New Democratic Party. The social democrat was inclined to view Canada as a national community whose social agenda and Constitution should be responsive to the will of a national majority, unimpeded by governments based on recalcitrant local majorities. At this time, social democracy found almost all its political support in English Canada.

Frank Scott, a founder of the CCF and a leading constitutional scholar, was one of the earliest exponents of this point of view. He was among the handful of experts permitted to appear before the Special Committee of the House of Commons set up in 1935 to consider the constitutional amending process. Scott urged that, except for a few 'minority rights,' Canada's Constitution should be amended by a simple majority vote in the Canadian Parliament without any participation of the provinces.[15] By minority rights, Scott did not mean provincial rights but the rights of cultural minorities within the provinces. Amendments affecting minority rights should be approved by the federal Parliament and all of the provincial legislatures.

Leaders of the two mainstream national parties would not go as far as Scott and the CCF. While they wanted a more flexible formula than the provincial compact theory would yield, they were still wary of the strength of provincial rights sentiment, especially in Quebec. The motion creating the House committee on the Constitution in 1935, which received all-party support, neatly captures the balance of concern among national politicians:

> That in the opinion of this house, a special committee should be set up to study and report on the best method by which the British North America Act may be amended, so that while safeguarding the existing rights of racial and religious minorities, and legitimate provincial claims to autonomy, the Dominion Government may be given adequate power to deal effectively with urgent economic problems which are essentially national in scope.[16]

The final three lines of the motion speak to the primary objective of constitutional change – strengthening the powers of the central government. Such changes, however, were not to be accomplished in violation of provincial autonomy. The reference to 'racial and religious minorities' was the political code of the day for French Canada. Despite the exigencies of the depression years, the concepts of a covenant of provinces and a covenant of founding peoples were still alive in the constitutional conscience of Canada's political leaders.

That support for provincial rights could endure, even in times that were least propitious for a federal division of governmental authority, demonstrates how rooted federalism had become in the Canadian political culture. This support was in marked contrast to developments south of the border. In the United States, the birthplace of constitutional federalism, a popular national leader could take actions that led to the removal of jurisdictional restrictions on the legislative powers of Congress. When crucial components of President Roosevelt's New Deal legislation were overturned by the United States Supreme Court (some of them on the grounds that they violated states rights), Roosevelt threatened to pack the Supreme Court with justices of his own political persuasion. He did not have to follow through with the threat, because some of the incumbent nine justices found reasons for upholding the federal legislation[17] Since then, the US Congress has been virtually free of states rights restrictions on its powers, and the United States has been as centralized as John A. Macdonald hoped Canada would be.

Canada had its New Deal too – a pale imitation of Roosevelt's introduced by Bennet's Conservatives – but the government was defeated at the polls in 1935.[18] Mackenzie King's Liberal government, far from implementing the New Deal legislation, referred it to the courts on the grounds that it might violate the constitutional rights of the provinces. When the Judicial Committee found that much of it did, King, instead of threatening to change the judges, responded in quintessential Canadian fashion and appointed a royal commission (Rowell-Sirois). Even that federal initiative on constitutional matters was too much for some of the provinces.

Despite the close balance of countervailing constitutional forces, constitutional changes continued to be made through the middle decades of the century. This was a period of micro-constitutional politics. The changes were made one at a time, with a minimum of public involvement. There was no talk of bringing in a whole new constitution, although some feared – especially in Quebec – that the piecemeal changes were heading towards a wholesale abandonment of true federalism. All the constitutional initiatives during this period were centralist. Still, the most significant of them were accomplished through a process that recognized the provincial governments' share in Canadian sovereignty.

For the first time, changes were made to the most delicate area of all – the division of powers between the two levels of government. These changes expanded the central government's role in legislating for the welfare state and followed the direction recommended by the Rowell-Sirois Commission. In 1940 the BNA Act was amended to give the federal Parliament exclusive jurisdiction over unemployment insurance, a legislative field denied it by the Judicial Committee at the depth of the Depression. In 1951 section 94A was added to the BNA Act giving the federal Parliament concurrent jurisdiction with the provinces in the field of old-age pensions. Unlike the other two concurrent powers in the BNA Act, agriculture and immigration, where in case of conflict federal law prevails, the reverse would be true in the field of pensions. In 1964 section 94A was expanded to cover survivors and other supplementary old-age benefits as well as disability benefits irrespective of age. Even for an amendment that did not impinge directly on provincial powers, a 1960 change in the BNA Act providing for compulsory retirement at the age of seventy-five of judges appointed by the federal government to the provincial superior courts, the unanimous consent of the provinces was sought and obtained.

Under the still unpatriated Constitution, all of these amendments were formally enacted by the United Kingdom Parliament, though the British action was in response to a resolution of the Canadian Parliament requesting the amendment. The federal resolution, in turn, came only after the federal government had obtained each province's consent to the proposed amendment. In seeking this consent, the federal government was complying not with a legal rule but with what it regarded as a political imperative.

At this time, obtaining the unanimous consent of all the provinces was not an impossible task. Provincial consent was not obtained through high-profile conferences with all the players at the table and a wide range of constitutional issues on the block. On the contrary, the federal government sought each province's consent in turn for each amendment, and, with few exceptions, this consent was quietly given by provincial executives agreeing in correspondence, not by the provincial legislatures. Only British Columbia with the 1940 unemployment insurance amendment, Manitoba and Saskatchewan with the 1951 pensions amendment, and Quebec with all the amendments from 1951 on sought legislative approval.[19] All these procedures are in marked contrast to the constitutional politics that prevailed before and after patriation of the Constitution in 1982.

The federal government in the 1940s was bold enough to push through a series of constitutional amendments without provincial consent. Though none of these amendments directly affected the powers of provincial governments or legislatures, they did fly in the face of the doctrine that the Constitution was a pact or treaty among the provinces. In 1943 the British Parliament, responding to a request of the federal Parliament, passed an amendment to the BNA Act postponing the redistribution of seats in the House of Commons constitutionally required after each decennial census. A similar unilateral federal initiative in 1946 led to the British Parliament replacing section 51 of the BNA Act. This is the section that governs the number of seats each province has in the federal House of Commons. The new section was designed to base the distribution on a more strictly proportional basis. It is interesting to note that Quebec, one of the provinces that gained from the 1946 amendment, was the only one to protest officially against the lack of consultation with the provinces. Quebec was now supplanting Ontario as the chief advocate of the compact theory.

In 1949 two more constitutional amendments were made through unilateral federal actions. The first, which provided for Newfoundland's union with Canada, has been discussed already. The criticism of federal unilateralism was relatively muted in this instance because section 146 of the BNA Act explicitly authorized the British government to admit Newfoundland to the Canadian union on the basis of 'addresses' from the Canadian Parliament and the Newfoundland legislature.[20] The second 1949 amendment was far more controversial. This amendment amounted to a 'mini patriation' of the Constitution in that it gave the federal Parliament the power to amend the BNA Act – except for certain sections – without going to Britain and without the consent of the provinces.

Foremost on the list of those parts of the Constitution which were exempted from this unilateral federal amending power and which would remain under the British Parliament's custody were the exclusive legislative powers of the provinces, denominational school rights, and the right to use English and French in federal, Manitoba, and Quebec institutions. In addition, two fundamental features of parliamentary democracy at the federal level were exempted: the requirement that there be a session of Parliament once a year; and the requirement that no House of Commons continue beyond five years, except in the event of an emergency recognized by two-thirds of the House. The new federal legislative power to amend the Constitution of Canada, subject to the exceptions listed above, was added to the list of exclusive federal legislative powers in section 91 of the Constitution. To underline its primacy it was placed at the top of the list, becoming section 91(1); the former section 91(1) – Public Debt and Property – was renumbered section 91(1A).

The federal government's rationale in obtaining this amending power without consulting the provinces was that it was obtaining power over those parts of the Constitution that are of concern to the federal government only. All along, section 92 of the Constitution, setting out exclusive provincial powers, had given each provincial legislature power to amend 'the Constitution of the province, except as regards the Office of Lieutenant Governor.' So, the federal argument went, in obtaining the power to amend those parts of the Constitution of concern only to the federal government, the federal level of government was simply catching up to the provinces.

The problem with this argument is that it is far from clear which parts of the Constitution are of exclusive concern to the federal government. Is the Senate, for instance, of concern only to the federal government? Although it is a branch of the federal legislature, it is the branch designed to give equal representation to all regions of the country, regardless of population. The provinces, especially the smaller ones, might argue that they have a special interest in the Senate. That indeed was what the Supreme Court of Canada decided in 1979 when it ruled that the federal Parliament could not use its unilateral amending power in section 91(1) to abolish or restructure the Senate.[21] In 1949 it was not specific issues such as Senate reform that agitated the provincial governments; it was the altering of basic constitutional issues such as the amending process, without the participation of the provinces. That kind of unilateralism threatened the provincial governments' claim to a fundamental share of Canadian sovereignty.

From the federal government's perspective, section 91(1) could be viewed as a pre-emptive strike. The Liberal government was no longer led by the canny and cautious Mackenzie King but by Louis

St Laurent, whose very image as a French-Canadian elder statesman might dampen Quebec criticism of federal constitutional
initiatives. St Laurent's advisers, sensing they were riding a centralist wave, felt confident about the possibility of persuading the
provinces to accept a reasonable overall solution to the amending
formula question.

The traditional machinery of constitutional bargaining was called
into play, and a federal-provincial conference met in Ottawa in
January 1950. Its purpose, according to St Laurent, was 'to seek
together to devise a generally satisfactory method of transferring
to authorities responsible to the people of Canada the jurisdiction
which may have to be exercised from time to time to amend those
fundamental parts of the Constitution which are of concern alike
to the federal and provincial authorities.'[22] Custody of the Constitution was to be transferred not to the people of Canada, but to
those responsible to the people.

The constitutional conference established a committee of attorneys-general to work out an amending formula. The committee
slogged away through 1950 on the intricacies of a complex amending formula, but in the end these efforts came to naught. The
conference to which the committee was to report back never re-
convened. A number of the provinces continued to press for a
more inflexible amending system than federal officials could accept. Public interest in patriating the Constitution was still quite
low. Besides, the federal government was now finding alternative
means to formal constitutional amendment for restructuring the
federation in a centralist direction.

One such change made without a formal constitutional amendment was the abolition of appeals to the Judicial Committee of the
Privy Council. In 1949 the federal Parliament passed legislation
ending all appeals to Great Britain and making the Supreme Court
of Canada the highest court. Two years earlier the Judicial Committee itself had ruled that this legislation was within the federal
Parliament's legislative jurisdiction under section 101 of the BNA
Act. This change had great centralizing potential. The English-
Canadian legal scholars who had pressed for the change argued
that Canadian judges, sensitive to the country's needs, would abandon the Judicial Committee's strict observance of provincial rights.[23]

The Liberal government, anxious not to arouse provincial suspicions, was at pains to deny the centralizing potential of acquiring judicial autonomy for Canada. It turned aside a proposal from the Conservative opposition to make the Supreme Court legally bound to observe Judicial Committee precedents, as well as a Quebec backbencher's proposal for provincial participation in the selection of Supreme Court justices. Government spokesmen argued that neither change was necessary, since the Supreme Court would simply adhere to the law of the Constitution. These denials of a possible centralist bias were not convincing. The fact remained that the judicial umpiring of federal-provincial disputes was now in the hands of a body whose members were all appointed by one of the parties to these disputes – namely, the federal government. To adherents of strict federalism, who were increasingly concentrated in Quebec, this was unacceptable.[24]

In the years immediately following, there was little opportunity to test whether a truly supreme Supreme Court would make a significant difference in the way the Constitution was interpreted. In the 1950s and on into the 1960s, the most important federal initiatives were in the realm of fiscal federalism, a realm in which judicial review has minimum application. Fiscal federalism has to do with the taxation and expenditure activities of government. The division of powers in this dimension of federalism is governed more by politics and economics than by constitutional law. Both politics and economics in this period favoured the federal government's aggressive use of the full amplitude of its powers.

In 1941, under the plenary power the federal government enjoys during a wartime emergency, the provinces were 'persuaded' to let the federal government collect all direct taxes in the country in return for 'tax rental' payments. Similar federal-provincial tax agreements were negotiated after the war. Although Ontario and Quebec refused to participate in the agreements covering the years 1947–52, and Quebec alone stood aloof in 1952–7, these arrangements had, in the words of J.A. Corry, 'a strongly centralizing effect, increasing the leverage of the national government on the policies of the provincial governments as well as on the economy of the country.'[25]

On the expenditure side, the postwar years witnessed a tremendous increase in federally initiated shared-cost programs with the provinces. Some, like the building of the Trans-Canada Highway, were not of a continuing nature. Others, like the federal grants to universities that began in 1951, the hospital insurance program introduced in 1958, and an array of social service and income support programs, would enable the federal government to have a major and long-term influence on how provincial governments allocate resources in what, constitutionally, are their exclusive legislative responsibilities.[26] For the balance of power in the Canadian federation, this exercise of fiscal clout by the federal government was far more important than any formal constitutional amendment.[27]

The only major resistance to these developments came from Quebec. That resistance came not from a progressive Quebec trying to expand its powers but from a reactionary Quebec government led by Maurice Duplessis, a government on the defensive in constitutional politics. The Duplessis government responded to growing centralism through that classic Canadian instrument of reaction – a royal commission. The rationale of the Tremblay Commission, appointed in 1953, was to check fiscal federalism and the continuous encroachment of the federal welfare state on provincial autonomy. The commission's basic conclusion was that, in its constitutional practice, Canada must return to the strict observance of federalism. Only in that way could Quebec enjoy its fundamental right under the Confederation compact to secure its distinct French-Canadian culture. That culture was defined as fundamentally 'communal,' based on 'three great traditions – family, autonomous work and the parish.'[28] Quebec must be protected not only from centralism but from secularization, industrialization, and creeping socialism as well.

In many respects the Tremblay Report can be viewed as a museum piece. Within a few years, Quebecers would begin electing provincial governments responsive to the forces of modernity Duplessis and the Tremblay commissioners were determined to resist. Nonetheless, the nationalist mentality that permeated every page of the Tremblay Report would endure – an insistence that the French Canadian's primary identity and loyalty lay with Quebec, and a corresponding rejection of the competing claims of

Canadian nationalism. Within Quebec, new elites, liberal, secular, and bourgeois in outlook, would soon pour new wine into this nationalist vessel, with profound implications for Canada's constitutional politics. Instead of urging a return to the traditional Constitution, Quebec governments would press for radical constitutional change.

All of this lay a few years ahead. For constitutional politics at the beginning of the 1960s it was business as usual. Federal-provincial committees of attorneys-general beavered away on an all-Canadian constitutional amending formula. By the autumn of 1964 enough progress had been made for a solution to be submitted to a summit conference of first ministers held at Charlottetown to celebrate the centennial of the Fathers of Confederation conference held in that city in 1864. At the conclusion of the conference Prime Minister Lester B. Pearson and the ten provincial premiers 'affirmed their unanimous decision to conclude the repatriation of the BNA Act without delay.'[29] The autonomous community of Canada was now to take its Constitution into its own hands – or at least the hands of its own political elites. The Canadian nation-building project commenced one hundred years earlier was now to be brought to a tranquil and consensual conclusion – or so it seemed until constitutional politics were lit afire by the Quiet Revolution in Quebec.

6 Mega Constitutional Politics, Round One: Fulton-Favreau to Victoria

On 14 October 1964 headlines in Canadian newspapers proclaimed the end of Canada's long struggle to find an acceptable constitutional amendment formula. The federal justice minister, Guy Favreau, and his ten provincial colleagues, meeting in Ottawa, unanimously agreed to a complex formula (the Fulton-Favreau formula) for amending all parts of the Constitution in Canada.[1] The Constitution was coming home.

This announcement turned out to be false news. Patriation was not to occur for another eighteen years. It did not happen in the 1960s because the government of Quebec withdrew its support for the formula and, at that time, the federal government accepted the principle that fundamental changes in the Constitution of Canada must not be made without the consent of the Quebec government.

It was a great irony that Quebec should be the province to veto the Fulton-Favreau formula. The formula appeared to give Quebec precisely what compact theorists and staunch exponents of provincial rights had always insisted upon – a requirement that no changes be made in the federal division of powers without the consent of all the provinces. Changes affecting the use of the English or French language would also require unanimous consent. Most other amendments would be subject to the 7/50 rule – consent of the federal Parliament plus the legislatures of two-thirds (seven out of ten) of the provinces representing at least 50 per cent of the Canadian population. A touch of flexibility was added by a clause permitting the delegation of legislative power from provinces to the federal Parliament and vice versa.[2]

The Fulton-Favreau amending formula guaranteed Quebec that

its historic constitutional interests – the provincial powers secured at the time of Confederation and the status of the French language – could not be altered without its consent. For a Quebec whose primary objective in constitutional politics was to defend the covenant of Confederation, it was enough; but it would not satisfy the Quebec now manifesting in its politics the consequences of the Quiet Revolution.

The social and economic conditions giving rise to Quebec's Quiet Revolution went back many years.[3] From the 1920s, forces of urbanization, industrialization, and secularization accumulated until, by the 1960s, they had transformed Quebec into a modern society that, except for language, was scarcely distinguishable from the rest of North America. As with other modernizing societies around the world, this decline in traditional distinctiveness was accompanied by an increased political assertiveness and emphasis on self-government.[4] The nationalism of Quebec's provincial elites shifted from the nationalism of *survivance* to a nationalism of development and expansion.[5] In constitutional terms, the priority was no longer to secure the powers acquired at Confederation but to increase Quebec's powers: the 'state of Quebec' should assume a comprehensive responsibility for the functions of the modern state, and the Québécois, to use the slogan of that day, should become 'maîtres chez nous.'

Premier Jean Lesage of Quebec, a Liberal who had previously served as a cabinet minister in the federal government, headed the first Quebec government of the Quiet Revolution. He found he had ample constitutional power for his initial reforms – the nationalization of Quebec's hydroelectric industry and the establishment of Quebec's first secular education ministry. In the fall of 1964 the Lesage government, which, incidentally, numbered René Lévesque among its members, agreed in principle to the Fulton-Favreau formula as the basis for patriating Canada's Constitution. Gradually, in the months that followed the Ottawa conference, public criticism of the formula began to build in Quebec.

Intellectuals, editorialists, and then opposition leaders, including the right-wing Union Nationale, now talked of the Québécois taking more of their collective interests under their own control. To do this, Quebec would need more powers and clearer recognition of its status as the homeland of French Canadians. Patriation of the BNA Act was regarded as primarily English Canada's nation-building project. For Quebec to accept it now would be a serious strategic error, especially with an amending formula that Daniel Johnson, the Union Nationale leader, labelled 'une camisole de force,' a strait-jacket. Once the Constitution was patriated, English Canada would probably lose interest in it. With such a rigid amending formula, Quebec might then find it impossible to obtain the substantial constitutional changes required for its nation-building project.

By the end of 1965 the heat of this criticism was sufficient to convince Lesage that Quebec would have to withdraw its support for the Fulton-Favreau formula. In January 1966 he informed Pearson that 'the government of Quebec has decided to delay indefinitely the proposal for constitutional amendment.'[6]

Lesage's change of heart meant much more than simply another failure to agree on a constitutional amending formula. The circumstances that prompted the change indicated that Quebec's price for supporting patriation would be nothing less than a restructuring of the Canadian federation to give sufficient scope for Quebec nationalism. Quebec's constitutional aggressiveness accelerated under the Union Nationale régime of Daniel Johnson, which replaced the Lesage Liberals in 1966. Johnson called for sweeping constitutional changes to be premised on a two-nations conception of Canada. Quebec would need powers commensurate with its status as the home of one of Canada's two founding peoples. Johnson's book, Égalité ou indépendance, took the form of an ultimatum: the only alternative to restructuring Canada along two-nations lines was the separation of Quebec from Canada.[7]

Following Quebec's rejection of the Fulton-Favreau formula, Canada's constitutional politics entered a new phase of mega constitutional politics.[8] Constitutional politics at the mega level has the qualities of a soap opera: if engaged in over a long period of time it becomes extremely boring; yet all along it remains gripping as to the final outcome – which never seems to come. Little did Canadians know when they entered this phase in the mid 1960s that it would carry on with few intervals of normalcy for a quarter of a century. Indeed, so accustomed has the present generation of

Canadians become to this kind of constitutional politics that many have come to think it is the normal Canadian condition. But it is not the norm, either for Canada or anyone else.

Virtually all countries that take their constitutions seriously engage from time to time in piecemeal, small-scale efforts to re-form them. In the United States, for example, since that gruesome episode of mega constitutional politics, the Civil War, every gener-ation has concerned itself with debating one or two constitutional changes.[9] Most recently, equal rights for women and constitutional impediments to budget deficits have been the principal constitu-tional preoccupations. Similarly, in Great Britain, the questions of adopting a constitutional bill of rights or of shifting to a system of proportional representation have found a place on that country's political agenda. Canada, too, has enjoyed long periods of ordi-nary, low-level constitutional politics. Indeed, that is how I would describe Canada's constitutional politics through most of its first century.

Constitutional politics at the mega level is distinguished in two ways from normal constitutional politics. First, mega constitutional politics goes beyond disputing the merits of specific constitutional proposals and addresses the very nature of the political community on which the constitution is based. Mega constitutional politics, whether directed towards comprehensive constitutional change or not, is concerned with reaching agreement on the identity and fundamental principles of the body politic. The second feature of mega constitutional politics flows logically from the first. Precisely because of the fundamental nature of the issues in dispute – their tendency to touch citizens' sense of identity and self-worth – mega constitutional politics is exceptionally emotional and intense. When a country's constitutional politics reaches this level, the constitu-tional question tends to dwarf all other public concerns.

Mega constitutional politics raises the fundamental question of whether the citizens of a nation-state share enough in common, in terms of their sense of political justice and collective identity, to go on sharing citizenship under a common constitution. That is why the media in Canada often refer to this kind of politics as the 'national unity' issue. Elsewhere, I have dubbed it 'the politics of frustration,'[10] for the divisions in the political community that fuel constitutional politics of this intensity make consensual resolution difficult. In the words of Keith Banting and Richard Simeon: 'Lack of consensus makes constitutional change necessary. The same lack makes resolution supremely difficult.'[11] Resolution becomes even more difficult when the mechanisms of constitutional change move from elite accommodation to more democratic and participatory procedures. Such a move becomes inescapable as the country's constitutional philosophy shifts from the organic constitutionalism of Burke to the social contract of Locke. Then the question the people must answer is: 'Can we become a single sovereign people?'

Many countries engage in mega constitutional politics from time to time and either break up or continue on the foundation of a new constitutional consensus. The latter is certainly what the United States did after the Civil War. Belgium has experienced this kind of constitutional politics in recent years. The former USSR and Yugoslavia are surely experiencing such politics right now, as is South Africa. Great Britain and other Western European countries will enter this type of politics in the political unification stage of the European community. But none of these countries has been engaged in mega constitutional politics so intensely and for so long as Canada.

Canada's struggle was not fully engaged until the thesis of Quebec nationalism was countered by the antithesis of pan-Canadian constitutional nationalism. Such a confrontation was in the making when in 1965 three Quebecers – Jean Marchand, Gérard Pelletier, and Pierre Trudeau – reversed the path Jean Lesage had taken and moved from Quebec to Ottawa. Trudeau soon took over the leadership of the Government of Canada and launched a constitutional counter-offensive against Quebec nationalism.

Trudeau had been one of the intellectual leaders of Quebec's Quiet Revolution. The strand of that revolution which he firmly embraced and eloquently expounded was not Québécois ethnic nationalism but the need for democratic reform within Quebec. 'Democracy first,' he wrote in a 1958 issue of Cité Libre. 'After that it will be up to the sovereign people to opt freely for the choices they prefer.'[12] He became increasingly antagonistic to the aspiration of Quebec nationalists to build an ethnically homogeneous state on the territory of Quebec. Trudeau regarded the 'ethnic chauvinism' inherent in this project as a kind of tribalism – an emotive and reactionary force that would undermine individual freedom and prevent Quebecers from moving forward to enjoy the full fruits of advanced technology and functional rationalism.[13]

Although Trudeau's desire to counter Quebec nationalism persuaded him to enter national politics as a federal Liberal, it was some time before he or his new political colleagues joined the constitutional battle. In an essay written in 1965 only a few months before his departure for Ottawa, he stated that 'we must not meddle with the constitution just yet.' To do so, he argued, 'will provide an escape valve for our energies, and useful diversionary tactics for those who fear the profound social reforms advocated by the progressive elements in our province.'[14] Nor was the government he joined, first as parliamentary secretary to Pearson and then as justice minister, in any hurry to resume constitutional negotiations after Quebec's rejection of the Fulton-Favreau formula. The Pearson government strenuously opposed Ontario premier John Robarts's initiative in organizing an interprovincial 'Confederation of Tomorrow' conference in Toronto in the fall of 1967 and sent just four 'observers.'[15]

The Confederation of Tomorrow conference was one response of English-speaking political leaders to Quebec's neo-nationalism. The conference posed the question, 'What does Quebec want?' The logic in asking that question was the view that the breakup of the country could be prevented only by accommodating the constitutional demands of the less extreme Quebec nationalists.[16] This perspective then, as now, finds most of its support in Ontario and Anglo-Quebec. It was a perspective on constitutional politics that Trudeau consistently repudiated.

Canadians did not find out at the Robarts conference what Quebec wants, but for the first time they could watch the proceedings of a constitutional conference on their television screens. The people were now admitted to constitutional politics as voyeurs. Though many did not like what they saw, the proceedings staged in the high-tech, high-rise surroundings of the new Toronto-Dominion Centre had a great deal of pizzaz as a media event. Under pressure from the two large central Canadian provinces, Ottawa now accepted 'the inevitability of some form of constitutional review.'[17] A federal-provincial constitutional conference was called for early 1968. The media success of Robarts's conference guaranteed a large audience for the next stage in the constitutional struggle.

The Pearson Liberals had begun to lay the groundwork for a new federal constitutional initiative when, soon after forming their first minority government in 1963, they established the Royal Commission on Bilingualism and Biculturalism. In 1965 the B and B commissioners had reported on the initial results of their probe of English-French relations in Canada. 'Canada,' they stated, 'without being fully conscious of the fact, is passing through the greatest crisis in its history.'[18] They described the crisis in terms resembling Lord Durham's analysis a century and a quarter before, as a conflict between two majorities: the French-speaking majority in Quebec and the English-speaking majority in all of Canada. For French Canada the question was whether it was 'going to think of itself as maintaining a vital solidarity among its dispersed parts, although centred in Quebec, or as an exclusively Quebec society.' The question for English Canada was whether it could accept the central concept of 'equal partnership.'[19] Pierre Trudeau, who as federal justice minister headed the task force preparing the federal position for the 1968 constitutional conference, would have clear and distinctive answers to these questions.

The shape of the Trudeau-fashioned federal initiative was indicated when he addressed the Canadian Bar Association in September 1967. If there was to be a constitutional review, his first priority would be a constitutional bill of rights. Such a bill would include the rights of individuals both as democratic citizens and as members of Canada's English- and French-language communities. By making agreement on the fundamental rights of the Canadian citizen the first step towards basic constitutional reform, 'we will,' Trudeau argued, 'be testing – and, hopefully, establishing - the unity of Canada.'[20] From this point until 1982, when the Charter of Rights and Freedoms was finally added to the Canadian Constitution, Trudeau never wavered in making a constitutional bill of rights his number one constitutional priority. And throughout, 'the fundamental rationale for this constitutional strategy was the perceived value of such a measure as a popular and unifying counter to decentralizing provincial demands in the Canadian constitutional debate.'[21]

The full scope of this strategy was revealed in the Pearson government's policy statement, *Federalism for the Future*, released on the eve of the constitutional conference that opened in Ottawa on 5 February 1968.[22] A broad constitutional review, and not simply patriation, would now be undertaken, but this review was not to be driven by Quebec's agenda. *Federalism for the Future* did not ask what Quebec wanted, in the style of Robarts's conference. Instead, it asked what constitutional changes would strengthen the sense of Canadian community. And its answer was first and foremost a constitutional statement of the rights of the Canadian citizen. Just behind that reform must come the strengthening of the central institutions of the federation, in particular the Senate and the Supreme Court of Canada. These priorities should now be at the top of the constitutional agenda. Only after making progress on these unifying reforms was attention to be given to the divisive issues related to the federal division of powers. Patriation with an all-Canadian amending formula was not even mentioned.

When the constitutional conference opened in Ottawa on 5 February 1968, though Pearson presided as chairman, Trudeau was the main federal spokesman. In a dramatic televised confrontation with Quebec premier Daniel Johnson, Trudeau rejected the Quebec nationalists' constitutional agenda. The future of French Canadians was to be secured not collectively through an autonomous provincial homeland but through their participation as individual citizens in a Canada-wide community guaranteeing recognition of their language rights from sea to sea. Trudeau's performance at this conference was instrumental in pushing him to the forefront of the contest to choose a new leader of the Liberal party and a new prime minister of Canada. In Trudeau, English Canada had found a constitutional hero. More than that, in his ideas they would find the makings of a new constitutional ideology. The question for Canada would be whether that ideology could also win the hearts and minds of Trudeau's own people, the Québécois.

The Trudeau vision of Canada gave birth to a rival nationalist ideology to that of Quebec nationalism. As an intellectual, Trudeau had mused about the inherent incompatibility of federalism and nationalism. Federalism requires rationalism and works through compromise; nationalism thrives through emotion and fosters intolerance. Nonetheless, Trudeau contended that 'federalism is ultimately bound to fail if the nationalism it cultivates is unable to generate a national image which has immensely more appeal than the regional ones.'[23] It was precisely such a 'national image' that Trudeau began to advance as he took the leadership of the constitutional counter-offensive against Quebec nationalism.

At the core of the Trudeau vision were individual rights – liberal-democratic rights and bilingual language rights defined and maintained by federal institutions. Equal enjoyment of these rights should be the primary bond of citizenship in the Canadian nation-state. In this credo, the right to use English or French in educating one's children and in communicating with government, wherever one lives in Canada, would ensure that the individual Canadian could have full access to all Canada offers. Language rights so conceived, far from recognizing Quebec's special status as the homeland of French Canadians, aimed at promoting the mobility of Canadians, so French Canadians would not be locked into the Quebec 'reservation' and English-speaking Canadians would feel welcome in Quebec. Trudeau and the governments he led embraced only the first of the Bs, bilingualism, in the B and B commission's mandate. Canada, in their vision, was fundamentally a multicultural, not a bicultural community. Multiculturalism had the electoral advantage of responding to that section of the Canadian community, by now more than one-quarter of the population, whose ethnic background is neither British nor French. It had an additional advantage as a constitutional strategy. As Kenneth McRoberts put it, 'by recognizing a multitude of cultures, multiculturalism could rein in the notion of duality and nullify Quebec's claim to distinctiveness on the basis of culture.'[24] There was no room for the 'two nations' concept in the Trudeauian view of Canada.

Despite Trudeau's intellectual intentions, his pan-Canadian nationalism, translated into the crude realities of mass politics, could be invested with the very passion and intolerance that Trudeau feared in nationalist movements. His ideology's insistence on the primacy of individual rights was blind to the individual's need for cultural security and respect, a need which may be particularly acute for those who feel their minority culture is threatened with extinction by a dominant culture.[25] In time, the contest between the nationalism of Trudeau and his Quebec adversaries would come to be charged with the sense of moral rectitude that flows from strong commitments to opposing conceptions of political justice and fundamental rights. A constitutional struggle of this kind, in which each side insists on a principled victory is, as the United States discovered, difficult if not impossible to contain within the accommodations of federalism. The secular religions of individual rights and ethnic self-determination could divide Canadians more deeply than catholicism and protestantism divided their nineteenth-century forebears. Trudeau's nationalism and that of his Québécois adversaries asked the citizen to declare a primary loyalty – the one to Canada, the other to Quebec. The essence of a deeply federal community is not to require its members to make such a categorical choice.

The full implications of this collision of nationalisms would not be felt until later rounds, when the constitutional struggle was engaged at a more popular level and rival leaders competed to win popular support for their ideals. In this first round of mega constitutional politics, while Quebec public opinion was a significant factor in beginning and ending the discussions, public interest outside Quebec – largely through the agency of television – was just beginning to develop. The formal set pieces remained thoroughly elitist: first ministers, attorneys-general, and government experts negotiating through the procedures of what Richard Simeon aptly termed 'federal-provincial diplomacy.'[26]

This period marks the apex of what Canadian political scientists call 'executive federalism.' By the mid 1960s meetings of federal and provincial ministers and their expert advisers on virtually all topics became so numerous they were supplanting legislatures as the primary arena of Canadian policy making.[27] The machinery of executive federalism, with its own federally dominated secretariat, was cranked up and applied as never before to constitutional negotiations. Beginning with the February 1968 conference and running through until the final conference at Victoria in June 1971, the constitutional review dominated federal-provincial relations. During that period, by Simeon's score card, the process spawned seven 'summit' meetings of first ministers, nine meetings of ministerial committees, fourteen of continuing committees of officials, fifteen of officials' subcommittees, plus innumerable informal interactions.[28]

At this stage, public criticism of executive federalism as the principal instrument of constitution making was relatively muted. Representatives of municipal governments protested their exclusion from the process as did leaders of some of the opposition parties. The one gesture towards a more inclusive process of constitutional review was the establishment in 1970 of a Special Joint Committee of the Senate and the House of Commons, chaired by Mark Mac-Guigan and Senator Gildas Molgat, to review all aspects of the Constitution. Over the next two years the MacGuigan-Molgat Committee conducted public hearings across the country, but its activities were detached from the mainstream of constitutional negotiations in the federal-provincial meetings. It was the latter that received most of the media's and the public's attention. The people did not yet claim their sovereignty.

Within the contained environment of federal-provincial negotiations, elite accommodation on a broad constitutional agenda was proving to be even more difficult to attain than when the agenda focused solely on the amending formula issue. Trudeau's proposal for a charter of rights had not yet penetrated the popular imagination, and there was no public pressure on provincial leaders to support a bill of rights. This group of provincial politicians, in contrast to those who would be involved in constitutional politics twenty years later, was not predisposed to accept a constitutional bill of rights as a good change in the Canadian system of governance. While they had no difficulty supporting the principles embedded in the democratic rights portion of Trudeau's proposal, they were deeply concerned about the way in which entrenchment of these rights would undermine their cherished ideal of legislative supremacy.

As for the language rights in the Trudeau charter, there was coolness bordering on hostility to the rights themselves. This was especially so for the premiers of the western provinces, where the largest francophone minority, Manitoba's, numbered just 3 per cent of the population. The only agreement on language rights that could be wrested from the premiers at the February 1968 conference was recognition of the 'desirability' of implementing the B and B commission's recommendations 'in ways most appropriate to each province.'[29] The federal government forged ahead in this area on its own and, in 1969, without a constitutional amendment,[30] had Parliament enact the Official Languages Act. This act gave the first explicit recognition, at the statutory though not the formal constitutional level, of English and French as Canada's 'official languages.' Its main practical import was to require the delivery of federal government services in both official languages all across Canada. While the act did a great deal for 'recognition of the French fact within the federal government,'[31] it was not a consensus builder in constitutional politics.

By 1969 it was clear there was no possibility of reaching a consensus on the federal government's full constitutional agenda. Most of the provincial governments were far more concerned with bread-and-butter economic issues than with constitutional reform. Pushed to the constitutional table by the federal initiative, their attention focused increasingly on the basic elements of fiscal federalism – the taxing and spending powers. Here, cross-cutting regional interests quickly emerged. Premiers of provinces with a strong economic base pressed for a larger share of the direct tax field. British Columbia's 'Wacky' Bennett called for a total withdrawal of the federal government from the personal and corporate income-tax fields. Representatives of poorer provinces, particularly from Atlantic Canada, pressed for the retention of strong federal fiscal powers to support the redistribution of wealth to have-not regions. These provinces were alarmed by a federal proposal, which resurfaced in the federal constitutional proposals of September 1991,[32] to limit its own spending power by requiring a 'national consensus' of provincial legislatures for conditional grants in areas of provincial jurisdiction.[33] Quebec, as was to be expected, took the most autonomist position, questioning the very presence of the federal government through its fiscal powers in areas of provincial responsibility. At the end of the first day of the December 1969 constitutional conference, Ontario's John Robarts, the one who had initiated the whole process of constitutional review in 1967, showed he was now older and wiser. 'We won't come to any rapid conclusions,' he said. 'It just is not possible, with the great variation of opinions among governments. Some of our differences may never be reconciled and we may, in fact, never be able to reach agreement.'[34] To which, nearly a quarter of a century later, we can only say amen.

The deepest conflict underlying these talks was the contest between the nation-building projects of Trudeau and the Quebec government. Most of the time this fundamental ideological conflict about the very meaning of Canada was kept beneath the surface. At the level of political leadership there was a real mismatch. While Trudeau's political stock was never higher, Quebec provincial leadership was extremely weak. Just after the constitutional review began, Daniel Johnson took ill and withdrew from active politics. Following his death in September 1968, education minister Jean-Jacques Bertrand took over as interim leader of the Union Nationale. He was not confirmed as leader until mid 1969. As a result, no Quebec nationalist leader took Trudeau on. Quebec officials sullenly attended the meetings with position papers calling for a massive transfer of powers to the provinces; but with Trudeau, his ministers, and his officials directing the meetings, there was no chance that Quebec's constitutional agenda would be seriously addressed.

Claude Morin, Quebec's deputy minister of intergovernmental affairs during this period (and later René Lévesque's minister of intergovernmental affairs), has poignantly expressed the frustration of shadow-boxing through this round of constitutional negotiations. Towards the end of his bitter memoir, he writes: 'So it was that right through the forty months of constitutional review Quebec and Ottawa were arguing in parallel, Quebec continuing to hope for basic discussion of power sharing and political reorganization, and Ottawa trying to move as far as possible along its chosen path while at the same time being careful never to admit the constitutional problem in its full-blown political dimension.'[35] The Trudeau game-plan was clearly to step right around Quebec's demands for more power, the cause that had given rise to a broad constitutional review, by winning support for constitutional proposals built on an alternative vision of Canada. But the popular support he would need for success in that venture, especially in Quebec, could not be secured in the closed quarters of executive federalism. In that forum, where the implicit decision-making rule was the unanimous agreement of all the governments, it was increasingly clear that success in a comprehensive constitutional overhaul could not be achieved.[36]

In 1970, as the third inconclusive year of the constitutional review dragged on, even the federal government was losing patience with the process. The time for closure had come. The idea of a full constitutional review would have to be abandoned, but perhaps a small package of changes could be put together which would be enough to bring the Constitution home to Canada on a consensual basis. With the election in April 1970 of a Liberal government in Quebec led by Robert Bourassa, whose constitutional slogan was not 'equality or independence' but 'profitable federalism,' the political conditions for closure on this basis seemed relatively propitious.

The shape of a limited constitutional package emerged at a working session of first ministers in February 1971. Elements of a constitutional bill of rights, a commitment to overcoming regional disparities, and constitutional recognition of the Supreme Court would be included with yet another attempt at the amending formula to pave the way for patriation. This was in line with the federal agenda. But to keep Bourassa at the table there had to be one element from Quebec's agenda and that would be a proposal for increasing provincial control over social policy.

Social policy was a crucial field of policy for Quebec. This was the domain of public policy in which the Quiet Revolution was having its fullest flowering. In this field a new generation of Quebecers, trained in modern administrative sciences, could take charge of matters traditionally left to the church. Yet to build the components of a modern welfare state coherently, the province needed to control all the components of social welfare policy, rather than being caught in the web of federal and provincial programs that had grown up since World War II. Already there was a constitutional model in place to accomplish this goal: section 94A of the BNA Act. This section, it will be recalled from chapter 5, was added to the Constitution in 1951 and gave both levels of govern-

ment jurisdiction in the field of old-age pensions, with the proviso
that provincial laws would prevail over any conflicting federal
legislation.

When section 94A was extended in 1964 to supplementary and
survivors' benefits, Quebec had the constitutional space in which
to introduce a comprehensive pension scheme and opt out of the
Canada Pension Plan established that year by the federal government for the rest of Canada. With this basic building block in
place and under the able leadership of Claude Castonguay, Quebec's minister of social affairs, Quebec aimed at pulling together
all the various income support, occupational training, and welfare
policies into a coherent program, including those that remained
under federal control. This would require extending section 94A
to the one field of social policy, unemployment insurance, which
since 1940 has been under exclusive federal legislative jurisdiction,
as well as to family allowances and occupational training programs
which the federal government had mounted through its spending
power. By making all these matters shared fields of jurisdiction
with provincial paramountcy, Quebec could opt out of all federal
social programs and expand the de facto special status it already
enjoyed in the pensions field. To remove any fiscal disincentive for
taking this course, Quebec proposed that the federal government
should transfer to the government of a province opting out of
federal programs sufficient funds to support equivalent provincial
programs.

Needless to say, the Quebec social policy proposal did not fit
neatly into Trudeau's scheme of things. The federal government
had indicated it was willing to attach constitutional limits to the
use of its spending power by requiring some sort of national consensus for new federal programs in areas of exclusive provincial
responsibility. It was also willing to provide fiscal compensation for
provinces not wishing to participate in new federal schemes – but
the compensation must go to the individual citizen, not the provincial government. For the federal nation-building objective, it was
essential that the federal government be seen by all citizens as a
provider of essential elements of the modern welfare state. Giving
up its exclusive power over unemployment insurance and permitting the dismemberment of the Canada-wide initiatives it had taken

in manpower training and income support did not sit well with that objective. Nevertheless, social policy was added to the items from the federal agenda to form the constitutional package to be considered at the full-dress constitutional conference scheduled for June 1971 in Victoria, British Columbia.

Between February and June the details of the constitutional package began to take shape through a negotiating process that closely resembled the process leading up to the Meech Lake Accord. The bargaining was very much on a closed-door basis, most of it bilateral in nature, except, unlike Meech, when it was Quebec leaders who shopped their proposals around the various capitals. The process in the spring of 1971 was basically federally driven and it was the federal justice minister, John Turner, who toured the provinces in search of consensus. The aim, as with Meech, was to emerge from this cocoon of shuttle diplomacy with a fully worked out set of constitutional proposals that might have a chance of securing unanimous approval at a highly publicized first ministers' meeting.

And the process appeared, if only for a brief moment, to have been successful. With much fanfare, the ten provincial premiers and Prime Minister Trudeau assembled in British Columbia's legislative chamber on 14 June. For three days the first ministers debated the constitutional proposals, often in full view of the television cameras. Then, on 17 June, they went into a closed session, emerging after thirteen hours with the text of the Victoria Charter. The bargaining was over. There was agreement to take the charter back to each capital to see whether it had full government support. Trudeau, despite the many compromises he had made, was reasonably satisfied with the charter, and there was general enthusiasm among most of the provincial delegations. Only Quebec's Robert Bourassa was 'guarded and non-committal.'[37]

It is worth recalling the contents of the Victoria Charter. Even though it would soon be relegated to the dustbin of Canada's constitutional history, all of its items would appear again in some form or other in subsequent stages of the constitutional debate. The charter serves also as a benchmark of the constitutional thinking of Canada's political elites at the end of the first round of the mega constitutional struggle.[38]

Taking pride of place at the top of the charter were democratic rights and language rights. To this extent the 'Trudeau vision' was served, but compared with what was to come ten years later this was a mini charter of rights. It included only the fundamental freedoms of thought, conscience, expression, association, and assembly (all subject to what legislatures might think necessary in the interests of public safety, order, health, morals, or national security), plus guarantees of universal suffrage, federal and provincial elections every five years, and annual sessions of the legislatures. The charter declared English and French official languages, but its specific language rights were a monument to dissensus. Ontario and the four Atlantic provinces would join Quebec, Manitoba, and the federal Parliament in recognizing the right to use both languages in the legislature. The three westernmost provinces refused to go even this far towards bilingualism. The federal government would print provincial statutes in the minority language if a province refused to do so. Only New Brunswick and Newfoundland would go so far as giving authoritative status to both versions. New Brunswick and Newfoundland were also the only provinces which would entrench the right to use both languages in their courts, though such a right already existed for Manitoba, Quebec, and federally established courts. There would be a new right to communicate in either language with the head office of government departments and agencies, but not in Nova Scotia or the four western provinces. Minority education rights were not mentioned. This sorry checkerboard of rights ended with a touch of hopefulness: a mechanism whereby provinces could in the future opt in to a more extensive coverage of minority language guarantees.

After the rights came a lengthy section dealing with the Supreme Court of Canada. This section represented the second priority on Trudeau's constitutional agenda – strengthening the federation's central institutions. Senate reform had not yet been seized upon by the provinces of 'outer Canada' as the means of checking central Canadian domination of national policy making. By the 1960s, however, the Supreme Court had begun to show signs of a centralist bias. Its 1967 decision in the Offshore Mineral Rights Reference had brought into question the court's credibility as a neutral arbiter of federal-provincial disputes.[39] The Victoria proposals aimed to overcome this doubt by entrenching the court in the Constitution (instead of its continuing as a creature of the federal Parliament) and by giving the provinces, through a most cumbersome set of procedures, a role in the selection of its justices. This part of the charter also made a small gesture towards special status for Quebec: three of the court's nine justices should come from Quebec, and these three justices should form the majority in any cases involving Quebec's distinctive civil law.[40]

The Victoria Charter contained a short pledge on the part of both levels of government to promote 'equality of opportunity and well being for all individuals in Canada' and to reduce regional disparities. Hidden away in small print in an attached schedule was abolition of the federal powers of reservation and disallowance. Trudeau was willing to give up this power of federal surveillance over the provinces in exchange for their being bound by a charter of rights. A decade later when they insisted on inserting a legislative override in the charter, he would withdraw this offer.

At the end of the Victoria Charter was yet another proposal for an all-Canadian amending formula. This formula was considerably more flexible than the Fulton-Favreau formula. Unanimity would not be required for any amendments. The basic rule for most constitutional amendments would be approval by the federal House of Commons (the Senate would have only a ninety-day suspensory veto), and approval by the legislatures of any province that ever had 25 per cent of Canada's population, at least two Atlantic provinces, and at least two western provinces with 50 per cent of the western population. Since only Ontario and Quebec had 25 per cent of the Canadian population, this formula was, in effect, a not so subtle way of ensuring a constitutional veto for these two provinces. In 1982 Trudeau was forced to abandon this formula in favour of one more faithful to the principle of provincial equality. The Victoria amending formula continues to resurface as the search goes on for a consensus in defining the constituent elements of the Canadian body politic.[41]

In 1971 the amending formula was not the deal-breaker. That honour was reserved for an article tucked away in the middle of the Victoria Charter dealing with jurisdiction over social policy. The proposal went a little way towards accommodating Quebec's aspiration for constitutional space in which to exercise a plenary control over the province's social policies. Family, youth, and occupational training allowances would be added to pensions in section 94A. In effect, since the federal Parliament had no explicit constitutional authority to legislate in these fields, this was an expansion of federal legislative powers, albeit one that would continue to be subject to provincial paramountcy. An obligation was introduced for the federal government to give the provinces ninety days' notice before introducing legislation in these concurrent fields. But the proposal fell far short of covering the whole field of social policy and provided no mechanism for fiscally compensating provinces which did not participate in federal initiatives.

It took little time for Quebec to reject the Victoria Charter. At Victoria, the first ministers gave one another ten days to see whether their cabinet colleagues sufficiently supported the proposals to submit them to their legislatures for approval. There was no legal requirement to obtain approval of the provincial legislatures. With the Constitution still unpatriated, the approval of the British Parliament was the only legal requirement. Still, it was felt that approval of the terms of patriation by Canada's elected legislative bodies would give the new constitutional arrangements a stronger democratic root in Canada. Ten years later, when patriation actually occurred, this step was omitted to avoid advertising the fact that the terms of patriation were unacceptable to Quebec's National Assembly. In 1971 the extent of provincial legislative support was never tested. On 22 June, after an all-night meeting of his cabinet, Bourassa telephoned Trudeau to tell him his government had rejected the Victoria Charter.

Bourassa's official communiqué singled out the uncertainty involved in judicial interpretation of some of the language in the social policy provisions as the main reason for rejection.[42] This was a characteristically technocratic explanation of a political response to a broad-based nationalist agitation in the province. There was not enough in the Victoria Charter to satisfy the aspiration of many Quebecers for a federal restructuring that would give Quebec the freedom to put its distinctive stamp on a modern set of public policies. Overnight, a front to reject Victoria was formed. It included the Corporation of Quebec Teachers, the Confederation of National Trade Unions, and the Federation of St-Jean-Baptiste Societies. Full-page advertisements appeared in newspapers comparing Victoria with the imposition of conscription in World War II and calling for a 'general mobilization of the people of Quebec.'[43] Translated into the idiom of mass communications, technical constitutional issues quickly assume symbolic, mythic proportions. Claude Ryan, at the time editor of *Le Devoir* and later to succeed Bourassa as Quebec Liberal leader, said that Bourassa's 'non' expressed the profound convictions' of the whole Quebec people.[44] Even though Ryan was overstating the strength of anti-Victoria sentiment, the political thunder aroused by the Quebec nationalists was enough to persuade a government whose main political opposition was now René Lévesque's separatist Parti Québécois to withhold its support for this Trudeau-directed patriation package.

Quebec's rejection was enough to torpedo the deal. The political convention that Quebec's approval was necessary for major constitutional change, if not the rule of unanimity, was at that time firmly in place. Round one of the mega constitutional struggle was over.

7 Round Two:
New Constitutionalism

After the collapse of the Victoria Charter, everyone, it seemed, had had enough of constitutional politics. For the next few years constitutional politics was not front and centre in Canadian politics. It would take the election of the Parti Québécois to power in Quebec in November 1976 to quick-start another round of mega constitutional politics. In the five-year intermission that preceded this event, changes took place in the political, economic, and legal circumstances of the country that would produce an agenda of constitutional concerns considerably more complex and urgent than that of round one.

A measure of the lack of interest in constitutional issues in the aftermath of Victoria is the deafening silence that greeted the report of the Special Joint Committee of the Senate and the House of Commons on the Constitution of Canada in 1972. This committee, chaired by Senator Gildas Molgat and MP Mark MacGuigan, had been Canada's first attempt at popular participation in constitution making. The committee held meetings in forty-seven cities and towns across the country, received 8000 pages of evidence, and heard evidence from 1486 witnesses at meetings attended by 13,000 Canadians. The committee concluded that 'the people now want a new constitution,'[1] and went on to lay out detailed recommendations for a comprehensive new constitution.

The Molgat-MacGuigan committee was slightly ahead of its time. The time for new constitutionalism did not come until the latter half of the 1970s, when the separatist victory in Quebec moved federal and provincial governments to play the new constitutionalism game. The Molgat-MacGuigan report exuded a wonderful naïvety, a sense that a whole new Constitution adding the 'functionally contemporary' to the best of the past could be worked out in a calm and rational fashion. If Canadians have learned anything from the last twenty-five years, it must surely be that constitutional politics at the macro level do not work that way.

Still, many ideas in the report were portents of things to come, particularly the principle of 'self-determination.' Clearly, increasing support in Quebec for Quebec's separation from Canada prompted the committee to deal with this topic. By the 1970s the separatist cause had moved from the fringes of Quebec politics and terrorist actions to the Parti Québécois, a democratic political party with a good chance of achieving power through electoral means. The Parti Québécois, the committee observed, 'has made the exercise of right of self-determination the corner-stone of its creed.'[2] The committee pointed out that self-determination of a people is not the same as self-determination of a province. The right of self-determination of peoples is what is recognized in the International Covenant on Civil and Political Rights adopted by the United Nations in 1966. Quebec province as a whole could not claim this right. The French-Canadian people is not coextensive with the boundaries of Quebec and, further, 'there are within the Province of Quebec other groups which would possess an equal claim with Francophones to self-determination.'[3] Contemporary Canadians in the fifth round of their great constitutional struggle have cause to revisit these early ruminations on the messy principle of self-determination.[4] It is one thing to ask whether all Canadians can be a sovereign people; an equally valid question is whether all Quebecers can be a sovereign people.

In the 1970s there was little understanding of the rights of Canada's aboriginal peoples. The example Molgat-MacGuigan gave of a community within Quebec with a right to self-determination was not aboriginal peoples but the province's one million anglophones, 'who at least in the western part of the province have sufficient cohesion to constitute viable communities.'[5] The next section of the report dealt with 'native peoples.' The committee was at least one step ahead of the federal government, which at that time totally excluded aboriginal peoples from its constitutional agenda.

Aboriginal peoples as such had no place in the 'Trudeau vision' of the Canadian community. The future offered to native persons in the Trudeau government's 1969 white paper was that of undifferentiated individuals enjoying the equal rights of all Canadian citizens.[6] Molgat-MacGuigan acknowledged that an alternative approach, viewing 'the native people as collectivities ... does appear preferable to many of the native peoples themselves.'[7] The committee did not endorse that alternative view but simply recommended that no constitutional changes concerning native peoples be made until their own organizations had completed their research on aboriginal rights in Canada.

At this stage it was the judicial branch of government, not the political branches, that set the pace in recognizing the collective rights of Canada's aboriginal peoples. In 1973 the Supreme Court of Canada in the Calder case[8] brought down a landmark decision giving clear recognition to the existence of aboriginal title in Canadian law. The justices split three-to-three on whether the aboriginal title of the Nishga people to their ancestral lands in British Columbia's Nass valley had been extinguished by laws of the old colony of British Columbia.[9] This was enough to persuade the Trudeau government to change its policy. Whereas Trudeau in 1969 had said, 'We can't recognize aboriginal rights because no society can be built on historical "might have beens,"'[10] his government after the Calder decision agreed to enter into 'comprehensive' land-claims negotiations with aboriginal groups 'where rights of traditional use and occupance had been neither extinguished by treaty nor superseded by law.'[11] This comprehensive land-claims policy, by recognizing the legal foundation in white-settler law of the rights of aboriginal peoples, was at least a beginning of a broader recognition of aboriginal societies as founding peoples.

Canada's aboriginal peoples may turn out to be among the few beneficiaries of Canada's protracted constitutional struggle. Opening up both the substance and the process of constitutional politics would eventually provide opportunity for aboriginal peoples to assert their right to consent to the conditions on which they might be part of the Canadian community. It is unlikely that such an opportunity would have occurred had Canada's constitutional debate not addressed fundamental questions about the nature of the country and kept those questions open for so long. The entry of the aboriginal peoples onto the constitutional playing-field was just beginning in the 1970s. Over the next two decades the strengthening of the aboriginal peoples' political organizations and expectations would amount to nothing less than a second 'quiet revolution,' with as profound implications for Canada's constitutional turmoil as that which earlier converted Quebec to constitutional radicalism.

It was in the traditional arena of constitutional politics – federal-provincial relations – that changing circumstances had a more immediate impact on the constitutional struggle. While both Quebec and the federal government, the chief protagonists of round one, were relatively quiescent following the collapse of the Victoria accord, a third force was stirring. The western provinces were becoming constitutionally restless. At the Confederation of Tomorrow conference in 1967, Saskatchewan premier Ross Thatcher's comment, 'if we had a hundred problems, the constitution would be the hundred and first,'[12] bluntly summed up the West's constitutional apathy at that time. In the early 1970s the constitutional mood of western Canada was moving from apathy to grievance.

Two factors account for the change. The first had to do with economics. The dramatic increase in the world price of oil resulting from the Organization of Petroleum Exporting Countries (OPEC) price increases made the three westernmost provinces, sitting on top of substantial petroleum reserves, concerned about whether the existing Constitution adequately secured provincial control over this great new source of wealth.[13] Ottawa's initial reaction to the international oil crisis gave rise to this concern. The federal government's policy was to protect Canadian oil consumers from the crisis by keeping the Canadian domestic price well below world levels. It introduced an oil export tax to finance this policy – in effect subsidizing consumers, most of whom reside in Ontario and Quebec, at the expense of western producers. Then, to ensure that Ottawa rather than the provinces had access to the major share of tax revenues generated by the oil boom, Ottawa provided that oil companies could no longer deduct royalties paid to the provinces from their federal income tax. Further constitutional alarm bells sounded later in the decade when the

Supreme Court of Canada in two decisions found that provincial schemes to tax and regulate resource industries were beyond the provinces' constitutional powers.[14] Well before the last Trudeau government delivered the coup de grâce – its National Energy Policy – many westerners were convinced that the Constitution left them dangerously exposed to the rapaciousness of central Canada.

This view was fortified by a second factor that was basically political: the almost total failure of the Trudeau Liberals to elect members from the western provinces. This draining away of Liberal support in western Canada pre-dated the Trudeau government's resource policies and may have had as much to do with Trudeau's apparent preoccupation with bilingualism, a program of little salience in the West, where the German and Ukrainian communities are larger than the French. Whatever the cause of this political phenomenon, westerners increasingly turned to constitutional remedies. The central institutions of the federation had to be restructured to give the West and the East a stronger voice in national policy making. A reformed Senate was coming to be looked upon as the logical place for the less populous provinces of 'outer Canada' to check the domination Ontario and Quebec, with over half of the Canadian population, could exercise over the House of Commons. Some called this growing movement of constitutional discontent 'western alienation,' but it could be a misleading term. Unlike Quebec nationalism, which aimed to lessen participation in the Canadian community, the western movement had as its main aspiration 'greater inclusion in, rather than withdrawal from, the broader Canadian society.'[15]

The constitutional restlessness stirring the western provinces was not confined to that region. The pendulum of power and initiative that swings back and forth from central to provincial governments in the Canadian federation was once again swinging towards the provinces. Following World War II, the federal government's dominance had been sustained by Keynesian economic management and leadership in building the Canadian welfare state. The momentum of those policies was now spent. By the mid 1970s the federation was experiencing a high tide of 'province-building.'[16] Between 1965 and 1974, provincial and local government spending as a percentage of GNP increased from 15.1 per cent to 23.1 per cent, while federal government spending declined from 16.2 per cent to 15.5 per cent.[17] The provinces were still keen to obtain fiscal support for provincial programs from the federal government by way of transfer payments or tax room, but as they built their own bureaucracies, modernized their governments, and brought in specialists to manage the relationship with Ottawa, cooperative federalism gave way to a more combative style of intergovernmental relations.

One measure of just how combative federal-provincial relations were becoming is the frequency with which the two levels of government began to fight each other in the courts. Between 1975 and 1982, the Supreme Court of Canada decided eighty constitutional cases, almost all of them dealing with the federal division of powers – two more than it heard in its first quarter-century as Canada's final court of appeal.[18] Moreover, provinces were not simply interested in defending their jurisdiction in the courts. Through the 1970s virtually all of the provinces, no matter how economically dependent some of them were on Ottawa, began to seek expanded jurisdiction in some areas – be it Newfoundland's desire to control offshore resource development, other Atlantic provinces' interest in greater control over fisheries, or the concern of a number of provinces in strengthening jurisdiction over communications and family law.

In attributing this kind of constitutional discontent to 'the provinces,' it is important to bear in mind that the term means provincial governments, not necessarily the people who live in the provinces. Alan Cairns in 1977 made a powerful case for the proposition that 'province-building' was primarily a top-down process: the demands it generates are shaped by provincial politicians and civil servants.[19] The empirical research on citizens' attitudes assembled by David Elkins and Richard Simeon at this time showed that Canadians remained quintessentially federal in outlook, with a strong sense of allegiance to both levels of government.[20] During this period of province building a strong current of economic nationalism was also building on the left in English Canada, although it was not strong enough to have much influence on government policy.[21] Later, in the fourth round of mega constitutional politics, this body of English-Canadian nationalism would play a decisive role in rejecting the Meech Lake Accord.

In the 1970s, constitutional politics was still highly elitist, and it was the aspirations of governments, not people, that really counted. These aspirations had now developed to the point where Quebec had plenty of company in insisting that patriation be accompanied by substantive constitutional change. Any doubts on the matter vanished when the provincial premiers met in 1975 in St John's, Newfoundland. The virus of constitutional discontent is most contagious at such meetings. The premiers had received an invitation from Prime Minister Trudeau to attend a constitutional conference confined to that old chestnut, patriation and the amending formula. In reply, the host premier, Frank Moores, conveyed the following message: 'While all the Premiers agreed that ... patriation was a desirable objective, it was generally felt that this issue should be dealt with in the context of a more general review of such aspects as the distribution of powers, control of resources and other related matters.'[22] Trudeau, having temporarily lost his appetite for broad-based constitutional review, did not take the premiers up on this offer.

At this point the patriation project seemed stymied by the cross-cutting constitutional objectives of Ottawa, Quebec, and the other provinces. If nothing dramatic had happened, constitutional politics would likely have drifted along below the mega level until another generation took over. But one event in Quebec launched the country on yet another gripping round of that heavy, symbolically charged constitutional stuff.

On 15 November 1976 the Parti Québécois, led by René Lévesque, came to power. There was now no question as to what the Government of Quebec wanted. Its constitutional objective was to make Quebec a separate state enjoying an economic association with what would remain of Canada. The PQ made it easier for those who were not *indépendantistes* to vote for it by promising to proceed to separation only after winning approval for independence in a referendum. At this time, no one seriously questioned the legitimacy of a majority-rule referendum as the way of determining the constitutional future of all Quebecers – francophones, anglophones, allophones, and aboriginals.

The PQ's election victory, in the words of Donald Smiley, 're-sulted in more constitutional discussion among Canadians than at any time in the country's history.'[23] The coming to power of Quebec separatists increased tremendously the sense of urgency in English-speaking Canada about the need for major constitutional change. The 'Trudeau vision' had neither won the hearts and minds of the Québécois nor deflated the cause of ethnic national-ism. Indeed, while Trudeau had been licking his wounds after Victoria, Bourassa's Liberal government in Quebec was bringing in Bill 22, making French the official language of Quebec – a mea-sure the PQ's Bill 101 would soon extend much further.[24] There was now a sense, as never before, that the constitutional choice for Canada was either a totally new Constitution reshaping the Canadi-an federation in a way that dealt satisfactorily with Quebec and the other major sources of constitutional discontent or the dismember-ment of the federation and the separation of Quebec from Cana-da. The constitutional stakes seemed very high indeed: Canadians would either make a new social contract or risk the breakup of their country. The period of new constitutionalism was at hand.

At first it was the 'chattering classes' – lawyers, writers, profes-sors, students, people who have time for this sort of thing and believe they have expertise to offer – who began to explore broad new constitutional alternatives. There was, as Cairns reports, 'a virtual explosion of conferences, seminars and publications on constitutional ailments and cures as the public-spirited and the self-seeking sought to get their views on record.'[25] In October 1977, for example, concerned citizens from Canada assembled at the Univer-sity of Toronto for a week-long conference that produced a 500-page book, *Options Canada*. President John Evans's introduction to this volume anticipated an opening up of the constitutional pro-cess. The conference's work, he wrote, would contribute 'to the grass-roots debates and searchings that are going on all over the country: for it is these grass-roots debates ... that are ultimately the arbiters of our destiny.'[26] The people were to be involved as more than voyeurs in constitution making.

But the politicians had other ideas. Constitution making was too important to be left to the people. By 1977, government task forces and commissions were working away on constitutional proposals.

In July the federal government established the Task Force on Canadian Unity, chaired by Jean-Luc Pepin, a former member of Trudeau's cabinet, and John Robarts, the former premier of Ontario. The Pepin-Robarts Task Force was given a broad mandate to 'obtain and to publicize the views of Canadians regarding the state of their country' and to provide 'ideas and initiatives ... on the question of Canadian unity.'[27] While Pepin, Robarts, and their colleagues were touring the country feeling the public pulse on constitutional reform, Trudeau was preparing his own proposals. Having been persuaded to partake in 'new constitutionalism,' he was determined to do it his way.

His way was revealed to Canadians midway through 1978 with the release of a booklet, *A Time for Action*.[28] This glossy booklet, dripping with maple leafs and available at the local post-office, summoned Canadians to a 'renewal of the Canadian Federation.' The central thesis of the 1972 report of the Special Joint Committee on the Constitution was now government policy. Renewal of the federation required nothing less than an entirely new Constitution. The establishment of a new Constitution was to be accomplished in two stages. The leading elements of Trudeau's earlier agenda were to constitute phase one, except now they were to be done unilaterally by the federal government using the limited power to amend the Constitution it had obtained in 1949.[29] This phase would include a statement of fundamental objectives of the federation, a remodelling of federal institutions, and, naturally, a Charter of Rights that at first would apply only at the federal level.

Details of phase one were fully set out in a Constitutional Amendment Bill, Bill C–60,[30] which followed fast on the heels of *A Time for Action*. Among the highlights of Bill C–60 were a new federal upper house, the House of the Federation, jointly elected by the House of Commons and the provincial legislatures; a constitutionally entrenched Supreme Court of Canada enlarged to eleven justices, whose appointments would require consultation with provincial governments as well as ratification by the House of the Federation; and codification into constitutional law of the basic conventions of responsible government. The proposed statement of 'fundamental aims' – the first of countless 'Canada clauses' to come – began, as might be expected in a Trudeau document, with an affirmation of unity ('the people of Canada ... declare and affirm ... their expectation for a future in common') and concluded with a small recognition of Quebec nationalism ('a permanent national commitment to the endurance of the Canadian French-speaking society centred in but not limited to Quebec').[31] As in the Meech Lake Accord, these statements of fundamental characteristics of the federation were not to be put in a preamble to the Constitution but in its first substantial sections.

Phase two of the process would 'cover all those sections of the Constitution on which the federal government and the provinces must discuss together what should be done.'[32] This would include the division of powers and the amending formula. The second stage would be capped by a final act of patriation that would not just bring the Constitution home, but would bring home a totally new Constitution by 1 July 1981.

Following this federal initiative, the constitutional clouds burst and a torrent of constitutional proposals rained down on the land. Some came from private sector organizations, others from provincial governments and political parties. It would be tedious and pointless to summarize this long line of documents, but a few highlights will give a sense of the swirling vortex of opinion at this stage in the constitutional debate.

The most comprehensive of the private ventures was *Towards a New Canada*, prepared by a committee of the Canadian Bar Association.[33] The lawyers had the temerity to propose a non-monarchical head of state – the only group to do so. That proposal proved to be the kiss of death, causing the lawyers' handiwork to be repudiated by their own organization. The time for republicanism in Canada had not yet come. The provincial governments' proposals were put together with the help of selected experts but without any broader public consultation. They did not for a moment accept the assumption of Trudeau's phase one that central institutions of the federation such as the Supreme Court or the Senate, could be restructured unilaterally by the federal government. On the contrary, reform of these institutions figured prominently in many of the provincial publications. There was at this time a veritable 'epidemic of Senate reform.'[34] It was no surprise that the model favoured by most provinces was not Trudeau's but one based on

West Germany's *Bundesrat* – a chamber of provincial government appointees.[35] At this point, no government proposed a directly elected upper house.

Although the threat of Quebec separation had triggered this second round of constitutional politics, most of the provinces, in fashioning their own proposals, gave little weight to responding to Quebec. If some of their proposals, such as increased provincial control over natural resources and communications, corresponded with Quebec demands, that was more by coincidence than design. Ontario and New Brunswick were somewhat of an exception; being closer to Quebec and with numerically significant francophone minorities, they tended to be more supportive of cultural dualism as a fundamental constitutional principle.[36]

The Government of Quebec had nothing to contribute by way of proposals to restructure the Canadian federation. Premier Léves-que waited until the efforts at federal-provincial negotiation had failed to release *Quebec-Canada: A New Deal*, setting out Quebec's constitutional proposal.[37] Here, for the first time, the objective of sovereignty-association was sketched out. This was the softest of sovereignty options, designed to make separatism more palatable to faint-hearted nationalists. Though acceding to formal sovereign-ty, the nation of Quebec would be tied closely to Canada economi-cally. The economic association would be regulated by an interna-tional treaty providing for a common market and a common cur-rency. It was recognized that political institutions would be needed to manage the economic association – a community council, a commission of experts, a monetary authority, and a court (to settle treaty disputes). Some of these institutions – the council and the court – were to be structured on a parity basis (equal represen-tation for Quebec and Canada), but in others, notably the mone-tary authority, Quebec would be a junior partner with seats allocat-ed according 'to the relative size of each economy.'[38] This was the plan that the PQ government would submit to the people of Que-bec in the forthcoming referendum as the basis for negotiating Quebec's separation from Canada. It was prepared with no consid-eration as to how it might be received by the rest of Canada, which, as usual, was perceived by Quebec nationalists as homoge-neous and centralist.

It remained for the Quebec Liberal party, then in opposition, to bring forward a Quebec federalist program for a new Canadian Constitution. The party's proposals, released early in 1980, were known as the Beige Paper.[39] As might be expected from a party led by Claude Ryan, who had spearheaded the attack on the Victoria Charter, the Beige Paper called for some decentralization of power, especially in the fields of social policy and culture. It proposed increased powers for Ottawa in setting national economic policy and emphasized Quebec's role in central institutions such as the Supreme Court and a new, provincially appointed, Federal Council replacing the Senate. Although the paper insisted that a new Canadian constitution give Quebec the powers needed for 'the protection and affirmation of its distinct personality,' it also insisted that this not be done in a way that would 'contradict the fundamental principle that all partners within the federation are fundamentally equal.'[40]

The contrast between the Beige Paper proposals and those of another constitutional committee of the Quebec Liberal party eleven years later (the Allaire Report)[41] is truly remarkable. The gulf between the two is not so much the greater degree of decentralization called for in the Allaire Report as fundamentally different perceptions of the political community on which the new Constitution is to be based. For Ryan's 1979 Quebec Liberals, the community is Canada, a Canada based on two founding peoples. For Allaire, the community is Quebec. Its proposals 'are presented as 'a blueprint for the society we want for Quebec.' As for Canada, or the 'rest of Canada,' it 'is and will remain our neighbour.'[42] Over a decade, the emotional dynamics of Canada's constitutional politics moved the constitutional outlook of Quebec's Liberal party (although not necessarily the Bourassa government) much closer to the Parti Québécois's sovereignty-association than to Claude Ryan's Beige Paper.

The constitutional position closest to the Beige Paper at the time it was issued emanated from a federal body – the Pepin-Robarts Task Force on National Unity. The constitutional position advanced in its report, *A Future Together*, issued early in 1979, closely resembled the Beige Paper in substance as well as in spirit. It too proposed some decentralization of powers in the social policy and cultural areas, but more central power over the economy and a strengthening of central institutions. Its principal recipe for national unity was not a charter codifying the equal rights of individual Canadians but recognition of the country's regional divisions and its linguistic and cultural diversity. Although set up 'to advise the Government [of Canada] on unity issues,'[43] this was hardly the advice the Trudeau government was looking for. The task force appointed to consult with the people, like the Quebec Liberal party, was out of power.

Power in constitutional politics, as in most other matters, still rested in the hands of Canada's eleven first ministers. In the fall of 1978, amidst the frenzy of new constitution drafting, Trudeau and the provincial premiers returned for yet another round at the constitutional bargaining table. At this meeting Trudeau agreed to modify his phase one–phase two program and to work towards the negotiation of fourteen items, including division-of-powers issues pushed by the provinces. To coordinate this renewed effort at elite accommodation, the first ministers established a Continuing Committee of Ministers on the Constitution. The CCMC was chaired by Roy Romanow, attorney-general of Saskatchewan, and the federal minister of justice, initially Otto Lang and then Marc Lalonde.

The agenda of constitutional negotiations was now as wide as it has ever been. The priorities of Trudeau's federal government were there: the Charter of Rights, the Senate, the Supreme Court, the codification and Canadianization of constitutional monarchy, a commitment to the reduction of regional disparities through equalization payments, and, of course, patriation with an amending formula. But provincial concerns were also represented: proposals to restrict the exercise of the federal spending power and declaratory power (under which Ottawa took control of facilities such as grain elevators and uranium mines by declaring them to be 'works ... for the general Advantage of Canada')[44] as well as proposals to expand provincial jurisdiction over communications, fisheries, family law, and natural resources on land and offshore. New constitutionalism at the constitutional bargaining table had been reduced to a grab-bag of issues reflecting each government's pet constitutional project – except, of course, Quebec's separatist objective.

For three months the CCMC worked away at this agenda, producing 'best effort' drafts on each of the items. These texts, in the
words of Romanow and his co-authors, Whyte and Leeson, 'represented a high degree of consensus and accommodation,' and in
substance shared a common direction – 'a devolution of federal
government authority.'[45] Even so, the drafts did not provide the
basis for a federal-provincial accord. At the constitutional conference held in February 1979, the first ministers agreed to disagree.
Trudeau gave notice that his government was preparing a second
list of items to strengthen the Canadian economic union and
Ottawa's power 'to manage the overall economic interests of
Canada.'[46]

The round of constitutional negotiations that culminated in
February 1979 is as close as Canada's political leaders came during
the Trudeau era to reaching a comprehensive agreement on constitutional reform. It was the only time during Trudeau's years as
prime minister that his government seemed willing to go a reasonable distance towards accepting the decentralizing demands of the
provincial premiers as a condition for achieving a constitutional
settlement and patriation. The mellowing of Trudeau's constitutional position had more to do with a diminution of his political
resources than any change in his own or his colleagues' view of
what is best for Canada. In February 1979 the Trudeau government
was just three months away from electoral defeat – a defeat the
pollsters had been predicting for several years. Early in that year
the Supreme Court dismantled the unilateral, first phase of Trudeau's constitutional strategy by ruling that the federal Parliament
could not use its limited amending power to alter a part of the
constitutional fabric as integral to the Canadian federal system as
the Senate.[47] At the same time, the tumultuous breakup of Trudeau's marriage had drained away this remarkable leader's moral
energy.[48]

While Canada's political leaders at the end of the 1970s came
closer than ever before to reaching a consensus on a new Confederation pact, still they did not come all that close. To begin with,
there was Quebec. In principle, Quebec was supportive of some of
the decentralizing changes advocated by other provinces, but there
was no way the government of René Lévesque would approve a

new federal constitution for the Canadian nation before it had endeavoured to secure a clear mandate from the people of Quebec for taking Quebec out of the Canadian federation. Moreover, among the other provincial governments and Ottawa, there was no consensus on the nature of the federal union they wished to renew. Take Senate reform, for example. Many of the provinces as well as the federal government had come to attach considerable importance to establishing a new federal upper house. But whereas the model favoured by British Columbia and the Quebec Liberal party would be truly a 'house of the provinces' in which delegates of the provincial governments would represent 'their regions' in national policy making, others wanted a federal second chamber that, being elected, would strengthen the ties between national legislators and citizens in all regions of the country. These competing approaches to Senate reform were built on very different understandings of the Canadian political community.

In retrospect one cannot help but be struck by the naïvety that pervaded this period of new constitutionalism. Many Canadians who participated in the effort of comprehensive constitutional renewal underestimated just how difficult it is to establish peacefully and democratically a new constitution for a people who are divided about the fundamental nature of the political community they wish to share. No liberal democratic state has accomplished comprehensive constitutional change outside the context of some cataclysmic situation such as revolution, world war, the withdrawal of empire, civil war, or the threat of imminent breakup. A country must have a sense that its back is to the wall for its leaders and its people to have the will to accommodate their differences. The Parti Québécois' coming to power in 1976 galvanized, for a moment, governments and the chattering classes into constitutional action. But the people themselves, though casually consulted, were not yet engaged. That would begin to change, at least for Quebecers, at the beginning of round three.

8 Round Three:
Patriation

The year 1980 was a watershed in Canada's constitutional politics. That year marked an end in the attempt to achieve agreement between the federal government and all the provinces on a complete restructuring of Confederation as the basis for patriation. The way was opened for a resolution of the constitutional crisis, but the solution was doubly incomplete: the accord was restricted to a limited number of issues, and it was not entered into by the Government of Quebec. Two political events in the first half of the year had a decisive bearing on these developments: Pierre Trudeau won an election and René Lévesque lost a referendum.

The combination of these two events transformed the balance of power between the two Canadians whose competing visions of Quebec were at the heart of the constitutional debate. Trudeau's miraculous resurrection from the political dead cannot be attributed to his constitutional ideas. His election strategists urged 'that he keep silent on the constitution, the issue that he had insisted on stressing [in the losing campaign] the previous May.'[1] Trudeau reluctantly agreed and won the election. But he was not the kind of leader who needed a mandate from the electorate to pursue the cause of his life. He returned to power with a will to resolve the constitutional issue on his terms in what he sensed would be his last term as prime minister.

René Lévesque, in contrast, nearing the end of his term in the spring of 1980, was like a poker player who is forced to reveal the value of his hole card. That card in the constitutional game was the measure of support within Quebec for his sovereignty-association option. When the referendum occurred, he had to turn that card face up and reveal that it was worth only 40 per cent. Lévesque remained at the constitution table, but from that point on he played with a weak hand.

Christian Dufour refers to the Quebec referendum as 'the essence of sovereignty: the enjoyment of the right to self-determination.'[2] It was the first occasion since their conquest by Britain and abandonment by France that the Québécois were consulted directly, if not clearly, on their constitutional future. Though a large minority in Quebec did not identify with Quebec as a cultural 'nation' and though the outcome concerned all of Canada, the referendum was treated as an exercise in self-determination by the Canadiens, the historic Quebec people.

Both protagonists were French-Canadian leaders who were urging their people towards competing national destinies. The Parti Québécois continued to evoke the ideal of ethnic self-determination, holding out the possibility of Quebec taking its place proudly in the community of nations as a modern, distinctive North American state – a state which, in Lévesque's words, would be 'the second most important French-speaking country in the world.'[3] Against this vision, the federalist forces, led formally by Claude Ryan but effectively by Pierre Trudeau and his justice minister, Jean Chrétien, reminded Quebecers of their opportunity to continue to participate in a larger national enterprise based on the encounter of the French and English realities and now enriched by the contributions of many other cultures. This encounter, Trudeau proclaimed, 'has become the fabric of our life as a nation, the source of our individuality, the very cornerstone of our identity, as a people.'[4] For the most part, the referendum was a civilized struggle among eloquent men and women passionately contesting noble ideals. But it is not the kind of contest a society can afford to have very often.

For the Quebec people as a whole the result of the referendum was clear: 59.6 per cent said 'no' to sovereignty-association while only 40.4 per cent said 'yes.' For French Quebec, however, the result was not clear: it is estimated that a bare majority – perhaps 51 per cent – had in fact voted 'yes.'[5] Moreover, it would be wrong to interpret a 'no' vote as an unconditional 'yes' to remain in Canada. On the contrary, many who voted that way did so because they believed, naïvely in retrospect, that Trudeau's campaign promise to 'renew the constitution' meant, among other things, changes in the division of powers to accommodate some of Quebec's demands.

There has been much debate about that promise and whether, in the light of Trudeau's subsequent actions, Quebecers were deceived or betrayed by him. Trudeau's commitment was made with dramatic effect in the Paul Sauvé Arena on the evening of 16 May, just four days before the referendum vote. 'Appearing to discard his written notes, he glared out at his audience and waited for a moment of calm.'[6] Then came these words:

> I know that I can make a solemn commitment that following a 'No' vote we will immediately take action to renew the constitution and we will not stop until we have done that.
>
> And I make a solemn declaration to all Canadians in the other provinces: we, the Quebec MPs, are laying ourselves on the line, because we are telling Quebecers to vote 'No' and telling you in the other provinces that we will not agree to your interpreting a 'No' vote as an indication that everything is fine and can remain as it was before.
>
> We want change and we are willing to lay our seats in the House on the line for change.

It is true that 'renew the constitution' does not necessarily mean giving Quebec more powers, and that Trudeau's constitutional ideas in the past had pointed in a very different direction. But it is also true that in the referendum campaign he did not remind Quebecers that his constitutional priority was a Charter of Rights designed to make French Canadians feel at home anywhere in Canada. Nor did he explain to Quebecers his disdain for the decentralizing proposals in the report of the Pepin-Robarts Task Force on National Unity or in the Beige Paper issued by the Quebec Liberal party, whose leader captained his referendum team. If on the night of 16 May he had made it clear he had not changed his mind on these matters, it is most unlikely that the crowd in the arena would have risen with tears in their eyes and given him a standing ovation. Candour often stands in the way of crowd-swaying eloquence.

The one certain implication of Trudeau's commitment was the immediate initiation of the third round of mega constitutional politics. On 9 June 1980 the first ministers gathered at 24 Sussex Drive and cranked up the tired old machinery of federal-provincial constitutional negotiations. The Continuing Committee of Ministers on the Constitution (CCMC), now a travelling road-show co-chaired by Jean Chrétien and Roy Romanow, prepared 'best-effort' drafts through the summer. The agenda included most of the grab-bag of items that had been on the table in 1978–9 as well as a couple of new entries. One was a new constitutional preamble for which, at one point, there were 'twenty-seven differing themes and suggestions.'[7] The final federal draft included recognition of Canada's 'distinct French-speaking society centred in though not confined to Quebec.'[8] The other new item was the federal government's concern to strengthen Ottawa's powers to manage the economy and enhance the economic union. The mood of the Trudeau government, after its electoral success and its victory in the Quebec referendum, was far less accommodating to the devolutionary demands of the provinces.

The climax of the CCMC mandate was to be a first ministers' conference in Ottawa from 8 to 12 September 1980. This turned out be a real anticlimax, to no one's great surprise. What is surprising is that eleven years later, a federal minister of constitutional affairs, Joe Clark, could refer to first ministers' meetings as 'a way that we know works.'[9] Any observer of these meetings in recent years would have difficulty sharing Clark's confidence in this method of reaching constitutional accommodation.

The September 1980 meeting must rank as one of the most acrimonious on record. Even before the eleven first ministers assembled in front of the television cameras in the flag-bedecked Ottawa Conference Centre, two sour notes from the previous day had poisoned the atmosphere. Trudeau had stormed out of a formal dinner, without eating the birthday cake prepared for Saskatchewan premier Alan Blakeney, and a federal document prepared by Michael Kirby, head of the Federal-Provincial Relations Office, was leaked to the media. The Kirby memorandum concluded that consensus on the agenda was 'by no means certain' and recommended that the federal government should be pre-

pared to proceed unilaterally, blaming the failure of the conference on 'an impossibly cumbersome process' or 'the intransigence
of the provinces.'[10] The conference ended when Trudeau rejected
a memorandum banged together by the premiers across the street
at the Château Laurier and representing their best agreement on
the various items. Trudeau dismissed the so-called 'Château consensus' as just another provincial 'shopping list.'[11]

Less than a month later Canada's patriation log-jam was, in
effect, broken. On the night of 2 October, Trudeau announced on
national television his government's intention to proceed unilaterally with patriation and a few constitutional changes, dubbed the
'people's package.' The package contained an all-Canadian amending formula (which included a federally initiated referendum to
break a deadlock between Ottawa and the provinces), a Charter of
Rights, and a declaration of the principle of fiscal equalization.
Trudeau intended to have these changes endorsed by the federal
Parliament, where his party had a clear majority, and then, with or
without provincial consent, to request that the British Parliament
make them the law of the Canadian Constitution.

Trudeau's approach was now truly Gaullist in nature. By appealing over the heads of provincial politicians directly to the people,
he aimed to forge a popular consensus in support of constitutional
changes that would 'complete the foundations of our independence and of our freedoms.'[12] The reference for Trudeau's 'our'
was a national community composed of individual Canadians owing
their primary allegiance to Canada and its central institutions. In
substance and in method he challenged the understanding of
Canada as a fundamentally federal community.

At the core of Trudeau's constitutionalism was the individual
Canadian citizen as the bearer of the most fundamental constitutional rights. Charter rights to basic political freedoms, due process
of law, protection against discrimination, mobility throughout the
country, education in English or French, and communication with
government in either language anywhere in Canada pre-empted
the rights and limited the powers of all governments. There was
nothing here to recognize Quebec's special place in Confederation
as the homeland of a founding people. And that, of course, was no
accident. Trudeau's ideological mission in going to Ottawa was

precisely to woo his compatriots away from a Quebec conception of their national identity.

The other main parts of the people's package were similarly cast. The principle of equalization embodied a commitment to 'promoting equal opportunities for the well-being of Canadians' regardless of where they lived in Canada. In effect, this proposal would recognize in the Constitution what had become, since 1957, the established practice of fiscal federalism in Canada: transferring wealth by way of 'equalization payments' from the 'have' to the 'have-not' provinces to ensure that they all 'have sufficient revenues to provide reasonably comparable levels of public services at reasonably comparable levels of taxation.'[13] This principle of national social welfare is profoundly Canadian and one not found in the United States, committed as it is to the free flow of market forces.

The third part of 'the people's package,' the formula for amending the Constitution after formal custody was transferred from Britain, was based on the proposal contained in the 1971 Victoria Charter, though with an interesting populist wrinkle. Up to a point the constitutional process would remain intergovernmental: amendments would require the agreement of the federal Parliament and the legislatures of Ontario, Quebec, and two Atlantic and two western provinces. But if the governments became deadlocked, the federal government could take its proposals directly to the people in a referendum and seek majorities in the four regions of the country. If within two years the provinces did not agree to this formula, then the people themselves would be invoked as the final arbiters of who should have custody of their Constitution. Trudeau's formula would be pitted in a national referendum against whatever proposal might be agreed to by eight of the provinces representing 80 per cent of the population, thereby assuring a Quebec and Ontario veto.[14]

The constitutional process Trudeau proposed to follow in giving effect to the rest of his package represented an even more categorical denial of Canada's federal nature. Important changes in the powers of the provinces (the Charter of Rights would significantly limit their powers) would be made without their consent. And the mechanism for developing and refining these proposals would not be the traditional intergovernmental meetings but open, televised public hearings before a committee of the Canadian Parliament. In Trudeau's constitutional process, provincial barriers were not to come between the citizens and the representation of their constitutional will through the Parliament of Canada.

For the thirteen months following Trudeau's pronouncement, Canadians were absorbed in an intense constitutional crisis. At the heart of the crisis was the contest between Trudeau's new populist constitutionalism and the traditional constitutionalism of Canadian federalism.

The Trudeau government did all it could to broaden the political support for its constitutional program. From the outset it had the support of two provincial governments – New Brunswick's and Ontario's. New Brunswick's premier Richard Hatfield, responsive to the demography of Canada's most dualist province (65 per cent English, 35 per cent French), was enthusiastic about the entrenchment of bilingualism, a feature of the Charter of Rights and Freedoms. Ontario's William Davis, as premier of the central and largest province, cast himself in the role of honest broker in the constitutional debate. Ontario's support for the people's package was more readily secured by omitting from the Charter of Rights any provisions committing Ontario to official bilingualism – a commitment Ontario's Conservative government was most unwilling to make. At the national level, some bipartisan support for the Trudeau initiative was secured when Ed Broadbent, leader of the New Democratic Party, was brought on side on condition that a constitutional amendment adding slightly to provincial power over natural resources would be added to the package.[15] This condition was not enough to win the support of either Saskatchewan's Blakeney, leader of the only provincial NDP government, or the federal NDP caucus.[16] Beyond the political elites, public opinion was courted by a mass advertising campaign. Great Canadian geese flapped across billboards, bringing the Constitution home with everyone's rights and freedoms guaranteed forever.

The crucial instrument in the process of building legitimacy for the federal initiative was the special parliamentary committee that sat through the late fall of 1980 and early winter of 1981. This committee, made up of ten senators and fifteen MPs (in all, fifteen Liberal, eight Conservative, and two NDP), was in several respects a new phenomenon in Canada's constitutional politics. Parliamentary committees on the constitution were certainly not new, but this was the first to have all its hearings – a total of 267 hours over fifty-six days – televised.[17] Unlike those at previous committees, most submissions came not from academics, governments, or ordinary citizens but from interest groups. The committee permitted only five individuals to appear as witnesses (two each chosen by the Liberals and Conservatives and one by the NDP). The interests represented covered a wide spectrum: native peoples, the multicultural community, women, religions, business, labour, the disabled, gays and lesbians, trees, and a number of civil liberties organizations. Most of those who appeared pressed for a stronger Charter of Rights, and a number of them actually saw their ideas adopted.

Indeed, the remarkable feature of this parliamentary committee and the key to its political efficacy was the extent to which its government majority was willing to accept (one might even say desired to accept) amendments to the government's proposal. What better way to foster the image of a people's package? Among the accepted changes were the following:

· a clause championed by feminists specifying that all the rights and freedoms in the Charter 'are guaranteed equally to male and female persons';[18]
· constitutional recognition of 'the aboriginal and treaty rights' of aboriginal peoples;[19]
· a provision of the Charter directing that it be interpreted 'in a manner consistent with the preservation and enhancement of the multicultural heritage of Canadians';[20]
· entrenchment of official bilingualism in New Brunswick;[21]
· the addition of 'mental or physical disability' to the list of unconstitutional grounds of discrimination;[22]
· a strengthening of the rights of the criminally accused, including a clause mandating the exclusion of evidence obtained in violation of Charter rights;[23] and
· a modification of the general limits on Charter rights placing the onus of proof on governments to justify encroachments on rights and dropping the implication that parliamentary supremacy must be retained.[24]

The government's enthusiasm for constitutionally protecting rights and freedoms did meet some political limits. Neither homosexuals nor the unborn gained explicit recognition of their rights, and, most significantly, the price of maintaining NDP support was rejection of a Conservative party amendment protecting property rights.[25]

These concrete changes in the constitutional proposals secured through interest-group activity in the parliamentary arena did more than expand the base of political support for the Trudeau government's unilateral initiative. The process itself created a new public expectation about popular participation in constitution making – an expectation that the architects of the Meech Lake Accord would ignore to their peril. It also produced a new set of players in the constitutional process – the interest groups whose rights claims gained constitutional recognition and whose perspective is distinctly indifferent to federalism. As Alan Cairns's writings have shown, this development poses a fundamental challenge to the traditional pattern of constitutional politics in Canada.[26] The groups who were successful in 1980–1 acquired a stake in the Constitution which rivals that of provincial governments and throws into question a process of constitutional change monopolized by federal and provincial government leaders.

Resistance to the Trudeau government's constitutional initiative was led at the national level by the official opposition, Joe Clark's Progressive Conservative party, and by the governments of eight of Canada's ten provinces. The opposition campaign was a difficult one to mount in that it focused entirely on process rather than substance. The chief contention of Clark and the opposing premiers, the 'gang of eight,' was that in proceeding unilaterally with constitutional changes affecting the provinces, Trudeau was violating a fundamental principle of Canadian federalism, albeit one that was not formally written in the Constitution. Trudeau's opponents did not dare attack the centrepiece of the people's package, the Charter of Rights and Freedoms. Intellectuals could argue that a constitutional bill of rights would result in a substantial shift of power from elected legislatures to appointed judges,[27] but these arguments cut little ice with the general public, who indicated in poll after poll overwhelming support for the idea of a charter of rights even though they knew little about its actual contents.[28] Nonetheless, in opposing Trudeau's unilateralism, Clark and his provincial allies drew on a federal ethic deeply imbedded in Canada's political culture. By the end of December 1981 the opinion polls that showed the popularity of the Charter of Rights were also showing that majorities in all regions were opposed to Trudeau's unilateralism.[29] In the struggle for the hearts and minds of the citizens, Charter rights did not yet trump provincial rights.

Trudeau's opponents were hampered in another respect. The gang of eight included René Lévesque's separatist Quebec government. Even though the Parti Québécois had temporarily put independence on the back burner, it was hardly a credible partner in any project to reform the Canadian Constitution. The highest common denominator of any such project Quebec's separatists could support was bound to be extremely low.

That indeed turned out to be the case when, in April 1981, the gang finally unveiled their alternative to the federal proposal. They proposed to patriate the Constitution with an all-Canadian amending procedure but with no other constitutional changes until sovereignty over the Constitution had been transferred to Canada. Under their amending formula, most amendments could be made by the federal Parliament together with two-thirds of the provinces representing half of the population. This formula differed from Trudeau's in that it treated all provinces in the same way and gave no province an explicit veto. Lévesque, fresh from an electoral victory and half-heartedly playing the only constitutional game in town, accepted this formula. He was subsequently much maligned for checking Quebec's historic claim to a constitutional veto in the cloakroom of the Château Laurier (where the gang of eight participated in a public signing of their proposal) along with his galoshes.[30] However, the formula did retain a defensive veto for Quebec in that a dissenting province could opt out of an amendment transferring jurisdiction to Ottawa and receive full fiscal compensation. This feature, together with the pressure on Lévesque to form a common front with provinces that could not abide a Quebec veto, explains his action.

The dissident provinces, like the federal government, drew on public funds to mount advertising campaigns against the federal proposal. Billboards went up across Quebec showing a federal fist crushing the Quebec flag. Canada's constitutional politics were becoming more participatory than ever before. A crucial consequence of this development was now much in evidence. When constitutional advocates compete in the arena of public opinion they do so largely on symbolic terms.[31] Mass advertising and television news clips reduce complex constitutional arguments to simplistic slogans and emotive graphics.

Trudeau's opponents did not confine their campaign to Canada. A vigorous lobbying effort, spearheaded by Quebec, was launched in Britain to persuade members of the British Parliament not to accede to a request from the Canadian Parliament to amend Canada's Constitution in matters of direct concern to the provinces that lacked provincial support. Native groups also submitted their case for the protection of historic treaty rights to the British Parliament and courts.[32] The case for the British Parliament not acting as a rubber stamp and automatically approving any request for a constitutional amendment emanating from the federal government was based on solid constitutional logic. The entire rationale for retaining Britain's trusteeship of the Canadian Constitution and not proceeding with patriation in 1927 was that Canadians had not agreed on who or what should be the sovereign constitutional authority in Canada (see chapter 5). For the British Parliament to regard itself as bound by the will of the Canadian Parliament on all constitutional questions would be, in effect, to accept that Parliament as constitutionally sovereign and to deny the very purpose of British trusteeship. This, indeed, was precisely the conclusion reached by a committee of the British Parliament chaired by Anthony Kershaw.[33] The Kershaw Committee reported that a request for an amendment affecting the federal structure should be conveyed with 'at least that degree of Provincial concurrence (expressed by governments, legislatures or referendum majorities) as that required for a post-patriation amendment.'[34]

Jean Chrétien as Trudeau's minister of justice wasted no time in issuing a paper that attempted to rebut Kershaw.[35] It is unlikely that either this paper or the Kershaw Report was read by more than a handful of academics and government lawyers. The more effective counter to Kershaw and the whole British gambit was to play on the strong sentiments of Canadian nationalism and resistance to British interference. Trudeau knew well how to play on these themes. In a clever turn of phrase he likened the Kershaw Report to a current science-fiction movie, *The Empire Strikes Back*.[36]

In the end, it was resort not to the British Parliament but to the courts that checked Trudeau's unilateralism. Three provinces – Manitoba, Newfoundland, and Quebec – submitted questions concerning the constitutional validity of the Trudeau government's methods to their provincial courts of appeal. The crucial question was whether provincial consent was a 'constitutional requirement' for a request to the British Parliament to change the Constitution in the ways contemplated by the federal government. By April 1981 the three courts had given their answers: the Manitoba court (three judges to two) and the Quebec court (four to one) said provincial consent was not a constitutional requirement, but the three judges of Newfoundland's court took the opposite view.[37]

Both sides then prepared to appeal to the Supreme Court of Canada. During the spring and summer of 1981, while the contending governments made their submissions to the court and the justices worked on their opinions, the constitutional debate was closed down. The Conservatives agreed to stop their filibuster in the House of Commons and Trudeau indicated he would not proceed with his initiative if the court found the unilateral procedure unconstitutional. The fate of Trudeau's proposals now rested squarely in the hands of the nine Supreme Court justices. Never before had 'the main stream of national political life flowed so relentlessly up to a Supreme Court decision.'[38] The closest parallel in American history was the Dred Scott case that preceded the Civil War.

On 28 September 1981 the Supreme Court rendered its decision. As befits a court now emerging as a key player on the national political stage, it chose to deliver its verdict, for the first time ever, on national television – an occasion marred somewhat when one of the justices tripped over a wire and disconnected the sound system, so that for the next forty-five minutes the country had to read the chief justice's lips. When the country finally unravelled the decision, it realized that the court had spoken with a forked tongue. Seven justices to two, it held as a matter of strict black-letter law that there was no requirement of provincial consent. But another majority made up of six justices found that in terms of constitutional convention, the unwritten fundamental rules concerning the proper use of legal power that have always been an essential element in the British and Canadian constitutional traditions, there was a requirement of a 'substantial degree' of provincial consent.[39] The court's decision gave half a loaf to each side. For the Trudeau government it amounted to a legal green light but a political red light.

Ten years later Trudeau would claim that the justices who wrote the majority opinion on constitutional convention 'blatantly manipulated the evidence before them so as to arrive at the desired result.'[40] At the time of the decision, he was much more deferential to the court. In his initial response – a televised press conference from Seoul, South Korea – he acknowledged that a convention requiring provincial consent for amendments affecting provincial powers had existed.[41] Even though the Supreme Court, by asserting that constitutional conventions were not enforceable in the courts, removed any legal barriers from his proceeding without provincial consent, Trudeau decided to respect the majority's opinion on convention and try one more time to reach agreement with the provincial premiers.

And so, once again, in the first week of November 1981, the stage was set in the Ottawa Conference Centre for yet another first ministers' constitutional conference. This time there was an important difference in the rules governing the proceedings. The Supreme Court's ruling in the Patriation Reference case stipulated that only a 'substantial degree' of provincial consent was required, thereby relaxing the strict rule of unanimity implicitly accepted by participants in previous conferences. The significance of that rule change became clear on the third day of the conference – more precisely on the evening of the third day and early morning of the fourth – when seven premiers from the gang of eight broke with Quebec and agreed to an accord with the federal government.[42]

Much has been written about the forging of that November accord. For many Canadians it was a historic compromise paving the way for patriation. For many Quebecers it became 'the night of the long knives,' leaving Quebec isolated within the Canadian constitutional process. Some think that the turning point in the Conference came midway through the third day when René Lévesque, without consulting his colleagues in the gang of eight, accepted in principle an idea Trudeau had been dangling before the premiers – resolving their differences through a national referendum.[43] Lévesque was as much a constitutional populist as Trudeau. If rising for Trudeau's referendum bait is what destroyed Lévesque's relationship with his fellow premiers, it indicates just how wedded the latter were to the tradition of elite accommodation.

The accord between the federal government and the nine provinces was truly an achievement of elite accommodation. For both sides it was a genuine compromise, forged by Roy McMurtry and Roy Romanow, the attorneys-general of Ontario and Saskatchewan, respectively, and Jean Chrétien, the federal justice minister, in 'a small, secluded room' in the conference centre – hence the title 'kitchen accord.'[44] On Trudeau's part, he had to abandon his amending formula for one advanced by his provincial opponents and also stomach some major modifications of his Charter of Rights. For the dissident provinces the accord meant abandonment of their own priorities for constitutional reform (of which Senate reform was probably the most important) and acceptance of a Charter of Rights that a number of them, especially Manitoba's Sterling Lyon and Saskatchewan's Alan Blakeney, regarded as an imprudent modification of parliamentary government.

Under the amending formula agreed to in the accord, most amendments would require the agreement of the federal Parliament (in which the Senate would have only a suspensory veto) and the legislatures of two-thirds (seven) of the provinces representing half the population. This was the gang of eight's amending formula, with one modification – there would be no financial compensation for a province that chose to opt out of an amendment transferring power to Ottawa. For Trudeau any kind of opt-out smacked of the checkerboard federalism he had railed against on the opening day of the conference. For Quebec, the revision of the formula Lévesque had earlier accepted meant that, besides giving up a veto over future constitutional changes as vital to its interests as Senate reform, a formidable fiscal cost would be attached to the use of the defensive veto. Moreover, to nail down the lid on Quebec's constitutional vulnerability, the amending formula itself and a few other matters (most importantly, the monarchy and the composition of the Supreme Court) were made subject to the rule of unanimous provincial consent.[45] So, what Blakeney often referred to as 'the tyranny of unanimity' would be briefly lifted to put through a change in the amending process very much against Quebec's interests and then reimposed to ensure that the new process would be difficult, if not impossible to change in the future. The empowerment of the people through a deadlock-breaking referendum was abandoned with not a whimper from the people.

One modification of the Charter made particularly to mollify Newfoundland attached an affirmative action rider to the mobility right, so that provinces with above-average unemployment could protect jobs from out-of-province job-seekers.[46] The other Charter change agreed to in the 'kitchen accord' was much more controversial – the 'override' or 'notwithstanding' clause that became section 33 of the charter. This section permits any provincial legislature or the federal Parliament to enact legislation which will operate notwithstanding that it may violate certain Charter rights. This legislative override was made subject to two restrictions. First, it cannot be used against democratic rights such as the right to vote or the mobility and language rights so essential to Trudeau's pan-Canadian nationalism. Second, an override expires after five years unless re-enacted by the legislature. For some, the override even with these restrictions contradicts the basic purpose of a constitutional bill of rights – of placing certain fundamental rights and freedoms beyond legislative encroachment.[47] For others with less faith in the judiciary's wisdom in striking the right balance between competing rights and social interests, the override is a prudent democratic fail-safe device.[48] However, the fact that the override was adopted in a closed-door deal among political elites meant that the public was not exposed to this debate. Given the popularity of the Charter and growing distrust of politicians, the circumstances of the override's adoption could only lower its legitimacy.

After the conference adjourned on 5 November the federal

government, with the concurrence of the provinces, brought forward two changes in the kitchen accord with a view to making it more acceptable to Quebec. One was to provide fiscal compensation for a province opting out of a transfer of powers relating to 'education or other cultural matters.'[49] This arrangement would still leave Quebec vulnerable to transfers of power in the social policy field. The other change was to accommodate the Quebec government's policy of requiring new immigrants, regardless of their mother tongue, to educate their children in French schools. The Charter right of English-speaking immigrants to educate their children in English would come into effect in Quebec only when authorized by the Quebec legislature or government.[50] To this extent Trudeau was willing to accept Quebec's distinctness and a checkerboard Charter in order to secure Quebec's consent to a constitutional deal, but the Lévesque government refused to accept the accord as amended.

Two further changes were made to the constitutional package that were not the product of intergovernmental negotiations. On the contrary, these changes were prompted by adverse reactions to the first ministers' decision to apply the legislative override to the explicit guarantee of sexual equality in section 28 of the Charter and to drop entirely constitutional recognition of aboriginal rights. Both decisions were reversed through the pressure of public agitation. For the coalition of women's organizations who mounted the campaign for the retaking of section 28, their success was important not so much for its substance – section 28 might well turn out to be more useful to men than to women[51] – but as evidence of their newly won power in the constitutional process.[52] Similarly, the restoration of aboriginal rights was more significant for the change it indicated was taking place in constitutional politics than for its substance. Some of the premiers could be persuaded to accept the restoration only by insertion of the word 'existing' before aboriginal rights.[53] While the new wording had the agreement of ten governments, it was accepted by only one aboriginal organization: the Métis Association of Alberta.[54] The three national aboriginal organizations representing status and non-status Indians and the Inuit were united in opposition to the entire package. Nonetheless, the limited success of the 'Indian lobby' in reversing the first ministers' decision to avoid any formal constitutional recognition of aboriginal rights demonstrated that public support for aboriginal peoples in the constitutional process extended well beyond the aboriginal community itself.

With these adjustments to the accord reached by Trudeau and all of the premiers except Quebec's, the package of constitutional changes went forward quickly for enactment into Canadian constitutional law. This was done in two stages. First, in early December 1981, resolutions supporting the package were passed in both Houses of the Canadian Parliament. The majority in the House of Commons was large, with 246 members in favour and only 24 (seventeen Conservatives, five Liberals, and two New Democrats) opposed. The second step took place in Britain, where the United Kingdom Parliament for the last time formally amended the Canadian Constitution. The Canada Act declared the amendments approved by the Canadian Parliament (now packaged as the Constitution Act, 1982) to be the law of Canada and stated that never again would the British Parliament enact Canadian laws.

There was relatively little fuss in Britain. Margaret Thatcher refused Quebec's request to delay action on the Canadian Constitution until the courts had dealt with its challenge to the constitutional propriety of proceeding without Quebec's consent.[55] British parliamentarians were much more moved by the position of Canada's aboriginal peoples, but were deterred from trying to block the Canada Act by a British court ruling that the Crown's treaty obligations to natives were now the responsibility of the Government of Canada.[56] The Canada Act passed through both Houses of the British Parliament in March 1982. On 17 April 1982, beneath an ominous grey Ottawa sky, Queen Elizabeth in a signing ceremony on Parliament Hill proclaimed the Canada Act in force.

A remarkable feature of this process of achieving patriation was the absence of any role for the provincial legislatures. In the past, when the federal Parliament passed resolutions requesting the British Parliament to amend Canada's Constitution, a few provincial legislatures (most often Quebec's) passed supporting resolutions, but there was no systemic practice of obtaining the approval of provincial legislatures for such amendments.[57] However, in the 1971 attempt to achieve patriation, the agreed-upon procedure had called for the passing of identical resolutions by the Parliament of Canada and all the provincial legislatures.[58] Although there was no legal requirement for approval by the provincial legislatures, it had been felt that ratification in and by the elected provincial legislatures would give the patriated Constitution a stronger democratic root in Canada. Approval by the provincial legislatures was quietly eliminated from the patriation round in 1981 for one obvious reason: it would display the embarrassing dissensus in the country about the conditions of patriation. The one provincial legislature that did vote on the resolution approved by the federal Parliament was Quebec's National Assembly, which on 25 November 1981 passed a 'decree' (70 to 38) rejecting it, a decree that the federal justice minister, Jean Chrétien, said would have the same effect as 'a decree saying there will be no snow over Quebec this winter.'[59] In the future, as the provincial premiers in the Meech Lake round almost forgot, ratification by provincial legislatures would be a requirement for amendments under the patriated Constitution.

And so the third mega round of constitutional politics ended, unlike the previous two or the one to follow, with some concrete constitutional changes. Many Canadians have the mistaken impression that Canada adopted a whole new Constitution in 1982. That is wrong. Most of the original 1867 Constitution was retained intact. The changes in the Constitution made in the patriation round were as follows:

· Canada's Constitution was patriated, meaning no longer would it be formally amended in Great Britain. In the future, most amendments would require the approval of the federal Parliament (with the Senate having only a suspensory veto) and seven provinces representing 50 per cent of the population. A few amendments (notably changes to the monarchy, the composition of the Supreme Court, or the amending formula itself) would require unanimous provincial approval.
· The Canadian Charter of Rights and Freedoms was added to the Constitution.
· The 'existing' rights of Canada's aboriginal peoples were constitutionally recognized.

- The principle of fiscal equalization among the Canadian provinces was constitutionally recognized.
- The provinces obtained a concurrent power to regulate interprovincial trade in natural resources and to levy indirect taxes on these resources.
- The original Constitution and its amendments were repackaged, with the British North America Act being retitled the Constitution Act, 1867.

No doubt these were important changes in Canada's Constitution, but they left untouched many of the issues that had been on the constitutional agenda. The Supreme Court of Canada was left in an anomalous position: although there were now rules for changing it through constitutional amendment, the court itself was still not established in the formal Constitution. A Senate that not even the senators could any longer defend was left in place. And, aside from a slight change concerning natural resources, the division of powers, the primary target of Quebec's constitutional aspiration since the Quiet Revolution, was unchanged.

There was a more profound sense in which the patriation round was inadequate as a resolution of Canada's central constitutional debate. The constitutional changes made in 1982 did not answer the question that had been left hanging since 1927 when Canada became, in principle, an autonomous community: What kind of a political community was Canada? What are its defining features and essential constituent parts? Legally, the umbilical cord that had tied Canada to Britain was now severed. In that sense, patriation was complete. But the patria had not yet defined itself – at least not in a way that was clearly consented to by all sections of the Canadian people. By 1982 Canada had achieved legal autonomy: even if the British Parliament were to do the unthinkable and rescind the Canada Act, Canadian courts would not give effect to such an act. Still, Canada had not yet achieved autochthony: it did not yet have a constitution whose authority derives from the people themselves.[60]

It might be objected that patriation in 1982 did bring with it a new definition of the Canadian political community: a society of equal rights-bearing citizens represented in provinces of equal status but expressing their collective national will primarily through the majoritarian institutions of the federal government. This vision of the Canadian political community was shared by many who supported the Trudeau initiative and the constitutional changes in 1982. But the passage of the Constitution Act, 1982, did not mean that the Trudeauian view of the Canadian people was now universally shared by the people themselves. The very act of repudiation by Quebec's National Assembly strengthened the sense of many Quebecers that they are a people whose right to self-determination requires expression through the majoritarian institutions of Quebec. And the aboriginal peoples whose political organizations also repudiated the terms of patriation had just begun to exercise their right to government by consent.

Round three was over, but a Canadian social contract had not been accomplished. Indeed, the very circumstances under which patriation was accomplished – the deep cleavage that would linger over its value and its justice – might make it more difficult than ever for Canadians to constitute themselves a sovereign people.

9 Round Four:
Meech Lake

The threshold question concerning the Meech Lake round of constitutional politics is whether it could have been avoided. The patriation round was dictated by promises made during the Quebec referendum. Because of the circumstances in which the Meech Lake round failed, a fifth round, the one in which Canadians are currently embroiled, was bound to follow. But was the Meech Lake round necessary?

A lot of Canadians think it was not. Some attribute Meech Lake to the vain wish of a single politician, Brian Mulroney, to secure his place in history by accomplishing what Pierre Trudeau could not – namely, reaching a constitutional accommodation between Quebec and the rest of Canada. To believe that Meech was unnecessary one need not subscribe to such a simplistic great-fool theory of history. Nor is it necessary to accept Trudeau's immodest verdict that after his 1982 constitutional reforms, 'the federation was set to last a thousand years.'[1] A plausible case can be made that after 1982, the 'Quebec problem' was best dealt with through benign neglect. In time, with memories of the 'night of the long knives' fading and demographic trends reducing the prominence of the indigenous French Québécois in their own province, Quebec nationalism would die and, with it, the need for any constitutional reconciliation.

It is just as plausible to argue, however, that if, in the wake of the bitter feelings engendered in Quebec by the 1982 changes, English-Canadian politicians had from the start spurned the first modest proposals from Quebec for a renewal of Confederation, then the 1991–2 crisis of national unity would have come five years earlier. And, further, that with Quebec federalists having nothing to offer, it would have been even more likely to lead to dismemberment of the federation. We know that Meech left the country more bitterly divided than at any time since Confederation. We can only speculate on whether it could have been held together without Meech. On that question, no one is entitled to be dogmatic.

The local government of a section of the federation constituting a quarter of its population and the home province of a majority of its largest linguistic minority had denied the legitimacy of fundamental constitutional changes. Moreover, the legitimacy of the 1982 constitutional changes was not significantly enhanced by the Supreme Court of Canada's ruling. The Lévesque government, just after the 'night of the long knives' when the other nine provinces and Ottawa agreed to go ahead without Quebec, had asked the Quebec Court of Appeal whether Quebec had a veto under the unpatriated amending process (see chapter 8). On 7 April 1981, just ten days before the Constitution Act, 1982, came into force, Quebec's Court of Appeal gave its answer: no, Quebec did not have a veto. On 6 December 1982, with the horse well out of the barn, the Supreme Court in an unsigned 'Opinion of the Court' upheld the Quebec Court of Appeal's ruling.[2]

To understand the limited force of the Supreme Court's decision it is essential to recognize that the Quebec Veto case was not about the formal law of the Constitution but about its unwritten, political conventions. In its 1981 Patriation Reference decision, the Supreme Court found there was a constitutional requirement to obtain a substantial degree of provincial consent for requests to the British Parliament to amend the Canadian Constitution in matters affecting provincial powers. It based that finding on constitutional convention. And how are constitutional conventions identified? The court answered that question by adopting British constitutionalist Sir Ivor Jennings's test: 'We have to ask ourselves three questions: first, what are the precedents; secondly, did the actors in the precedents believe that they were bound by a rule; and thirdly, is there a reason for the rule? A single precedent with a good reason may be enough to establish the rule.'[3]

In the Quebec Veto case, the court could easily dismiss Quebec's argument that convention required unanimous provincial consent. But the second leg of Quebec's case posed a more severe challenge: the contention that, for the degree of provincial consent to be substantial, Quebec must be one of the provinces supporting the amendment. There were certainly precedents for this contention, most recently the decisions not to go ahead when Quebec withdrew its support for the Fulton-Favreau formula in the 1960s and refused to endorse the Victoria Charter in 1971. Moreover, a strong reason could be advanced for a Quebec veto rule – namely, Quebec's special place in Confederation as the only province with a French-speaking majority. Wrestling with that argument would have taken the Supreme Court to the heart of Canada's constitutional debate and forced the judges to pronounce upon the fundamental nature of the Canadian political community. But the Supreme Court managed to avoid that issue by ignoring questions of precedent and principle and, indeed, the last sentence in Jennings's test. The justices decided the case entirely on the narrow grounds that they could not find political leaders outside Quebec who were involved in the precedents stating they were bound by a Quebec veto rule. It was not the Supreme Court's most convincing performance.[4] It was a political response to a political challenge dressed up in judicial clothing.

The ultimate arbiters of constitutional conventions, as the Supreme Court itself acknowledged, are not courts of law but the court of public opinion.[5] In the period immediately following patriation, the verdict in this arena was unclear. Public protest in Quebec against the 1982 changes was not widespread and support for Quebec independence was declining. Yet Trudeau and his colleagues did nothing in this period to sell Quebecers on the merits of the 1982 changes. No one should have counted on the Supreme Court to squelch Quebec nationalism or persuade the Quebec majority that the Constitution Act, 1982, was an adequate fulfilment of Trudeau's promise to renew Confederation. On the basis of public opinion polls taken in Quebec during the months following patriation showing that the people of Quebec 'firmly agreed with the 1982 constitutional amendment,' Trudeau felt that no such persuasion was necessary.[6] He did not appreciate that just as Quebecers had voted for him federally and for Lévesque provincially, they might support the contents of his constitutional changes, especially the Charter, while still supporting Quebec nationalist objectives.

In the immediate post-patriation period the only serious action in constitutional politics involved not the Québécois but that other component of the population whose consent to be part of the Canadian people has not yet been freely given – the aboriginal peoples. The Constitution Act, 1982, recognized that the further 'identification and definition of the rights' of aboriginal peoples was a piece of unfinished constitutional business which must be addressed.[7] It stipulated that within a year, the prime minister was to convene a constitutional conference to deal with the matter.[8] Besides the provincial premiers, representatives of the aboriginal peoples and of the northern territories were to attend the conference. Seats at the federal-provincial conference table were status badges neither group would forget.

This conference took place in March 1983. It produced an agreement on a constitutional amendment – the first amendment to be made under the patriated Constitution. The agreement was subsequently ratified in the federal Parliament and all the provincial legislatures except Quebec's. Quebec attended this and subsequent conferences on aboriginal issues only as an observer, but did not participate in the agreement. It's abstention was based not on opposition to the enhancement of aboriginal rights but on the unwillingness of its government to participate in a constitutional process to which Quebec's National Assembly had not consented. Quebec's refusal to participate was of no legal effect, since the amendment was made under the seven-province/half-the-population rule.

The 1983 amendment expanded the 1982 recognition of aboriginal rights in two ways. First, it gave constitutional recognition to rights included in land-claims agreements.[9] These modern agreements would now have the same status as treaties. Rights set out in land-claims settlements – for instance, the limited right of self-government extended to the Cree and Inuit in northern Quebec under agreements signed in the 1970s – were now constitutionally protected.[10] To ensure that these rights were entrenched, the amendment added a provision to the Constitution requiring that before any amendment is made to sections of the Constitution bearing directly on the rights of aboriginal peoples,[11] a constitutional conference must be held composed of the first ministers and representatives of the aboriginal peoples.[12] The second change stipulated that aboriginal and treaty rights 'are guaranteed equally to male and female persons.'[13] This part of the amendment was designed to ensure that the discrimination Indian women had experienced under the Indian Act and which had been upheld by the Supreme Court of Canada did not occur in the future.[14]

These changes, though significant, fell well short of the growing constitutional aspirations of Canada's aboriginal peoples. This fact was recognized in a further part of the 1983 amendment that committed the first ministers and northern territories to at least two more constitutional conferences with representatives of the aboriginal peoples.[15] In fact, there were three more conferences – in 1984, 1985, and 1987. All three focused on the issue of aboriginal self-government.[16] The federal government and many of the provinces were willing to place in the Constitution a *contingent* right to aboriginal self-government: such a right would have legal effect for any given aboriginal community if and when the details were negotiated with the federal government and the provincial governments concerned. Most of the aboriginal leadership, while recognizing the need to tailor the details of self-government to the circumstances of different communities, insisted that the Constitution must recognize the inherent right of aboriginal peoples to self-government. Indeed, some contended that such a right is already included in the 'existing aboriginal rights' recognized in the Constitution.

For the public viewing these proceedings on television, it was difficult to understand this debate. According to polling evidence, by 1987 a significant majority of Canadians agreed that the right to aboriginal self-government should be included in the Constitution. So did most governments. What, then, was all the argument about? Essentially it was not an argument so much as a clash of fundamentally different ideological and cultural starting points. Aboriginal leaders regard the right of their peoples to govern themselves as a moral right that they had long before Europeans arrived, and one they have never relinquished.[17] European assertions of sovereignty, including the assertion of sovereignty over Indians contained in Canada's present Constitution, did not remove that right.[18] Might does not make right. While the great majority of aboriginal people want to continue as part of Canada, they and their leaders wish to have their membership in the Canadian political community recognized as flowing from their freely given consent. That consent must be recognized in the Constitution as deriving from their inherent right to self-government, not from the goodwill of other Canadians and their governments. What is being asked for here is primarily a symbolic good, but one of great significance to many aboriginal people.

It is a difficult good for non-aboriginal Canadians to concede in the formal law of the Constitution. Their leaders approach the issue not from the perspective of philosophy but in terms of constitutional law. Putting an inherent right to self-government in the Constitution before at least roughing out the details involves too much uncertainty. Who knows what judges would make of such an abstract right? If aboriginal peoples are to have a share of sovereign power in Canada, better to work out in advance the powers and resources their self-governing communities are to have than to leave all this to the vagaries of judicial interpretation. The hegemonic European settlers might now be willing to accept the principle of aboriginal self-government, but their legal advisers remain cautious about how that right is expressed in enforceable law. The aboriginal peoples, for their part, might wish that in earlier times they had been as cautious about admitting the Europeans to their lands.

The March 1987 conference broke up without resolving this issue. A month later the country's constitutional energies transferred to the Meech Lake Accord and constitutional proposals stemming entirely from Quebec's constitutional discontents. During the controversy that for the next three years raged around that accord, Canadians would learn that the aboriginal question would not go away. Indeed, as it turned out, an important factor in the defeat of the Meech Lake Accord was opposition to the first ministers' decision to postpone action on the aboriginal constitutional front during the Meech round.

Changes in political leadership in Ottawa and Quebec City triggered the next major effort at a constitutional accommodation with Quebec. By 1985 the two great gladiators who had dominated the two previous rounds, Pierre Trudeau and René Lévesque, had departed from the lists. In February 1984 Trudeau took his walk in the snow and announced his decision to retire. In June of that year the Liberals chose John Turner to replace him. Turner, unlike Trudeau and the man he defeated for the leadership, Jean Chrétien, had none of his ego invested in the 1982 Constitution, but he was not to be prime minister for long. Turner lost the general election of September 1984 and the new Conservative leader, Brian Mulroney, became prime minister. While the constitutional issue was not a big factor in the election, Mulroney, in what proved to be a successful effort to strengthen his party's Quebec base, recruited candidates of a Quebec nationalist persuasion. During the campaign he undertook to negotiate an accommodation with the Lévesque government that would enable Quebec to 'sign' the 1982 Constitution 'with honour and enthusiasm.'[19] But it was not René Lévesque with whom he would seek to fulfil this promise. In 1985 Lévesque retired and in December of that year his successor, Pierre-Marc Johnson, lost the provincial election to the Liberals led by a recycled Robert Bourassa. Bourassa, too, in the course of his campaign, made a commitment to resume constitutional negotiations.[20] The stage was now set for a Quebec round.

The Quebec round began quietly on a May weekend at Mont Gabriel, a ski resort north of Montreal, where a group of academics, government officials, journalists, and business representatives from across the country gathered to discuss the future of Quebec and Canada.[21] Here, Gil Rémillard, Bourassa's minister of intergovernmental affairs, presented Quebec's five conditions for accepting the 1982 Constitution. These conditions came directly from *Mastering Our Future*, the constitutional position adopted by the Quebec Liberal party on 3 March 1985 and the platform on which the Liberals had fought and won the provincial election later that year. While these conditions had already had an airing in Quebec and acquired a certain legitimacy there, this was their first exposure to the rest of Canada.

The first and most controversial condition was constitutional recognition of Quebec as a 'distinct society.' 'We must be assured,' said Rémillard, 'that the Canadian constitution will explicitly recognize the unique character of Quebec society and guarantee us the means necessary to ensure its full development within the framework of Canadian federalism.'[22] Second, Quebec's role would be strengthened in the field of immigration. Third, it would have a role in the selection of the three Quebec judges on the Supreme Court of Canada. Fourth, Quebec would be able to opt out of federal spending programs in areas of exclusive provincial jurisdiction without suffering a fiscal penalty. Finally, Quebec would recover its veto on constitutional amendments on matters affecting the province's interests.

To the little group of constitutional aficionados at Mont Gabriel, these 'conditions' seemed a reasonable basis for beginning another round of constitutional discussions. Though the conditions were not without their problems, they were less radical than other constitutional proposals that had emanated from Quebec in recent years.[23] The question was: Would the country, especially the country outside French Quebec, see them that way?

The answer to that question would not come for another year. The next step was not to put the Quebec proposals out for public discussion but to develop them through quiet diplomacy. The very quietness of this process – its closed and elitist nature – helped to produce the negative response that eventually came from English Canada.

It is easy now with the wisdom of hindsight to see how out of tune that process was with the times. But in the spring of 1986 those who saw themselves as the major players in the constitutional process, the first ministers and their advisers, did not realize how much the conditions of constitutional politics in Canada were changing. They did not appreciate how seriously those groups of what Alan Cairns calls 'Charter Canadians,' especially women's groups, aboriginal peoples, and the multicultural community, took their recent enfranchisement as constitutional players. Nor did they sense how difficult it might be to combine the traditional practice of executive federalism with the new requirement in the constitutional process for ratification of amendments in provincial legislatures. Perhaps, most fatally, they did not understand how proposals that might be seen as moderate in an era dominated by the politics of federalism could appear in a different light in a Canada where Charter rights for many citizens have come to eclipse provincial rights.

For Robert Bourassa, the process of shuttle diplomacy was one he knew well from the Victoria Charter round. Roles now were reversed and Quebec officials rather than federal emissaries shopped proposals around the provincial capitals. From the outset the Quebec effort had the blessing of the Mulroney government and was quietly co-managed by Mulroney's minister for federal-provincial affairs, Senator Lowell Murray, and his senior official, Norman Spector. The chief Quebec emissary, Rémillard, was well situated to represent this Ottawa-Quebec alliance, having served until a few months before the 1985 Quebec election as Mulroney's constitutional adviser. The objective of the quiet diplomacy was to shape Quebec's five conditions into constitutional proposals that could be supported by all the provinces.

It was a classic exercise in elite accommodation, this time more secret than ever. Because the Bourassa government feared that rejection of Quebec's minimalist proposals for constitutional reform would play directly into the hands of its separatist opponents, it did not want the details of proposals publicly revealed until an intergovernmental consensus on them had been achieved. Most of the participants, accustomed to cabinet domination of the legislature, assumed that the support of first ministers could be readily translated into legislative ratification. In the end the process produced an accord among the first ministers but not within the country.

The accord was reached in two stages. The first stage was accomplished in the summer of 1986. Warmed up by visits of the Quebec team to their capitals, the provincial premiers assembled in Edmonton in August for their annual interprovincial bun feast. At the conclusion of their conference they issued a communiqué that became known as the Edmonton Declaration. It said, 'The premiers unanimously agreed their top constitutional priority is to embark immediately upon a federal-provincial process, using Quebec's five proposals as a basis of discussion, to bring about Quebec's full and active participation in the Canadian federation.'[24] The ten provincial governments now agreed to a Quebec round of constitutional negotiations. Stage two involved reaching an agreement on detailed constitutional amendments. This took place through numerous bilateral meetings and one major multilateral negotiation among ministers and officials in March 1987. The finale came on the last day of April 1987, when Mulroney invited the provincial premiers to join him for a day of constitutional discussions at the government's conference centre on Meech Lake, just north of Ottawa in the Gatineau Hills. After hours of intense negotiations in which Mulroney, calling on the skills he had honed as a labour negotiator, was the driving force, the first ministers emerged proud, smiling, and a little stunned. They had done it! They had reached a constitutional accord through which, to use the prime minister's rhetoric, 'the bonds of Confederation will be strengthened and the unity of our people ... enhanced.'[25]

Canada now had the Meech Lake Accord before it. When we examine the accord, it is easy to see what had happened to Quebec's 'conditions' through the months of negotiations since Mount Gabriel. In a nutshell, they had been provincialized. They had been made agreeable to the provincial premiers by respecting the principle of provincial equality and, with one exception, extending to all the provinces the powers sought by Quebec.

Let's begin with immigration. Since Confederation, immigration had been a field in which both Ottawa and the provinces could legislate, with federal law being paramount in case of conflict. In recent years a number of provinces, including Quebec, had negotiated bilateral agreements with Ottawa defining their respective roles in the selection and integration of immigrants.[26] The Quebec agreement, known as the Cullen-Couture Agreement, had been put in place under the Trudeau government. Quebec wanted to replace it with an arrangement giving the province a greater role in immigration. The Meech proposal was to establish that every province had the right to make a new agreement with Ottawa, and that once made, an agreement would be constitutionally entrenched in the sense it could be changed only by mutual consent of the two parties.[27]

Similarly, with the Supreme Court proposal, all the provincial governments, not just Quebec's, would have a say in filling Supreme Court vacancies. Still, there was in this part of the accord an element of special status for Quebec. Ever since the Supreme Court was established in 1875 there had been a statutory requirement that at least a third of its members must come from Quebec. The purpose of this rule was to ensure that the court would have competence in Quebec's distinctive civil law. The requirement that three of the court's nine judges be from Quebec was now to be placed in the Constitution. These judges would be appointed by the federal government from names submitted by the Quebec government. The other six judges would be appointed from lists submitted to the federal government by governments of the common-law provinces.[28]

Quebec's long-standing objection to the use of the federal spending power in areas of exclusive provincial responsibility would now be met by a constitutional provision permitting any province to opt out of new national shared-cost programs in areas of exclusive provincial jurisdiction and receive reasonable compensation, providing it introduced a program of its own that was compatible with 'national objectives.' With regard to the amending formula, instead of restoring Quebec's veto, all the provinces would be given a larger veto than they had acquired in 1982. The list of matters requiring unanimous provincial agreement was to be enlarged, notably by adding Senate reform and the creation of new provinces. Further, the opportunity to opt out of amendments passed under the seven-province/half-the-population rule would become less costly for all provinces by providing reasonable fiscal compensation for amendments centralizing any provincial power, not just powers relating to education and culture.

The accord's omission of Senate reform represented a major concession by Alberta's premier, Don Getty, who had publicly pledged to make Senate reform a condition for accepting Quebec's conditions. Under the Meech proposals the requirement of provincial unanimity would make Senate reform considerably more difficult. To win Getty over, Mulroney included an interim amendment that until such time as Senate reform was accomplished, the federal government would appoint senators from lists submitted by the premiers. Mulroney promised to adopt this practice at once, even before the amendment was passed. Tacked on to the end of the accord was a further commitment to have Senate reform on the agenda of future constitutional conferences. A similar commitment was made to discuss fisheries (reflecting the bloody-mindedness of Newfoundland's Brian Peckford) and 'such other matters as are agreed upon' at first ministers' conferences to be held at least once a year. The first ministers seemed set on dancing around the constitutional mulberry bush forever.

The one element of the accord which, by its very nature, could not be provincialized was the distinct society clause. Its whole purpose was to give constitutional recognition to Quebec's special place in the Canadian federation. However, in the negotiating process this clause was Canadianized. Alongside recognition of the 'distinctive nature of Quebec society as the principal although not exclusive centre of French-speaking Canadians' would be recognition that 'a fundamental characteristic of the Canadian federation is the existence of French-speaking Canada, centred in but not limited to Quebec, and English-speaking Canada concentrated in the rest of Canada but also present in Quebec.'[29] These defining features of Canada were to be placed not in the preamble to the Constitution, where their weight would be minimal, but as the first substantive section of the Constitution.[30] In this position the statements were to serve as an interpretation clause (akin to recognition of Canada's multicultural heritage in the Charter of Rights) – a guide to judges in interpreting the entire Constitution.

The first ministers' accord was not quite complete. They arranged to meet a few weeks later on 2 June in Ottawa to put the finishing touches on the language of their constitutional proposals. As the accord experienced its first public exposure in the days leading up to the June meeting, the rumbling sounds of the political battle it would provoke could be heard. In Quebec's National Assembly, the only legislature to consider the Meech accord before its final draft, while the government majority was supportive, the main concern of experts appearing before a constitutional committee was that the accord did not go far enough in securing Quebec's distinct culture.[31] Outside the Quebec legislature very different concerns began to be voiced. Aboriginal peoples and northerners complained about being totally left out. Though the two opposition leaders in the House of Commons, the Liberals' John Turner and the NDP's Ed Broadbent, were quick to praise the accord, they soon began to hear from constituents concerned that the accord would balkanize Canada, jeopardize national social programs, and undermine the primacy of the Charter of Rights. The big clap of thunder came on 27 May when a full-page denunciation of the accord by Pierre Elliott Trudeau was published in Montreal's *La Presse* and the Toronto *Star*. Trudeau was utterly scathing. In trying to come to terms with Quebec nationalists who were 'perpetual losers,' the accord was a 'total bungle.' It would render the Canadian state 'totally impotent,' destined to be governed by 'political eunuchs.'[32] Although this was not careful constitutional analysis, it was the kind of rhetoric that would make Trudeau, in this his third coming, the spiritual guru of the anti-Meech forces.

On 2 June the first ministers with their entourage of advisers assembled in Ottawa to 'clarify' their accord. They did not meet in the flag-bedecked conference centre with its ample provisions for media coverage but in the inner regions of the Langevin Block, which houses the offices of the prime minister and his advisers – not a happy choice of venue for the completion of an accord designed to mend rifts within a divided people. It took sixteen hours for the elites to accommodate their differences. In the early hours of 3 June they emerged with the final version of the Meech Lake Accord.[33]

Nearly all the effort in the Langevin Block focused on the spending power and distinct society proposals. The change finally agreed to in the spending power provision seems picayune. A province which opted out of a national shared-cost program in one of its own areas of responsibility and wanted to recover the federal contribution would have to mount a program of its own that met not just 'national objectives' but 'the national objectives.' Adding one word, 'the,' was a small concession to those, like Manitoba's Howard Pawley, who wanted to preserve a strong leadership role for the federal government in social policy, despite the fact that most aspects of social welfare are under provincial jurisdiction. Many who took this view would have preferred the word 'standards' to 'objectives,' but 'the national objectives' at least connoted something reasonably definite and defined by the federal Parliament.

The other change was to the distinct society clause. Essentially what happened here is that a little piece of fudge became a big piece of fudge. A clause which, from the beginning, no one really understood was laced about with further ambiguities. Canada-wide duality was now phrased in terms of recognizing 'the existence of French-speaking Canadians' (not French-speaking Canada) 'centred in Quebec but also present elsewhere in Canada,' and 'English-speaking Canadians' (not English Canada), 'concentrated outside Quebec but also present in Quebec.' The 'role' of the federal Parliament and provincial legislatures to 'preserve' this duality would now be affirmed in the Constitution. In addition, the Constitution would recognize 'that Quebec constitutes within Canada a distinct society' and affirm the 'role' of the legislature and government of Quebec 'to preserve and promote' the distinct identity of Quebec. In case anyone was confused about what all this meant, clauses were inserted to make it clear that none of the above derogated from the powers of either level of government or affected the rights of aboriginals and the multicultural community enshrined in the 1982 Constitution. Nothing was said about increased powers for Quebec,[34] or the implication that other rights, such as women's, might be affected.

Removing some ambiguities only created others. If constitutional accords are like peace treaties, this was indeed a very tenuous peace – one that no amount of minute drafting and piles of qualifiers could hold together once the work of the peacemakers was exposed to the popular political process. The three subsequent years of acrimonious constitutional debate left the two nations warring more intensely within the bosom of a single state than at the beginning of the accommodation process.

Some of what went wrong with the Meech accord can be attributed to the inexperience of political leaders in working with the new amending process. Under the new rules, only two components of the accord, the Supreme Court and the amending formula proposals, required unanimous provincial approval. The rest could be done under the seven province/half-the-population rule, but the first ministers insisted on putting all their proposals in a single package as an all-or-nothing deal. They did so because their accord was an intricate set of compromises and tradeoffs – 'a seamless web,' to use Lowell Murray's fateful phrase.[35] Pull at one strand

and it would all unravel. The logic was clear, but the result was to give every legislature in the land a veto over the package. To compound that problem, the legislatures were to be presented with a 'done deal' too delicate to touch lest it all come apart – hardly the way to gain legitimacy for the first ministers' handiwork.

At the Langevin meeting, Mulroney, Ontario's David Peterson, and Manitoba's Howard Pawley talked about the need for public hearings and further public debate.[36] Pawley had made legislative hearings a condition of his support for the accord because the Manitoba legislature had adopted a rule requiring public hearings before voting on any constitutional amendment.[37] Once the accord was approved by Quebec's National Assembly on 23 June 1987, however, Bourassa made it clear that 'Quebec will not consider any proposed changes that may arise out of public hearings in other provinces.'[38] Bourassa had done all his negotiating behind closed doors, and had left himself no manoeuvring room through the public phase of Meech.

Under the new amending rules, once a resolution supporting a constitutional amendment is adopted by one legislature, the other legislatures have up to three years to ratify it.[39] Three years is the maximum, not the minimum, amount of time for ratifying amendments. The first ministers had no agreed-upon schedule for ratification. By embarking on this process without a timetable, not only did they give ample time for opposition to mobilize but also, as Richard Simeon points out, they 'made it virtually inevitable that a number of elections would have been held and thus that governments not part of the initial bargaining, and not committed to its success, would have been elected.'[40]

The Meech accord did indeed fare badly in the three provinces that had elections during the ratification process. In October 1987 New Brunswick's Richard Hatfield was wiped out and the Liberals led by Frank McKenna won every seat in the legislature. A few months later, in the spring of 1988, Pawley's NDP government was defeated in Manitoba. While the Conservatives under Gary Filmon (who was only lukewarm to Meech) formed a minority government, the Liberals shot past the NDP into second place largely on the basis of leader Sharon Carstairs's assault on Meech Lake. Following the retirement of Newfoundland's Brian Peckford, the

Conservatives were defeated in the April 1989 election and re-placed by the Liberals led by Clyde Wells. Wells soon became the effective leader of the anti-Meech forces across the country.

The only pro-Meech politician to win election during the period was Prime Minister Mulroney. But his party's victory in the November 1988 general election could not be interpreted as an electoral endorsement of Meech. The main issue in the election was the Free Trade Agreement with the United States. The leaders of the two opposition parties, John Turner and Ed Broadbent, both supported the Meech accord. This may in fact have reduced the legitimacy of Meech, as many who opposed it felt they had been denied an electoral means of registering their disapproval.

Where did all the opposition to Meech come from? To begin with, it came mostly from outside Quebec. Although the accord was not enormously popular in Quebec, the majority of Quebecers might have accepted Meech, without much enthusiasm, as Que-bec's minimal conditions for accepting the 1982 Constitution. But precisely because Meech was presented as Quebec's minimal condi-tions, when it became increasingly clear that what was minimal for Quebec was much too much for Canadians outside Quebec to swallow, the feeling grew in Quebec that the rest of Canada in rejecting Meech was rejecting Quebec.

The fundamental reason so many Canadians outside Quebec rejected Meech is that they did not accept its basic rationale. The great majority of English-speaking Canadians simply did not accept that the 1982 Constitution was imposed on Quebec against its will. Nor did most of them believe that a failure to accommodate Que-bec would lead to a breakup of the federation. For most English-speaking Canadians, it was enough that Trudeau, together with most of Quebec's representatives in the House of Commons, pro-moted and accepted the 1982 Constitution. As Stefan Dupré has poignantly phrased it, in rejecting the 'Myth of Imposition,' En-glish Canada compounded it by creating the 'Myth of Rejection.'[41]

To English-speaking Canadians who rejected Meech's rationale, the very notion of a 'Quebec round' of constitutional change, concentrating on Quebec's demands and ignoring constitutional changes like Senate reform favoured in other parts of the country, smacked of pandering to Quebec. The contents of the accord, above all its centrepiece, the distinct society clause, added to this sense of resentment. The dualistic vision of Canada which that clause incorporated – a Canada based on the English and French as its two founding peoples – was insulting to Canada's aboriginal peoples. Nor did it resonate well with those who were of neither English nor French extraction and who by the 1980s constituted nearly 40 per cent of the Canadian people. As the distinct society clause was translated into the symbolic terms of constitutional politics, it encroached on tender feelings of status. By giving constitutional recognition in the defining features of Canada to Quebec, the English, and the French, the clause was seen by many who did not fit into any of its categories as a putdown, as denying their fundamental importance to Canada. The Meech debate demonstrated just how inflammatory the politics of status can be, for it deals with that most cherished of psychic commodities – self-respect.

The accord was bitterly attacked by the newest of the constitutional stakeholders – the interest groups who had been successful in the struggle over the Charter of Rights. They had been excluded from the making of the accord and saw the fruits of their previous victory at risk in its ambiguities. These groups, especially women's organizations in English Canada, had much to do with the breaking of Meech. Another group of Canadians who felt victimized by Meech were those who live north of the sixtieth parallel in Yukon and the Northwest Territories. Their aspiration for provincehood, thwarted badly enough in 1982 when it was made conditional on the consent of seven provinces,[42] was now to be burdened further by requiring, under the Meech proposals, unanimous provincial approval. Northerners were dealt an additional indignity by the accord's failure to make provision for their nominees to be considered for Supreme Court appointments. Although the northerners were fewer than a hundred thousand in number, their rough treatment contributed to the accord's aura of injustice in English Canada.

Crucial also in the attack on Meech was the political left in English Canada. The left in Canada has never been much enamoured of federalism, and that, indeed, is true of the left in most federal states (see chapter 5). An accord adding to provincial powers had little appeal to left-wing liberals or social democrats. Their critique concentrated on the spending-power clause. Using 'national objectives' instead of 'national standards' in the wording of that clause, it was argued, meant a fatal weakening of the federal government's capacity to initiate Canada-wide programs like medicare which, they claimed, 'while lying within provincial jurisdiction, have come to be seen by Canadians generally as being important to a decent and dignified life for all Canadians.'[43] This was a potent argument in rallying social policy communities in English Canada against Meech. To activists in these areas, many of them women, the niceties of federalism – the idea that provinces ought to be free to choose their own means of meeting federally set objectives in provincial fields of jurisdiction – were of no consequence.

A growing surge of English-Canadian nationalism underlay the centralist attack on the Meech Lake Accord. In the 1988 election campaign, opposition to the Mulroney government's proposed Canada/United States Free Trade Agreement became intertwined with opposition to Meech Lake. Canadian nationalists attacked the Free Trade Agreement because, in their view, it destroyed the possibility of Canada's being a distinct society. Meech Lake and free trade were linked together as a double-barrelled threat to the collectivist social policies which, for the nationalist left in English Canada, constitute the key difference between the Canadian and American variants of capitalism. It is this linkage which pushed most of the left-wing intelligentsia in English Canada into the anti-Meech camp. In the past, many of these people had been sympathetic to accommodating Quebec nationalism, but they could not forgive Quebec for supporting free trade and giving Mulroney his 1988 election victory.[44] If that is what Quebec nationalism meant, they would prefer a Canada without Quebec, a Canada in which their own nationalist vision could be fulfilled.

On top of all these substantive points of attack there was, of course, Meech's objectionable process. The contradiction between the closed, elitist Meech negotiations and the open legislative process through which it was to be ratified became painfully clear when a number of legislatures, including the federal Parliament, conducted public hearings on the accord. Members of the public

and of opposition parties participating in these proceedings objected to being told they could talk about the accord all they wished
but not a word would be changed unless they spotted some 'egre-
gious error.' By insisting that the Meech accord be adopted regardless of how it fared in public discussions, its sponsors did more
than erode the accord's legitimacy. They reduced public respect in
the English-speaking provinces for the legitimacy of the parliamentary institutions the governments supporting Meech presumed to
dominate.

The real miracle of Meech is just how close it came to being
ratified despite its unpopularity in English Canada. It is entirely
possible that it would have been adopted had the Quebec unilingual signs issue not suddenly flared up at the end of 1988. By the
middle of 1988 the federal House of Commons and eight of the
ten provincial legislatures had ratified the accord. New Brunswick
and Manitoba were the only provinces that had not. Then, on 15
December 1988, the Supreme Court of Canada brought down its
ruling that Quebec's French-only sign law violated the Charter of
Rights, and all hell broke loose.[45]

In Quebec, Robert Bourassa, who in 1985 had promised English
voters that his government would permit bilingual signs and whose
government had discontinued the Parti Québécois policy of automatically attaching the Charter's override to every new piece of
legislation, now found himself under intense pressure from Quebec nationalists to invoke the override clause and restore those
sections of Bill 101 designed to preserve the French face of Quebec. On Sunday, 18 December, while Bourassa deliberated with his
divided caucus and cabinet, nationalists staged the largest rallies
since the 1980 referendum under the slogan 'Ne touchez pas à la
loi 101.' The next day Bourassa announced his decision: he would
invoke the notwithstanding clause to restore French-only commercial signs outdoors, but allow multilingual signs indoors, so long as
they were out of sight from the street. Bill 178, the indoor/outdoor
compromise, was far too small a change from Bill 101 for the
English and a cowardly retreat from that bill for the hard-core
nationalists. Nonetheless, it might well have met the rule set down
by the Supreme Court in the signs case that a law requiring predominantly (but not exclusively) French signs was a reasonable

limit on freedom of expression. Despite the loss of three of his anglophone cabinet members, Bourassa had Bill 178 passed by the National Assembly.

In English Canada the reaction was severe and equally tribal. Restoration of Quebec's unilingual sign law, which had been in place since 1977, rallied opponents of the Meech Lake Accord as nothing had before. In Manitoba, Filmon, with the agreement of the two opposition leaders, withdrew the resolution placing the accord before Manitoba's legislature. An all-party task force was set up to conduct public hearings on the accord throughout the province. As Patrick Monahan has written, after Bourassa's decision to use the notwithstanding decision, 'there was virtually no chance that the Meech Lake Accord would be ratified.'[46]

The transference of anger from Bourassa's use of the override to Meech was not a logical process. The override was there ready for use with or without the Meech Lake Accord, but Bourassa encouraged the linkage by suggesting that it might not have been necessary to invoke the override had Meech Lake been in force. Critics of the accord pounced on this remark as evidence of its sinister purpose[47] – ignoring the fact that the text of the accord specifically recognized Quebec's English-speaking minority and that the Supreme Court of Canada, two-thirds of whose judges would be from outside Quebec, not Robert Bourassa, would decide what it meant.

English Canada's wrath over Quebec's use of the override revealed the irony of the Charter of Rights. That Charter, Trudeau's Charter, designed to unify Canada, had become a profound source of disunity. This is not because the French-speaking majority in Quebec and the English-speaking majority in Canada were divided on the rights and freedoms inscribed in the Charter. Filmon, who a few years earlier as opposition leader in Manitoba had successfully crusaded against a constitutional amendment to protect the rights of the francophone minority in his province, was not a more ardent supporter of minority language rights than Bourassa. Empirical research shows that Quebecers, if anything, are more supportive of minority language rights than Canadians in other provinces.[48] It was not the substance of the Charter but the Charter as symbol, as icon, which in the heat and passion of mega constitutional politics became profoundly divisive. For a majority of English-speaking Canadians, Charter rights had displaced provincial rights as the fundamental constitutional rights. Trudeau's nationalism, based on equal rights of the Canadian citizen, may well have won the hearts and minds of English Canadians. But for the Québécois, if they had to choose between maintaining control over their cultural security or giving primacy to the Charter – and that was the choice the signs issue presented to them – the choice was clear. They would stick with the original bargain of Confederation: a province in which the French majority could maintain and develop its distinct identity was their fundamental constitutional value. And if that condition appeared unobtainable under a constitution shared with other Canadians, the majority of Quebecers would prefer to be a separate people with their own constitution.

Throughout 1989, events moved steadily against the Meech accord. Early in the year public hearings in Manitoba and New Brunswick got under way. Over 90 per cent of the witnesses appearing at these hearings attacked the accord and called for extensive changes.[49] The process showed how divisive popular participation in constitution making can be if it is carried on in balkanized enclaves. This was particularly evident in Manitoba, where no one from outside the province was allowed to be heard. The chances of Canadians constituting themselves a sovereign people under these circumstances are clearly nil.

In late October the Manitoba and New Brunswick committees released their reports. Manitoba's, as could be predicted, showed little interest in accommodating Quebec. It insisted on the primacy of the Charter, called for absorbing recognition of Quebec's distinctness into a larger 'Canada clause' recognizing the aboriginal peoples and Canada's multicultural heritage as equally distinct components of the country, and dropping altogether the spending-power provision and an extension of unanimity in the amending formula.[50] The New Brunswick report was much more conciliatory. It would keep the accord, but make acceptance of it conditional on negotiating a 'companion accord' to provide constitutional security for those who felt threatened by Meech – especially linguistic minorities and women.[51]

Just as Manitoba and New Brunswick were weighing in against

the accord, the premier of a third province, Newfoundland's Clyde Wells, launched his own vigorous attack. He addressed a public letter to Mulroney in which he replied in kind to those who contended that the accord was the only way of saving the federation. The accord, he wrote, 'would, at the very least, prevent forever the kind of Canada the vast majority of its people espouse and desire,' and 'at worst, it would result in the destruction of the nation in a relatively short period of time.'[52] Wells followed this up by debating Mulroney on prime time television at a November first ministers' conference in Ottawa – the first time the two men had discussed the Constitution face to face. Overnight, Wells became a constitutional hero. He stood on the high ground of principle: equal rights for every citizen, equal powers for every province. The existing Constitution deviates in many ways from these notions of equality, but they have enormous appeal to the current generation of Canadians – outside French Quebec. From this vantage point, Wells made the politicians who had put Meech Lake together look like grubby compromisers.

Wells insisted the accord must be changed to meet his principles or else he would have Newfoundland's legislature withdraw its support. Bourassa had left himself no room to manoeuvre, and would not move an inch. On 6 April 1990 Newfoundland's legislature rescinded its support for the Meech Lake Accord.[53]

Meanwhile, with the 23 June deadline just ninety days away, Mulroney launched a last-minute effort to save the accord. On 23 March he asked an all-party committee of the House of Commons to hold public hearings on McKenna's idea of developing a 'companion accord.' Such a companion or parallel accord would amount to a political commitment to support another set of constitutional amendments, simultaneously with or immediately after ratification of the Meech proposals. These subsequent amendments would be designed to deal with a number of the concerns raised by the Meech Lake Accord. Even though McKenna's list of concerns was relatively modest, designing amendments that would encompass them without, in effect, contradicting the Meech amendments would be about as easy as squaring the circle.

The parliamentary committee, chaired by Jean Charest, reached an all-party consensus only by extending a parallel accord to cover virtually all the concerns of the three dissenting provinces. Its report, released on 16 May, included a commitment to drop a Quebec veto over restructuring the Senate if Senate reform was not unanimously agreed to within three years. It also called for a declaration that the clause recognizing Quebec as a distinct society 'confers no extra powers on the province and does not interfere with the Charter of Rights and Freedoms.'[54] Though this may have accommodated the accord's critics, Bourassa quickly indicated that it was 'unacceptable' to Quebec.[55] The Mulroney government's apparent willingness to embrace the Charest committee's report led directly to the resignation of Lucien Bouchard, Mulroney's Quebec lieutenant, from the cabinet. Bouchard would soon became leader of the Bloc Québécois, a new Quebec political party built around Quebec nationalists in the House of Commons (defecting from both the Conservatives and the Liberals) and committed to Quebec independence.

In these most inauspicious circumstances, Mulroney persuaded the provincial premiers to join him for one more round of that great spectator sport of Canadian politics – a first ministers' constitutional conference. This conference was to break all previous records for longevity and for television ratings. One of its other distinctive features was the presence of leaders of the opposition parties from two of the provinces. Gary Filmon, leading a minority government, had good reason to bring along Sharon Carstairs and Gary Doer, leaders of the Liberals and the NDP, respectively. He would need the support of at least one of their parties to get anything ratified in the Manitoba legislature. Ontario premier David Peterson, who headed a majority Liberal government, invited NDP leader Bob Rae and Conservative leader Mike Harris to participate in the Ontario delegation. The presence of opposition leaders, albeit only in a consultative role and not seated at the bargaining table, was a throwback to the Confederation conferences attended by multipartisan delegations from the colonial legislatures and perhaps a harbinger of a broader process of elite accommodation to come in the next round.

With less than three weeks to go before the time on Meech ran out, this conference had the suspense and pressure of the closing minutes in a Stanley Cup hockey final. It began on the evening of

Sunday, 3 June, with a dinner at the Canadian Museum of Civilization on the banks of the Ottawa River in Hull, Quebec. That night
at least there was agreement to continue the talks. And continue
they did – for seven days and seven nights. On Monday the conference venue shifted to the first ministers' home arena – the conference centre in downtown Ottawa. But they chose not to put their
differences and their efforts to bridge them on public display, and
throughout the week the first ministers met in closed sessions in
a windowless room on the fifth floor. Technically, their meetings
were not a conference but a meeting to see if there was enough
common ground to have a formal conference. The public was
'tethered to the talks by an electronic umbilical cord,'[56] its information confined to titbits the participants tossed to media scrums
as they emerged for a meal, some sleep, or their counsellors' advice.

At an hour and a half to midnight on Saturday, 9 June, the first
ministers assembled for the first time in the flag-bedecked hall on
the main floor of the centre to issue a final communiqué. It
seemed they had done the impossible: the politicians who had
negotiated Meech three years earlier and the provincial premiers
elected since then now agreed on the conditions that would enable
the holdout provinces to ratify the Meech Lake Accord. They
agreed to proceed with a whole new set of constitutional initiatives
immediately following legislative ratification of the Meech proposals.[57] Those initiatives were as follows:

· a House of Commons committee would conduct public hearings
  across the country on what should go into a 'Canada clause'
  giving constitutional expression to the defining features of the
  Canadian community;
· a commission composed of equal delegations from the provinces
  with appropriate numbers from the federal Parliament and the
  territories would conduct hearings and develop proposals for an
  elected Senate;
· constitutional meetings with the aboriginal peoples would be resumed;
· constitutional amendments would be adopted to strengthen the
  entrenchment of sex equality in the Charter of Rights and mi-

nority language rights and to deal with the future of the northern territories; and
· further reviews of the amending formula would be undertaken.

What a plate full of future constitutional business! Even if Meech had gone through, a fifth mega round of constitutional politics would have followed swiftly on its heels. It is also evident from the references to a House of Commons committee and an interlegislative commission holding public hearings at the development stage of constitution making that the first ministers were collectively moving to a more open constitutional process.

Despite the euphoria on the evening of 9 June, the Meech accord was not ratified. One of the holdout provinces, New Brunswick, ratified quickly on 15 June. Frank McKenna had become a strong convert to the cause of salvaging Meech, but the same cannot be said for the political leadership in the other holdout provinces. Clyde Wells affixed an asterisk beside his signature on the 9 June communiqué. The asterisk was to explain that he endorsed only the commitment made by the premiers of the three holdout provinces in part one of the document to submit the Meech accord 'for appropriate legislative or public consideration and to use every possible effort to achieve decision prior to June 23, 1990.'[58] Wells would not say whether he would support the accord when it was resubmitted to the Newfoundland legislature.

The Manitoba troika of Filmon, Carstairs, and Doer, while not enthusiastic about Meech, agreed to support it in the Manitoba legislature. Canada's aboriginal people had not been a party to the Ottawa agreement or to Meech Lake; now one of their leaders, Elijah Harper, the only aboriginal member in the Manitoba legislature, had some leverage on the constitutional process and knew how to use it. When Filmon on 12 June asked the Manitoba legislature for unanimous consent to consider the Meech proposals without the normal two days' notice, Harper recorded the only 'no' vote. The following week, Harper, despite a six-point federal offer of action on aboriginal concerns, opposed any short-cutting of the legislative hearings on constitutional proposals required under the legislature's rules. With 3500 names, mostly of aboriginal persons, listed to be heard, the hearings would extend far beyond

23 June. Unanimous consent was not required to curtail the length of the hearing, but none of Manitoba's leaders was willing to offend the aboriginal people or compromise their commitment to an open constitutional process. Though the Meech accord was finally put before the legislature, Filmon, citing the reference to appropriate public discussion in the 9 June communiqué, refused to force a vote on it before the 23 June deadline.

In Newfoundland there was no procedural roadblock. Wells considered and then rejected a Newfoundland referendum on the accord. He brought the accord before the legislature, releasing government members from party discipline but indicating his own vote would likely be in the negative. The principal advocates for Meech Lake in the Newfoundland Assembly were first ministers from the mainland. New Brunswick's Frank McKenna, Ontario's David Peterson, Saskatchewan's Grant Divine, and, finally, Mulroney himself – on 21 June – flew to St John's to make their pitch for the accord. Wells kept waiting to see what Manitoba would do before calling for a vote. On the afternoon of 22 June with just hours remaining, Mulroney's minister of federal-provincial relations, Lowell Murray, announced on national television that the federal government 'would ask the Supreme Court of Canada to rule that the deadline could move to September 23, the anniversary of the date Saskatchewan ratified the accord in 1987.'[59]

The federal government would do this only if Newfoundland ratified the accord before the day was out. For Wells, this was the last straw. The only logic in pressuring his province but not Manitoba to observe the 23 June deadline was the cynical political logic that it was safer to offend Newfoundlanders than the aboriginal peoples. Wells refused to bow to that pressure. Newfoundland's legislature adjourned without a vote and Meech was dead.

Even if the accord had been ratified it could hardly have constituted a popular social contract. After three years of debate, it was not in accord with the constitutional preferences of the majority within or without Quebec. A poll conducted in April 1990 reported that 59 per cent of Canadians opposed the Meech Lake Accord and 71 per cent wanted a national referendum on it.[60] While the accord was considerably more popular in Quebec, where 49 per cent supported it, Quebec independence was even more popular.

The sovereignty-association option rejected by 60 per cent of Quebecers in 1980 was now favoured by two-thirds of the population.[61]

To suggest it was somehow undemocratic for the legislatures of two provinces representing just 8 per cent of the Canadian people to block constitutional changes approved by legislatures representing all the rest is to miss the point that many of the people were driven to through the Meech round: a loss of faith in the representative capacity of elected legislatures. Here, in yet another respect, Quebec was a distinct society, for that loss of legitimacy did not apply to Quebec's elected legislature. For Quebecers the crucial question now was whether its National Assembly should represent an independent, sovereign people. For all Canadians the time was at hand to see whether they wished to form a single sovereign people. That question could be postponed no longer.

10 Round Five:
The Canada Round I

Simply by calling the fifth round of mega constitutional politics the Canada round is to react to the previous round. The Meech round was called by its sponsors the Quebec round because they saw its purpose as winning Quebec's support for the changes made to the Constitution in 1982. But that very feature of the Meech accord made it highly contentious in Canada outside Quebec. The majority of Canadians outside Quebec did not accept the rationale of Meech and resented its derivation from Quebec's demands. If this part of Canada was to give its support to further constitutional reform, the changes would have to respond to a broader, more comprehensive set of aspirations than those of Quebec nationalism. Hence, after Meech, for constitutional reformers to get a hearing outside Quebec, they had to talk about a Canada round.

Indicative of just how divisive Canada's constitutional discourse had become is that during this Canada round, Canada outside Quebec came to be called the 'Rest of Canada' or ROC. After Meech, the commonest constitutional aspiration of the people in ROC was to put the Constitution back in the freezer and get on with life. But these people were not to have their way. In this era of popular constitutionalism, when constitutions are to be based on the consent of the people, the two parts of the Canadian people whose membership in the Canadian community was originally based on coercion would not accept the Constitution as it stood. The Québécois and Canada's aboriginal peoples would demand another round of constitutional change whether the Rest of Canada liked it or not.

It did not take long for aboriginal people to demonstrate their continued determination to their own pre-Meech constitutional round. In July 1990 the Mohawks at Oka clashed with Quebec police over barricades erected to prevent a golf course from being built on land claimed by them.[1] The Oka Mohawks were soon joined by Kanewake Mohawks who closed the Mercier Bridge connecting Montreal to the south shore of the St Lawrence. The Mohawk standoff, first with the Quebec police, then with the Canadian army, continued through the summer. It was finally ended by force, not by a consensual agreement. But the support the Mohawks received from the aboriginal community across the country indicated that the prospect of maintaining civil peace between aboriginal and non-aboriginal Canadians was at risk if the aboriginal demand for a new constitutional order based on mutual consent continued to be ignored.

As for Quebec, even before the death of Meech, Bourassa's Liberal party had a committee working on constitutional alternatives in the event that Meech failed. Three days after Meech died, 200,000 Quebecers waving the Quebec flag and chanting 'in-dé-pen-dance' paraded through the streets of Montreal in the annual Jean-Baptiste Day celebration. The loudest cheers were reserved for Parti Québécois leader Jacques Parizeau and for Lucien Bouchard, the Mulroney minister who had resigned when he saw Meech being diluted.[2] Before that week was out, Bourassa announced he would get together with Parizeau to form a broad commission – a Quebec 'estates general' – to consult the Quebec people on a full range of constitutional options.[3] The only options ruled out would be the status quo and annexation to the United States. Quebec was not about to retire from the constitutional struggle. On the contrary, in the wake of the Meech failure, Quebec was – as predicted – about to raise the ante.

The Quebec threat was not well received in the Rest of Canada. Generally, people do not take kindly to negotiating with a 'knife to their throat.'[4] Outside Quebec there was absolutely no way political leaders could obtain public support for another round of constitutional reform dealing solely, or even primarily, with Quebec's demands. For English-speaking Canada, the constitutional agenda in the Canada round had to be shaped by more than Quebec and aboriginal concerns. One aspiration to which that agenda had to respond was the desire of 'outer Canada' – the eight provinces of the West and Atlantic regions – to counter what was seen as central Canada's domination of the federation and to obtain a more effective role in national policy making. Senate reform has become the principal vehicle for meeting that concern.

A second and more pervasive force in English-speaking Canada during the Canada round was a growing sense of Canadian nationalism. Canadian nationalism is a complex body of sentiment with a left, a centre, and a right. On the left are the social democrats with their aspiration for Canada-wide standards of social policy and a strong collectivist central government. In the middle are the Charter Canadians with their Trudeauian belief in equal individual rights as the fundamental constitutional value. And to the right are the business community and the economists with their desire for a more efficient Canada better able to compete in the global economy. In constitutional politics Canadian nationalism, unlike the other sources of constitutional discontent, is fuelled less by a sense of grievance over past injustice than by a sense of thwarted ambition. It was this sense of thwarted aspiration for a stronger Canada, on the left and within the Trudeauian centre of English Canada, that defeated Meech Lake.[5] Political leaders in English Canada ignore this sentiment at their peril.

Quebec nationalism, aboriginal self-government, regional alienation, and Canadian nationalism: How can these four sources of constitutional grievance and aspiration be accommodated to one another? Clearly, no accord is possible if any of these constitutional causes is pushed too far. This is particularly true of Quebec and Canadian nationalism. If these two nationalist tendencies remain strong and uncompromising, the Canadian federation cannot be held together by consent.

Accommodating these forces within a common constitution would be a daunting challenge even for a federation cheerfully practising the elitist politics of consociational democracy – the top-down form of democracy considered by political scientists to be most effective in reconciling the segments of a deeply divided nation-state.[6] Canadians, however, insist on a more participatory form of constitution making. Elite accommodation operating through the machinery of executive federalism is a major casualty of the Meech round. Still, eager as so many Canadians may be to do their constitutional politics democratically, they are learning that 'negotiating a popular accord will be ever so much more difficult than rejecting an elitist accord.'[7]

The constitutional process in the Canada round reversed the stages of the Meech round: this time public discussion of constitutional options – lots of it – preceded negotiation of an agreement. Indeed, after nearly two years of public discussion, many Canadians wondered if the negotiation stage would ever be reached. This public discussion proceeded in two distinct stages – some might say in two distinct solitudes. Quebec, responding to the failure of Meech with a widespread sense of grievance and rejection, had a huge head start. Most of Quebec's formal public consultations were carried out between the fall of 1990 and the spring of 1991. Only towards the end of Quebec's process was the Rest of Canada, in the sourest possible mood, drawn into the debate.

In Quebec the public consultation process proceeded in two forums. The first was the Constitutional Committee of the Quebec Liberal Party, chaired by Jean Allaire. After the death of Meech, the committee intensified its activities. It developed audio/video presentations of the full range of constitutional alternatives and took these to meetings in every constituency in the province. The Allaire Committee also met with business and union leaders and with academic experts. The second and broader forum was the Bélanger-Campeau Commission established by Quebec's National Assembly on 4 September 1990. This was the 'estates general' agreed to by Bourassa and Parizeau. Besides the two party leaders and sixteen other members of the assembly (nine Liberals, six Parti Québécois, and one Equality party), its membership of thirty-six included representatives of business, labour, the cooperative movement, the arts, education, and municipalities as well as three Quebec members of the federal Parliament (one Conservative, one Liberal, and Lucien Bouchard, by now leader of the Bloc Québécois, the new Quebec separatist party operating at the federal level). The non-politician members of the commission, including its co-chairmen, Michel Bélanger and Jean Campeau, two leading

Quebec businessmen, were appointed by Bourassa in consultation with Parizeau. Notably absent from the commission's membership were any representatives of Quebec's aboriginal peoples.

The Bélanger-Campeau Commission's public hearings began in early November and continued through the winter months. Although the six hundred individuals and groups who made submissions represented virtually every constitutional viewpoint, the majority favoured either a high degree of autonomy for Quebec within a restructured federation or outright independence.[8] Both Bélanger-Campeau and Allaire focused entirely on Quebec's constitutional future. The Allaire Committee's primary criterion in assessing constitutional options was 'the political autonomy necessary for the development of Quebec's identity.'[9] Bélanger-Campeau's mandate was 'to examine and analyze the political and constitutional status of Quebec.'[10] There was no reference to Canada in these terms of reference. The aim was to define the space in which Quebec could fulfil its destiny. If the space needed could be found in Canada, fine. If not, it must be claimed outside Canada.

Quebec's constitutional consultation in the winter of 1990–1 should be seen as the constitutional culmination of its Quiet Revolution. The nationalist energies released by that mutation in Quebec politics were held in check but not defeated by Trudeau's pan-Canadian nation-building project. The imposition of Trudeau's constitutional vision in 1982 aroused Quebec nationalism, and the rejection of the Meech accord released it from the discipline of moderation. The title of the Allaire Committee's report, *A Quebec Free To Choose*, said it all. Quebec – more precisely the French-speaking Quebec majority – was now choosing its national destiny 'serenely' and with little regard for how its choice might be received by the Rest of Canada.

A striking new feature of the Quebec nationalism evident in this exercise was the participation of a new Quebec business class. Since the early 1960s a dynamic group of French-speaking entrepreneurs had emerged in Quebec. They headed a number of Canada's fastest-growing companies and were at the cutting edge of financial innovation. Compared with the social scientists and professionals in the forefront of Quebec nationalism a generation earlier, this new business class was less *étatiste*, less enthusiastic about expanding the public sector. Still, it worked in close cooperation with the Quebec government and drew much of its corporate financing from semi-public pools of capital such as local savings banks, provincially tax-sheltered schemes, and public sector pension funds. To be sure, not all the members of this new Quebec business class were committed sovereigntists, but the achievements of this class and the active support of some of its prominent members – like Michel Bélanger and Jean Campeau – for greater Quebec autonomy infused Quebec nationalism with a sense of economic confidence it never had before.[11] In the words of Pierre Fortin, one of Quebec's leading economists, 'the province now understands it has all the human, technological, and financial bases it needs to generate its own economic development as a mature member of Canada and the world community.'[12]

The influence of this business mentality is clearly evident in the reports produced by both Allaire and Bélanger-Campeau. The Allaire Committee's report was released at the end of January 1991. The report attacked the concept of the interventionist, welfare state. 'Market globalization,' it argues, requires an effective, competitive administrative machinery while public intervention often leads to dependence and biases the behaviour of socioeconomic agents.'[13] Allaire's formula for Quebec's future was political autonomy for Quebec within a strengthened Canadian economic union. It is a formula that comes close to the sovereignty-association proposed by the Parti Québécois in the 1980 referendum.

The political autonomy proposed for Quebec would mean giving the provincial government 'full sovereignty' over virtually all aspects of social policy and economic development. Allaire listed twenty-two policy areas to be brought under exclusive Quebec authority.[14] This agenda is somewhat less horrific than was initially made out. Only one of the areas – unemployment insurance – was under exclusive federal jurisdiction.[15] A number of subjects on the list – for example, municipal affairs, education, natural resources, and health – were already exclusively or primarily under provincial jurisdiction. The Fathers of Confederation never contemplated government being active in areas such as research and development, culture, and the environment. The existing Constitution does not refer to these or most of the other subjects in Allaire's list, yet in modern times both levels of government have been active in these fields. In essence what Allaire proposed was a massive withdrawal of the federal government's involvement in most areas of concurrent jurisdiction and all areas of exclusive provincial jurisdiction – especially in its power to spend public money. The report is silent on whether this federal withdrawal would apply to the other provinces. The proposals are phrased entirely in terms of Quebec's needs.

There is little of the traditional emphasis on Quebec's distinct and historic culture in Allaire's rationale for this consolidation of power in Quebec's hands. The central argument is couched in terms of McLuhan's 'global village': the need for coherent units of government close to the people to enable a society to participate effectively in an increasingly interdependent world. The emphasis is on overcoming expensive overlaps of responsibilities that have produced confusion and huge deficits in the Canadian federation. The Allaire Report did insist that the survival and full development of 'francophone Quebec society' require that Quebec obtain the constitutional protection it sought in the Meech accord for its role over immigrant selection as well as the 'repatriation' of its control over culture and communications.[16] However, the report promised to safeguard 'the historic rights of Anglophone Quebeckers' and 'the right of allophone communities to develop themselves as cultural communities.'[17] As for Quebec's aboriginal peoples, they were to be treated as 'distinct nations entitled to their culture, their language, their customs and traditions, as well as the right to direct the development of their own identity.'[18] Ironically, in promising to develop as a multinational, multicultural society, Allaire committed Quebec to becoming not a distinct society but a mirror image of Canada – except with a French-speaking majority.

Allaire provides only the sketchiest picture of how the Rest of Canada would function under the proposed constitutional restructuring. The federal government would retain exclusive jurisdiction over defence, foreign trade, and currency, and some of its responsibilities for native affairs, immigration, financial institutions, justice, fisheries, the postal service, telecommunications, and transport. The federal government would also continue to be responsible for equalization – for ensuring that all provinces, without resorting to above-average levels of taxation, could fund public services up to the level of the more affluent provinces. The report does not consider how the federal government, with the tight restrictions Allaire would apply to its taxation powers, would find the revenues (or the political will) to support the huge fiscal transfers required for equalization.

Nor did the Allaire Report give much thought to the central institutions of the restructured federation. It would simply abolish the Senate: so much for outer Canada's interest in obtaining a stronger voice in Canadian affairs! By assuming – most unrealistically – that all the other provinces would agree to the same massive dismantling of federal programs as Quebec wants, it avoids any question of Quebec representatives playing a lesser role in the federal legislature than MPs from other provinces. The Supreme Court of Canada would be replaced by a 'tribunal' confined to settling constitutional disputes and enforcing statutes of 'the new central state.' As for managing the economic union, Allaire proposed only a central bank with a board made up of regional delegates but independent of political authorities. The report recognized that an effective economic union requires harmonizing monetary and fiscal policy as well as many aspects of social, economic, and environmental policy, but it has nothing to say about the political institutions through which this harmonization would be accomplished. The authors of the Allaire Report appear totally oblivious to the difficulty Europe has experienced in developing democratic and accountable institutions to manage its economic union.[19]

On the weekend of 9 and 10 March 1991, the Liberal party of Quebec held a convention in Montreal to debate the Allaire Report. It was not much of a debate. The party's youth wing took over the event. The young Liberals commandeered the microphones and forced closure on issues before senior members of the party, including former leader Claude Ryan, could speak.[20] Although 2771 delegates registered for the meeting, by the evening of the first day less than half that number were in the hall and most of them were under thirty years of age. To no one's great surprise, most of the fifty-six proposed amendments to Allaire – nearly all of them designed to soften its sovereigntist tone – were defeated. Only two amendments of any significance were accepted: one retaining a charter of rights for the restructured Canada and another opening up the possibility of reforming rather than abolishing the Senate.[21]

Premier Bourassa dropped in at the end of his party's convention to give a closing address in which he attempted to distance himself and his government from the uncompromising sovereigntist spirit that had pervaded the meeting. Fortunately for him, the convention's final decision was to withdraw a motion making the Allaire proposals Quebec's 'complete, final and non-negotiable position.'[22] Bourassa was left some room to negotiate, but in this round the Meech process would be totally reversed: rather than negotiating first in private on the basis of Quebec's minimum demands, he would begin in public with Quebec's maximum demands for a restructuring of the federation.

After the televised sessions of the Liberal party convention, the release two weeks later of the Bélanger-Campeau Commission's final report was something of an anticlimax. The body of the report is a ringing declaration, an anthem, to Quebec nationalism. 'Quebecers,' the report declared, 'are aware that they form a distinct national collectivity.'[23] It traced the quarter-century of frustration in trying to negotiate constitutional arrangements appropriate for that sense of national collectivity, and declared that the stalemate must now be broken. With 'serenity' Quebecers must choose their future. But the commission could not agree on the substance of the constitutional future Quebecers should choose. This, of course, is what one would expect given the commission's political mixture of federalists and outright separatists. A substantial majority – including Bourassa, Parizeau, and members of their parties – could agree only on the process Quebec should follow in choosing its future.

That two-track process was embodied in Bill 150 enacted by Quebec's National Assembly in May 1991. The first track is sovereigntist. Bill 150 committed the Quebec government to holding a referendum 'on the sovereignty of Quebec' between 8 and 22 June 1992 or between 12 and 28 October 1992.[24] If the results favoured sovereignty, Quebec was to acquire it 'one year to the day' from the holding of the referendum. To prepare for that option a committee of the legislature was established to examine all matters relating to Quebec's accession to full sovereignty. The second track was committed to exploring the federalist option. For this purpose another legislative committee was to examine 'any offer of a new constitutional partnership' made by the Canadian government.[25] The only kind of offer the committee was to consider was one that 'is formally binding on the Government of Canada and the other provinces.'[26] The intent here appears to be that Quebec would not publicly negotiate with the Rest of Canada but simply respond, on a take it or leave it basis, to proposals ratified by the federal Parliament and other provincial legislatures.

Bill 150 does not provide for a Quebec referendum on a federalist option. Herein it differs from the process recommended in the Allaire Report and adopted by the Quebec Liberal party. Allaire called for a referendum 'before the end of the fall of 1992' should the Rest of Canada agree with the constitutional reforms proposed by Quebec. The purpose of this referendum would be to ratify an accord reached with the Rest of Canada. The possibility of a Quebec referendum on a federalist constitutional solution was kept open by including in the preamble to Bill 150 clauses recognizing the Quebec government's retention of 'its full prerogative to initiate and assess measures to promote the best interests of Quebec' and the National Assembly's 'sovereign power to decide any matter pertaining to a referendum and to pass appropriate legislation if necessary.'[27]

By the spring of 1991, with the completion of the Allaire and Bélanger-Campeau reports and the setting of a fall 1992 deadline for the completion of this constitutional round, Quebec had laid down the gauntlet to the Rest of Canada. The Rest of Canada, to put it mildly, was not impressed. It was in no mood to get down on its knees to seek a reconciliation with Quebec. Just how out of phase with Quebec the prevailing mood was in the rest of the country became clear as the federal government began its first constitutional initiatives in the Canada round.

Towards the end of 1990 the Mulroney government, still licking its wounds over Meech, took two seemingly uncoordinated and unplanned steps. On 1 November Mulroney unveiled 'A Citizens' Forum on Canada's Future.' Composed of its chairman, Keith Spicer, an academic/journalist currently serving as chairman of the

Canadian Radio-television and Telecommunications Commission, and 'an advisory group' of eleven other Canadian notables,[28] the Citizens' Forum was to be just that – an opportunity for Canadians from all regions and walks of life to speak out on the future of their country. It was to report on what it heard by 1 July, Canada Day, 1991. The second initiative was more traditional and focused: a parliamentary committee to review the constitutional amending process. The committee, co-chaired by Senator Gérald Beaudoin and MP Jim Edwards, was established on 17 December 1990 and, like the Citizens' Forum, was to report by 1 July 1991.

On the day the Citizens' Forum was announced, Spicer said, 'There's a very high potential for fiasco.'[29] And so there was! Spicer began 'his search for the soul of Canada' by flying off to read poetry with the natives in Tuktoyaktuk, an Inuvialuit community in the far north.[30] This was far too imaginative a launch for sober-souled Canadians. It was followed by open discord among the commissioners and the resignation of one of the group's most prominent members, west-coast media guru Jack Webster. All this was happening at the very time the Bélanger-Campeau Commission was opening to great public acclaim in Quebec. The contrast was sharp. As Graham Fraser put it, 'While Spicer was being ridiculed, his commissioners variously resigning or attacking each other, Quebec's Commissions seemed to be walking off into a sovereignist sunset.'[31]

Despite its rocky start, the Citizens' Forum did engage a large number of Canadians – 400,000 in all – in discussing the future of their country.[32] But the participation of Quebecers and aboriginals, the two parts of the Canadian community whose constitutional discontent drove the constitutional process, was relatively low. Quebecers, who constitute 25 per cent of Canada's population, made up only 11 per cent of Forum participants. For many of the politically active citizens in the Rest of Canada, the forum was a catharsis, in the commissioners' own words, 'a therapeutic exercise in airing grievances.'[33] Their grieving was not about the Constitution itself but about the inordinate amount of time their political leaders were spending on the Constitution at the expense of other issues, especially the economy and the environment. Yes, they were prepared to go some way in accommodating Quebec and even further in accommodating aboriginal peoples. But there was a clear limit to how far they would go: 'For most participants outside Quebec, Quebec's presence in confederation cannot be bought at the price of damaging or destroying those things they value most about the country, and in particular, must not be bought by sacrificing individual or provincial equality.'[34] As for the direction of constitutional change, a general decentralization of power was out. The majority of Rest-of-Canada participants, stated the forum's summary, desire 'a strong central government which will act with resolution to remedy the country's economic ills, help to unify its citizens, and reduce the level of discord among groups or regions.'[35]

Far from resolving Canada's constitutional debate, the Citizens' Forum demonstrated just how difficult a consensual resolution would be. While Allaire and Bélanger-Campeau were demonstrating the continuing strength of Quebec nationalism, the forum showed that English-Canadian nationalism was also alive and well. So also – outside Quebec – was the Trudeau-Wells ideology of individual rights and equal provinces. What seemed nearly dead at this point was the prospect of a constitutional accord between the Quebec and Rest-of-Canada majorities.

Compared with the Citizens' Forum, the Beaudoin-Edwards parliamentary committee on the amending process was a low-key affair. Beaudoin-Edwards is more significant for the concerns it addressed than for its report or recommendations. In Quebec there was still an insistence that Quebec must recover its constitutional veto. That, indeed, was a basic demand of Allaire. In the Rest of Canada, the central concern was the legacy of Meech – an insistence on a more participatory constitutional process. In the Citizens' Forum this feeling was often expressed in negative terms as a loss of faith in elected politicians and the parliamentary process. Those bidding for the people's support would have to adopt procedures more compatible than first ministers' conferences with the principle of popular sovereignty. The favoured devices were a referendum and a constituent assembly made up predominantly of non-politicians.

The Beaudoin-Edwards Report addressed both concerns. For the amending procedure it recommended replacing the seven-province/half-the-population rule with a system of regional vetoes first put forward in the 1971 Victoria Charter.[36] Under this formula, most amendments would require the support of the House of Commons and the legislatures of Ontario, Quebec, two of the four Atlantic provinces, and two of the four western provinces. Quebec would get its veto, but only if the Rest of Canada agreed to abandon the principle of provincial equality. Beaudoin-Edwards realized that no change could be made in the amending process in isolation of other constitutional changes. Indeed, if all sections of the Canadian people could agree on a new amending system, they would have agreed on what kind of a sovereign people they were and their constitutional travails would be over. Because changing the amending formula is one of those few provisions requiring unanimous provincial consent, it is likely to be done, if done at all, only after other changes have been made by the easier seven-province/half-the-population rule.

The more timely recommendations of the Beaudoin-Edwards Committee concerned changes in the constitutional process that could be introduced immediately without any formal constitutional amendment – namely, the referendum and the constituent assembly. The committee called for enactment of federal legislation enabling 'the federal government, at its discretion, to hold a consultative referendum on a constitutional proposal.'[37] The legislation would require a double majority: an overall majority and a majority in each of the four regions (Atlantic, Ontario, Quebec, and the West). The results of the referendum would not be binding on Parliament or the provincial legislatures. However, a constitutional package approved by the double majority would acquire a great deal of political legitimacy and, as a result, would have a much easier passage through the ratifying legislatures. Although Beaudoin-Edwards did not stipulate that the referendum take place before legislative ratification, that seemed implied, particularly since one province, British Columbia, had legislation requiring a province-wide referendum before its legislature could act on any proposals to amend the Constitution.[38] An issue entirely ignored by Beaudoin-Edwards – a particularly thorny question – was how a federal referendum on the constitution would relate to provincial referendums such as British Columbia's and Quebec's.

The overwhelming weight of submissions to the Beaudoin-Edwards Committee pushed home the realization that 'public dissatisfaction with the first ministerial negotiation methods of developing constitutional amendment proposals is so high that any proposals now brought forward would be in immediate jeopardy, irrespective of their merits, if they were seen by the public as being a product solely of eleven first ministers making deals behind closed doors.'[39] The committee's majority, however, turned thumbs down on the idea of a constituent assembly as a mechanism for broadening public participation in shaping constitutional proposals. Instead, it recommended yet another federal parliamentary committee to hold public hearings on any constitutional proposals emanating from the federal government and to interact with aboriginal leaders and committees established by provincial and territorial legislatures.[40]

In rejecting the constituent assembly idea, the majority on the Beaudoin-Edwards Committee reacted to two elements included in many of the proposals for this type of forum. One was the inclusion of representatives of special interest groups. The parliamentarians, not surprisingly, rejected 'the idea that people can only be represented by other people like themselves.'[41] They also rejected the assumption that 'ordinary citizens' directly elected to a constituent assembly would somehow be non-political. That second assumption was not present in the New Democratic Party's minority report. The New Democrats proposed a constituent assembly with an even division between elected parliamentarians and representatives of aboriginal peoples, northerners, and other minorities.[42] Both the majority and the minority on the committee ignored the idea of an assembly or conference, intermediate between a first ministers' meeting and a large constituent assembly, made up of delegations from the constituent legislatures, the northern territories, and aboriginal peoples.[43] Yet it was meetings of legislative delegations at Charlottetown and Quebec City that put Canada together in 1864 (see chapter 3), and assemblies of this kind were also instrumental in the founding of the United States and Australia.[44] This generation of Canadians may yet find such a conference to be the best instrument for negotiating the terms of a new Canadian social contract.

A month before the Beaudoin-Edwards Committee released its final report, the federal government, in the Throne Speech opening Parliament on 13 May 1991, announced its constitutional process. The key element in that process was the very mechanism recommended by Beaudoin-Edwards. Over the summer, the federal cabinet would develop a set of constitutional proposals and, in September, turn them over to a joint parliamentary committee 'that will be established to consult with Canadians.'[45] Also included in the government's statement was a vague promise of a more direct form of democratic consultation. Following receipt and consideration of the parliamentary committee's report, Parliament would be 'asked to approve enabling legislation to provide for greater participation of Canadian men and women in constitutional change.'[46]

The parliamentary committee itself would attempt to overcome the 'democratic deficit' that had come to tarnish federal-provincial constitutional negotiations. It would 'be mandated to meet in public sessions with its counterpart provincial or territorial committee or, where no such committee exists, with counterpart legislators. It will, also, meet with aboriginal groups.'[47] For the first time since Confederation an attempt would be made to conduct constitutional negotiations through interlegislative rather than intergovernmental channels.

The provincial, territorial, and aboriginal sides of this negotiating process were beginning to take shape. Quebec's National Assembly, serenely indifferent to developments in the Rest of Canada, by the spring of 1991 had a committee waiting for 'binding offers' from the federal government. By the fall of 1991 all the provinces and both northern territories had established some kind of process to explore constitutional options. These provincial and territorial initiatives came in all shapes and sizes.[48] Manitoba, Ontario, Prince Edward Island, and the two northern territories used committees of elected legislators.[49] Alberta and British Columbia used executive task forces, followed by legislative committees. The New Brunswick and Newfoundland committees, like Quebec's Bélanger-Campeau Commission, had a mixture of legislators and citizens, while the committees established in Nova Scotia and Saskatchewan were made up entirely of citizens from outside the legislature. Both the British Columbia and Saskatchewan efforts were eclipsed by autumn elections, producing in each province NDP governments whose first priority was the economy, not the Constitution. The most significant part of British Columbia's effort was a series of special studies written by experts on various aspects of the Constitution.[50]

While the participants in these initiatives would no doubt assess constitutional options from the perspective of their region, they were far more Canadian-minded than their Quebec counterparts. A concern to reconcile differences and save the federation was particularly marked in the mandates of the committees established in the Maritimes, the region of the country most threatened by Quebec separation. All these outside-Quebec committees were, to use Alan Cairns's phrase, at least playing the same constitutional game as the federal government – they were trying to renew the Canadian federation, not maximize their own autonomy or local self-interest.[51] At the same time, they were not going to snap to attention when a federal proposal came along and abandon their own agendas and timetables. Fruitful interaction between them and the proposed federal committee was highly problematic.

By early July, Joe Clark, now installed by Mulroney in the constitutional affairs portfolio, had agreed to a parallel process for aboriginal peoples.[52] Organizations representing the four streams of aboriginal peoples – the Assembly of First Nations (status Indians), the Native Council of Canada (non-status Indians), the Métis National Council, and the Inuit Tapirisat of Canada – would carry out intensive consultations with their peoples and then interact with the parliamentary committee established to discuss the federal government's constitutional proposals.[53] Later in the summer the federal government established another instrument to probe aboriginal issues: a Royal Commission on Aboriginal Peoples. The commission, co-chaired by Georges Erasmus, former chief of the Assembly of First Nations, and Quebec judge René Dussault, was given a broad mandate to examine all aspects of the aboriginal peoples' condition and was empowered, as it went along, to comment on constitutional reform 'in a timely fashion.'[54]

It had taken five mega rounds of constitutional politics, but Canada's aboriginal peoples were at last winning recognition of their right to government by consent. Reaching an accord with aboriginal peoples on how to make that right operational would be a difficult process. Aboriginal peoples are committed to a highly consensual form of decision making that does not dovetail easily with the more top-down, tightly scheduled procedures of non-aboriginals. The first nations' assertion of their right to self-determination posed a formidable challenge to the claims of Quebec sovereigntists. With few exceptions, aboriginal peoples in Quebec wish to enjoy their right to self-government within Canada – not within a sovereign Quebec. They are not nations that can be yanked out of Canada against their will by a provincial majority. By the fall of 1991, Ovide Mercredi, the new chief of the Assembly of First Nations, was making that point perfectly clear – to the distress of many Quebecers. It is a point that threatens both the territorial integrity and the political stability of an independent Quebec.

For the first time since the early 1970s, when the Molgat-Mac-Guigan Committee declared that the right to self-determination adhered to peoples, not provinces,[55] the question of an independent Quebec's borders, long a taboo subject, was on the table. It was not only Quebec's aboriginal peoples who were forcing this issue. Claims were also being heard that Quebec's English-speaking minority, concentrated in the southwest corner of the province, should not be forced to leave Canada.[56] Quebecers, indeed Canadians, were discovering how troublesome the principle of self-determination can be. Quebec sovereigntists were now insisting that it is provinces not peoples which have the right to self-determine.

On 24 September 1991, in the midst of this frenzy of constitutional activity at the provincial, territorial, and aboriginal levels, the federal government unveiled its constitutional proposals. They were presented in a glossy blue book entitled *Shaping Canada's Future Together*.[57] If the Canadians as now constituted are to have a future together, it will most likely be on the basis of constitutional proposals that develop in reaction to this set of proposals. In sharp contrast to the Trudeau government's proposals in the first three mega rounds and Quebec's five conditions in the Meech round, this set of federal proposals was put forward on a highly tentative basis. Not only was this an imperative of the democratic constitutionalism Canadians were now insisting upon, but it also reflected the political weakness of the sponsoring government. By the fall of 1991 the Mulroney government had plummeted to 14 per cent in the polls. No government launching a constitutional initiative had ever operated from such a weak political base. If anything, the prime minister was running behind his government. Wisely, he stepped away from centre stage in the constitutional drama, at least for the moment, and let his constitutional minister, Joe Clark, be the spear-carrier for the new proposals.

The federal package was large and diffuse – twenty-eight recommendations in all. Only the Trudeau government's plan in round two for a totally new constitution was more comprehensive. Some of the recommendations did not require formal constitutional amendment. Proposals to relax party discipline in the House of Commons and to make the parliamentary process less executive-dominated required only the will of the governing party. The same was true of the proposal to have regional input on appointments to the Bank of Canada's board of directors. The more controversial idea of focusing the bank's mandate on price stability could be done by amending an ordinary act of Parliament. At the other extreme, two of the recommendations, both carry-overs from Meech Lake, could be implemented only through constitutional amendments subject to the unanimity rule: entrenching the Supreme Court's composition, including its three Quebec positions, in the Constitution; and the changes to the constitutional amending formula proposed in the Meech accord.[58] The government, determined this time to avoid the strait-jacket of unanimity, separated these two items from its main or core package. All the remaining proposals for constitutional amendment required only ratification by the House of Commons and the legislatures of seven provinces with 50 per cent of the population.

The contents of this core package fell under eight headings:

1 *Canada clause* A clause to be inserted at the beginning of the Constitution (although not the preamble) stating 'who we are as a people.' A diffuse shopping list of proposed contents included recognition of Quebec's special responsibility 'to preserve and promote its distinct society.'
2 *Distinct society* A clause to be inserted in the Charter of Rights

stating that the Charter shall be interpreted in a manner consistent with the preservation and promotion of Quebec as a distinct society and the preservation of Canada's linguistic duality. Quebec's distinctiveness was defined to include a French-speaking majority, a unique culture, and a civil law tradition.

3 *Charter changes* The Charter of Rights to be amended to guarantee 'property rights.' The section permitting legislatures to override certain sections of the Charter to be changed so that its use requires not a simple majority but 60 per cent of members of the legislature.

4 *Aboriginal self-government* A general aboriginal right to self-government to be entrenched in the Constitution. Before the right becomes enforceable in the courts, up to ten years should be allowed to define the scope and limits of this right through agreements between aboriginal peoples and governments with overlapping jurisdiction.

5 *Senate reform* Senators to be elected with 'more equitable provincial and territorial representation than at present' and guaranteed representation for aboriginal Canadians. The Senate should not be a confidence chamber or have any role in financial legislation, and only a suspensory veto on 'matters of national importance.' In all other matters it would have full legislative powers, and would be given a mandate to ratify appointments to federal regulatory boards and agencies. On cultural issues, majorities of all senators and of francophone senators would be required.

6 *Supreme Court of Canada* When vacancies occur, appropriate provincial and territorial attorneys-general should submit lists of five nominees. The federal government would appoint from such lists, unless no lists were provided within ninety days. This constitutional amendment would be made under the seven-province/half-the-population rule.

7 *Economic union* By far the most creative part of the package, this element had three parts:
  i *Section 121* The free-trade clause in the original constitution (s.121) should prohibit restrictions on the free movement of 'persons, goods, services and capital.' The federal Parliament should be able to exempt a federal or provincial regulation from

this prohibition on the agreement of seven provinces with 50 per cent of the population.

ii *Section 91A* The federal Parliament should be given a new power (s.91A) to enhance the economic union on any matter it declares 'to be for the efficient functioning of Canada.' This power could be used only when approved by seven provinces with 50 per cent of the population. A dissenting province could opt out for three years.

iii *Council of the Federation* A new institution to be created to manage the economic union and to coordinate intergovernmental affairs. Like the Council of the European Community, it would be made up of ministers from the federal and provincial governments. The territories would be non-voting members. Unlike the European Council, it would have no permanent staff or headquarters. It would have the power to harmonize provincial budgetary policy with federal fiscal and monetary policies. Its decisions would require agreement of the federal government and seven provinces representing 50 per cent of the population.

8 *Division of powers* A hodgepodge of recommendations to provide a more flexible, better coordinated, and more decentralized federation. These proposals included a total withdrawal of a federal role in manpower training, a partial federal withdrawal from six other fields (tourism, forestry, mining, recreation, housing, and urban affairs), the possibility of constitutionalizing bilateral power-sharing agreements in immigration and culture, and an amendment to permit the two levels of government to delegate powers to one another. Federal spending in areas of exclusive provincial jurisdiction would be more restricted than under the Meech accord by being made subject to the seven-province/half-the-population rule, with compensation for opting-out provinces whose programs meet national objectives.[59]

Quite a package! Something for everyone (well, almost everyone), but maybe not enough for anyone. For Quebec, the five conditions of Meech were covered, although some of them – notably the distinct society's narrowing definition and confinement to the Charter – in a diluted form. Further, the proposals provided some of the decentralization and retrenchment of federal authority sought by Allaire. However, this was offset by the threat to Quebec's autonomy in economic policy posed by the economic union proposals. Aboriginal peoples were given a right to self-government, but it was not recognized as inherent and would be inoperative in law for up to ten years. For the provinces of outer Canada there was Senate reform, but a far cry from the 'triple E' approach (elected, equal representation for the provinces, and fully effective) favoured by many westerners and Newfoundland. Proposing 'equitable' representation fudged the equality issue and the institution would be trivialized by giving it no more than a delaying power in matters of national importance.

The economic union proposals promised some appeal to more business-oriented nationalists in English Canada, but contained a lot of gimmickry that would not stand up to critical examination. Section 91A, the federal power to enhance economic efficiency, might frighten Quebec nationalists, but with its opt-out clause and the need for seven provinces to endorse its use it would equally strike Canadian nationalists as faint-hearted. The simplistic rewriting of section 121, the internal free-trade guarantee, raised the spectre of an enormously expanded role for the judiciary in reviewing government regulation.[60] And the idea of having the federation's big decisions on economic and social policy made by a ministerial federal council – a Brussels on the Ottawa – did not fit the democratic mood of contemporary Canada.

As might be expected of proposals emanating from a Conservative government, the recommendations had little to offer the left in English-speaking Canada. The entrenchment of property rights and tight restrictions on the federal spending power were bound to be attacked from the left. After the fall elections, with the NDP in power in three provinces (Ontario, British Columbia, and Saskatchewan) and in a position to block any constitutional amendments, the constitutional agenda of the left in English Canada could not be ignored. By attempting to accommodate Quebec's autonomist demands through a general decentralization of the federation, the proposals risked offending more than the nationalist left in the Rest of Canada. If the Citizens' Forum is to be believed, Canadians of all political persuasions outside Quebec do not want a weaker national government.

Thus, the federal package, while containing many of the elements of a possible resolution, was far from an optimal fit for the state of constitutional opinion in the country. It still had a long way to go. And go it would – first, as promised, to a joint parliamentary committee. The committee would be chaired by a veteran Quebec constitutionalist, Senator Claude Castonguay, and a Manitoba MP, Dorothy Dobbie. Though its thirty members would provide strong representation of the Conservatives, Liberals, and NDP, in the present context of federal politics it was by no means an all-party committee: Lucien Bouchard's Bloc Québécois and Preston Manning's Reform party would not be on it. With polls indicating that the Bloc Québécois was leading all federal parties in Quebec and the Reform party was similarly ahead in Alberta and coming on strong throughout the West and Ontario, these gaps in the committee's political coverage could not be regarded as minor. The committee would have until the end of February 1992 to see how the federal package of constitutional proposals might be modified to accord better with the will of the people.

The trail of Canada's constitutional odyssey is littered with the wreckage of constitutional vehicles that went off the rails, but for sheer disaster nothing can top the miserable performance of the Castonguay-Dobbie Committee. Most citizens with an interest in the Constitution had by now talked themselves out on generalities and were not prepared on short notice to discuss a complex set of twenty-eight proposals. Provincial, territorial, and aboriginal consultations were still in full swing, so the time was not ripe for inter-legislative negotiations. When the so-called unity committee hit the road, its members were squabbling, its logistics dreadful, and its meeting places half empty. Its national tour was terminated in early November when no one showed up at a meeting in Manitoba. The opposition members were now threatening to quit unless Dobbie was replaced and the committee's operations totally revamped. At the end of November, Castonguay, citing health reasons, resigned. He was replaced by another experienced Quebec constitutionalist, Senator Gérald Beaudoin.

The unity committee was salvaged when the government agreed to reform the committee in the direction urged by the NDP. The committee would resume its activities at the beginning of 1992, but its regular hearings would be supplemented by five conferences, each in a different region of the country. Each conference would focus on one component of the federal package: the division of powers, economic union, Senate and other institutional changes, distinct society/Charter/Canada clause, and aboriginal rights. In effect, these conferences would be mini constituent assemblies. They would bring together politicians (mostly federal), experts, interest-group leaders, and 'ordinary citizens' – the latter chosen by the sponsoring conference from persons answering newspaper advertisements. Each conference would be organized by an independent research organization.

As the new year began there were signs that conditions in the country were more propitious for a consensual solution to the constitutional crisis. By January 1992 most of the provincial and territorial consultations had been completed, with reports that were conciliatory in tone and not completely at odds with one another or with the federal proposals. Ontario, departing from its traditional honest-broker's role, took the most distinctive stance. Both its premier, Bob Rae, and its all-party legislative committee insisted that a 'social charter' be added to the constitutional package, to balance the emphasis on competition in the economic union proposals and the decentralization of legislative powers. The social charter would amount to a constitutional pledge to maintain national standards in health care, education, social services, and environmental protection.[61] Providing such a commitment was not judicially enforceable – and that indeed appears to be its sponsors' intention[62] – it could be digestible by Quebec federalists while providing some comfort to the nationalist left outside Quebec.

Quebec's sovereigntist mood was less strident than it had been a year earlier. To a degree, the depth of the economic recession had dampened some of the enthusiasm for radical constitutional change. Economic hard times and the ugly implications of aboriginal claims and the boundaries issue meant that sovereignty was no longer something that could be considered with serenity. The Bourassa government, while continuing to reject out of hand the centralizing aspects of the economic union proposals and provincial equality in a reformed Senate, was showing signs that it would give serious consideration to a modified federal package.[63] There was also some progress on the aboriginal front, with a number of provinces and the federal government indicating they were now prepared to entrench an inherent right to aboriginal self-government in the Constitution.[64]

In this more accommodating environment, the Beaudoin-Dobbie 'unity committee' resumed its activities, conducting hearings in provincial capitals and attending special conferences on five consecutive weekends from mid January to mid February. The hearings flushed out the provincial premiers, who indicated the tough intergovernmental negotiations that lay ahead.[65] The mini constituent assemblies were more conciliatory than the premiers and proved a success – most importantly with the media. This was indeed a surprise for a country grown accustomed to constitutional disasters.

One reason the conferences went well is that the country was ready for them. For over a year Canadians had been talking about constitutional questions. Besides the official constitutional forums sponsored by governments and legislatures, there had been a myriad of panel discussions, study groups, and town-hall meetings sponsored by all kinds of organizations – business and labour, schools, universities, churches, synagogues, service clubs, interest groups, and neighbourhood organizations. Canada surely had a lock on the entry in the Guinness Book of Records for the sheer volume of constitutional talk. Of course only a few of those involved in the talk could be among the two hundred or so attending each weekend conference, but those who came had been informed and animated by the discussions. They were not 'ordinary Canadians.' Who is? They were Canadians with an extraordinary interest in matters constitutional. Many came with well-formed positions but in a more accommodating mood than the citizens who had been invited in the previous round only to kick at the Meech accord from the outside. Discussing constitutional issues in close encounters with Canadians from all parts of the country is far more conducive to compromise than 'spilling out your guts' at the microphone before a home-town crowd.

The first conference, in Halifax, on the division of powers, provided the clearest indication of a more accommodating mood. The majority of delegates recognized what had been becoming increasingly obvious – that Quebec and the Rest of Canada could not reach a constitutional accord on the basis of strict adherence to the principle of provincial equality. The country now became familiar with a concept the experts had been bandying about for some time: asymmetry.

Asymmetrical federalism – which has always been a feature of the Canadian federation – means that the provinces do not all exercise exactly the same powers.[66] Constitutional amendments giving Quebec, and only Quebec, additional powers would be a hard, direct asymmetrical solution. A softer, indirect form of asymmetry could be achieved by a section 94A solution. Under section 94A (added to the Constitution in 1951 and extended in 1964),[67] old-age pensions and supplementary benefits were made concurrent fields of jurisdiction. In case of conflict in these areas, the normal rule of federal paramountcy was reversed so that provincial law could prevail over federal law. Only Quebec has availed itself of the power available under this section and developed its own public pension scheme. If areas of jurisdiction demanded by Allaire were added to section 94A, again Quebec might be the only province that exercised all the powers. The conference's executive summary seemed to have this softer version of asymmetry in mind when it stated: 'There was a strong view that asymmetry in the take-up and administration of federal and provincial powers by Quebec, and where desired, for the other provinces and territories was not a problem.'[68]

The Halifax conference ignored certain problems with asymmetrical solutions. There must be some transfer of revenues to support any province taking over program responsibilities from Ottawa. If the list of areas that Quebec alone takes over from Ottawa is long, either in law or in practice, then the question arises whether Quebec participation in the institutions of central government should be reduced. Though the conference did not resolve these questions, it did create some legitimacy for a constitutional solution that is closer to an optimum fit than a general decentralization of powers or a failure to respond at all to Quebec's demand for more autonomy.

The consensus position emerging from the Calgary conference on institutions favoured a strong elected Senate 'that asserts regional influence in national decision-making.'[69] This gathering of citizens was prepared to go much further than the federal cabinet in empowering a second elected legislative chamber to check the executive-dominated House of Commons. The tough and unre-solved questions concerned how the country is to be represented in this new upper house. Among staunch triple E supporters there was some recognition that Quebec could not be forced to accept equal representation of the provinces. More fundamentally, the proposal to include aboriginal seats in a reformed Senate opened up the question of whether territory or sociological category should be the basis of representation. Women delegates forced this issue on the agenda. Fundamental as this issue is, it is one Cana-dians were ill-prepared to settle in this constitutional round.

A week later, the Montreal conference on economic union dem-onstrated that a balance must be struck between the right and left wings of Canadian nationalism. Freer trade within Canada must go hand in hand with greater protection for the country's social pro-grams. 'These two are a package,' said Vancouver economist John Helliwell, summing up the conference, 'and one cannot be ob-tained without the other.'[70] The one component of the economic union proposals that would likely survive was strengthening the constitutional prohibition against internal trade barriers. Quebec and the Rest of Canada agree on this objective, provided a more appropriate body than courts is established to interpret and apply the free-trade principle. But the nationalist left in English-speaking Canada insisted that Canada be more than a commercial union. A guarantee of internal free trade must be balanced by some elements of Ontario's social charter proposal.

The fourth conference in Toronto got down to the challenge of constitutionally defining Canadian identity. Just how emotive the negotiation of the country's constitutional symbols can become was seen at the opening panel of aboriginal leaders, when Ovide Mer-credi asked that his people be given a share of that valuable consti-tutional coinage – recognition as a distinct society. It immediately became evident that while Quebec is well past being satisfied by symbolic recognition as a 'distinct society,' its majority will demand that its special status not be devalued by being shared with any other part of the federation. The Canadians at this conference, unlike those who defeated Meech Lake, were willing to recognize Quebec as a distinct society and in even stronger terms than envisaged in the federal proposals. They were also willing to recognize the aboriginal peoples' inherent right to self-government. While there was strong support for protecting the rights of the French minority outside Quebec and the English minority in Quebec, this did not translate into a dualist, English-French, conception of the whole of Canada. If a consensus could be discerned at this conference, it was one which recognizes that the deep diversity of the Canadian people or peoples is a condition not just to be tolerated but to be celebrated as the core of Canadian identity. Aboriginal, Québécois, and Rest of Canada Canadians could share constitutional sovereignty as citizens of a multinational state.[71]

It had not been possible to work out arrangements for a conference focusing on aboriginal questions. Instead, Joe Clark promised a special public meeting on aboriginal issues sometime before 10 April, the date then set by the federal government for releasing its revised constitutional proposals. The fifth conference, in Vancouver, was dedicated to knitting together the positions emerging from the earlier conferences. This it did and, to use co-chair Rosalie Abella's phrase, 'the little conferences that could' handed over their conclusions to the Beaudoin-Dobbie Committee.[72] The constitutional ball was now handed back to the federal political elites.

And they almost dropped it! For two weeks in closed-door sessions on Parliament Hill the thirty MPs and senators considered the views expressed in the public conferences. Throughout, they were in close communication with their party leaders, including in the Liberals' case their old leader, Trudeau, on the telephone from Montreal. In essence the Beaudoin-Dobbie Committee's discussions were a negotiation among the leaders of the three old-line, national political parties. With the Mulroney government now standing at 11 per cent in the opinion polls, it was essential to broaden political support for the federal constitutional proposals. This gave the Liberals and the NDP a great deal of leverage in the negotiating process. The wrangling within the committee room and the corridors of Parliament rose to a crescendo as the committee approached the 28 February deadline set earlier by Parliament. An hour before midnight of the final day, the unity committee emerged with a 'unanimous report' – well, almost unanimous, and almost a report. The report was not printed until a day and a half later, and there were dissents on some significant details.[73] Dissents on other points were avoided by suggesting options rather than recommending detailed solutions.

The 125-page report of the Beaudoin-Dobbie Committee, entitled *A Renewed Canada*, called for changes in every component of the federal government's package.[74] Some of these changes were relatively minor, others major. The recommended changes, for the most part, followed the general contours of the discussions in the five public conferences. That fact had the potential to give the committee's recommendations an extra measure of political legitimacy. Some of that potential was dissipated, however, by the unseemly last-minute scramble in putting the committee's report together and the lack of consensus on some important points.

To the emotionally treacherous challenge of defining the country in a Canada clause, the committee's response is extravagant. It recommends both a poetic constitutional preamble and, for those who prefer to be defined in prose, a declaration to be inserted as section 2 of the Constitution. The poetry strikes an ambivalent note with respect to popular sovereignty; it begins: 'We are the people of Canada / drawn from the four winds / a privileged people / citizens of a sovereign state.'[75] The implication of these words is that the people are the authors of the Constitution even though it is the state, rather than its citizens, that is declared to be sovereign. The proposed section 2, a 'declaration' of 'our characteristics as Canadians and the things we hold dear,'[76] struggled earnestly to ensure that no one was left out or offended. As can be seen by its treatment of Quebec, this may well be an impossible task of symbolic engineering. There is to be recognition of 'the special responsibility of Quebec to preserve and promote its distinct society,' but also 'a profound commitment to the vitality of official language minority communities.'[77] Unlike the distinct society clause in the Meech Lake Accord, the declaration does not direct judges to give weight to the clause in interpreting the Constitution.

The Beaudoin-Dobbie Report supported the federal government's proposal to limit 'distinct society' as an interpretation clause to the Charter of Rights and Freedoms, and it accepted the proposal of defining Quebec's distinctness in an implicity limiting way to include language, culture, and civil law. The committee thus retained the one clear way in which the federal proposal offered Quebec less than Meech. This distinct society clause, unlike that in Meech, would not apply to the division of powers, a part of the Constitution of more concern to Quebec than the Charter. The Beaudoin-Dobbie Report muddied the water further by throwing into the same clause, as a counterwieight to recognizing Quebec's distinctness in having a French-speaking majority, recognition of 'the vitality and development of the language and culture of French-speaking and English-speaking minority communities throughout Canada.' Again, as in Meech, the effort to provide symbolic gratification to groups harbouring conflicting hopes and fears ended up in piling fudge on fudge. Perhaps the Toronto conference on rights, identity, and values got it right when it dismissed both the distinct society and Canada clauses as 'bedtime reading for the judges.'[78]

The changes to the Charter of Rights proposed by the federal government did not fare well with the committee. Only the Conservative members of the committee were in favour of putting property rights in the Charter. These members also favoured adding a right to privacy. At the other end of the political spectrum, the NDP members wanted to exempt the Charter's equality rights from the legislative override. As for making the override more difficult to use, the committee thought that consideration of this and other issues should be postponed. Given that the country has more than enough unavoidable constitutional issues to resolve, it would surely be wise to put off tinkering with the Charter to another day.

On aboriginal self-government, the Beaudoin-Dobbie Report was much more forthright. Here, in being bolder than the government's original proposal, it reflected the consensus developing in the country. The committee called for a clause that would make it clear the existing aboriginal rights recognized in the 1982 constitutional changes include 'the inherent right of self-government within Canada.'[79] A process for working out the details of self-government through negotiations of aboriginal peoples with federal, provincial, and territorial governments was also recommeneded. There was no suggestion, however, that the opportunity to litigate claims based on the inherent right was contingent on completion of these negotiations. Most significantly, the committee recommended that aboriginal peoples not simply be consulted on constitutional amendments affecting their rights (as is now required under section 35.1 of the Constitution Act, 1982) but that no changes in these rights be implemented without their consent.[80] This went some way to extending the principle of government based on consent to Canada's aboriginal peoples, although it fell short of giving them a share of constitutional sovereignty equal to that of the federal and provincial legislatures.

On the thorny issue of Senate reform, the Beaudoin-Dobbie Report advanced only a little beyond the federal proposal. All its members (including its appointed senators) agreed that senators should be elected; however, it wanted a federal second chamber that would not just enhance regional representation but would also improve social representation. Thus it proposed a system of proportional representation based on multi-member (four would be the norm) constituencies, in the hope this would encourage parties to put up lists of candidates that would promote gender equality and represent 'Canada's social and cultural diversity.'[81] If the aboriginal peoples agreed, they should be given special representation. Senate elections would be held at different times from elections for the House of Commons and would be for fixed terms with a maximum length of six years. The committee rejected equality of the provinces as the principle of territorial representation in a reformed Senate. Instead, it offered optional formulas for an 'equitable' system giving smaller provinces disproportionate weight and enabling the West to hold central Canada (Ontario and Quebec) in check.

Committee consensus broke down on the question of an elected Senate's powers. The committee appeared more willing than the federal government had been to give the Senate significant legislative powers. But a close look at the fine print reveals that the position adopted by the Conservative and NDP members of the committee was really not very different from the federal proposal. While the report stated that 'the powers of a reformed Senate should be similar to those of the House of Commons on all bills except supply bills,'[82] it would require that the Senate vote on ordinary legislation within six months and on supply bills within thirty days. In the event of a deadlock – and this is the crucial point – the Conservatives and NDP would empower the House of Commons to override the Senate. This override might require an extraordinary majority in the House (some suggested 60 per cent), except for supply bills that would require a simple majority. The Liberals, in contrast, held out for a more powerful Senate which, except on supply and budget bills, would have an absolute veto. The committee agreed with the government proposal for double majorities on cultural matters and Senate ratification of appointments to federal agencies. A Senate proposal that contains only one of the Es (elected) in the triple E Senate concept surely has little hope of winning the support of the West or the East in Canada.

The Supreme Court, the other institution up for constitutional reform, was treated much the same as in the federal proposal. The Beaudoin-Dobbie Report went along with the proposal, essentially a carry-over from Meech, that Supreme Court justices be appointed by the federal government from provincial lists. It recommended a deadlock-breaking device that was missing from the proposal: in the event that the federal government was unwilling to appoint any of the provincial nominees, the chief justice could fill the vacancy with an interim replacement from the lower courts. The committee also adopted the part of the Meech proposal on the Supreme Court which is of great significance to Quebec – constitutionally entrenching the court's existing composition, with Quebec guaranteed three of the nine seats on its bench. The committee recognized, however, as had the federal government, that this part of the Supreme Court proposal would be subject to the unanimity rule and therefore should be detached from the main package of proposals. The Supreme Court proposals, such a bone of contention in the Meech round, were by now eclipsed by the Senate debate. The Canadian people still have only the dimmest sense of the importance of judicial power. As a result, the entrenchment of the Supreme Court in the Constitution could slip through on the coattails of more contentious items.

It is on the economic union proposals that the parliamentary committee departed most from the federal government's recommendations. In a nutshell, it stripped the economic union proposal down to essentials and balanced it with a social charter. Gone, without so much as a comment, are the proposal for a sweeping new federal power to promote the efficient functioning of the union and the Council of the Federation that was to manage the union. The proposal to expand section 121, the constitutional prohibition against internal trade barriers, survived, but with a lot of exemptions, including marketing boards and government monopolies. The committee, emulating the Free Trade Agreement with the United States, recommended a non-judicial body for settling disputes arising under the internal free-trade guarantee.

The committee's recommendation for a constitutional social covenant came directly out of Ontario's proposals and the Montreal conference. The social charter idea was a logical concomitant to a stronger economic union. Facilitating the free flow of commerce both within states and between states, however attractive to the business community, was sure to arouse concern on the left side of politics. Left-wing groups feared that a level economic playing field might force governments to push social programs and environmental regulations down to the level of the jurisdiction imposing the lightest burden on industry. To counter this tendency, the report recommended a social charter to establish decent social and environmental standards. A commitment to maintaining such standards across the country might also make a devolution of power to the provinces easier for Canadian nationalists to swallow.

The social covenant recommended by the Beaudoin-Dobbie Report would commit governments in Canada to provide the following: comprehensive and universal health care, adequate social services, high-quality education, protection of collective bargaining rights, and the integrity of the environment. The committee used the term social covenant rather than social charter because it recognized that unlike the rights in the Charter of Rights, which can be judicially enforced against government, a statement of what governments are positively obliged to do for citizens is not something that should be judicially enforced. It recommended that an intergovernmental agency be established to assess and report on the performance of governments in meeting their obligations under the social covenant. Only with this soft, political mode of enforcement would such a proposal have a chance of being acceptable to Quebec.

The committee, in its eagerness to strike a balance in constitutional symbolism, recommended that the same part of the Constitution in which the social covenant is to be lodged (section 36 of the Constitution Act, 1982) also contain a 'declaration' of economic values. This declaration would commit governments to cooperating to enhance the economic union (here is the ghost of the Council of the Federation) and to ensure mobility, full employment, and reasonable living standards. Again 'enforcement' would be through an intergovernmental monitoring commission. It is difficult to imagine such a clause giving comfort to anyone but its authors.

The parliamentary committee experienced its heaviest weather when it turned to the division of powers. Generally it called for less all-round decentralization than the federal government had proposed. In only one field – culture – was a majority of the committee willing to contemplate the hard form of asymmetry and recommend a power that, at least for a time, would be recognized only for Quebec. The Conservatives and NDP supported the idea of constitutionally affirming Quebec's exclusive jurisdiction in relation to 'cultural matters in Quebec.'[83] This jurisdiction would not really be exclusive: the federal government would continue to spend money on culture and to regulate broadcasting in Quebec, subject to agreements worked out with the province. The Liberals preferred to make cultural affairs a concurrent field of jurisdiction for all the provinces. Provincial power would be paramount in the field, but subject to the federal Parliament retaining full control over national cultural institutions.

On other matters, the committee's approach to accommodating Quebec was through a softer form of asymmetrical federalism to be implemented by what might be called 'make-a-deal federalism.' In the area of labour market training, for example, the committee recommended a constitutional amendment that would permit any province to affirm its exclusive jurisdiction in the field. A province wishing to take up this option would have to work out an agreement with the federal government on fiscal compensation. Again the exclusivity of provincial jurisdiction was illusory, since the federal Parliament would retain full power over labour market training relating to unemployment insurance or any other area of federal jurisdiction. Federal politicians were finding it difficult to relinquish Ottawa's grip on policy instruments in fields of so-called exclusive provincial jurisdiction.

Instead of ending federal spending in the areas of tourism, forestry, mining, recreation, housing, and urban affairs (all of which are primarily under provincial jurisdiction), the Conservatives and NDP recommended bilateral agreements defining federal and provincial roles. They liked this 'make-a-deal federalism' so much that they recommended it also be applied to energy, regional development, and family policy and that a device for protecting agreements from unilateral amendment be added to the Constitution. The Liberals, surprisingly, preferred giving Quebec a firmer constitutional base at least in the field of regional development (spending money on depressed areas of the province) by making it a concurrent field with provincial paramountcy. The committee would retain the proposal carried over from Meech to constitutionalize bilateral agreements on immigration.

The committee also went back to the Meech accord proposal for its recommendation on new federal spending programs in areas of exclusive jurisdiction. The federal government would not need provincial approval for these new federal invasions, but a province could opt out and receive fiscal compensation providing it introduced a program meeting the objectives of the new Canada-wide program. Such new programs would be constitutionally protected from unilateral change by the federal government. This latter provision would please those policy communities in English-speaking Canada who resent cutbacks in federal spending, but the whole approach was likely far too centralist for Quebec. Quebec would hardly be mollified by two morsels of power the committee tossed in: the inland fisheries and personal bankruptcy. In these fields it recommended that the provinces obtain a share of jurisdiction, but subject to federal paramountcy.

What a dog's breakfast! Certainly there was a lot of flexibility in this treatment of the division of powers – the committee also retained the proposal to permit delegation of powers between Parliament and the provincial legislatures – but also much confusion and uncertainty. While 'make-a-deal' federalism' maximizes flexibility, it minimizes constitutional security. It would be a miracle if Quebec would settle for such uncertain arrangements in areas where, for twenty-five years, it has sought a secure constitutional foundation for its jurisdiction.

Finally, on the constitutional amending formula, the Beaudoin-Dobbie Report was more willing than the federal government to contemplate an explicit Quebec veto. It put forward five options, each of which would give Quebec a veto over changes in the Senate or the Supreme Court. One option was an extension of the unanimity rule as contained in the Meech Lake Accord and proposed by the federal government. Other options would extend a veto power exclusively to Quebec. However well this bit of hard asymmetry might be received in Quebec, it was bound to be controversial in the Rest of Canada. There seemed no way it would be acceded to in advance of amendments on Senate reform. By the same token, while it seems to make sense to detach the amending formula (along with the Supreme Court's composition) from the large package of amendments that do not require unanimous provincial approval, approving that package without giving Quebec its constitutional veto would likely be impossible to sell in Quebec.

The Beaudoin-Dobbie Report, then, was another instalment in the constitutional soap opera that left Canadians still struck between a rock and a hard place. The quest for a new social contract had a long way to go. The Beaudoin-Edwards Committee was just the first stage of negotiations in the Canada round. All that could be said at this point is that the federal proposals had cleared the first hurdle in the constitutional steeplechase without completely falling apart. But higher hurdles lay ahead. Even if the government and the two major opposition parties in the federal Parliament accepted the unity committee's proposals, the two parties experiencing the greatest growth in their political support outside of Parliament, the Bloc Québécois and the Reform party, were free to pull the committee's report apart from opposite directions. Beyond the federal political parties, negotiations with representatives of the provinces, territories, and aboriginal peoples still had to take place. These negotiations were scheduled to begin in March 1992. It was most unlikely that the government of Quebec would be an active participant. Waiting for an offer from the Rest of Canada was the politically correct posture Bourrassa must assume. As the Rest of Canada's leaders tried to cobble together an accord, he could merely whisper his feelings in their ears.

11 The Canada Round II:
The Sovereign People Say No

On 26 October 1992 the Canadian people, for the first time in their history as a political community, acted as Canada's ultimate constitutional authority. In the referendum conducted on that day a majority of Canadians in a majority of provinces said 'no' to the Charlottetown Accord. Though there may have been some doubt as to what was required for a decisive 'yes' vote, there was no doubt whatsoever that this result was a decisive 'no.' The Charlottetown Accord was dead.

In rejecting the Charlottetown proposals, Canadians showed that, acting as a constitutionally sovereign people, they could achieve a negative result. The jury is still out on whether this negative consensus can become an enduring positive consensus to continue as a people sharing a common constitution. It would surely be a delicious irony – and so Canadian an outcome – if Canadians were at last to constitute themselves a sovereign people through an affirmation of the status quo.

It is too early to say whether the referendum has produced some finality – even a decade or two – to Canada's constitutional travails. What is clear is that the present generation of Canadians will not try again to reach an accord on a broad package of constitutional changes designed to prevent a unity crisis. If in the near future Canada plunges once again into the constitutional maelstrom, it will be because there is an actual, not an apprehended, crisis of national unity. Such was the effort and the agony of the 'Canada round' that most of Canada's politicians and most of its people have no stomach to return to the constitutional struggle unless some part of the country forces the issue.

The Canada round was the most exhausting of the five rounds of mega constitutional politics Canada has endured since the 1960s. Precisely because it came after four previous rounds, its negative result heightened Canadians' awareness of the inherently frustrating nature of constitutional politics. Never before had so many struggled so hard to produce, apparently, so little. It may yet turn out, however, that the very effort that went into this attempt at national reconciliation – the collective learning it engendered – will produce more positive results than most Canadians could appreciate at the time.

One feature of the Canada round that made it so trying on the country was the way it careened from stage to stage, from crisis to crisis, directed more by the panic of deadlines than by thoughtful statecraft. Looking back on this process, no one could say it was an exemplary way for a constitutional democracy to go about revising its highest law. The process, disjointed and panicky though it was, provided a far wider degree of public participation than any of the earlier efforts to arrive at a constitutional consensus. Nonetheless, the structural flaws in the Canada round's process go a long way to explaining its negative outcome.

Think of the process as being shaped like an hourglass. The top part of the glass was fairly wide, representing the public consultation stage of the process when most of the proposals contained in the Charlottetown Accord were discussed and debated. When these proposals were handed over to political leaders and government officials for negotiation and refinement, the glass narrowed. It came to its narrowest point in the summer of 1992 when the final terms of the Charlottetown Accord were hammered out in a process dominated by first ministers. From that narrow neck the process widened out again in the referendum campaign. This bottom part of the glass, though much shorter, was much wider than the upper half.

The short, wide bottom and the tiny neck were not the only unusual features of this hourglass. A much more serious flaw in the process was the structure of the upper part of the glass – the public consultation, negotiation, and refinement stages. The process represented by this part of the glass for most of its length was divided into nearly watertight compartments: Quebec and the rest of Canada. As we saw in chapter 10, immediately following the Meech Lake Accord there was little connection between the public discussions of constitutional options in the two parts of Canada. Not only were they different in time and in forum, but, most significantly, they addressed different questions. In Quebec, through the Bélanger-Campeau Commission and the Allaire Committee, a process that had run its course by the spring of 1991, discussion focused almost exclusively on the question of what Quebec needed to fulfil its constitutional aspirations. In the rest of Canada, through Spicer's Citizens' Forum and the various provincial, territorial, and parliamentary committees culminating in the Beaudoin-Dobbie Committee proposals at the end of February 1992, the critical question was how to reform the Constitution in a manner acceptable to all parts of the Canadian community.

As the process narrowed in the negotiating and refinement stage, the Quebec section of the glass was nearly empty. Only when it reached the narrowest point of the neck did Quebec, in the person of Premier Robert Bourassa, engage in the process. By then Bourassa confronted what was very nearly 'a done deal' – a set of proposals striking a delicate balance among constitutional interests in the rest of Canada. At this stage another deal was made, but only, as we shall see, by pulling a rabbit out of a hat and introducing a novel constitutional proposal for which the public, neither in Quebec nor in the rest of Canada, had been prepared. Is it any wonder that this accord of governments could not, in two months, be converted into an accord of peoples?

The Beaudoin-Dobbie Committee tabled its report in the federal Parliament at the end of February 1992. Six months later, on 28 August, the Charlottetown Accord was signed. The negotiations that produced the accord fell into three distinct stages. The participants in the first stage were delegations representing Ottawa, all the provinces except Quebec, the two northern territories, and four Aboriginal[1] organizations (the Assembly of First Nations representing status Indians, the Native Council of Canada representing non-status Indians, the Inuit Tapirisat of Canada, and the Métis National Council). These multilateral negotiations extended over three months from 12 March until 12 June, when they sputtered to a conclusion unable to produce a consensus on Senate reform.

Stage two was a reversion to the classic first ministers' conference, with two important modifications – Quebec did not attend, and Joe Clark, not Prime Minister Mulroney, represented the federal government. This second stage lasted just over a week, from 29 June to 7 July, and was devoted to breaking the impasse on the Senate. This it did – at least as between Ontario and Ottawa on the one hand and the provinces favouring a 'triple E' Senate on the other. The third stage, the only one in which Quebec participated, began with first ministers' meetings in late July and early August. These meetings paved the way for four days of intense negotiations in Ottawa from 18 to 21 August that produced an accord between the Quebec government and all the participants (the federal government, the other provinces, the territories, and the four Aboriginal organizations) in the earlier multilateral talks. The final meeting at Charlottetown on 28 August to finalize this accord was essentially a ceremonial event.

While the shift from the public discussion and parliamentary committee stage to multilateral negotiations inevitably meant a narrowing of the process, participation at this stage was considerably wider than in the four previous rounds. Inclusion of the Northwest Territories, Yukon, and the four native organizations meant that these were not simply federal-provincial meetings. Further, the development of proposals for ministerial consideration was parcelled out to four committees – on Aboriginal issues, division of powers, institutions, and miscellaneous matters.[2] The sixteen delegations were entitled to have two members on each committee, and many of these sitting members had backup support staff. With between one and two hundred persons involved, the process was considerably wider than a first ministers' meeting. Nonetheless, in terms of both openness and the representative character of participants, the process was much closer to the classic Canadian instrument of elite accommodation than to the constituent assembly model. Through the spring of 1992 all Canadians could glimpse of the process was an army of tight-lipped officials carrying heavy black bags as they moved their interminable meetings from city to city.

Aboriginal participation in the multilateral negotiations was in itself a measure of how far the Aboriginal peoples had come in gaining recognition as constituent components of the Canadian political community. That indeed was a major gain, but it was not without difficulties. Once the Aboriginal leaders sat down at the intergovernmental negotiating table they were forced to act like first ministers with mandates to speak for relatively centralized political systems. This milieu fosters a leadership style that is far less consultative than Aboriginal tradition. If the medium is the message, this mode of decision-making for Aboriginal peoples is highly assimilative.

This problem was particularly severe for Ovide Mercredi, the national chief of the Assembly of First Nations. Mercredi was the most effective Aboriginal leader in convincing non-Aboriginal Canadians of the justice and wisdom in recognizing the Aboriginal peoples' inherent right to self-government. But he was less success-ful in convincing his own people – particularly rival leaders within the AFN – of the value of his achievement. The AFN is the most confederal of the native organizations and its membership is more inclined to a consensual tradition of decision-making. A meeting of the AFN attended by 435 native leaders from across Canada held just a week before the referendum refused to endorse the Char-lottetown Accord,[3] and in the referendum itself polling stations on Indian reserves (where AFN status Indians reside) recorded a 60 per cent majority against the accord.[4]

There was another serious problem with the form of Aboriginal participation. The much postponed public meeting on Aboriginal issues, which was to have been part of the Beaudoin-Dobbie pro-cess, was finally held in Ottawa on the weekend following the launch of the ministerial meetings. The centre of attention at this highly publicized media event was a group attacking not the ex-clusion of Aboriginal peoples from their share of sovereignty but the exclusion of Aboriginal women from the constitutional process. Leaders of the Native Women's Association of Canada (NWAC) used the occasion to argue the case for the separate representation of native women at the constitutional table. Women were promi-nent in the delegations of the four national organizations which, according to what had hitherto been an unchallenged constitu-tional practice, were to represent Aboriginal peoples in the forth-coming talks. The president of the Inuit Tapirisat was a women and another native woman, Nellie Cournoyea, was the leader of the Northwest Territories' government. But NWAC insisted that the other Aboriginal organizations were not sufficiently sensitive to the possibility that a guarantee of Aboriginal self-government might endanger the equality rights of Aboriginal women.

Rebuffed by the politicians, NWAC took its case to court. Following an initial loss in the Trial Division of the Federal Court, it appealed to the Federal Court of Appeal. On 20 August, just as the first ministers were settling the final details of the Charlottetown Accord, the Federal Court of Appeal ruled in NWAC's favour, holding that its exclusion from the constitutional review process infringed the freedom of expression (but not the equality rights) of Aboriginal women under the Charter of Rights.[5] The only remedy the judges offered was a declaration of the Charter violation. However, the court victory added considerably to the legitimacy of NWAC's cause and cast doubts on the legitimacy of the constitutional process and its product.

Aboriginal representation was not the only problematic feature of the multilateral process. These intergovernmental meetings much more than those in any of the previous rounds were dominated by provincial governments – the governments of all the provinces except Quebec. In the run-up to the Victoria Charter, Prime Minister Trudeau's agenda dominated the entire process. In the second round in the late 1970s, federal and provincial perspectives were fairly evenly balanced as Trudeau and the provincial premiers arm-wrestled one another to a draw. In the patriation round, though the provincial premiers forced Trudeau to compromise, still it was his 'People's Package' that shaped the constitutional settlement. In the Meech round, the dominant forces in shaping the intergovernmental agenda and driving it forward were Quebec and the Mulroney government. But now, in the so-called Canada round, Quebec was not even at the table until the very end and the federal government was there without any great sense of commitment to the process or a clear agenda of its own.

Indeed, it was Ontario's premier Bob Rae, not Prime Minister Mulroney, who insisted that the Beaudoin-Dobbie recommendations be submitted to a process of intergovernmental negotiations. It was Rae who turned up at the first meeting with a well-defined program for the process. Instead of playing Ontario's traditional honest-broker role, Rae came with his own constitutional priorities – Aboriginal self-government and the social charter. That is not to say Ontario was the only province with a strong sense of purpose in these talks. The three prairie provinces, Alberta, Saskatchewan and Manitoba, as well as Newfoundland, all came with a strong commitment to a triple E Senate. The main dialectic in these meetings was between Ontario and provinces with a strong desire to curb central Canada's power in Ottawa.

As for the federal government, its role in the multilateral process was distinctly ambiguous. At the ministerial level the federal government was represented by the constitutional affairs minister, Joe Clark. In this respect the federal government was in the same position as a number of provinces whose delegations were headed by a minister other than the premier. But Clark did not have as straightforward a relationship with his first minister and cabinet colleagues as his provincial counterparts had with theirs. While Clark was working away at the intergovernmental negotiations, his prime minister and Quebec cabinet colleagues were hinting at a very different way of ending the constitutional impasse 'if the very, very challenging efforts of the minister responsible for constitutional affairs should prove to be unsuccessful' – a national referendum.[6]

Throughout the multilateral process, Clark's efforts were haunted by the possibility that Mulroney and the Quebec Tories really did not want him to succeed. Cynics could attribute this dilemma to Mulroney's unrealistic aspiration to play the role of constitutional messiah. A more strategic explanation would be Mulroney's and his Quebec colleagues' apprehension that if Clark succeeded it would be by agreeing to proposals – particularly a triple E Senate – which would be utterly unsaleable in Quebec. Moreover, both Ottawa and Quebec preferred to let Ontario do the 'dirty work' of seeing how far the other provinces could be pushed to accommodate Quebec.

A firm commitment to the process was not the only thing the federal government lacked in these negotiations. It also lacked any agenda of its own. The constitutional blueprint it had released in September 1991, *Shaping Canada's Future Together*, contained proposals for a new federal power and institution to enhance the economic union. Six months later all this was gone. The Beaudoin-

Dobbie parliamentary committee had, as we have seen, stripped all the meat off this part of the federal proposals.[7] The federal government – at least as represented by Clark – showed no inclination to put any of these proposals back on the table. Clark's objective now was primarily to achieve conciliation among contending provincial and Aboriginal positions.

The most problematic feature of the ministerial meetings was the absence of Quebec. Even though Quebec was not physically at the table, the Quebec question – what would be required to win the support of its government and a majority of its people – was very much on the minds of most delegations.[8] While the talks were going on, the Bourassa government was conducting its own round of bilateral talks with the federal government and several provinces, notably Alberta, New Brunswick, Ontario, and Prince Edward Island. These bilateral dealings on the side did not go down well with the other parties to the multilateral process.

By remaining on the sideline of that process rather than being a party to it, Bourassa could maintain the posture of waiting to inspect the 'best offer' from the rest of Canada before deciding whether to proceed with a referendum on sovereignty. That knife-at-the-throat strategy was just fine so long as Quebec sovereignty – or something very close to it – was a real option for Bourassa. But by the spring of 1992, a year after Bélanger-Campeau and Allaire, there were signs that, for the Bourassa government, the heady days of moving serenely towards sovereignty were over. Bourassa was back in the renewed federalism camp. In this context, staying outside the multilateral process entailed a serious risk. An accord produced by the process would likely be presented to him as a *fait accompli* – an accord that could be changed only minimally and yet one that only minimally reflected Quebec's constitutional agenda. Such an accord would be a shaky platform on which to mount a Quebec referendum campaign for renewed federalism.

The agenda for the multilateral process was shaped by the Beaudoin-Dobbie proposals. Parties to the talks were free to introduce proposals that Beaudoin-Dobbie had not considered. Some provinces, for instance, brought forward a demand for a share of jurisdiction over the export of natural resources. But such proposals lacked the legitimacy of those discussed in the public conferences held earlier in the year and were discarded.

By early June the ministerial meetings had reached agreement on seven issues: the division of powers, the social and economic union, Aboriginal self-government, a Canada clause, recognition of Quebec's distinct society, first ministers' meetings, and the Supreme Court of Canada. The agreements reached on these issues formed the bulk of what, ten weeks later, would emerge as the Charlottetown Accord.

That the process was dominated by provincial governments other than Quebec's can be seen most clearly in what was agreed to on the division of powers. Not even the smidgen of asymmetrical federalism in the Beaudoin-Dobbie Report was retained. Any accretions to or affirmations or protection of provincial jurisdiction that could be secured, including the field of culture, were to be obtained for all the provinces, not just Quebec. Even though Quebec did not participate in the negotiations, still it was generally recognized that any agreement with a ghost of a chance of ultimately winning Quebec's support would have to contain the basic elements of the Meech Lake Accord. Thus there was ready agreement on the two division-of-powers items from Meech – a provision permitting provinces to opt out of new federal spending programs in areas of provincial jurisdiction without fiscal penalty, and a commitment of the federal government to negotiate bilateral immigration agreements with the provinces. With this latter provision, however, the agreed text now stipulated that a province negotiating an agreement 'should be accorded equality of treatment in relation to any other province which has already concluded an agreement, taking into account the different needs and circumstances of the provinces.'[9] In other words, special treatment for Quebec was to be kept to an absolute minimum.

The other division-of-powers provisions followed the Beaudoin-Dobbie Report quite closely. The 'big ticket' items were again labour-market training and culture. And again, the basic approach was 'make-a-deal' federalism: provincial jurisdiction in these fields would be constitutionally affirmed and federal withdrawal from them would be facilitated, wherever requested, by agreements providing fiscal compensation. The equality-of-treatment principle would apply to these agreements too. A limited federal role would be preserved in each area: responsibility for unemployment insurance in the case of labour-market training and development, and 'national cultural institutions' in the case of culture.[10] Six other fields of provincial jurisdiction in which the federal government had become active, what insiders referred to as the 'six sisters' – forestry, mining, tourism, housing, recreation, and municipal and urban affairs – were to be subject to the same régime of negotiated agreements facilitating federal withdrawal. Two fields of federal jurisdiction which the Beaudoin-Dobbie Report had proposed be transferred to the provinces – inland fisheries and personal bankruptcy – were dropped from the discussions. For their part, the provinces persuaded the federal government to limit or abandon its 'imperial' powers: the 'declaratory' power under which the federal government could take control of provincial works would remain, but in the future its use would require provincial consent; and the federal power to reserve or disallow provincial laws[11] would be removed altogether from the Constitution. Finally and most important to the provinces were elaborate provisions to constitutionally secure federal-provincial agreements on a wide range of matters, including regional development and federal funding of provincial welfare programs.[12]

This intricate rejigging of the division of powers was not based on any profound rethinking of Canadian federal theory. Basically it represented what a group of provincial ministers and their officials could wrest from a relatively pliant federal government. The details of the proposals would be impenetrable to all but constitutional aficionados. At the symbolic level, the decisive level in a referendum campaign, this part of the negotiated package would not play well. Outside Quebec it could be attacked, unfairly, as a massive dismantling of federal power. In Quebec, even though a detailed analysis would indicate that through these proposals Quebec could recover much of the control over cultural and social policy it had lost to Ottawa's spending power, the proposals could not be portrayed as a great gain for the province. Because they depended so much on negotiated agreements, the proposals did not give Quebec the security it has sought in controlling policy under its existing constitutional powers, nor did they provide for any of the transfers of federal jurisdiction to Quebec advocated by Bourassa's own party through its adoption of the Allaire Report.[13]

And yet, on this critical matter of the division of powers, the issue of greatest concern to Quebecers, these were the proposals Bourassa would be stuck with if he was to take a federalist option to a Quebec referendum.

Another indication of the provinces' domination of the multilateral process was the federal government's further retreat on its own constitutional priority – the proposals to strengthen the economic union. The Beaudoin-Dobbie Report had discarded proposals for a new federal power to promote the efficient functioning of the economic union and a Council of the Federation to manage the union. Now even the idea of strengthening section 121, the free-trade guarantee already in the Constitution, was in limbo. In the multilateral meetings the provincial premiers pressed for so many exemptions that they might have ended up with a clause that weakened rather than strengthened the existing constitutional protection of internal free trade. And so the talks concluded on 11 June with no consensus on revising section 121.

Premier Rae's social charter, in contrast, came through with flying colours. The meetings endorsed a constitutional declaration of social and economic policy objectives very much like that proposed by the Beaudoin-Dobbie Report.[14] The design of a mechanism to monitor the covenant would be left to a future first ministers' conference. The provinces were also able to extract further concessions from the federal government by way of expanding the commitment to economic equalization under section 36. Equalization would now extend to the territories and entail a commitment to establish 'a reasonably comparable economic infrastructure' in each province and territory, and the federal government would be committed to consult with the provinces before introducing legislation relating to equalization payments.[15] These provisions represented at least significant symbolic gains for the economically weaker provinces and the northern territories.

The Aboriginal peoples were also able to consolidate some of their gains in the multilateral negotiations. Most importantly, they secured provincial support for constitutional recognition of the Aboriginal peoples' 'inherent right of self-government within Canada' and recognition that Aboriginal governments would constitute one of three orders of government in Canada. In effect, if these proposals were implemented, Canada would become a federation with governmental power divided three ways among a central government and the provincial and Aboriginal governments – each sovereign within its constitutional sphere of jurisdiction. But the provincial governments were uneasy about this Aboriginal self-government right becoming legally enforceable before its specific scope was negotiated, so a clause was inserted delaying justiciability of the right for three years.[16]

Detailed rules governing the process of negotiating Aboriginal self-government agreements made it clear that the negotiations 'should take into account the different circumstances of the various aboriginal peoples.'[17] Self-government negotiations would be triggered by the Aboriginal peoples, and the federal and provincial governments would be constitutionally committed to participate 'in good faith' in these negotiations. The distinct interests of the Aboriginal organizations participating in the talks were evident in a number of provisions. For treaty Indians there was a commitment from the federal government to abandon its narrow, one-sided interpretation of treaty obligations and to establish a process for implementing treaties in a 'broad and liberal manner' according to their original 'spirit and intent.'[18] For the Métis people there was a clarification of their inclusion in the ambit of the federal Parliament's responsibility for Aboriginal people under section 91(24) and a clause committing Ontario, the four western provinces, and the federal government to negotiate a broad accord with 'the Métis Nation.'[19] Another clause made it clear that all residents of an area could participate in the institutions of Aboriginal self-government, regardless of their ethnicity. This provision had special relevance for Inuit and other native peoples negotiating self-government arrangements where the resulting institutions would be public institutions of government.

Two thorny aspects of First Peoples' issues were not entirely resolved. One was the difficult ideological question of how the Charter of Rights should apply to the Aboriginal order of government. The other was the practical question of the fiscal basis of Aboriginal governments. The treatment of the first issue shows the deep ambivalence in the dominant culture's readiness to respect the Aboriginal peoples' capacity for genuine self-government. Yes, the Charter of Rights would apply to Aboriginal governments, and, yes, the Aboriginal governments would have access to section 33, the Charter's notwithstanding clause, but on 'conditions to be determined.'[20] One reason for the uncertainty here was that section 33 permits elected legislatures to override the Charter, but Aboriginal governments might follow forms of democracy more direct or consensual than legislatures.[21] To facilitate a solution, the English version of Charter rights governing elections and legislatures would have to be brought into line with the French version because the latter makes it clearer that these clauses apply only to federal and provincial legislatures. Section 25 of the Charter, which is already muddy enough, was to be further muddied. This section – which has been in the Charter since the beginning – *already* provides that 'any aboriginal, treaty or other rights and freedoms that pertain to the aboriginal peoples' are not to be abrogated or derogated from by 'certain rights and freedoms' in the Charter. To this non-derogation clause, a phrase was now to be added stating that it would apply 'in particular' to Aboriginal rights 'relating to the exercise of their languages, cultures or traditions.' How that might affect the Aboriginal right to self-government 'was still being discussed.'

And, if this was not confusing enough, the issue of protecting women's rights in Aboriginal communities continued to haunt the proceedings. Again, an earlier constitutional amendment in 1983 stipulated that Aboriginal rights recognized in the Constitution 'are guaranteed equally to male and female persons.'[22] But the Native Women's Association, though only on the outer edge of the meetings, continued to contend that the rights of Aboriginal women needed to be secured against the possibility of Aboriginal governments dominated by male chiefs. One of the Aboriginal self-government sections was headed 'Gender Equality,' but the text simply said 'To be determined.'[23]

Besides the nineteen clauses on Aboriginal self-government, other parts of the agreement were designed to give Aboriginal peoples a full role in the institutions of the federation. A non-derogation clause would be added to the Constitution to ensure that division-of-powers amendments did not affect the rights of Aboriginal peoples. In the federal Parliament, Aboriginal representation was to be guaranteed in the Senate (the details to be worked out later) and the possibility of Aboriginal representation in the House of Commons was also to be considered. Aboriginal interests were to be better secured in relation to the Supreme Court, whose decisions can have a decisive bearing on the content of Aboriginal rights. The federal government made a commitment to examine the possibility of enabling an Aboriginal Council of Elders to make submissions to the Supreme Court when it is considering Aboriginal issues. Provincial and territorial governments committed themselves to establish a process for consulting with Aboriginal peoples in preparing lists of candidates to fill vacancies on the court. Finally, 'Aboriginal consent' would be required for constitutional amendments that 'directly affect the Aboriginal peoples.' This, of course, was a crucial corollary of recognizing that Aboriginal peoples had a share of sovereign power in the Canadian state.[24]

On the symbolic side of the constitutional settlement the constitutional lawyers took over from the poets. Gone was the Beaudoin-Dobbie Report's constitutional preamble with its paean to 'the people of Canada drawn from the four winds.' In its place was an interpretation clause that 'would guide the courts in their future interpretation of the Constitution.' This Canada clause listed 'fundamental Canadian values.' At this point seven items made the list:

· parliamentary democracy and Canadian federalism
· the Aboriginal peoples and related rights
· Quebec's distinct society
· linguistic duality
· racial and ethnic equality
· equality of women and men
· the equality of provinces, while recognizing their diverse characteristics

This list is a wonderful testament to Canada's essential ambivalence on just about everything – it is indeed an essay in ambivalence. But no one in their right mind could seriously believe that the list would provide useful guidance to the judiciary in interpreting the Constitution. Its real point was to attempt symbolic gratification of the groups who contested the nature of Canada as a political community.

This exercise in defining the essence of a deeply diverse society was rapidly proving to be a 'mug's game.' Already, the Canadian Ethnocultural Council representing thirty-seven ethnic groups was complaining about its being left off the list.[25] Later on, multiculturalism would be incorporated. But then people with disabilities would protest the exclusion of their right to equality. If the disabled had been included, homosexuals, seniors, juniors, and Lord knows who else would complain about their exclusion. Could there be any better way of stirring up suspicion and resentment than handing out dollops of ill-defined constitutional status to certain segments of the population at the beginning of a revised constitution?

The Canada clause was not the only place where Quebec's cultural distinctiveness would be recognized. The talks adopted the Beaudoin-Dobbie proposal for a special non-derogation section of the Charter 'to assure that it is interpreted in a manner consistent with the preservation and promotion of Quebec as a distinct society.'[26] And, to assuage the fears of the linguistic minorities, the same clause instructed the judges to interpret the Charter in a manner consistent with 'the vitality and development of the language and culture of French-speaking and English-speaking minority communities throughout Canada.' So, in this particular effort at symbolic engineering, the constitution drafters had almost crawled back to Meech Lake. The difference now was that other issues were displacing the distinct society as the focus of constitutional acrimony.

As might be expected in a forum dominated by provincial governments, the participants had no difficulty agreeing to perpetuate their process. The first ministers' conference, that quintessential instrument of executive federalism, would be entrenched in the Constitution. The prime minister would be required to convene at least one a year. Unlike the Meech accord, which would have required that an FMC on the Constitution be held every year, the agenda of these annual FMCs was left open. Also, the territorial governments would be full participants, and representatives of the Aboriginal peoples would be invited to participate in items directly relevant to them. This restriction on Aboriginal participation shows the limit to which the federal and provincial governments were prepared to treat Aboriginal peoples as full partners in Confederation.

The seventh item on which the multilateral talks reached agreement was the Supreme Court. The federal government would name judges from lists submitted by provincial and territorial governments. Some method of making interim appointments would be worked out for situations in which lists were not submitted on a timely basis. Quebec's three places on a nine-judge court would be constitutionally entrenched. Agreement on this last point meant that four-fifths of the Meech Lake Accord was in the emerging package. But the fifth point, a Quebec veto over constitutional amendments affecting national institutions, remained unresolved because it was tied to Senate reform. And on crucial aspects of the Senate issue, the ministerial meetings could not reach agreement.

At this stage in Canada's constitutional politics Senate reform had become an issue of deep symbolic significance. For political elites, particularly in western Canada and to a lesser extent in the Atlantic provinces, Senate reform stood for a restructuring of the federation to overcome the perceived domination of national affairs by central Canada. That objective required a federal upper house which could serve as an effective political counterweight to a lower house based on representation by population. Not only must such a Senate be elected (an imperative of a democratic age), but the provinces must be represented in it on the basis of equality and their representatives must have real power. This political project would not be an easy one to sell to either the politicians or the people of Ontario and Quebec. Ontarians would have to accept that their province with ten million people would have the same power in the Senate as Prince Edward Island with 130,000. For Quebecers, the triple E Senate proposal threatened more than their power – for many, it threatened their very identity. Treating Quebec as simply a province like all the others appeared to deny Quebec's special place in Confederation as the homeland of a founding people.

In the multilateral negotiations, five provinces – Alberta, Manitoba, Newfoundland, Nova Scotia, and Saskatchewan – stuck firmly to the full triple E proposal. Their Senate had to be elected, its members equally distributed among the provinces, and it had to be fully effective – that is, with full power to block the House of

Commons.[27] The federal government could not endorse such a plan – less because of any deep-seated notion of how such a Senate might transform parliamentary government than from a strong sense of how objectionable such a proposal would be to Quebec. However, it was Premier Rae of Ontario who assumed the main burden of resisting the triple E plan.

Progress was made in reaching a consensus on some aspects of Senate reform. It was agreed that senators should be elected through a system of proportional representation that would better 'reflect the diversity of Canada's population, notably taking account of gender equality.'[28] At this stage, the thinking was that Senate elections would be held on their own every five years and be quite independent of House of Commons elections. There was also agreement on powers that the Senate would not have: it would not be a confidence chamber with the power to bring down a government, and on revenue and expenditure bills it would have only a thirty-day suspensive veto. But the definition of revenue and expenditure bills was narrowly drawn to exclude 'fundamental policy changes' to the tax system such as the Goods and Services Tax and the National Energy Program. There was even some agreement – at the margins – on the Senate's positive powers. As a gesture towards recognition of the country's bicultural character, there was acceptance of the Beaudoin-Dobbie idea of a double majority (a majority of francophone senators voting and a majority of senators voting) for federal legislation 'that materially affects French language and culture.'[29] Also, the Senate would play a role in ratifying certain federal appointments – specifically, the governor of the Bank of Canada and others, such as heads of cultural institutions and regulatory agencies, to be set out in federal legislation. But after three months of negotiations, agreement had still not been reached on two crucial issues of Senate reform – the Senate's powers with regard to ordinary legislation and the allocation of seats among the provinces. It was on these two issues that this first phase of the multilateral negotiations ended in deadlock on 12 June.

Failure to agree on the Senate meant that one element of the amending formula was also left unresolved. The meetings did agree to accept the Meech Lake proposal – so important to Quebec – that provinces opting out of *any* amendments (not just those relating to culture and education) made through the seven-province/half-the-population (7/50) formula would receive reasonable fiscal compensation. Also, the participation of the northern territories in the talks was evident in an agreement to return to the pre-1982 position and make the creation of new provinces possible simply through an Act of Parliament. At this stage there was agreement that the admission of new provinces would trigger a change in the 7/50 rule to one requiring three-quarters of the provinces representing 50 per cent of the population. But on the question of extending the rule of unanimity to amendments affecting the Senate and other national institutions, the triple E Senate supporters insisted, as a quid pro quo, on acceptance of their Senate plan.

For two weeks in June there was a hiatus in the constitutional negotiations. The Mulroney government, always ambivalent about the multilateral process, now showed signs of riding the other horse in its constitutional stable.[30] On 3 June Bill C-81, legislation enabling the federal government to hold a referendum, was passed by the House of Commons and, with Senate approval, became law on 23 June. Just eight months earlier the Conservatives' Quebec caucus had rejected a Canada-wide constitutional referendum as somehow interfering with Quebec's right to hold a referendum. Now there was speculation that Mulroney might be thinking of patching together a deal with Bourassa and taking it over the heads of the other premiers directly to the people. Such Gaullists delusions, if they existed, were completely out of touch with reality. Mulroney was no de Gaulle and there was virtually no chance of his being able to win support for an Ottawa–Quebec City constitutional deal from the other provinces – either their legislatures or their electorates – whose approval is legally required for ratifying constitutional amendments in Canada.

The real problem with the Mulroney government's late conversion to a constitutional referendum was that the development of constitutional proposals was completely detached from the referendum process. The politicians, officials, and experts closeted together negotiating the constitution through the spring and early summer of 1992 were not consciously working towards a referendum. The product of their labours – an agreement containing some sixty clauses sprinkled with asterisks marking unfinished business to be settled by more negotiations in the future – was not a document designed for popular ratification by the people. An agreement fashioned through this process was treated by its drafters as a contract between heads of governments and organizations that expected to have the final say on the matter. The penalty of pursuing a two-track approach to constitutional revision – elite negotiations and popular ratification – was that they came together too late to provide the foundation for a real social contract.

At the end of June, Prime Minister Mulroney himself made a brief appearance on the constitutional stage. He would try to revive intergovernmental negotiations with the threat that if they failed to reach an agreement his government would put its own proposals before a special session of Parliament in mid July. At the beginning of this second stage of the multilateral process, the Aboriginal organizations and territorial governments were left out. Only the provincial premiers were invited to have lunch with the prime minister at 24 Sussex Drive on Monday, 29 June. All came except Bourassa. The Quebec premier, assuming the politically correct Quebec posture, was still playing the nation-to-nation game waiting for the 'best offer' from the rest of Canada.

Mulroney's luncheon meeting seemed to work. The premiers agreed to make another attempt to break their deadlock on the Senate. They would do this not with Mulroney but with his constitutional minister, Joe Clark. The prime minister stayed around just long enough to greet Queen Elizabeth II on 1 July and celebrate the country's 125th birthday before flying off to Munich for a G7 Economic Summit from 6 to 8 July, and on to Helsinki for the Heads of Government Summit of the Conference on Security and Co-operation (CSCE) from 8 to 10 July. His quick exit left the country wondering how committed he was to the success of Clark's and the premiers' efforts.

It did not take long for Clark and the premiers to reach agreement on the Senate. At a meeting in Toronto on Friday, 3 July, Rae explored the conditions under which Ontario might be able to accept provincial equality in the Senate. This session prepared the ground for a meeting the following Monday in Ottawa. Instead of using the conference centre in downtown Ottawa with all its painful memories from the Meech Lake round, the first ministers and the territorial and Aboriginal leaders spirited themselves away in the Pearson Building, which houses the Department of External Affairs. The meeting extended into 7 July. Just as Mulroney was winding up the second day of his G7 meeting in Munich, he and the rest of Canada learned that Joe Clark and the premiers had reached an accord.

The key to the Pearson Accord, as it came to be known, was acceptance by Ontario and by Joe Clark of the principle of provincial equality in the Senate. This was a fateful and risky development given that all along there had been indications that this principle would be difficult, if not impossible, for Quebec to accept. Still, it was probably the only basis on which the governments of the other provinces could have reached an agreement.

The agreement proposed to reduce the Senate in size and to allocate seats on the basis of provincial equality rather than the Fathers' of Confederation precept of sectional equality. A Senate of 102 members (Ontario and Quebec each having twenty-four, blocks of twenty-four assigned to the four western provinces and to the three Maritime provinces, plus six for Newfoundland and one each for the northern territories) would give way to a Senate of eighty-four members with eight from each province and two each for the territories. It might become slightly larger if and when Aboriginal senators were added. The larger provinces were to be given some compensation by increasing the size of the House of Commons from 295 to 312 'to better reflect the principle of representation by population.'[31] Ontario would get ten of these new seats, British Columbia and Quebec three each, and Alberta one.

The main bargain Rae struck with the triple E Senate advocates was on the legislative powers of this new Senate. To obtain agreement on the provincial equality precept, the premiers flying the triple E flag had to accept a small e for effectiveness. The elected and provincially equal Senate would give up the full legislative power possessed (but seldom used) by the existing appointed Senate. On only one category of legislation would a simple majority of senators be able to defeat a bill. That would be bills involving

'fundamental tax policy changes directly related to natural resources.'[32] Insistence on a senatorial veto over these laws reflected
the deep legacy of western resentment over the Trudeau government's National Energy Policy. To defeat any other ordinary legislation, 70 per cent of the senators present would have to vote
against the bill. If between 60 and 70 per cent were opposed, there
would first be an effort to reconcile differences with the House of
Commons and, if that failed, then the two houses in a joint session
would settle the matter by simple majority vote.

The Pearson Accord contained three other curious changes in
the Senate proposal from the 12 June rolling draft. Senators now
were to be elected by 'a method of single transferable vote.'[33] It is
doubtful that many of the politicians who signed the accord knew
much about this system other than that it was some form of proportional representation which they believed could be made to
'reflect diversity' and take account of 'gender equality.' Certainly
most of the Canadian people did not have a clue as to how the
single transferable vote system works.[34] The other changes were to
have Senate elections take place at the same time as House of
Commons elections and to ban senators from serving in the cabinet. These changes are somewhat contradictory. Electing senators
in a general election would tie in Senate campaigns to the contest
among political parties for seats in the House of Commons. This
would tend to undermine the objective of having senators give
priority to regional interests over loyalty to the platform of any
national political party. At the same time, barring senators from
the cabinet would prevent any of the senators, no matter how
prominent they might be in a national party, from serving in the
cabinet, the crucible of national policy-making. Further, it would
create an elected second chamber, quite unlike Australia's triple
E Senate, in which the government had no ministers to explain or
defend its policies. The new Senate was to be more of a congres-
sional than a parliamentary body – an instrument through which
'outer Canada' (as well as ethnic minorities and women) could
check and balance a government dominated by the central Canadian majority. Perhaps the kindest thing one can say about this
Senate plan is that it does not appear to have been carefully
thought through.

Agreement on the Senate made it possible to resolve the amending formula issue. With reform of the Senate (they hoped) in place, this generation of Senate reformers was happy to make any future modifications of their handiwork nearly impossible by entrenching the rule of unanimity for constitutional amendments related to the Senate.

The Pearson Accord made only a few other changes in the rolling draft of proposals agreed to at the end of the first stage of the multilateral process on 12 June. The delay in the justiciability of the Aboriginal right to self-government was extended from three to five years – a change that somewhat belied the prime minister's undertaking to Aboriginal leaders that their absence from the negotiating table (in the meetings immediately preceding the Pearson Building conference) would not adversely affect agreements reached on Aboriginal issues. The addition of 'respect for individual and collective human rights' to the list of characteristics to be included in the Canada clause further displayed the hopelessness of overcoming the angst aroused by this project of symbolic gratification. Even more dissatisfying was the one other significant change in the rolling draft: the reappearance of a new section 121 'that prevents the erection of interprovincial trade barriers.'[35] Mulroney had made it clear that this was the one change in the proposals which his government must have. The guarantee of free trade across the federation was to be included, but hedged in by thirteen qualifications protecting virtually every conceivable form of government intervention in the economy. The provincial premiers had accepted the federal government's priority proposal by making a mockery of it.

On 8 July, when Canadians watched Prime Minister Mulroney at Munich respond on their television screens to Joe Clark's success in reaching agreement on the Pearson Accord, instead of the prancing prince of Meech Lake celebrating his saving of Confederation they saw a prime minister who 'looked surprised and disconcerted.'[36] Whether he should have looked surprised – whether he had been kept fully informed of the Pearson Building negotiations by Paul Tellier, his former *chef de cabinet* and now Clark's senior adviser – is a question for future historians to answer. But we do know that Mulroney had every reason to be disconcerted. Clark's success put him on the horns of a dilemma. If he repudiated the agreement Clark had reached with the premiers, he would jeopardize any chance of obtaining support for constitutional proposals from the rest of Canada. But a Senate based on equality of provincial representation would be a tough sell – some would say an impossible sell – not just with the Quebec government but with his Quebec cabinet colleagues and caucus.

Mulroney had little choice but to soldier on and do what he could with the constitutional file Clark handed him. There would be no special session of Parliament to consider an Ottawa/Quebec constitutional option. Instead, the federal government would work quietly behind the scenes to see what could be done to break Bourassa's boycott of the multilateral process. This required walking a tightrope at the public level. Any sign that the federal government was backing away from the Pearson Accord – above all, its provision for an equal Senate – would bring on a sharp attack from the other premiers. And Bourassa would not return to the negotiating table if Mulroney declared that the Pearson Accord was a 'done deal' that could not be reopened.

Bourassa himself had run out of options. In a few weeks his party would convene to decide on the constitutional question to be put to the people of Quebec in the referendum now scheduled for 26 October. By this time he knew there was no point in supporting constitutional proposals along the lines of the Allaire Report unless he was prepared to see them repudiated by the rest of Canada and to move forward to full Quebec sovereignty. Now that his flirtation with sovereignty was over, he really had only one option left. The only 'renewal of federalism' proposals he could put to Quebecers with any credibility that they might be adopted in the rest of Canada would have to be based on the Pearson Accord. All he could do was rejoin the multilateral process and see what could be done with the help of the federal government to make the accord more palatable to Quebecers.

On 4 August, Bourassa agreed to have lunch with the other premiers and Mulroney at the prime minister's Harrington Lake summer home. Although he still 'rejected outright' the proposal for an equal Senate, Bourassa agreed to another meeting with the first ministers at Harrington Lake on Monday, 10 August.[37] At this meeting agreement was reached – subject to the approval of the federal cabinet – on holding a full-scale constitutional conference of first ministers and Aboriginal and territorial leaders. Two days later, cabinet approval was obtained and the stage was set for the final step in the multilateral negotiations – the step that would turn the Pearson Accord into the Charlottetown Accord.

Although the final signing of the Charlottetown Accord would take place on 28 August in the city that gave it its name, the crucial deals that brought it to fruition were made in four days of negotiations beginning on Tuesday 18 August in the Pearson Building in Ottawa. The most difficult issue to resolve was clearly the Senate. On Tuesday night the press scrum scurrying about the Pearson Building could smell a deal brewing in the closed negotiating chamber. Bourassa might agree to the unthinkable – an equal Senate – if Quebec was guaranteed 25 per cent of the seats in a joint Parliament (the House plus the Senate). On Wednesday the details of a tentative agreement were released. The negotiators had pulled a rabbit out of the hat. The rabbit may have been a deal-maker, but – and this its creators could not appreciate – it would turn out to be a referendum-breaker.

This rabbit, the deadlock-breaking deal on the Senate, deserves a closer look. It would provide for an equal but a smaller Senate – six senators for each province and one for each territory. Reducing the Senate in size from the existing 104 (and eighty-four in the Pearson Accord) to sixty-two would be reciprocated by adding exactly the same number of seats – forty-two – to the House of Commons (as compared with an additional seventeen in Pearson). The additional forty-two seats were to be the initial stage in adjusting representation in the House 'to better reflect the principle of representation by population.'[38] Ontario and Quebec would each obtain eighteen of these new seats, while four would go to British Columbia and two to Alberta. There would be a further redistribution of seats in the House of Commons based on the 1996 census.[39] But Quebec was to be guaranteed for all time – and here was the rabbit's most contentious feature – no fewer than 25 per cent of the seats in the House of Commons (not as had been rumoured the House plus the Senate).

The political rationale for keeping the total number of parliamentarians at 399 was to enable the accord's supporters to say they would not be increasing the number of federal politicians. The politician-drafters sensed that in an age when citizens have become cynical about representative democracy, this could be a good selling point for their plan. But to understand why Quebec (and Ontario) pressed for as large an increase in the Commons as was politically possible it is necessary to consider the reduction agreed to in the Senate's powers. As in earlier versions of the rolling draft, the Senate by simple majority could block bills changing tax policy on natural resources, and a majority of francophone senators could block legislation materially affecting French language and culture – small sops to the West and to Quebec. But gone now was the Senate's veto on ordinary legislation. Defeat or amendment of legislation by the Senate, no matter how large the majority, would automatically trigger a joint sitting of both chambers – without any reconciliation process. In these joint sittings the outcome would be determined by simple majority vote. Given the deadlock-breaking role of joint parliamentary sessions, the larger the House of Commons (and the larger Ontario's and Quebec's shares of seats in the Commons) the weaker the power of senators elected to represent the interests of 'outer Canada.' The third E (for effectiveness) in the triple E Senate project, already reduced to a small *e* in the Pearson Accord, had become even smaller in the Charlottetown Accord.

TABLE 1

Redistribution of Seats under the Charlottetown Accord

| | Population | % | House of Commons Seats | | | |
			Current	%	Proposed	%
Quebec	6,912,300	25.3	75	25.4	93	27.6
Ontario	10,062,000	36.8	99	33.6	117	34.7
Alberta	2,558,200	9.4	26	8.8	28	8.3
British Columbia	3,290,500	12.0	32	10.8	36	10.7
Saskatchewan	992,900	3.6	14	4.7	14	4.2
Manitoba	1,095,000	4.0	14	4.7	4	4.2
Nova Scotia	906,800	3.3	11	3.7	11	3.3
New Brunswick	727,700	2.7	10	3.4	10	3.0
PEI	130,100	0.5	4	1.4	4	1.2
Newfoundland	575,100	2.1	7	2.4	7	2.1
Yukon	27,600	0.1	1	0.3	1	0.3
NWT	55,900	0.2	2	0.7	2	0.6
Total	27,334,100	100	295	100	337	100

It is not easy to give a rational explanation for the distribution of the new House of Commons seats. As table 1 shows, the additional seats would mean that only Ontario and Quebec would increase their proportions of House of Commons representation. Alberta and British Columbia, already underrepresented, would be even worse off in the larger house – despite their additional seats. These two provinces would end up with a worse ratio of members per capita than Ontario. Quebec's 25 per cent guarantee – which Bourassa had to have – could have been met without making such disproportionately large increases in Ontario's and Quebec's representation in the House. The Quebec guarantee would be difficult enough to sell in the West without asking Alberta and British Columbia to pay an unnecessary extra penalty. The first ministers might have benefited by spending a little more time with their pocket calculators.

Bourassa obtained one other significant concession on the Senate. Senators could be elected either directly by the population or indirectly by members of the provincial or territorial assemblies. While the indirect method would be open to all provinces, Bourassa left no doubt that it would be Quebec's choice so that its senators could be viewed as delegates from Quebec's National Assembly. Federal legislation would govern the direct method of electing senators. But no longer would there be any constitutional commitment to proportional representation. Instead, provinces and territories could modify the electoral system 'to provide for gender equality' – a provision more apt to puzzle and alienate the mainstream than to win the support of feminists.

Besides the Senate, the other part of the rolling draft on which Bourassa sought and won significant changes was the First Peoples section. While Quebec has gone further than any other province in actually facilitating Aboriginal self-government (particularly through the two major land-claims settlements in northern Quebec), Quebecers have the most difficulty, ideologically, in accepting Aboriginal peoples as founding peoples of Canada on a par with *les Canadiens,* or in according Aboriginal governments a constitutional status equal to that of a province – especially the Province of Quebec. Bourassa was sensitive to this concern and wanted to put some clear parameters around the Aboriginal peoples' 'inherent right to self-government.' On this point he was supported by other premiers, especially Newfoundland's Clyde Wells, who were also concerned about the scope of what seemed an unlimited jurisdiction.

Given the strength of the commitment to the Aboriginal self-government right that had built up through the earlier months of negotiations, the effort to hem in the right could not be pressed very far. The first change agreed to was a 'contextual statement' setting out the purposes of the jurisdiction to be exercised by 'duly constituted legislative bodies of Aboriginal peoples.'[40] Their purpose was twofold: to 'safeguard and develop their languages, cultures, economies, identities, institutions and traditions' and to 'develop, maintain and strengthen their relationship with their lands, waters and environment.' This contextual statement was to serve as a guide to the courts when the self-government right, after five years, became justiciable. Even then the courts were directed to do what they could to promote a negotiated settlement before adjudicating the issue. Two negative restrictions were attached to the self-government right: it was not, in itself, to create any new land rights – a crucial matter for Quebec's interest in developing northern hydroelectric projects – and Aboriginal laws would be invalid if they conflicted with federal or provincial laws 'essential to the preservation of peace, order and good government in Canada.'[41] This latter restriction may have been a good public relations move in non-Aboriginal Canada, but for Aboriginal peoples it placed a grey and murky cloud over their 'inherent right.'

This third stage in the multilateral process produced only a few other modifications in the rolling draft. The negotiators had another fling at the tired old Canada clause. Bourassa was able to secure, as he said he must, the exact language of Meech Lake affirming 'the role of the legislature and Government of Quebec to preserve and promote the distinct society of Quebec.'[42] And the distinct society was now defined as including a 'French-speaking majority, a unique culture and a civil law tradition.' In return, he had to accept the countervailing claim of linguistic minorities. 'Canadians and their governments' would be 'committed to the vitality and development of official language minorities throughout Canada.'[43] Bourassa's patience was so taxed in conceding this much that he would not go on and agree to insert the same language committing governments as well as citizens in the remaining subsections of the Canada clause. This would enable a legion of nit-picking constitutional lawyers in the referendum campaign to howl that the drafters had established a 'hierarchy of rights' in the Canada clause.

The division of powers, always the centre of attention for Quebecers engaged in the renewal of federalism, basically stood as in previous drafts. A commitment was added to develop a 'framework' to guide the use of federal spending in areas of exclusive provincial responsibility. Among other things, this framework would require Ottawa to 'respect provincial priorities.'[44] The only other addition was a clause committing federal and provincial governments to coordinate their activities in regulating telecommunications. The emphasis in this renewal of federalism remained squarely on negotiating deals to remove or restrain federal encroachments on provincial jurisdiction rather than on transferring jurisdiction to the provinces. From the perspective of the Allaire Report, the accord would appear very barren indeed.

The accord would also appear barren from the point of view of Canadians seeking a strengthening of the economic union. Mulroney made a little headway in trimming down the exemptions to a 'strengthened' section 121, but Bourassa was unwilling to accept a provision that threatened to produce 'an economy managed by judges.'[45] The effort to reduce interprovincial barriers to trade was dropped from the constitutional proposals and relegated to the list of fifteen matters to be dealt with through 'political accords.' So much for the federal government's constitutional priority.

Finally, the amending formula, where the whole constitutional odyssey began so many years before, was to be made even tighter. Not only changes in the Senate but nearly all changes in the structure of national institutions, including Quebec's 25 per cent guarantee in the House of Commons, in the future would require unanimous approval of all the provinces and the federal Parliament. The only exception would be the nomination and appointment of Supreme Court judges, which would be subject to the 7/50 amending procedure. Among other things, this procedure would make it difficult for the territories to become full members of Confederation. They could become provinces through a simple Act of Parliament, but increases in their Senate representation and full participation in the amending process would be subject to the rule of unanimity.

By Friday night, 21 August, the elements of what was to be known as the Charlottetown Accord were in place. It remained only for officials to translate the deals struck by the political leaders into the language of a formal agreement. This did not take long as it was a matter of making only a handful of changes in the Pearson Accord. On 27 August the political leaders flew to Charlottetown to review the text. Charlottetown was chosen because the premiers were scheduled to have their annual conference in the Island capital and, besides, there was the hope that some of Charlottetown's lustre as the cradle of Confederation would rub off on this latest effort to renew Confederation. On 28 August the Charlottetown Accord was signed.

At this point in the Canada round it was clear that whatever emerged from the multilateral negotiations would be submitted to the people in a Canada-wide referendum. Two provinces, British Columbia and Alberta, were legislatively bound to have referendums before their legislatures could consider any constitutional amendment. Quebec was bound to have a constitutional referendum by 26 October 1992. Indeed, the whole point of Bourassa's re-engagement in the multilateral process was to avoid being stuck with only a sovereignty option for the Quebec referendum. On the weekend following Charlottetown, at a convention of the Quebec Liberal party, Bourassa was able to persuade 90 per cent of the delegates to abandon Allaire and throw the party's support behind the much more moderate Charlottetown Accord.[46] A few days later he began the process in the National Assembly of amending Bill 150 to provide for a 26 October referendum on the Charlottetown Accord rather than on Quebec sovereignty. The federal government had been poised for some time to put the machinery of its new Referendum Act into action.[47] The act was designed to accommodate a federal referendum, with a simultaneous referendum in Quebec or any other province that wished to use its own referendum machinery.

Quite apart from the provincial commitments and the readiness of the federal referendum law, there were two broader reasons for Canada to have a referendum at this point in its constitutional odyssey. First, there was the question of political legitimacy. Meech Lake, it should be remembered, had been attacked as much, if not more, for its non-democratic process as for its substance. While the public had certainly been consulted – almost overconsulted – in the early stages of the Canada round, the Charlottetown Accord had been preceded by six months of closed-door elite negotiations. Key terms of the accord – above all Quebec's 25 per cent guarantee in the House of Commons – had never been exposed or explained in any public forum. Approval by the people in a referendum would provide the highest measure of democratic legitimacy.

As the opening chapters of this book have argued, Canadians – or at least most politically active Canadians – have come to aspire to a more democratic form of constitutionalism than their forebears. Most Canadians today would subscribe to Clyde Wells's aphorism that 'the Constitution belongs to the people.' This does not mean, as some have suggested, that in the future every constitutional amendment, no matter how minor or limited in scope, will require a referendum. But it probably does mean that proposals which alter fundamental terms of the Constitution – which bear on the very nature of what the country is all about – will require direct approval by the people. Canadians, like so many European peoples, may well insist on this form of popular sovereignty. No doubt there is a very big risk in taking such questions to the people, but, in a democratic age, there is the opposite risk, which European leaders may soon incur, of founding a new order of things on a weak foundation of public support.

The other rationale for the referendum was to avoid prolonging the constitutional debate and to obtain closure on the Canada round. By the autumn of 1992 the Canadian people and their leaders, constitutionally speaking, were all tuckered out. There was a widespread desire in the land to bring the big constitutional debate to some kind of conclusion. A successful referendum, of course, would have to be followed by ratification in the federal Parliament and the provincial legislatures, but legislative ratification for proposals approved by the people would likely be quick and perfunctory. Terminating the Canada round would not mean finality for the constitutional process. As the opponents of the Charlottetown Accord never tired of pointing out, the accord was full of loose ends that would require further negotiations. It was not unreasonable to think, however, that once the big issues of principle in the accord were accepted, the country might get some relief from the exhaustion of mega constitutional politics. By the same token, there was also a good chance that after such a gargantuan effort a negative result would produce at least a temporary constitutional truce. In the referendum there were many 'yes' and 'no' supporters who thought their side's victory would lead to constitutional closure.

With respect to the governing legislative rules, the referendum was a two-nations affair. The federal government respected Quebec's right to have the referendum regulated by its own law on popular consultation, the legislation under which the 1980 Quebec referendum had been conducted.[48] Alberta and British Columbia, however, agreed not to use their referendum laws.[49] Thus the federal proclamation directing a referendum for 26 October applied to all of Canada except Quebec.[50] Though the laws regulating the referendum campaign would be different in Quebec and the rest of Canada, all voters would be asked the same question: 'Do you agree that the Constitution of Canada should be renewed on the basis of the agreement reached on August 28, 1992?' That question had been agreed to by the first ministers and was formally approved by the House of Commons on 10 September by a vote of 233 to 12.[51]

The principal difference between the federal and the Quebec referendum laws is that Quebec's law imposed a much tighter and more partisan organization on the referendum campaign. Under the Quebec Act, members of the National Assembly headed up two committees, one for 'yes' and the other for 'no.' Each committee was restricted to an expenditure limit of fifty cents per voter, and all expenditures on the referendum campaign in the province had to be authorized by the 'yes' or 'no' committee. Naturally, Bourassa and his Liberal party colleagues led the 'yes' forces, while Jacques Parizeau and his Parti Québécois members led the 'no' side. Thus, in Quebec, the referendum campaign was fought very much along party lines.

The federal government in drafting its referendum legislation feared that confining effective participation to two committees might run afoul of the Charter of Rights. So, under the federal law, while no person or group could spend more than $5000 except through a referendum committee, and committees were restricted in the amounts they could spend to 56.4 cents per voter in the districts for which they registered,[52] an infinite number of committees were allowed. The three major parties in the federal Parliament – the Conservatives, Liberals, and NDP – got together to form a 'yes' committee headed not by active politicians but by retired political leaders and distinguished citizens from all parts of the country.[53] This official, multi-partisan, 'yes' committee anchored the organization of the 'yes' campaign. But on the 'no' side were a plethora of committees covering an even broader spectrum of political opinion than the 'yes' committee. Outside Quebec, the only partisan political opposition to the Charlottetown Accord came from Preston Manning's Reform party and the leaders of the Liberal opposition parties in the British Columbia and Manitoba legislatures. Accordingly, the referendum contest was cast primarily in terms of the country's national political leadership against the highly diverse and uncoordinated efforts of interest groups and activists alienated from that leadership.

Neither the federal nor the Quebec law made the results of a referendum binding on the government or legislature. In this technical, legal sense, then, the referendum was merely consultative – a plebiscite rather than a referendum. If the constitutional amendments proposed in the Charlottetown Accord were approved in the referendum, they would not become law until they were ratified by the federal Parliament and the provincial legislatures. However, from a political standpoint, a clear verdict by the electorate would be respected by the legislators. What would amount to a clear verdict? What kind of a majority was required for a referendum victory? On this question the Referendum Act was silent. Since a few items in the accord (notably the amending formula changes – so crucial to Quebec) were subject to the unanimity amending rule, the official line of the 'yes' side was that a 'yes' majority was needed in every province. Even so, the politicians on the 'yes' side were careful not to give a definitive answer to what might be done if only one province, say British Columbia, voted 'no.' With that kind of outcome there might well have been an effort to negotiate with the outrider province (perhaps even a couple of provinces) and to have a second referendum there rather than to abandon the whole project (just as European leaders are endeavouring to do with Denmark's rejection of the Maastricht Treaty). There has to be a little stretch in the rule of unanimity – otherwise it will be a hopelessly tight constitutional straitjacket.

The Canadian people did not show a great deal of gratitude for being consulted on the Constitution. The two-month-long referendum campaign was not a happy political event. The prevailing mood was one of crankiness. This was a period of political history – not only for Canada but for many Western democracies – in which the most popular leader was 'none of the above.' The leaders of all three national parties – Prime Minister Mulroney, the Liberals' Jean Chrétien, and the NDP's Audrey McLaughlin – were enjoying very low levels of public esteem. And the most important politician on the 'no' side in English Canada, Preston Manning, was doing little to raise the stock of the Reform party by attacking the Charlottetown Accord, cynically and inaccurately, as the 'Mulroney Deal.'

Many voters resented that they were faced with a complex package of sixty proposals put to them on an all or nothing basis. There was, of course, a good reason for this package deal. The contents of the accord represented a delicate compromise among conflicting constitutional visions and values. Take away any one component and the whole house of cards would come tumbling down. In this sense the Charlottetown Accord was just like the Meech Lake Accord except that the range of interests it attempted to accommodate was considerably wider. The political leaders who put the accord together were willing to accommodate their interests – were willing to give a little to get a little – because they were convinced national unity required a constitutional deal at this time and they could not see themselves negotiating a better deal in the near future. But these beliefs were not shared by the general public. One of the most telling bits of polling data released during the campaign was an item in the *Globe* poll showing that majorities of over 60 per cent in every part of the country thought that the consequence of a victory for the 'no' side would *not* be a boost for Quebec separatism but rather would indicate a need to renegotiate a better deal.[54] Nor did the people take kindly to anyone who tried to persuade them that voting 'no' would lead to the breakup of Canada. Prime Minister Mulroney's lowest moment in the campaign came when he made just such an effort. For dramatic effect he tore up a list of what Quebec could gain through the accord before the television cameras, suggesting that is what would happen to Canada if the accord were defeated.[55] Mulroney spent much of the remainder of the campaign trying to recover from this unappreciated threat.

There are important lessons here for practitioners of mega constitutional politics. Citizens are not likely to be in a mood to compromise their principles or interests in a major constitutional reordering unless they believe that dire consequences will flow from their refusal to do so. But it is not easy to cajole people into such a belief. Strong evidence of imminent crisis is required to give credibility to the constitutional reformers' forecast of gloom and doom should their handiwork be rejected. The South African president, F.W. De Klerk, at the present time would seem to be supported by such evidence. In the Canadian case, such evidence was lacking. Not only did the majority of Canadians not believe Quebec separation was imminent but a growing minority of Canadians no longer viewed the departure of Quebec as catastrophic even if it did occur.

The 'yes' side was also hurt by the absence throughout most of the campaign of the legal text of the constitutional changes proposed in the Charlottetown Accord. Bourassa's 26 October deadline left no time before the campaign got under way to translate the terms of the agreement signed by the political leaders at Charlottetown on 28 August into the precise language of constitutional amendments. Though any differences of meaning that might result from such a translation would be slight and of little import to the average voter, the 'no' side cleverly exploited the possibility that the proposals the people were being asked to consider – that is, the accord mailed to every voter – might differ in some subtle and unknown ways from the actual changes that would be made in the Constitution. One of the most effective television advertisements for the 'no' side showed a trusty farmer coming out of his barn after milking the cows muttering that he was not prepared to 'buy a pig in a poke.'

Working under pressure, around the clock, the legal advisers of the negotiating parties eventually produced a legal text – two weeks before the vote. However significant the legal text may have been for constitutional experts, for the vast majority of voters it was of little consequence. In style and format it was a much less accessible document than the Charlottetown Accord, and its modifications were too minor to influence overall appraisals of the accord.[56] Most of the changes were by way of additional detail. Some were designed to assuage particular sources of criticism. The Senate's powers, though not substantially changed from the Charlottetown deal, were made more parallel with those of the House of Commons – something that Newfoundland's Clyde Wells pressed for very strongly. For instance, unlike the present Senate, the new Senate would have a veto over constitutional amendments in relation to the House of Commons or Senate.[57] The most publicized change was an attempt to mollify critics who believed the Aboriginal self-government provisions endangered the rights of Aboriginal women. A section was added, for greater certainty, to ensure that nothing in the Aboriginal self-government amendments was to derogate from the equality rights protected in sections 15 and 28 of the Charter.[58] Needless to say, this change did not win over the Native Women's Association of Canada, whose members continued to oppose the accord because of their exclusion from the process that produced it.[59]

The referendum campaign, like all political campaigns in contemporary mass democracies, was dominated by television. Television is a medium in which deliberation over fine points of legal text has no place. In the two widely televised debates – one in each 'nation' – the 'yes' side did not do badly. NDP leader Audrey McLaughlin at least fought to a draw with Reform party leader Preston Manning, and most pundits scored Robert Bourassa a little ahead on points in his toe-to-toe with the PQ's Jacques Parizeau. But for most of the public the debate was carried on through the newscasts' ten-second 'sound bites,' the snappy one-liners from participants in televised 'town halls' and the spot ads squeezed between innings of the Toronto Blue Jays' (successful) quest of the World Series baseball championship. Though free broadcast time was allocated equally among supporting and opposing committees, the 'no' side seemed to have an edge in the television wars. To begin with, it is easier in a few seconds to trash a particular constitutional proposal from the perspective of some region or interest than it is to talk people into accepting a compromise. On the advertising front, the home-made, grass-roots feel of the 'no' ads appealed more to the anti-establishment mood than the slick, big-agency efforts of the 'yes' committee. The non-politician, good-citizen types who headed up the 'yes' committee hardly ever appeared on camera, the telecasters preferring to get their news bites from Mulroney and the other political leaders. The bias in news production strengthened the feeling that the campaign pitted the political elite's 'yes' against the people's 'no.'

In terms of newsworthy events, so much more important than ideas to the mass media, again the 'yes' side did not fare well. The most dramatic personal intervention was Pierre Trudeau's brief re-entry on the constitutional stage – a cameo appearance on 2 October at Maison Egg Roll, a Chinese restaurant in Montreal. As in the Meech Lake round, the former prime minister poured buckets of cold water over the constitutional efforts of his successors. Political scientists tracking the movement of opinion during the campaign found the biggest drop in 'yes' support outside Quebec occurred immediately after Trudeau's speech.[60] Trudeau was still very much English Canada's constitutional hero. The most damaging exit, Premier Don Getty's announcement early in the campaign of his intention to retire, left the 'yes' side with a lame-duck leader to battle Preston Manning in Alberta. The 'yes' side also suffered the worst 'accident': the leaked transcripts of intercepted telephone conversations in which Diane Whilhelmy, Quebec's deputy minister of intergovernmental affairs and Bourassa's senior constitutional advisor, lamented to colleagues how her boss had 'caved in' in agreeing to the Charlottetown Accord.[61] The Wilhelmy affair only lengthened the odds against the 'yes' side winning in Quebec.

But none of this – the lack of a legal text, the Wilhelmy affair, Trudeau's speech, Getty's cop-out, the split among Aboriginal peoples, Mulroney's opening gaffe, the unpopularity of the 'yes' side's politicians, the 'no' side's TV advantage – was as crucial to the outcome of the referendum as the Charlottetown Accord itself. It is doubtful whether even a flawless campaign on the 'yes' side could have garnered an adequate majority for the accord. For the deal at the centre of the accord – the compromise that produced the elite accommodation, the rabbit that the rest of Canada's political negotiators pulled out of the hat to get Quebec on board – could not be sold to the people. The Charlottetown Accord was defeated because, outside Quebec, it was perceived as giving Quebec too much, while inside Quebec it was perceived as not giving Quebec enough.

Nothing alienated voters in the rest of Canada so much as the guarantee to Quebec of 25 per cent of the seats in the House of Commons. The *Globe* poll published on 9 October showed majorities outside Quebec against this provision ranging from 71 per cent in the Atlantic region to 89 per cent in British Columbia. No other provision of the accord was so roundly rejected. While the 25 per cent guarantee was approved by 76 per cent in Quebec, that provision was not nearly enough to win a majority for the accord in Quebec. There the crucial voters were those interested in a renewal of federalism. For a long time, renewing federalism had meant substantially increasing the powers of the Quebec government within Confederation. What the Charlottetown Accord promised was not a lot more power in Quebec City but special status for Quebec within the central institutions of Canadian government. Bourassa had done nothing to wean Quebec federalists to this new constitutional strategy.

Though there was some movement of opinion during the campaign outside Quebec – particularly in Ontario and the Prairie provinces – Quebec remained solidly opposed from start to finish.[62] Indeed, the publication of poll after poll showing the 'no' side ahead in Quebec by ten to twenty percentage points may, towards the end, have had a negative effect on the 'yes' vote outside Quebec among voters whose prime motive for supporting the accord was to reach an accommodation with Quebec. For Canadians of this persuasion the second best outcome to a victory for the accord was its rejection by majorities in both parts of Canada. And, of course, that was exactly the outcome they got.

TABLE 2

Results of the 26 October Referendum

	% Yes	% No
Alberta	39.6	60.2
British Columbia	31.9	67.8
Manitoba	37.9	61.7
New Brunswick	61.3	38.0
Newfoundland	62.9	36.5
Nova Scotia	48.5	51.1
Ontario	49.8	49.6
PEI	73.6	25.9
Quebec	42.4	55.4
Saskatchewan	45.5	55.1
NWT	60.2	39.0
Yukon	43.4	56.1
National	44.8	54.2

On 26 October 1992 nearly fourteen million Canadians – 75 per cent of the eligible voters – exercised their franchise in Canada's first country-wide referendum on constitutional matters. The results, as set out in table 2, were clear enough: 54 per cent of the voters rejected the Charlottetown Accord. In only three Atlantic provinces – Newfoundland, New Brunswick, and Prince Edward Island – and Ontario did the 'yes' side win a majority. In Ontario the 'yes' victory was only by a hair and was due entirely to a massive 60 per cent vote for the accord in Metropolitan Toronto.[63]

The political leadership of the country had no difficulty interpreting this result. The Charlottetown Accord was dead. And so was Canada's fifth round of mega constitutional politics.

12 Canada Returns to Constitutional Normalcy

Canada's fifth round of mega constitutional politics was not entirely lacking in positive consequences. Although the Canadian people in this initial exercise of direct constitutional democracy rejected the Charlottetown Accord, the experience may have taught them something useful about their capacity to act as a constitutional sovereign people. As constitutional sovereign the Canadian people could say 'no' to all manner of constitutional proposals, but they could not say 'yes' to anything that touched those matters of national identity and constitutional vision on which they were so profoundly divided. Canadians were now a sovereign people in only a negative sense. They could and would insist on direct approval of constitutional proposals that changed the fundamentals of their constitution. But they can use their constitutional power only to reject, not to approve, changes in anything fundamental. If this lesson sunk in, the country might well eschew the crisis-ridden politics of mega constitutional change and return to constitutional normalcy.

The prevailing mood in Canada in the aftermath of Charlottetown certainly favoured such a return to normalcy. The phrase 'constitutional exhaustion' was on everyone's lips. Using the 'c' word was a guaranteed conversational turn-off at Canadian dinner tables. Hardly anyone wanted to talk about the constitution, except in Quebec. While many Quebecers, like Canadians everywhere else, were tired of constitutional battles, this was not true of dedicated sovereignists. Rejection of the Charlottetown Accord far from cooling their ardour, had strengthened their resolve to abandon attempts to negotiate, an accommodation with Canada and to press forward with their bold independence project. Whether Canada was to be plunged once more into a period of constitutional crisis now depended entirely on the ability of Quebec sovereignists to rally enough support in the province to force a secession crisis. No attempts would come from Ottawa or any other part of English Canada to head off Quebec separatism by offering accommodating packages of constitutional reform. That kind of mega constitutional politics was over. For the next three years the big constitutional game was played only in Quebec, as the Parti Québécois struggled to stage and win a Quebec referendum on independence.

Step one was for the Parti Québécois to return to power in Quebec. This it did in September 1994 when, led by Jacques Parizeau, the PQ defeated the Liberal government led by Premier Daniel Johnson, who had replaced Robert Bourassa. Though the election gave the Parti Québécois a solid majority – seventy seven seats to forty-seven for the Liberals and one for Mario Dumont's Parti Action Democratique – the popular vote was very close. The PQ's 44.7 per cent of the popular vote was just 0.4 per cent more than the Liberals' share of the vote. This did not deter Parizeau from pushing ahead quickly with his plans for a sovereignty referendum. Daniel Johnson, the defeated Liberal leader, in fact urged him not to renege on his election promise to hold a referendum within eight to ten months of coming to office.[1] Federalists within and outside Quebec tended to read the closeness of the popular vote in the election as showing that there was little chance of the sovereignists being able to win a referendum, and they wanted to remove this menace to constitutional peace as quickly as possible. Parizeau hardly needed the encouragement.

For the next year and a bit, until the Quebec referendum of 30 October, 1995, the prospect of Quebec secession was the compelling and all-absorbing issue in Canadian political life. But the two parts of the body politic – Quebec and the Rest of Canada – experienced the possibility of Quebec secession in entirely different ways. Never were Canada's two solitudes more evident. In Quebec, there was an intense debate about Quebec's constitutional future – about whether and on what terms it should continue to be part of Canada. Outside Quebec, Canadians were deeply concerned about the outcome of that province's debate – they cared about whether their country would hold together or break up. But there was no interest now in seeing what could be done to persuade Quebecers to say 'no' to the sovereignists, nor in softer alternatives to complete independence. If Canadians outside of Quebec were united on anything it was their desire for Quebec to decide whether it wanted in or out, and to make that decision soon.

A short and simple question was precisely what the Quebec referendum process would not produce. If Jacques Parizeau had had his way, Quebecers might have been given a clearer opportunity to opt for independence than was allowed by the referendum question that was eventually put before them. Parizeau's support for Quebec independence was unconditional. The sovereignty he sought for Quebec was not partial – it was not something to be accommodated with continuing political ties with Canada. On 6 December 1994, Parizeau unveiled his sovereignty plan. It took the form of a draft bill to come into force a year after its approval in a Quebec referendum. The bill was virtually a declaration of independence. Its first section declared that 'Quebec is a sovereign country.'[2] And the proposed referendum question was, 'Are you in favour of the Act passed by the National Assembly declaring the sovereignty of Quebec? YES or NO.'[3] The bill would authorize the Quebec government to negotiate an *economic* association between Quebec and Canada, but Quebec sovereignty would not be conditional on success in this negotiation. Unlike the 1980 referendum, there was no undertaking to seek approval of an agreement with Canada in a second referendum before proceeding with Quebec sovereignty.

The terms on which Quebec would become a sovereign country provided for a rather painless separation from Canada. Quebec's boundaries would remain intact, Quebec's citizens would remain Canadian citizens, and Quebec's currency would continue to be the Canadian dollar. Even Canadian laws would remain in force until amended or repealed by the National Assembly. And Quebec would take the necessary steps to participate as an independent country in the various international organizations and relationships to which Canada adheres, including the Commonwealth, NATO, and the North American Free Trade Agreement. These measures would be determined and carried out unilaterally by Quebec; all that would have to be worked out with Canada would be an apportionment of Canada's property and debts, and, possibly, an economic treaty.

Parizeau and his colleagues knew that this relatively straight, uncluttered road to sovereignty was not the first choice of a great many Quebec nationalists. They knew they would have to work hard to mobilize the support of a wide spectrum of Quebec opinion, and they had a plan for doing that. A massive public consultation process was organized. More than three hundred 'commissioners' from all walks of life would hold hearings on the draft bill in sixteen regions of the province.[4] Two special commissions were established for youth and the elderly, and representatives of all political parties and minority ethnic groups were invited to participate. When the public consultation process got under way in early February, it soon became clear that Parizeau and the Parti Québécois had serious rivals in shaping a sovereignist consensus: the Bloc Québécois, the Quebec sovereignist party holding a majority of Quebec seats in the federal Parliament, and its formidable leader, Lucien Bouchard.

Bouchard had always been a soft sovereignist. He was a supporter of sovereignty association – and, like René Lévesque and the PQ proposal in the 1980 referendum, the association with Canada he had in mind was political, not merely economic. A solution of this kind – a two-nation Canadian version of the European Union – has always been the most appealing constitutional vision for Quebec nationalists. Lucien Bouchard also had far more potential to draw Quebecers together than Jacques Parizeau. His political charisma went up a notch or two when in December 1994, he fell victim to a rare flesh-eating bacterium and had to have his left leg amputated.[5] He made a remarkable recovery and by February Bouchard had returned to the constitutional fray riding a wave of sympathy and admiration for the gallant way he had dealt with his tragic affliction.

Through the winter and spring of 1995 it was Bouchard and the soft sovereignty association option that came to the fore – despite the resistance of Parizeau. Far from producing a consensus on a sovereignty plan, the public consultation process exposed the many fissures in Quebec nationalism. Parizeau's sovereignty express was slowing down. On 6 April, the premier announced that the referendum, instead of taking place in June, would be postponed to the fall.[6] A few days later he indicated that he was now open to considering a political association with Canada as part of his sovereignty option.[7] Bouchard was by this time openly campaigning for a European-style union with Canada.[8] The denouement came in June, when leaders of Québéc's three nationalist parties, the Bloc Québécois, Parti Québécois and the Parti Action Democratique, met in Quebec City to ratify an agreement on the sovereignty campaign. They would all work together on achieving sovereignty but on condition that after a referendum win an economic and political partnership would be negotiated with Canada. This agreement would include a joint council and tribunal to manage the partnership.[9]

After a relatively quiet summer, the Parizeau government unveiled its new sovereignty and referendum plans on 7 September. The amended plan incorporated the modifications insisted upon by the Parti Québécois's more moderate partners. The first section of the new Bill 1 (An Act Respecting the Future of Quebec) authorized the National Assembly to proclaim the sovereignty of Quebec only after 'a formal offer of economic and political partnership with Canada' had been made and negotiated.[10] The negotiations must not extend beyond 30 October 1996 (a year after the referendum), and in the event that the negotiations 'proved fruitless,' the proclamation of sovereignty would still be made.[11] The terms on which Quebec was to become sovereign were substantially the same as those set out in the December 1994 bill: a painless continuation of Canadian citizenship, Canadian currency, and Quebec's boundaries – all to be determined unilaterally by Quebec. One notable change was an undertaking that Quebec's new constitution would guarantee the rights which Aboriginal nations enjoy under the Canadian Constitution – providing these rights 'are exercised in a manner consistent with the territorial integrity of Quebec.'[12] Aboriginal peoples' right to self-determination was to be more limited than Quebec's. The date of the referendum was now set for 30 October and the question to which Quebecers would be asked to answer 'yes' or 'no' would be: 'Do you agree that Quebec should become sovereign, after having made a formal offer to Canada for a new Economic and Political Partnership, within the scope of the Bill respecting the future of Quebec and of the agreement signed on June 12, 1995?'[13]

There was a clear implication in this question that if a majority answered 'yes,' Quebec could and would become sovereign through its own declaration of independence without any need to comply with the requirements of the Canadian Constitution. A challenge to the legality of this presumption had issued months earlier from a most ironic source, Guy Bertrand, a lawyer who in the 1980s had been a contender for the leadership of the Parti Québécois. The day after the PQ government announced its referendum plans, Justice Robert Lesage of Quebec's Superior Court brought down his judgment on the Bertrand challenge.[14] Justice Lesage found that Quebec's bid to secede unilaterally was unconstitutional and called on the government not to proceed with its unilateral declaration of sovereignty. However, the judge refused to grant the injunctive relief sought by Bertrand and order Quebec to halt the referendum. To do so, he reasoned, might cause more damage than the referendum itself. Quebec's second sovereignty referendum was now under way.

The second referendum differed from the first in some important ways. The question this time, though as fuzzy and convoluted as the 1980 question, was bolder in that it carried with it an implicit commitment to separating after a 'yes' win regardless of how negotiations went with Canada, whereas in 1980 there was a promise not to secede until a second referendum was held on the outcome of negotiations with Canada. That difference suggests that in 1995 the 'yes' side faced a harder sell. But other differences more than counterbalanced this point. These were factors relating primarily to political leadership. The political star of the 1980 referendum campaign was the Prime Minister of Canada, Pierre Elliott Trudeau. His direct interventions, though few in number and based on a vague and dubious promise to restructure Canadian federalism, were spectacular, and probably decisive. Trudeau literally stole the 1980 referendum from René Lévesque and the Parti Québécois. In 1995, the referendum star was not the Prime Minister of Canada but the leader of the Official opposition in the federal Parliament, Lucien Bouchard. The Bloc Québécois leader was now, as they say, at the top of his game. With his cane and a limp as reminders of his near brush with death just a few months earlier, he was virtually immune from personal attack.[15] To the softer Quebec nationalists whose support was so essential for a sovereignist win, Bouchard had much more appeal than the doctrinaire Parizeau. Bouchard talked strong but had the look of a bargainer. He could not captain the sovereignist team because Quebec's referendum law required that the 'yes' side be led by the premier. But as the campaign moved into its final three weeks, Parizeau, recognizing the limits of his own credibility as a leader who could cut a deal with Canada, named Bouchard Quebec's chief negotiator with the rest of Canada.[16] Bouchard was now the de facto leader of Team Sovereignty.

The leadership on the other side – the Save Canada team, to use Lawrence Martin's phrase – was ineffectual and deeply divided. Daniel Johnson was the official captain of this team, as required by the referendum law. But he was under more pressure to demonstrate his credentials as a Quebec nationalist than to trumpet the arguments for saving Canada. The leadership role so brilliantly performed by Trudeau in 1980 now fell to Prime Minister Jean Chrétien – and Chrétien was no Trudeau. His love of country was as deep and passionate as Trudeau's, but Chrétien lacked the intellectual and rhetorical skills which had won grudging admiration for his predecessor even from Trudeau's nationalist opponents in Quebec. Trudeau was a federalist with class, and something positive to offer – a restructuring of the federation. Chrétien, however, had nothing positive to offer as an alternative to the sovereignists' plan. For Chrétien and a great many Canadians, the Quebec nationalists' game of threatening to secede unless Quebec was offered a stronger place within the federation was over. Chrétien and his government refused to play and, until the final days of the campaign, resisted pleas of Daniel Johnson's Quebec Liberals, their 'partners' on the 'no' team, to offer Quebecers some constitutional goodies. The wreckage of the Meech Lake and Charlottetown Accords was argument enough to resist returning to the old constitutional game. And until the latter part of the campaign, the polls indicated that the 'no' side could win without offering an alternative to sovereignty/association.[17] The Save Canada team relied on the threat of dire economic consequences if the sovereignists won. But fear, even when based on reasonable speculation, never has the appeal of hope.

In the final week of the campaign, with polls showing the sovereignists five to six percentage points ahead, the federal government went into panic mode. For his last major appearance in Quebec, at Verdun just outside of Montreal, Chrétien agreed to deliver a speech which now said 'nothing was off the table with regard to the Constitution ...'[18] He made specific commitments to recognize Quebec as a distinct society, to restore Quebec's constitutional veto, and to transfer power over labour market training. With just five days to go, Chrétien, his eyes welling with tears, rallied his caucus in Ottawa for a final frantic fight to save the country. That night a tense and frightened Prime Minister delivered a five-minute television address to the country. The contrast with the upbeat and confident Bouchard who followed with a five-minute address of his own was striking. On Friday 27 October, with the referendum scheduled for the following Monday, tens of thousands of Canadians, many of them bused into the province from Ontario, staged a national unity rally in Place du Canada in downtown Montreal.[19] The demonstrators offered only love of country – but a country, as their bumper stickers and lapel buttons proudly proclaimed, that 'includes Quebec.' Given the closeness of the referendum vote, this last-minute 'hail Mary' event, organized by two of Chrétien's heartiest warriors, Brian Tobin and Sheila Copps, in defiance of Quebec's restrictive referendum rules, may well have been crucial in achieving a win for the 'no' side.[20]

And how close it was! On Monday 30 October, 5,086,980 Quebecers, 94 per cent of eligible voters, turned out to vote: 50.6 per cent voted 'no'; 49.4 per cent voted 'yes.' If a mere 31,000 of those who voted 'no' had changed their minds, the 'yes' side would have 'won.' Neither side could take much solace from such a result. Though the sovereignists had done much better than in 1980, when they got only 40.4 per cent of the vote (with an 86 per cent turnout), their leadership expressed bitter disappointment. 'It is true that we were beaten,' admitted Jacques Parizeau. 'But by whom?' he asked, and answered, 'money and ethnic votes.'[21] The premier went on to utter dark warnings about the 'temptation for revenge.' For the 'yes' side it was, in the words of *La Presse* columnist

Alain Dubuc, 'une victoire sans joie.'[22] A shaken Prime Minister Jean Chrétien told 'yes' voters that he now understood their 'profound desire' for change and promised that he would work to develop innovative solutions.[23]

It is a mistake to say – as some have said – that Canada came within a whisker of breaking up on 30 October 1995. If the 'yes' side had won the referendum the only thing about which we can be reasonably certain is that Quebec and Canada would have plunged into a period of great confusion, chaos, and conflict. To say that the Chrétien government was unprepared for a sovereignist win is a gross understatement. Chrétien had given ample indication that he would not accept a 'yes' win as mandating the break-up of the federation. But his government appeared to have no strategy for preventing a Quebec government headed by Parizeau from proceeding with its plan for unilateral separation. In the wake of a win for the 'yes' side by the narrowest of margins, with the Quebec government saying, 'we're on our way to independence,' and a federal government saying, 'oh no you aren't,' and passions inflamed by anglophone talk of partitioning Montreal and Quebec to keep the predominantly English-speaking areas of the province in Canada, it is likely that hotheads on each side would have taken to the streets to defend their conflicting claims of nationalist justice. The James Bay Crees had also made it clear that their historic homeland would be included in a sovereign Quebec only through armed force.[24] David Collenette, who was minister of defence at the time, tells us that he had prepared the army to protect federal property in Quebec from a sovereignist takeover.[25] But far from calming down the situation, a federal military presence on the streets of Quebec might have had the very opposite effect. Given the strong likelihood of communal violence in Quebec following a 'yes' win, the one thing we can say about the 'no' side's victory is that it meant that Canada's tradition of civility was not tested beyond its limits. In the long term, the example of that tradition – of avoiding violence in accommodating the very deep differences of identity and national sentiment that animate our people – may be our country's greatest contribution to human civilization.

The lesson to be learned from the closeness of the result in the 1995 Quebec referendum is the flip side of what Canadians should have learned from the 1992 Canada-wide referendum on the Charlottetown Accord. Just as the vote on the Charlottetown Accord showed that the Canadian people are much too divided to act positively as a sovereign people, the Quebec referendum demonstrated that the deep divisions within the Quebec body politic prevent its population from acting positively as Quebec's constitutional sovereign.[26] In ridings where francophones form less than 50 per cent of the population the 'no' side took 82.3 per cent of the vote.[27] And even in ridings that are 50 to 80 per cent francophone, the 'yes' side took only 41.1 per cent of the vote. It is only in the ridings which are over 80 per cent francophone that the sovereignists won a majority, and in most of these the majority was under 60 per cent. With these kinds of divisions, to regard the support of the slimmest of majorities for a vague and confusing question as a mandate to break up one of the oldest constitutional democracies in the world and force the entire population of Quebec to become citizens of a new state would amount to a clear case of majority tyranny.

It took a while for the lessons of the Quebec referendum – and of the Charlottetown Accord – to fully sink in. There was still some interest at the level of political leadership in continuing to play the old game of attempting to heal the country's deep divisions by some kind of constitutional restructuring. But the players now approached the national unity game with a great deal of wariness, looking for some new tricks to avoid becoming mired in the muck of mega constitutional politics. This was clearly evident in the federal initiatives Prime Minister Chrétien announced a month after the referendum to honour the promises of reform he had made at Verdun in the final days of the referendum campaign. First, the House of Commons would pass a resolution recognizing Quebec as a distinct society.[28] Second, Quebec's constitutional veto would be restored by an indirect method: legislation would be introduced binding the federal government to support constitutional amendments requiring the support of seven provinces representing 50 per cent of the population only when they have been consented to by Quebec, Ontario, two provinces representing 50 per cent of western Canada's population, and two provinces representing 50 per cent of Atlantic Canada's population. The third item was a promise to devolve labour-market training to the provinces – a matter of concern for Quebec that dates back to the aborted Victoria Charter of 1971.[29]

The Chrétien package of 'semi-constitutional' proposals went over like the proverbial lead balloon. It was immediately repudiated as too little, too late by Quebec sovereignists and failed to win endorsement by Quebec federalists as a satisfactory basis for re-engaging in a process of constitutional renewal. As for the other provinces, even though Chrétien had watered down the Meech Lake Accord's recognition of Quebec as a distinct society, several premiers still condemned it as endangering the principle of provincial equality.[30] Eventually, in September 1997, the premiers of the English-speaking provinces and heads of the two northern territories came up with their own version, the so-called Calgary Declaration, according to which 'All provinces, while diverse in their characteristics, have equality of status,' but at the same time, 'the unique character of Quebec society, including its French-speaking majority, its culture and its traditions of civil law' is recognized as 'fundamental to the well-being of Canada.'[31] In response, Lucien Bouchard, now ensconced in Quebec City as premier, growled, 'Quebec will accept nothing less than to be recognized as a people, as a nation capable of deciding its political future.'[32] Mercifully, this put an end to the futile attempt to solve Canada's so-called national unity problem by playing definition games and offering symbolic baubles.

The second part of Chrétien's package, the restoration of Quebec's constitutional veto – by indirect and convoluted means - was equally a fiasco. The very idea of Ottawa 'lending' its constitutional veto to the four 'regions' of Canada was bizarre. It seems to have come right off the top of the prime minister's head, catching even his justice minister, Alan Rock, by surprise. Roger Gibbins, an Alberta-based political scientist, pronounced it as 'little short of a constitutional *coup d'état* by the Prime Minister.'[33] Chrétien's initiative received a particularly bad reception in Alberta and British Columbia, the most rapidly growing Canadian provinces, where there is much popular resentment against being denied the same status as Ontario and Quebec. British Columbia seemed to bleat the loudest and so, within days, Justice Minister Rock had persuaded his Cabinet colleagues to lend Ottawa's veto to British Columbia too.[34] Thus the final version which was enacted into law in February 1996 as the Constitutional Amendments Act, 1996,[35] superimposes five regional vetoes on the operation of the 7/50 amendment rule in the Constitution.

So long as the Chrétien legislation stands, amendments to those crucial parts of the Constitution that concern the structure of the federation and federal institutions must have the support of the federal Parliament, British Columbia, Ontario, Quebec, at least two of the prairie provinces comprising 50 per cent of their combined populations (at current population levels this means Alberta plus either Manitoba or Saskatchewan), and at least two of the Atlantic provinces comprising 50 per cent of that region's population. The legislation is worded so that the regional approvals can be given by referendum. Given that there is now virtually a constitutional convention that important constitutional amendments are only legitimate when approved directly by the people, the political pressure for a national referendum to ratify major changes in the Constitution of Canada would likely be irresistible.[36] This means that the consent of majorities in seven provinces representing 92 per cent of Canada's population is now required for any important constitutional amendment. The legal basis for the regional vetoes is only an act of the federal Parliament which can be overturned by any subsequent parliament. But the political risk of removing any region's veto is so great that the new Chrétien rules for the constitutional game will be difficult if not impossible to change. One of the most enduring legacies of the 'little guy from Shawinigan' is to have placed Canada's sovereign people in a very tight constitutional straitjacket.

The Prime Minister had now delivered on two of the commitments he had made in the referendum campaign. Implementation of the third of his 'Verdun promises' – turning over to the provinces full control over labour-market development – began to unfold in 1996. Again formal constitutional amendment was avoided, and the reform was brought forward as part of a general overhaul of federal unemployment insurance, shifting policy to a much greater emphasis on assisting the unemployed to re-enter the workforce.[37] On 30 May 1996, the federal government announced that it was prepared to enter into agreements with the provinces enabling them to take over responsibility for employment training and other active employment measures, providing they met federal conditions. This reversion to the classic methods of intergovernmentalism was part of a two-track approach that was now emerging for dealing with national unity issues. The approach had a 'good cop – tough cop' character. Track one, or Plan A, as it came to be called, was the old game of accommodation and read-justment of the federal system, but a game now to be played by non-constitutional means. It was hoped that devolving responsibilities to the provinces, overcoming duplication and generally managing the federation more efficiently would be an effective way of sooth-ing constitutional discontents. But if Plan A failed, and Quebec sovereignists continued to push ahead with their project, then Plan B – the tough cop – would come into play. The key to Plan B was setting out the rules and conditions that would govern any attempt of a province to secede from the federation.[38]

To lead this new strategy Chrétien brought a remarkable new constitutional leader into his government, Stéphane Dion. Dion, a political science professor at the University of Montreal, and Pierre Pettigrew, a high-profile Montreal Liberal with a career in public finance, joined the Cabinet in January 1996. Chrétien's recruit-ment of these talented Quebecers resembles Prime Minister Pearson's move in 1965 to bolster his government's position in Quebec by inviting Jean Marchand, Gerard Pelletier and Pierre Elliott Trudeau to join the Liberal caucus in Ottawa. In coming to Ottawa to champion the federalist cause, Dion, like Trudeau, faced the challenge of countering the prevailing views of the media and chattering classes in francophone Quebec. He accepted this chal-lenge with a brilliance not seen in Ottawa since Trudeau's day. But having come of age politically when Trudeau was pushing for a more centralized federation, Dion was much more inclined to see the benefits of decentralization. He was also much more at ease than Trudeau had been with Quebec nationalism, and he was convinced that Canadian federalism was flexible enough to accom-modate Quebec's legitimate aspiration to serve as the homeland of one of Canada's founding peoples and the only jurisdiction in North America with a French-speaking majority.[39] Nonetheless,

Dion also recognized that Quebec, like Canada, was enriched by cultural and ethnic minorities who had collective rights that, in all justice, could not be ignored. He expounded these ideas in a remarkable series of public letters addressed to the Quebec premier, Lucien Bouchard. Though he argued forcefully that there was no logical reason for Quebecers to choose to separate from Canada, he underlined his government's willingness to respect the will of Quebecers if they 'expressed very clearly a desire to leave Canada.'[40] But he also insisted that no federation in the world allows a government of one of its constituent units to set the rules of secession unilaterally. And, even more provocatively, he pointed out that if Canada's boundaries can be changed, so can Quebec's.

It was over the question of the constitutional rules governing secession – Plan B – that Canada had its only heavy bout of constitutional politics after the 1995 Quebec referendum. The constitutions of most countries, including Canada's, do not explicitly spell out how part of the country can secede. Constitution makers are too optimistic for that and even when creating federal states envisage the union they are fashioning as eternal, or to use the language of the Australian Constitution, 'indissoluble.' Most attempts at unilateral secession, including that of the American South, have been dealt with by force rather than constitutional law. With a Quebec government still asserting its right to secede unilaterally following a sovereignist win in a referendum, which Lucien Bouchard said would take place as soon as there were 'winning conditions,' the Government of Canada decided that the time had come to challenge the legality of unilateral secession. If another Quebec referendum, as virtually everyone expected, was to occur soon and this time the 'yes' side won, Ottawa preferred that what happens next be governed by the rule of law rather than force. In May 1996, its backbone stiffened by Stéphane Dion, the federal government finally decided to join Guy Bertrand in his court challenge to Quebec's secession plan. Justice Minister Alan Rock said his government was willing to risk a confrontation with Quebec sovereignists 'because it had an obligation to defend the Canadian Constitution.'[41] In response, Bouchard threatened to call a snap election, but then backed off. In September Justice Minister Rock announced that rather than waiting to have the matter litigated up through the

Quebec courts, the federal government would use its power to refer questions directly to the Supreme Court of Canada. The Court would be called upon to answer three questions:[42]

- Under the Constitution of Canada, can the National Assembly, legislature, or government of Quebec effect the secession of Quebec from Canada unilaterally?
- Does international law give the National Assembly, legislature, or government of Quebec the right to effect the secession of Quebec from Canada unilaterally?
- In the event of a conflict between domestic and international law ... which would take precedence?

Rock was emphatic that it was not the intention of his government to block the democratic choice of Quebecers. 'This country,' he said, 'will not be held together against the will of Quebecers clearly expressed.'[43] But it was, he argued, in everyone's interest that such choice be made and given effect through a process that observes the rule of law.

Ottawa's decision to test the legality of an attempt by Quebec (or any other province) to secede from Canada unilaterally enraged the Bouchard government. For the sovereignists, Quebec's right to issue a declaration of independence on the basis of a majority vote of its people was an exercise of Quebecers' right to self-determination and rested on a higher law than Canada's Constitution. Besides, the official line in Quebec was to regard the Supreme Court as hopelessly biased – a virtual leaning tower of Pisa – in favour of the government which unilaterally appoints its judges. With the Government of Quebec refusing to take part and argue the sovereignist case, the Court appointed André Joli-Coeur, a committed sovereignist, to serve as an *amicus curiae* (friend of the court) to make the case for unilateral secession.[44] On the other side, in addition to a strong federal team led by an eminent Quebec lawyer, Yves Fortier, a large array of intervenors made submissions to the Court, as is usual with reference cases on big constitutional issues. These included the provinces of Manitoba and Saskatchewan, the Northwest Territories and Yukon, several Aboriginal groups, minority rights advocates – and the redoubtable Guy Bertrand.

On 20 August 1998, the Supreme Court rendered its historic decision.[45] It was a unanimous decision authored jointly by the Court's nine justices. To the question of whether Quebec, following a referendum vote by a majority of its citizens to secede, could unilaterally separate from Canada, the Court gave a firm 'no' answer. While the democratic principle requires that the will of a provincial majority expressed in a referendum be given 'considerable weight,' the Court recognized that other principles at the foundation of Canada's constitutional system are equally important – namely, the rule of law, federalism, and minority rights. The rule of law requires that any constitutional change, including removing a province from the federation, must be carried out according to the legal rules governing constitutional amendment.[46] As citizens of a federation, the Court reasoned, all Canadians, including Quebecers, exercise their democratic rights by participating in the building of two majorities, one national and one provincial. Both majorities must participate in fundamental constitutional change. Majoritarian democracy in Canada at both the federal and provincial levels must be balanced by respect for minorities whose rights are enshrined in the Constitution – namely the English in Quebec, the French in the other provinces and territories, and Aboriginal peoples. The combination of these principles means that for Quebec to declare its independence from Canada solely on the basis of a majority vote of the province's electorate would be to violate both the letter and the spirit of Canada's Constitution.

The Supreme Court also gave a firm 'no' to the question of whether under international law the principle of the self-determination of peoples gives Quebec a right to secede unilaterally. In answering this question the justices confronted the delicate question of 'whether, should a Quebec people exist within the definition of public international law, such a people encompasses the entirety of the provincial population or just some portion thereof.'[47] The Court found a way of sidestepping this fundamental question of constitutional philosophy. The right to self-determination as it has evolved under international law gives rise to a right to secede only for a people suffering oppressive colonial subjugation. Such conditions, the Court concluded 'are manifestly inapplicable in Quebec under existing circumstances.'[48]

The Supreme Court's decision was not entirely negative for the Quebec sovereignists. In what is undoubtedly the most creative part of its judgment – and the part which might well have enabled the Court, with its three Quebec members, to reach a unanimous result– the Court held that in the event of 'a decision of a clear majority of the population of Quebec on a clear question to pursue secession,'[49] the other participants in Confederation have an obligation to negotiate with Quebec. This obligation to negotiate, the justices reasoned, arises out of the fundamental principles of the Canadian constitutional system – democracy, federalism, the rule of law, and minority rights. Such negotiations would not be premised on the assumption that Quebec had an 'absolute legal entitlement' to secede, nor on an absolute denial of such a right. Their aim would be to see whether through good-faith negotiatons that observe Canada's fundamental constitutional values Quebec's constitutional status can be changed in a manner that is fair to the rights and interests of all Canadians affected by such a change. The justices acknowledged that these negotiations would be very difficult and, quoting from the submission of Saskatchewan's attorney general, could only succeed if the participants were sensitive to the 'threads of a thousand acts of accommodation' that 'are the fabric of a nation.'[50] The Court was vague about the parties to the negotiations. At one point it said that 'the other provinces and the federal government' would have an obligation to negotiate.[51] But given that the Constitution gives Aboriginal peoples a right to participate in discussions of constitutional proposals affecting their rights and the existence of constitutionally recognized treaty relations with Aboriginal peoples in Quebec, it would surely be obligatory to include Aboriginal representatives in the negotiations.[52] Moreover, given the now well-established practice of including the northern territories in Canada's intergovernmental conferences, representatives of Nunavut, the Northwest Territories, and Yukon should also participate.[53] The Court did not speculate on what might happen if there were a breach of the duty to negotiate, other than to say that such a breach might 'undermine the legitimacy of a party's action' and 'have important ramifications at the international level.' [54]

As a crucial landmark in Canada's constitutional odyssey, the Supreme Court's decision in the Quebec Secession case ranks in importance with its 1981 decision in the Patriation case.[55] In going where no high court in a constitutional democracy has gone before – namely to the legal rules governing secession – it was also a landmark decision for worldwide constitutionalism. In the Quebec Secession reference, as in the Patriation reference, the Court's constitutional statecraft produced a compromise which gave half a loaf to each side. This was evident in the political reactions to the decision. Though this was one of those rare occasions when the governments of Canada and Quebec shared positive feelings about anything constitutional, they did so for entirely opposite reasons. Premier Bouchard regarded the Court's recognition of a duty to negotiate with Quebec following a successful referendum as 'comforting to the sovereignist project,' helping to provide the winning conditions for a referendum which he said would be held if his party won the upcoming provincial election.[56] Prime Minister Chrétien, on the other hand, said that while the decision shows that Canada is not a prison for Quebec, it establishes 'a barrier that you have to go over before secession.'[57]

In its decision, the Supreme Court went out of its way to rule itself out as future arbiter of questions that might arise on the conditions that trigger the duty to negotiate, namely what constitutes a 'a clear majority on a clear question in favour of secession.' This question, said the Court, 'is subject only to political evaluation' and by the 'political actors' not by the courts.[58] The following year, one of the political actors, the federal government, in a move to legislate its treatment of the question, introduced the Clarity Bill. Under this legislation the House of Commons will determine whether a question relating to secession that a province intends to submit to its voters in a referendum 'would result in a clear expression of the will of the population of a province on whether the province should cease to be part of Canada and become an independent state.'[59] If a question fails to meet this test, the Government of Canada will not enter into negotiations 'on the terms on which a province might cease to be part of Canada ...'[60] In the event that a secession referendum takes place on a question that passes the clarity test, again the House of Commons will decide whether a win for the 'yes' side is large enough to be treated as 'a clear expression of a will by a clear majority' to separate from Canada.[61]

The Clarity Act does not stipulate a numerical requirement but implies that a bare majority of just over 50 per cent would not be enough. In its final section, the Act recognizes that if a clear majority on a clear question have expressed their will to leave Canada, secession must still be accomplished by amending the Constitution of Canada, and negotiations leading to the amendment must consider 'the division of assets and liabilities, any changes to the borders of the province, the rights, interests and territorial claims of the Aboriginal peoples of Canada, and the protection of minority rights.'[62]

The Clarity Bill was opposed in the House by the Bloc Québécois and the Progressive Conservatives, and after a rough ride in the Senate it was enacted at the end of June 2000. It was bitterly opposed by the Bouchard government in Quebec, which had been returned to power in the November 1998 election, although losing to Jean Charest's Liberals in the popular vote. The Quebec government enacted its own legislative missile, the Quebec Self-Determination Act. While the Quebec Act, which became law on 5 December 2000, does not explicitly express an intention to change Quebec's status unilaterally, it does assert that 'the Quebec people has the inalienable right to freely decide the political regime and legal status of Quebec.'[63] The Act also stipulates that in a referendum on Quebec's future, a majority is constituted by 50 per cent of valid voters plus one.[64] Premier Bouchard's acceptance of the Supreme Court's ruling (and indeed his entire leadership of the Quebec sovereignist movement) suggests that after a referendum win (on his question) his preference would have been to try to negotiate a change in Quebec's status in a reconstructed, two-nation Canada, rather than undertake a radical and unilateral break. The federal Clarity Act does not preclude the federal government's entering into such negotiations, but it does deny any constitutional obligation to negotiate a sovereignty/association proposal.

As the first year of the new millennium ended, the governments of Canada and Quebec had donned legislative armour and seemed poised for another heavy round of constitutional warfare. But after a lot of sound and fury, the battle did not take place. Early in January 2001, one of the constitutional gladiators, Lucien Bouchard, shocked his party and surprised his province and the country by announcing his retirement from politics.[65] Bernard Landry, who had been deputy premier and succeeded Bouchard, appeared to be a much more hard-line sovereignist. But as Landry watched the polls and the continuing lack of support for straight-up independence, he shifted to the softer Bouchard line. When those 'winning conditions' that he, like Bouchard before him, kept looking for still did not materialize, he was in no hurry to call another sovereignty referendum. Finally, with the PQ government's five-year term running out, Landry had to face the voters. In the April 2003 Quebec election the PQ were soundly defeated by the Liberals, led by the former federal Conservative Cabinet Minister Jean Charest whose appeal was at least in part a promise to end the heavy constitutional wars.[66]

There may be intellectuals who are keen to continue a political conversation about the great questions of who we are and who we could be,[67] but most Quebecers, like most Canadians everywhere, have had enough of this stuff for the time being. This does not mean the end of constitutional politics in Canada, but it does mean a reversion to the much more traditional kind of constitutional politics that for well-established constitutional democracies is the normal way of adapting and changing their constitutional systems. This is the mode appropriate for a political society that treats its constitution in a manner congenial to the philosophy of Edmund Burke rather than John Locke.

At the beginning of this book I introduced Burke and Locke as representing two different approaches to constitutionalism.[68] For the Burkean, a constitution is thought of not as a single foundational document drawn up at a particular point in time containing all of a society's rules and principles of government, but as a collection of laws, institutions, and political practices that have passed the test of time and which have been found to serve the society's interests tolerably well. For constitutional systems understood in this organic way, change is incremental and pragmatic, and consent is mostly implicit. When one of the 'bits and pieces' – to use Daniel Elazar's phrase[69] – is not serving the people well, an effort is made to fix it. From the Lockean perspective, however, the Constitution is understood as a foundational document expressing the will of the people, reached through a democratic agreement, on the nature of the political community they have formed and how that community is to be governed. Constitution making in this tradition is a profoundly democratic act in which a people comes together to express its sovereign will. The central argument of this book has been that up until the 1960s constitutional politics in Canada was basically Burkean, but for a generation – from the late 1960s to the mid-1990s – the prevailing constitutional aspiration in Canada and in Quebec was for a Lockean constitutional moment. That effort failed, for the now obvious reason that in neither Canada nor Quebec was there – or is there – a population capable of acting as a sovereign people in a positive Lockean way.

The elements of a constitution, understood as an organic system, fall into four categories:

- the formal Constitution and amendments to it,
- organic statutes that are not formal amendments of the Constitution but create or alter major institutions of government or regulate the way constitutional rules are used,
- political practices that have hardened into constitutional conventions and political agreements about the proper use of governmental powers, and
- judicial decisions interpreting the formal Constitution and the principles underlying the constitutional system as a whole.

Even before the big mega constitutional game fizzled out, contrary to the view that after the failure of the Charlottetown Accord Canada was in a 'constitutional deep-freeze,' normal constitutional change was taking place in 'bits and pieces' of all four categories of Canada's constitutional system.

Jean Chrétien's 1996 Constitutional Amendments Act, the federal Clarity Act, and Quebec's Self-Determination Act must surely count as organic statutes, and the Supreme Court's decision in the Quebec Secession Reference clearly makes an important contribution to the Canadian Constitution. Amendments were also occurring through section 43 of the Constitution Act, 1982, which deals with changes in any provision in the Constitution of Canada that applies to one or more provinces but not all of the provinces. Section 43 amendments require only the support of the federal

Parliament and the legislatures of the province or provinces affected. Between 1993 and 1998 four such amendments were adopted.

In 1993, the New Brunswick Act was amended to give 'equality of status and equal rights and privileges' to that province's English and French communities.[70] This was a constitutional amendment that had been promised in the aborted Charlottetown Accord. It made New Brunswick Canada's only officially bicultural as well as bilingual province, a development very much in keeping with the historic position of New Brunswick's Acadien people, who constitute 34 per cent of the province's population. In that same year, Prince Edward Island's Terms of Union with Canada were altered to permit a bridge to replace a ferry-boat service as P.E.I.'s link to the mainland. This change, involving as it did a wrenching challenge to Islander identity, came after a hotly contested provincial referendum. In 1997, in response to a unanimous resolution of Quebec's National Assembly, the federal Parliament supported an amendment making the constitutional guarantee of denominational school rights, one of the key components of the Confederation compromise, inapplicable in Quebec.[71] This constitutional amendment was, in effect, an adjustment to the secularization of Quebec society and the desire of English and French Quebecers to organize schools around language communities rather than religious communities. Secularization was also evident in the important change made to Newfoundland's 1949 Terms of Union with Canada. Term 17 had granted six Christian denominations the right to publicly supported school systems. In 1998, after a political struggle that for Newfoundlanders, was of mega constitutional proportions, the constitutional guarantee of a costly and divisive educational system was replaced by a requirement that non-sectarian courses in religion be offered and religious observances in schools be permitted where requested by parents. The 1998 amendment replaced a 1997 amendment providing for a system of inter-denominational schools. It was approved by a 73 per cent majority in a provincial referendum.

While none of these section 43 amendments involved changes to the structure of the Canadian federation, each was important to the people of the provinces involved. Provincial constitutions in

Canada, in marked contrast to state constitutions in the United States, as Nelson Wiseman has observed, 'barely dwell in the world of the subconscious.'[72] Many of their most important terms are conditions on which a province became part of Canada, and on these matters the federal Parliament continues to play a role.[73] The spate of amendments in the 1990s adjusting foundational constitutional arrangements of individual provinces shows how patriation has allowed an element of flexibility to continue in Canada's constitutional system and displays yet another facet of Canadian diversity. It should also be noted that Quebec, which had rejected the patriation package, did not spurn this aspect of the new, all-Canadian, amending process.

The Charlottetown Accord, it will be remembered, attempted a massive restructuring of the Canadian federation by constitutional amendment. Since the failure of the Accord significant adjustments have been made in the operation of the federal division of powers. These changes have been brought about by informal political agreements rather than constitutional amendments, and several of those that have been achieved through the low-key processes of intergovernmental relations incorporate parts of the rejected Accord. The Chrétien government's enthusiastic engagement in this approach to federal restructuring was, in Harvey Lazar's words, 'less an explicit strategy for winning the hearts and minds of the people of Quebec than an approach that presumed that good government and good policy would be as attractive to Quebecers as it would to all other Canadians.'[74] This reworking of federal relations would also demonstrate that a freeze on formal constitutional restructuring need not result in 'status quo federalism.'

Economic motives were as important as political considerations in steering this process of federal renewal by informal constitutional means. Many of the changes were motivated by the federal government's effort to reduce its staggering fiscal deficit and by new pressures from the global economy. One of the most important examples of the latter is the intergovernmental Agreement on Internal Trade (AIT) reached in July 1994, just a few months before the Parti Québécois returned to power in Quebec.[75]

Through the era of mega constitutional politics, the federal government under both Trudeau and Mulroney had tried to strengthen the economic union aspect of Confederation by amending the free trade clause (section 121) in Canada's founding Constitution. That section sets down the principle that 'Articles of the Growth, Produce or Manufacture of any one province ... be admitted free into each of the other provinces.' Section 121 has been virtually a dead letter of the Constitution. The courts (and Canadian business) have given it very little attention. In the modern period, decisions of the Supreme Court of Canada have treated the federal Trade and Commerce power very generously, making federal jurisdiction over international and interprovincial trade virtually a plenary power. Federal governments, however, have been too timid to use this power to dismantle the many ways in which the provinces have restricted free trade across their borders. During the patriation round of negotiations, the Trudeau government failed to get the provinces to agree to a strengthening of section 121. A much more watered-down constitutional commitment to strengthen Canada as an 'economic union' was a casualty of the Charlottetown Accord debacle. Eventually, the embarrassing possibility that Canada's internal market might be more restrictive of trade than the external markets which NAFTA and GATT were opening up for the country induced federal and provincial leaders to enter into an agreement to lower internal trade barriers.[76]

The Agreement on Internal Trade has been a big disappointment to economic liberals. It leaves ample scope for provincial governments to restrict access to provincial markets by pursuing 'legitimate policy objectives,' and it lacks effective monitoring and enforcement mechanisms. Still, AIT has contributed to Canada's economic integration in a number of areas, including government procurement, labour mobility, and the harmonization of professional and occupational standards. It represents about as much as can be achieved through the consensual ways in which Canadians have come to operate their federation.[77] For the foreseeable future, the Canadian economic union is likely to be fostered more by the economic constitution of the new global order and the discipline of membership in the World Trade Organization than by intergovernmental agreements or reform of the Canadian constitution.

Intergovernmental agreements were the core of the soft part – Plan A – of the federal government's constitutional strategy ad-

vanced under Stéphane Dion's leadership after the Quebec referendum. Of course, the instruments of this process, political agreements between and among governments, are not in the formal
sense constitutional amendments. But if the constitutional system is
understood in the larger Burkean sense as the understandings and
agreements that hold a political society together, this emergent
system of accords must be seen as having constitutional significance.[78] From the death of the Charlottetown Accord to the present
day, the intergovernmental process that has been unfolding has
had three general characteristics: first, on balance, and particularly
at the beginning, it has tended to decentralize power in a federation that is already highly decentralized; second, in intent it has
been almost religiously symmetrical – respecting the principle of
provincial equality and not offering deals to one province that are
denied to others; and third, it has been thoroughly elitist, government driven, and largely out of sight politically.

A process of federal 'rebalancing' with the first two of these
characteristics reflected what for a time was the prevailing political
climate in Canada. In the 1990s, the most dynamic challenges to
the political status quo came from the right-of-centre Reform Party,
the only party in English Canada that opposed the Charlottetown
Accord, and from similarly oriented Conservative governments led
by Mike Harris in Ontario and Ralph Klein in Alberta – all of whom
were strongly committed to shrinking government in general and
the federal government in particular. Devolving responsibilities to
the provinces, though not aimed at mollifying Quebec, also fitted
in well with a strategy of not provoking Quebec. But the third
characteristic – the quiet, behind-closed-doors nature of the intergovernmental process – was at odds with the growing unease in the
country about the need to address the 'democratic deficit' in Canadian governance. Roger Gibbins and Katherine Harmsworth warned
that if reforming the federation 'becomes the fodder for intergovernmental discussions rather than public debate, there is some risk
that the final product will face public repudiation should Canadians find the opportunity to express themselves.'[79]

The devolutionary dimension of federal rebalancing has been
primarily a matter of the federal government agreeing to stop
spending money on issues that are mainly if not entirely under

provincial jurisdiction.[80] Thus Ottawa largely withdrew from the sectors of mining and forestry, recreation, and tourism – all of which it had been prepared to do as part of the Charlottetown Accord. In other policy fields, where it is recognized that both levels of government have significant roles to play, progress was made in better defining functions and coordinating activities. A 1998 agreement on harmonizing environmental policy is a prime example. To implement Prime Minister Chrétien's promise to withdraw from job training, the federal government negotiated bilateral agreements with the provinces and territories (though not with the Harris government in Ontario) to enable them either to assume full responsibility for training measures financed by the Employment Insurance Fund or to develop co-management schemes with the federal government. Though devolution of this economy-related aspect of education may have contributed to more harmonious federal-provincial relations, it may also have adverse effects on Canada's global competitiveness. Gordon Di Giacomo points out how provincializing training for employment may hinder the development of policies for industrial sectors that cross provincial boundaries.[81] With unilateral initiatives such as the Canada Millennium Scholarship Foundation, Canada Research Chairs, Canadian Foundation for Innovation contributions to university infrastructure, and most recently establishment of the Canadian Council on Learning,[82] Ottawa has not been fastidious about treating other dimensions of education as exclusive provincial responsibilities.[83] In the 'knowledge age,' no federation can afford to do without effective national policies to promote higher education, research, and the learning skills of its citizenry.

A major move in the informal restructuring of the federation during this era of constitutional normalcy was the signing – with considerable fanfare – of the Social Union Framework Agreement (SUFA), in February 1999.[84] The 'social union' was a bit of constitutional hype borrowed – along with the 'economic union' – from the Charlottetown Accord. Only its elite inventors and a handful of academics had a clue what it meant. The 'Framework to Improve the Social Union for Canadians' targeted areas of social policy largely under provincial jurisdiction – education, health, and social welfare – in which the federal government, using its superior taxing capacity and a spending power subject to few constitutional constraints, had come to play a leadership role in building the Canadian welfare state. Over the years the principal opposition to Ottawa's interventions in these fields came from Quebec. The idea behind the Social Union was not to curtail federal involvement in social policy but to manage it in a more cooperative and consensual manner through a Council of Ministers.

The Social Union Agreement is a classical Canadian compromise: the legitimacy of federal spending in areas of provincial responsibility is accepted, but on two conditions – first, that a majority of provinces approve any *new* federal social policy initiatives that are to be funded through intergovernmental transfers, and second, that a government which already has a program in the area covered by the federal initiative can receive its province's share of the new federal funding for a related provincial policy that meets 'Canada-wide objectives.' The Agreement also deals with federal initiatives that distribute funds directly to individual citizens or organizations (for instance, the Millennium Scholarship Foundation). Under SUFA, the provinces must be consulted three months before such programs are introduced so that they have a chance to influence their design or offer alternatives. While these restrictions on federal spending went further than those that a Quebec Liberal government had insisted be included in the Meech Lake Accord, they did not go far enough for Lucien Bouchard's PQ government. SUFA was signed by the federal government and all the provinces except Quebec,[85] which insisted on maintaining its special status – de facto if not de jure. Writing nearly five years after the agreement, Harvey Lazar reports that although public awareness of SUFA is virtually nil, it has played a role in the effective implementation of several developments in social policy, including the National Child Benefit and some social housing initiatives.[86]

While SUFA has opened up new avenues for federal-provincial cooperation, it has not removed the main source of federal-provincial conflict – money. The provinces continue to press the federal government for more money or tax room for health, education, and urban problems they view as primarily their responsibility. But as the federal government emerged from an era of deficit reduction to one of budget surpluses, it has shown no enthusiasm for relinquishing its fiscal leverage to shape policy nationally in critical areas of social policy. Ottawa has also been under pressure from the mayors of Canadian cities to deal directly with them on pressing transit and housing needs. These federal inclinations were reinforced by the Romanow Royal Commission on the Future of Health Care, which reported in November 2002. A key political finding of the Commission was that Canadians have come to regard a universally accessible, publicly funded health care system as a valued component of their Canadian identity. Romanow recommended the establishment of a Health Council of Canada, to be made up of representatives of the public, the health sector, and governments.[87] The Council's purpose would be to provide national leadership in monitoring and improving the performance of health care systems across the country. Needless to say, provincial and territorial governments have been much more enthusiastic about obtaining more federal money than supporting a national institution to assess how effectively that money is spent. The stiffest opposition to a national Health Council came not from Quebec but from Alberta, whose government is strongly committed ideologically to expanding the private sector of health care. The Canada Health Council announced by Health Minister Anne McLellan at the end of 2003 is to consist of a federally appointed chair, representatives of the provinces and territories and an equal number of health-care experts and members of the public.[88] Quebec, maintaining its special status, is not represented on the Council but has agreed to share information with it. Alberta's chair is empty and its government, for the time being, uncooperative.

The one major collective initiative of the provinces in these efforts at reforming the federation was the establishment in 2003 of the Council of the Federation.[89] The impetus for this initiative came from Quebec, a Quebec now led by a Liberal premier committed to renewing rather than breaking up the Canadian federation.[90] The Council of the Federation is reminiscent of an initiative of another Quebec premier, Honoré Mercier, who organized the Interprovincial Conference of 1887.[91] The members of the Council are the leaders of the provincial and territorial governments. The federal government is not a member, though the Council hopes to meet annually with the federal Prime Minister and is generally seen as an instrument for coordinating provincial and territorial relations with Ottawa, particularly on fiscal issues. Cynics will regard the Council as a way of orchestrating the 'piling on' attacks on the federal treasury that are an annual ritual of federal-provincial affairs in Canada. But it could also be a useful means through which Quebec re-engages as a constructive member of Confederation.[92] There are many ways in which members of a horizontal federal council can learn from one another, establish best practices, harmonize and coordinate their policies, and perhaps even deal effectively with some of the interprovincial trade problems that have not been resolved through the Agreement on Internal Trade.

It is important to note that the Council of the Federation has thirteen members – the ten provinces, plus the three northern territories, Yukon, the Northwest Territories and Nunavut, the new territory of the Eastern Arctic inaugurated in 1999. Inclusion of the northern territories as full members of the Council consolidates the practice of including them as regular participants in Canadian intergovernmental affairs. This is a good example of how a political practice consistently adhered to by the political leadership of the country can crystallize into a constitutional convention. In this case, custom and convention provide handier constitutional instruments than formal constitutional amendments for dealing with the status of territories whose populations total just two-thirds that of Canada's smallest province, Prince Edward Island. As Gordon Robertson pointed out some years ago, giving jurisdictions with such small populations full provincial status in a constitutional amending process which is already something of a straitjacket might be a difficult pill to swallow.[93] Indeed, as one reviews the ebb and flow of power, policy, and ideology in the Canadian federation's operation over the past decade, it is difficult to conclude that Canada would be better off if its governments had tried to write the changes that have taken place into the concrete of formal constitutional amendments.

In this period of organic and piecemeal constitution development, some progress has been made towards achieving a more consensual, less colonial relationship of the Canadian state with Aboriginal peoples. Progress in this direction, however, has not been steady and is far from complete. For Canada, and for the world, working out a decolonized relationship of Indigenous peoples with the states within which they are embedded, even as we reach the end of the United Nations' Decade of Indigenous Peoples in 2004, remains very much a work in progress.[94] In Canada, the constitutional changes that have taken place have been achieved not through a grand set of amendments to the Constitution such as those that formed part of the Charlottetown Accord, but through agreements of individual Aboriginal peoples or groups of peoples with the Crown, a Crown now represented in Aboriginal affairs by federal and provincial governments. For Aboriginal peoples, the Charlottetown process, as we saw, was an alienating experience, and their leaders and their communities have shown no interest in returning to the mega constitutional table. Their preferred approach is that recommended in the 1996 Final Report of the Royal Commission on Aboriginal Peoples – namely 'people to people, nation to nation' relationships based on the principles of recognition, respect, sharing and responsibility.[95]

A year before the Royal Commission reported, the Government of Canada announced that it was prepared to recognize, without any litigation, that 'the inherent right to self-government' was one of the 'existing aboriginal rights' recognized and affirmed in section 35 of the Constitution Act, 1982.[96] The government reiterated this position in its official response to the Royal Commission report.[97] But, of course, the government's understanding of what the inherent right means is quite different from Aboriginal understandings of that concept. For Aboriginal peoples, as their views are summarized in the Royal Commission report, self-government and self-determination have to do with the responsibility they have from their creator for looking after their societies and the lands, waters, and creatures that sustain them.[98] Authority of this kind may be denied by others but cannot be taken away or granted to them by other governments or authorities. The federal government's approach, however, continued to be one of devolving powers to Aboriginal peoples rather than making room for Aboriginal peoples to recover control over their own societies according to their own evolving traditions.[99] At the outset it tried to restrict in a predetermined colonialist manner the subject matters on which it was prepared to negotiate self-government agreements. Since 1995, a large section of the Department of Indian Affairs and Northern Development has been devoted to 'implementing the inherent right' through negotiated agreements with Aboriginal peoples. But given the very different starting points of most Aboriginal communities and governments on the one hand, and of federal and provincial governments (as well as many of the citizens who elect these governments) on the other, progress in 'implementing the inherent right' has been slow and difficult.

Considerable progress has been made in the northern territories, where self-government negotiations have been woven into the settlement of land claims, and the absence of governments with full provincial status means that negotiations can be essentially bilateral. The creation of Nunavut, a new, self-governing territory carved out of the Northwest Territories and encompassing the entire Eastern Arctic (nearly a quarter of Canada's land mass), is the most spectacular development.[100] Nunavut is the result of a 1993 Agreement between Canada and representatives of the 22,000 Inuit people who constitute 85 per cent of the region's population. In the Agreement, ratified by 69 per cent of the eligible voters, the Inuit agreed to surrender native title to all of the land in the region. In return, ownership of 350,000 square kilometres (approximately 11 per cent of the total) selected by the Inuit as vital to their interests was vested in an Inuit land corporation. The Agreement also included a commitment by Canada to establish a Nunavut Government and Legislature with jurisdiction over most fields of policy. To afford time for the Inuit to prepare for taking the leading role in this new territorial government, Nunavut did not become operational until April 1999. While the governmental institutions of Nunavut were created by an Act of Parliament, the commitment to establish these institutions is entrenched in the 1993 Agreement which, as a modern treaty, has constitutional status under section 35 of the Constitution Act, 1982. The Inuit people, who had not developed a traditional system of structured governmental authority, were happy to adopt an essentially Westminster model of government, with a prime minister and cabinet responsible to a one-person-one-vote elected legislature.[101] They have put their own distinctive stamp on the operation of this system by avoiding the development of political parties, by making Inuktitut an official language, and by decentralizing as much of government as possible to the small hamlets dotted across their vast territory. The establishment of Nunavut is as close as Canada has yet come to facilitating Indigenous self-determination.

Elsewhere in the north, the process of accommodating Indigenous self-determination in territorial development has been slower and more complex. In Yukon, after many years of negotiations, the Council of Yukon Indians representing that territory's 6,000 native people (20 per cent of Yukon's population) entered into a treaty-like Agreement with the governments of Canada and Yukon on land and self-government. Under the Agreement, in addition to ownership of selected parcels of land, traditional harvesting rights, and cash compensation for surrendered lands,[102] each of the fourteen First Nations represented by the Council can negotiate agreements to assume a range of governmental responsibilities in its homeland area. As of 2001, four had done so.[103]

Less progress has been made in the third northern territory. Even with its eastern portion severed to form Nunavut, the Northwest Territories is still a vast jurisdiction, running the length of the Mackenzie River Valley from the Alberta/British Columbia border to the Beaufort Sea. A diverse group of Aboriginal peoples, including the Inuvialuit in the Beaufort Delta area, the Sahtu, Gwich'in, Tlicho, Deh Cho, Akaitcho, Lutselk'e, and Métis peoples, constitute approximately half of the territory's 37,000 people and nearly all of its population outside the principal urban centres of Yellowknife, Hay River, and Inuvik. Up until 1995, the federal government was willing to negotiate agreements only with peoples willing to surrender Aboriginal title claims in exchange for ownership of parcels of land, cash compensation, and a co-management role in traditional harvesting, but no self-government rights. In the 1980s and early 1990s, the Inuvialuit people in the Beaufort Delta, and the Sahtu Dene and Métis, and the Gwich'in Tribal Council along the lower Mackenzie entered into Agreements with Canada on this basis.[104] It was not until August 2003 that the first modern Aboriginal government was established in the Northwest Territories, when Prime Minister Chrétien flew to Rae, northwest of Yellowknife, to sign an Agreement giving the Tlicho, or Dogrib, nation control over 39,000 square kilometres of the lands and

waters between Great Slave Lake and Great Bear Lake.[105] The
Tlicho Government will have extensive law-making powers over
land use and local community affairs and a share of resource
revenues in an area of the Northwest Territories larger than Belgium that includes two diamond mines. Two years earlier, Canada
and the Deh Cho Dene, whose traditional lands cover a 100,000-
square-kilometre area in the southwest corner of the territories,
signed a Framework Agreement to enter into negotiations to clarify
treaty rights in the area and establish a 'public government based
upon Deh Cho First Nations laws and customs and other Canadian
laws' to be 'the primary government for the delivery of programs
and services to residents of the Deh Cho territory within the Northwest Territories.'[106] Work on Aboriginal self-government has been
proceeding in parallel with efforts to restructure the Government
of the Northwest Territories, a government in which Aboriginal
people hold a majority of the leadership positions. The most likely
outcome, still some years away, is a federally structured system of
government in which power is shared between a central territorial
government and governments resulting from agreements with re-
gionally based Aboriginal peoples. This will not be an easy or
inexpensive system to operate but it may well be one that makes
sense – constitutionally – in a territory with a population so evenly
balanced between urban-based non-Aboriginal people and Aboriginal peoples who are rebuilding their communities in traditional
country.

South of the sixtieth parallel the major breakthrough in making
room for Aboriginal self-government was the signing of the Nisga'a
Agreement in 1998 by representatives of the Nisga'a, British Columbia, and Canadian governments.[107] The Nisga'a Final Agreement is the first modern Canadian treaty covering land and
self-government which in its entirety has formal constitutional status. It is the culmination of many decades of struggle by the Nisga'a
people of the Nass Valley to gain recognition by Canada and British
Columbia of ownership of their land and of their right to govern
themselves.[108] As we noted in chapter 7, it was the Supreme Court's
recognition of the native title rights of the Nisga'a in the 1973
Calder case that led to the Trudeau government's decision to
launch a modern treaty process. It was not until the mid-1990s

when the federal government agreed to give constitutional recognition to self-government rights and the British Columbia government agreed to join the treaty process that an agreement was finally possible.[109] The Agreement recognizes Nisga'a ownership of just over 8 per cent of the lands they claimed. Much of the remainder was subject to overlapping claims of other First Nations. The part that the Nisga'a secured under their own ownership includes the areas where their villages are located and where they carry on forestry, farming, fishing, and other essential economic activities. The governmental system recognized in the Agreement is built along traditional lines, and though it is not a public government like Nunavut's, it recognizes the rights of non-Nisga'a residents to participate in areas of governance that 'directly and significantly affect them.'[110] The Agreement recognizes the authority of a Nisga'a system of government and its law-making powers over a wide range of matters, including public order, environmental protection, education, health, social welfare, language, and culture. On most subjects, federal and provincial laws prevail over conflicting Nisga'a law. But in matters essential to their collective life and identity, including management of their own lands, their constitution, citizenship in the Nisga'a nation, and the maintenance and fostering of their language, and culture, if there is any conflict with federal or provincial laws, the Nisga'a laws prevail. This means, in effect, that through the Agreement, the Nisga'a are recognized as having a share of sovereign law-making authority in Canada.

The Nisga'a Agreement, like the negotiated settlement of most constitutional disputes, was a compromise, and as such it was bound to attract criticism on both the Aboriginal and non-Aboriginal sides.[111] It was not easy for the Nisga'a to accept an Agreement in which they abandoned claims to much of their traditional country as well as many elements of their sovereignty as 'the full and final settlement in respect of the aboriginal rights, including aboriginal title, in Canada of the Nisga'a Nation.'[112] In the Nisga'a ratification referendum, the Agreement was approved by only 51 per cent of the 2,384 eligible Nisga'a voters.[113] But what was much too little for many Nisga'a was much too much for opposition political leaders in British Columbia and critics in the right-wing national press. The acknowledgment of even a sliver of sovereign law-making powers to be kept by an Aboriginal nation stuck in the craw of these critics. Gordon Campbell, Opposition leader in the British Columbia legislature at the time of the Agreement but soon to become provincial premier, challenged the Agreement in the courts on the grounds that it unconstitutionally recognized the supremacy of Nisga'a law in a few areas. Campbell's challenge was rejected in a landmark ruling by Justice Williamson of British Columbia's Supreme Court that the forming of Canada in 1867 did not extinguish the right of Aboriginal peoples to govern their own societies.[114]

Demands to meet the requirement in B.C. law that a referendum be held before its legislature deals with a constitutional amendment were met by the not very convincing argument that the Nisga'a Agreement was not an amendment of the Constitution of Canada. While in a narrow sense it can be said that the Agreement does not change anything in Canada's Constitution, it certainly adds to it. The argument against ratifying treaties with Aboriginal peoples by provincewide referenda that is much more in keeping with the underlying principles of Canada's constitutional system is that the fate of a small Aboriginal nation should not depend on the vote of an electorate numbering in the millions. It took the application of closure by the NDP government and a lengthy debate in the Canadian Senate to complete the ratification process in 2000. The Nisga'a Agreement is a significant achievement for Canada – and for the world – in Indigenous self-determination. But it has not led quickly to other settlements. For many Aboriginal peoples in Canada and for much of the non-Aboriginal community – and for opposite reasons – it was not seen at the time as an attractive model to emulate.

Much of the legal foundation of these negotiations with Aboriginal peoples came from decisions of the Supreme Court of Canada as it adjudicated disputes about what it meant for Canada in the Constitution Act, 1982, to recognize and affirm 'the existing aboriginal and treaty rights of the aboriginal peoples of Canada.'[115] For Aboriginal peoples, the unfolding jurisprudence of the Supreme Court on the meaning of their rights has been a roller-coaster ride. It started off quite favourably with the Supreme Court calling for 'a generous, liberal interpretation' of Aboriginal rights in the 1990 Sparrow case.[116] But even in this decision upholding the Musqueam people's right to fish for salmon in traditional ways with nets larger than those allowed under federal regulations, the Court made all Aboriginal and treaty rights subject to infringement by government actions which the courts find to be justifiable. Then, in a series of three cases decided in 1996, known as the Van der Peet trilogy,[117] the Court's majority adhered to a 'frozen rights' doctrine which threatened to reduce the constitutional rights of Aboriginal peoples to the bundle of activities that judges view as integral to the distinctive culture of an Aboriginal people at the time of its first contact with Europeans. That same year, in Badger, the Court seemed to drain much of the meaning from the Crown's fiduciary obligation[118] to protect the interests of Aboriginal peoples, and weakened treaty rights by not questioning the federal governments unilateral extinguishments of historic treaty rights.[119] The Supreme Court returned the following year with its decision in Delgamuukw, giving a wide interpretation to the scope of aboriginal title. 'What aboriginal title confers,' pronounced Chief Justice Lamer, 'is the right to the land itself.'[120] The constitutional entitlement of native peoples to recognition of their responsibility for ancestral lands and waters includes the right to use and develop sub-surface minerals. In fleshing out the meaning of native title the Court stepped away from its frozen rights doctrine and acknowledged that native societies are free to develop traditional land as they see fit so long as they do so in a way that does not undermine their historic bonds with the land. As is virtually always the case with the justice rendered to Aboriginal peoples in settler courts,[121] the Court's decision in Delgamuukw had a bitter-sweet quality. Native title is open to infringements by federal and provincial governments for 'objectives of compelling and substantial interest to (the) community as a whole ...' although in the case of a serious infringement the Crown's fiduciary obligation 'may require' not just consultation but 'the full consent of an aboriginal nation.'[122] The Supreme Court was clearly trying to encourage the settlement of land and self-government issues through negotiation rather than litigation, but by arming each side with such powerful verbal markers, its decision, at least in the short run, may well have had the opposite effect.

As a backlash of opinion built up against the partial success of

Aboriginal peoples at the negotiating table and in the courts, the Supreme Court began to show signs of sensitivity to loudly expressed popular opinion. This was most evident in its response to protests over its ruling in the 1999 Marshall case, that federal fishing regulations contravened rights of the Maliseet and Mi'kmaq peoples secured in eighteenth-century treaties with the Crown.[123] Confronted with an outbreak of communal violence between native and non-native fishers and angry attacks in the section of the press already stirred up by opposition to the Nisga'a Agreement, the Court wrote a second opinion (Marshall No. 2) explaining its refusal to rehear the case, but placing particular emphasis on the over-arching sovereign authority of the federal government to set justifiable limits on all Aboriginal rights, including treaty rights.[124]

The federal government itself seemed to sway with the political winds under the Chrétien government's last Minister of Indian Affairs, Robert Nault. Frustrated with the slow progress being made at the over eighty 'tables' where land and self-government issues were under negotiation, Nault tried to revert back to legislating solutions. The centrepiece of his 'suite' of legislative initiatives was the First Nations Governance Act designed to provide the hundreds of bands subject to the Indian Act with 'more effective tools of governance on an interim basis pending the negotiation and implementation of the inherent right to self-government.'[125] Nault and his cabinet colleagues soon found that this attempted reversion to colonial rule over native peoples would be met with stiff resistance. Aboriginal Canadians, like most Canadians, are concerned about the quality of their governments – their integrity and capacity for serving people's needs – but they are not willing to have the governance of their communities repaired by governments purporting to be their moral superiors.

In all parts of Canada, Aboriginal peoples have been working for some time to improve the way their communities are governed. In many instances, a central issue is to identify the collective 'self' which can provide the agency for exercising the right to self-determination. Nearly two centuries of colonial oppression fragmented many of the Amerindian nations. Indeed, one of the strategic aims of the Indian Act was to break up the Indian tribes into small reserve-based bands. Among the Inuit and Métis peoples, as well as among the First Nations, a good deal of 'nation-building' has been going on and must continue in order to constitute viable political societies capable of providing the public services needed by their people and of interacting effectively with other governments. A wide range of Aboriginal parties are at various stages of negotiating self-government arrangements. These include traditional Amerindian nations such as those participating in the revived British Columbia Treaty Process, treaty-based alliances of First Nations such as operate in Manitoba, new confederations of old nations such as the Anishinabek in Ontario, sections of larger nations such as the various Dene peoples in the NWT, province-wide groupings such as form Saskatchewan's Tribal Council and the Native Council of Nova Scotia, various Métis communities, and new political communities built by the Inuit people of Labrador and Northern Quebec, as well as some of the 'First Nation' bands operating under the Indian Act.

The constitutional process taking place through these various self-government negotiations, and sometimes independently of them, is Burkean in two senses. First, rather than being based on governmental arrangements pre-fabricated by officials in a distant capital, it is an organic process that draws on each people's own stock of collective wisdom and new ways of doing things learned through education and participation in the political life of Canada. Second, the process has practical ends in view – better provision of the goods, services, and opportunities people need to live secure, healthy, and fulfilling lives. Perhaps the most important lesson that the Royal Commission on Aboriginal Peoples had for Canadians is that improving the living conditions of the indigenous population and restoring indigenous peoples' capacity for looking after their societies and the resources that sustain them, far from being alternatives, are complementary dimensions of reform. There is no way of knowing where this process of constitutional evolution is going, but if it enables Indigenous people to give expression in contemporary Canadian law to values embedded in their traditional regimes, it could, as John Borrows shows, do much to enrich the constitutional culture of Canada.[126]

As issues of national unity have receded from the everyday political life of the country, Canadians have turned their constitutional attention to the quality of their democratic institutions. This is surely another benefit of Canada's return to constitutional normalcy. For, though Canada never experienced a golden age of democracy when its parliamentary bodies functioned in an ideal manner, tendencies in the operation of its parliamentary system that centralize power and minimize the role of citizens have become a major source of disquiet. Leading political scientists and newspaper columnists have critically analysed the transformation of Cabinet government into a system of party government in which the prime minister or premier and a small group of political advisers manage government and control policy-making.[127] It is a system in which the line between politics and administration is blurred, the power of ministers accountable to Parliament is dwarfed by that of faceless political aides close to the first minister, and in which the enforcement of strict party discipline undermines the capacity of elected legislatures to serve as deliberative bodies. The legitimacy of this domination of government by the leadership of the governing party is further reduced by a first-past-the-post electoral system in which the party that governs rarely garners even half the popular vote. One sign of public disaffection with these trends is a marked decline in voter turnout: only 54 per cent of the voting-age population turned out for the 2000 federal election – a 21 per cent decline since 1988.[128] The message has been heard by politicians. Two who came to power in the latter part of 2003, Dalton McGinty in Ontario and Paul Martin in Ottawa, both campaigned on promises to tackle the 'democratic deficit.'[129]

Fortunately, the democratic deficit can be tackled without resorting to the difficult process of formal constitutional amendment. Under section 44 of the Constitution Act, Parliament through ordinary legislation can pass laws 'in relation to the executive Government of Canada or the Senate and House of Commons.'[130] The only exceptions are the monarchical provisions of the Constitution, provisions governing the representation of provinces in each house of Parliament, the powers of the Senate and the method of selecting Senators, and the use of Canada's two official languages. Provincial legislatures have a similar power under section 45 'to make laws amending the constitution of the province,' subject to the exception (noted earlier) of their terms of union with

Canada, the office of lieutenant-governor, and language rights. Thus, much can be done through ordinary legislation, at both the federal and provincial levels, to change how parliamentary governments operate in Canada.

Not even legislation is needed to reform the internal functioning of parliamentary bodies. Through changes in the rules and political practices governing legislative bodies progress is already being made in reducing executive domination of the legislature. Backbench members of the government caucus gain more freedom to speak their mind, without jeopardizing responsible government, when fewer bills are treated as confidence measures. Legislatures fulfil their deliberative function in a less partisan, more independent manner when their committees are free to choose their own leadership. Backbench members of the government caucus appear and feel less like 'trained seals' when (as is now the case in Alberta and British Columbia) they have significant opportunities to influence government policy. If government leaders are sincere about reducing the 'democratic deficit' they will be open to much more change of this kind. What is needed more than anything else is a change in attitude, above all on the part of the leaders of political parties, who must recognize that they are responsible to the parliament the people have elected and that the policies by which we are governed should emerge from the cut and thrust of parliamentary debate. Reforms of this kind that, to use Churchill's word, aim at 'revivifying' parliamentary institutions will likely have more general appeal than radical moves away from parliamentary government to direct democracy such as recalling elected members through petitions or deciding policy issues by popular referenda.

A somewhat more radical reform being contemplated by several provincial governments, including the newly elected McGinty government in Ontario, is to have fixed four-year terms for legislatures. The Constitution requires only a maximum term of five years for both the House of Commons and provincial legislatures.[131] Under the system of responsible government Canada has inherited from Great Britain, prime ministers and premiers whose parties have a majority in the legislature can ask the Crown's representative to dissolve the legislature and hold an election whenever they think it is politically convenient.[132] Legislation that removes this power and requires elections at a fixed time would simply be a further instance of guarding against the autocratic use of monarchical powers that have fallen under the control of political leaders. I hazard a guess that Edmund Burke would applaud such a constitutional development. Those who might question attributing constitutional significance to such a change should bear in mind that the rules and principles that constitutionalized Canada's monarchical executive and established responsible government have all developed through informal constitutional conventions.

Headlines in Canadian newspapers and some recent book titles give the impression that the biggest constitutional change in Canada over the last decade or so has been the supplanting of parliamentary government with 'rule by the judges.'[133] This fear-mongering about a Canadian juristocracy borders on the hysterical. Readers of this book will know that from the beginning of Canada's constitutional odyssey the country's highest courts have had an important, although not a dominating or dictatorial influence, on the country's constitutional development. Since 1982 the power of judges has undoubtedly increased as the judiciary has been called upon to play an important role in interpreting aboriginal and treaty rights, and the rights and freedoms enshrined in the Charter.[134] Still, the judiciary's role in most areas of public policy – fiscal policy, health, social welfare, education, environment, economic development, transportation, defence, foreign trade, and foreign relations – remains marginal. In adjudicating disputes under the Charter of Rights it does play a leading role in criminal justice policy, including police powers, and in a number of moral controversies arising from social change. Abortion, euthanasia, and same-sex marriage are leading examples. On all of these issues, the judges' thinking about the scope and meaning of Charter rights and possible justifications for limiting these rights should be important contributions to how we deal with these issues, but not the last word. The framers of the Charter of Rights were wise enough to insert a clause[135] – a very Burkean clause – that leaves with elected legislatures the responsibility of reviewing the reasoning of the judges on these contentious issues about the meaning and limits of rights.[136] Unfortunately, Canada's political leaders have not been able to accept that responsibility.[137] They have given judicial decisions interpreting rights and reasonable limits on rights an unchallengeable, binding authority that they should not have. If, under the Charter, Canadians experience elements of a juristocracy, they should recognize that it is self-imposed and removable by a change in attitude. It might also help if Parliament were given a responsible role in the appointment of Supreme Court justices.[138]

The one structural change in the institutions of Canadian democracy whose time appears to have come is electoral reform. Canada, along with Great Britain and India, remains one of the few parliamentary democracies in the world with a first-past-the-post electoral system. In Canada, as in Great Britain, there is growing pressure to adopt a system that will produce legislatures – and governments – that more accurately reflect the political preferences of voters. Electoral reform is most likely to occur first at the provincial level. The Quebec government is committed to introducing a modified proportional voting system before the next election, the British Columbia and Ontario governments are engaged in public consultations on electoral form, and the New Brunswick and P.E.I. governments have established inquiries into voting system alternatives.[139] At the national level, the Law Commission of Canada has carried out a national consultation on electoral reform,[140] and there is strong support for proportional representation across the spectrum of opposition parties in the House of Commons and growing interest in the Liberal caucus.[141] The approach to reform which is most likely to win support in Canada is a 'mixed system' that retains constituency-based MPs but adds MPs elected through party lists to ensure that the portion of seats held by each party reflects their portion of the popular vote. The party lists can be on a national basis, as in New Zealand,[142] or on a regional basis, as recommended by Lord Jenkins's Royal Commission for Britain.[143] Changes in the way Canadians elect their parliamentary representatives can be achieved through ordinary legislation at both the federal and provincial levels. Indeed, one group of Canadians is arguing in the courts that the existing electoral system is unconstitutional because it denies supporters of small parties their right to 'equal benefit of the law' under the Canadian Charter of Rights and Freedoms.[144]

In the next lap of their constitutional odyssey Canadians can undertake and carry out considerable reform of their parliamentary institutions without resort to the tortuous instrument of formal constitutional amendment. But what about that one institution of parliamentary government which is just about everyone's first candidate for reform – the Canadian Senate? The Senate today is virtually the only upper chamber in the democratic world that is an appointed body with legislative power virtually equal in law to that of the elected lower house.[145] Many would regard it as the most flawed part of the constitutional handiwork of the Fathers of Confederation. The most popular reform proposals are to abolish the Senate or convert it to a directly elected body. As we saw in the previous chapter, the Charlottetown Accord proposed a 'triple E' Senate – elected, equal representation for each province, and an effective role in legislation (but less than the Senate has now). And as we also saw, the Charlottetown Accord was rejected by a majority of Canadians. Anyone who thinks that the 'triple-E' Senate should be salvaged from the wreckage of Charlottetown and offered up to Canadians again should think twice. It would take a truly heroic set of leaders to convince Quebecers that Quebec is just a province like the rest, or westerners that Quebec is more than that, or all Canadians to hold back on other constitutional reforms and deal only with the Senate. We are not likely to see a prime minister or premiers willing to take up this challenge in the foreseeable future.

If the Senate is to become a more respected and useful component of parliamentary government in Canada, reform will have to take place through those small 'c' forms of constitutional change being used to reform the elected branch. A recently published book on the Senate by David Smith opens up a new way of thinking about reforming the Senate through such means.[146] Smith challenges those who consider that the Senate can be reformed only by making it an elected body to let 'form follow function' and think first about the purpose of a second legislative body before deciding what form it should take. If we think of bicameralism in the Canadian context, Smith argues, the Senate's purpose should be understood as being to complement not challenge the House of Commons. It was never designed to represent provincial governments but to bring to the deliberation of national issues and legislation a depth of analysis, a range of experience and measured judgment, and a balance of regional outlooks lacking in the highly partisan exchanges of the elected chamber. Internal reforms of the Senate should be aimed at better performance of this deliberative role.

But what about the manner in which Senators are selected? One might agree with Smith that an election conducted by rival political parties is not the best way to create a second chamber that will function as a useful complement rather than a competitor to the House of Commons. But an appointing system which appears to be used primarily for rewarding faithful service to the governing party is unacceptable to most Canadians. There are a number of reform possibilities. It would not be unconstitutional for Prime Minister Martin to direct the Governor General to 'summon' to the Senate Canadians who have been selected by provincial electorates for this service.[147] Prime Minister Mulroney did this in 1990 when he had Stan Waters, the winner of an Alberta Senate election, appointed to the Senate. Prime Minister Chrétien's refusal to follow suit and appoint Mr Bert Brown and Professor F.L. (Ted) Morton, the winners of another Alberta Senate election in 1998, to fill Alberta vacancies was not based on constitutional niceties. John Ibbitson has suggested that the prime minister seek advice from all provincial governments before making Senate appointments, leaving it to each to determine the best mode of identifying worthy candidates.[148] But if we follow David Smith's analysis of the Senate's purpose, it would be better to consider an approach to reform that, instead of treating the Senate as an alternative forum of intergovernmental relations, aims more directly at recruiting experience and talent from various walks of life. One such possibility is for the prime minister to be advised by a non-partisan committee on the persons best qualified to fill Senate vacancies. Reform along this line has been recommended by the Wakeham Committee in Britain for appointments to a reformed House of Lords. The federal and provincial governments, without any constitutional amendment, have introduced advisory committees to obtain informed, non-partisan advice on appointing judges.[149] It is difficult to see any constitutional objection to similarly reforming the selection of persons worthy of being appointed to the Senate. All of these appointing systems would be more palatable, as would the status quo, if instead of serving until age seventy five (which results in an average tenure of fifteen years), Senators were appointed for shorter fixed terms. Under section 44 of the amending formula, such a change could be made by a simple Act of Parliament, albeit an Act for which the Senate's consent would be necessary.

After a generation of massive efforts to overhaul their country's constitution, Canadians have shifted gears and fallen back on older, quieter, less conflictual, and more piecemeal ways of adjusting and adapting their constitutional system. This does not mean that the great causes of constitutional unrest – Quebec nationalism, western alienation, and Aboriginal peoples' struggle for self-determination – have gone away. Quite to the contrary, in Quebec even a federalist premier like Jean Charest must constantly reassure his followers that he too is a Quebec nationalist. Western Canadians are keener than ever to have their aspirations given more weight in national affairs.[150] Aboriginal peoples have strengthened their resources and resolve to overcome their colonized condition. And Canadian nationalists continue to be concerned about how to manage these internal sources of division and at the same time be strong enough to assert Canada's sovereignty against the hegemonic power next door. The root causes of constitutional conflict have not disappeared, but Canadian society has learned that the concerns generated by these conflicting sentiments are not to be resolved all at once by a massive constitutional restructuring. We have come to share David Thomas's appreciation of 'constitutional abeyance.'[151] There is, let us hope, a revival of interest in addressing the sources of tension in the body politic by ordinary, everyday politics. A sign of such a revival is the decision of Paul Martin, a new prime minister from Quebec to make a westerner, Ann McLellan, deputy prime minister, and to make Aboriginal and urban affairs top priorities of his government.

The bits and pieces of constitutional change that take place through normal constitutional politics will not produce a constitution that makes all Canadians happy. We Canadians do not have a single constitutional document in which we can all see the vision of the political community we want Canada to be or become. We know

now that we cannot expect such a finish to our constitutional odyssey, for the simple reason that we do not share a common vision. The kind of constitutional patriotism[152] we sought through the era of mega constitutional politics is beyond us. But what is not beyond Canadians is to experience another kind of constitutional patriotism, one that comes from realizing that it is through our engaging in the odyssey itself, not reaching its final destination – our continuing openness to working peacefully and creatively with the diversity and pluralism of our place and time[153] – that we share a common civic identity and destiny.

Appendix

Consensus Report on the Constitution, Charlottetown, August 28, 1992

Preface

This document is a product of a series of meetings on constitutional reform involving the federal, provincial and territorial governments and representatives of Aboriginal peoples.

These meetings were part of the Canada Round of constitutional renewal. On September 24, 1991, the Government of Canada tabled in the federal Parliament a set of proposals for the renewal of the Canadian federation entitled *Shaping Canada's Future Together*. These proposals were referred to a Special Joint Committee of the House of Commons and the Senate which travelled across Canada seeking views on the proposals. The Committee received 3,000 submissions and listened to testimony from 700 individuals.

During the same period, all provinces and territories created forums for public consultation on constitutional matters. These forums gathered reaction and advice with a view to producing recommendations to their governments. In addition, Aboriginal peoples were consulted by national and regional Aboriginal organizations.

An innovative forum for consultation with experts, advocacy groups and citizens was the series of six televised national conferences that took place between January and March of 1992.

Shortly before the release of the report of the Special Joint Committee on a Renewed Canada, the Prime Minister invited representatives of the provinces and territories and Aboriginal leaders to meet with the federal Minister of Constitutional Affairs to discuss the report.

At this initial meeting, held March 12, 1992 in Ottawa, participants agreed to proceed with a series of meetings with the objective of reaching consensus on a set of constitutional amendments. It was agreed that participants would make best efforts to reach consensus before the end of May, 1992 and that there would be no unilateral actions by any government while this process was under way. It was subsequently agreed to extend this series of meetings into June, and then into July.

To support their work, the heads of delegation agreed to establish a Coordinating Committee, composed of senior government officials and representatives of the four Aboriginal organizations. This committee, in turn, created four working groups to develop options and recommendations for consideration by the heads of delegation.

Recommendations made in the report of the Special Joint Committee on a Renewed Canada served as the basis of discussion, as did the recommendations of the various provincial and territorial consultations and the consultations with Aboriginal peoples. Alternatives and modifications to the proposals in these reports have been the principal subject of discussion at the multilateral meetings.

Including the initial session in Ottawa, there were twenty-seven days of meetings among the heads of delegation, as well as meetings of the Coordinating Committee and the four working groups. The schedule of the meetings during this first phase of meetings was:

March 12	Ottawa
April 8 and 9	Halifax
April 14	Ottawa
April 29 and 30	Edmonton
May 6 and 7	Saint John
May 11, 12 and 13	Vancouver
May 20, 21 and 22	Montreal
May 26, 27, 28, 29 and 30	Toronto
June 9, 10 and 11	Ottawa
June 28 and 29	Ottawa
July 3	Toronto
July 6 and 7	Ottawa

Following this series of meetings, the Prime Minister of Canada chaired a number of meetings of First Ministers, in which the Government of Quebec was a full participant. These include:

August 4	Harrington Lake
August 10	Harrington Lake
August 18, 19, 20, 21 and 22	Ottawa
August 27 and 28	Charlottetown

Organizational support for the full multilateral meetings has been provided by the Canadian Intergovernmental Conferences Secretariat.

In the course of the multilateral discussions, draft constitutional texts have been developed wherever possible in order to reduce uncertainty or ambiguity. In particular, a rolling draft of legal text was the basis of the discussion of issues affecting Aboriginal peoples. These drafts would provide the foundation of the formal legal resolutions to be submitted to Parliament and the legislatures.

In areas where the consensus was not unanimous, some participants chose to have their dissents recorded. Where requested, these dissents have been recorded in the chronological records of the meetings but are not recorded in this summary document.

Asterisks *in the text that follows* indicate the areas where the consensus is to proceed with a political accord.

I: UNITY AND DIVERSITY

A. People and Communities

1. *Canada Clause*

A new clause should be included as Section 2 of the *Constitution Act, 1867* that would express fundamental Canadian values. The Canada Clause would guide the courts in their future interpretation of the entire Constitution, including the *Canadian Charter of Rights and Freedoms.*

The *Constitution Act, 1867* is amended by adding thereto, immediately after Section 1 thereof, the following section:

"2.(1) The Constitution of Canada, including the *Canadian Charter of Rights and Freedoms,* shall be interpreted in a manner consistent with the following fundamental characteristics:

(a) Canada is a democracy committed to a parliamentary and federal system of government and to the rule of law;

(b) the Aboriginal peoples of Canada, being the first peoples to govern this land, have the right to promote their languages, cultures and traditions and to ensure the integrity of their societies, and their governments constitute one of three orders of government in Canada;

(c) Quebec constitutes within Canada a distinct society, which includes a French-speaking majority, a unique culture and a civil law tradition;

(d)   Canadians and their governments are committed to the vitality and development of official language minority communities throughout Canada;

(e)   Canadians are committed to racial and ethnic equality in a society that includes citizens from many lands who have contributed, and continue to contribute, to the building of a strong Canada that reflects its cultural and racial diversity;

(f)   Canadians are committed to respect for individual and collective human rights and freedoms of all people;

(g)   Canadians are committed to the equality of female and male persons; and

(h)   Canadians confirm the principle of the equality of the provinces at the same time as recognizing their diverse characteristics.

(2) The role of the legislature and Government of Quebec to preserve and promote the distinct society of Quebec is affirmed.

(3) Nothing in this section derogates from the powers, rights or privileges of the Parliament or the Government of Canada, or of the legislatures or governments of the provinces, or of the legislative bodies or governments of the Aboriginal peoples of Canada, including any powers, rights or privileges relating to language and, for greater certainty, nothing in this section derogates from the aboriginal and treaty rights of the Aboriginal peoples of Canada.''

2. *Aboriginal Peoples and the Canadian Charter of Rights and Freedoms*

The Charter provision dealing with Aboriginal peoples (Section 25, the non-derogation clause) should be strengthened to ensure that nothing in the Charter abrogates or derogates from Aboriginal, treaty or other rights of Aboriginal peoples, and in particular any rights or freedoms relating to the exercise or protection of their languages, cultures or traditions.

3. *Linguistic Communities in New Brunswick*

A separate constitutional amendment requiring only the consent of Parliament and the legislature of New Brunswick should be added to the *Canadian Charter of Rights and Freedoms*. The amendment would entrench the equality of status of the English and French linguistic communities in New Brunswick, including the right to distinct educational institutions and such distinct cultural institutions as are necessary for the preservation and promotion of these communities. The amendment would also affirm the role of the legislature and government of New Brunswick to preserve and promote this equality of status.

B. Canada's Social and Economic Union

4. *The Social and Economic Union*

A new provision should be added to the Constitution describing the commitment of the governments, Parliament and the legislatures within the federation to the principle of the preservation and the development of Canada's social and economic union. The new provision, entitled *The Social and Economic Union,* should be drafted to set out a series of policy objectives underlying the social and the economic union, respectively. The provision should not be justiciable.

The policy objectives set out in the provision on the social union should include, but not be limited to:

· providing throughout Canada a health care system that is comprehensive, universal, portable, publicly administered and accessible;
· providing adequate social services and benefits to ensure that all individuals resident in Canada have reasonable access to housing, food and other basic necessities;
· providing high quality primary and secondary education to all individuals resident in Canada and ensuring reasonable access to post-secondary education;
· protecting the rights of workers to organize and bargain collectively; and
· protecting, preserving and sustaining the integrity of the environment for present and future generations.

The policy objectives set out in the provision on the economic union should include, but not be limited to:

· working together to strengthen the Canadian economic union;
· the free movement of persons, goods, services and capital;
· the goal of full employment;
· ensuring that all Canadians have a reasonable standard of living; and
· ensuring sustainable and equitable development.

A mechanism for monitoring the Social and Economic Union should be determined by a First Ministers' Conference.

A clause should be added to the Constitution stating that the Social and Economic Union does not abrogate or derogate from the *Canadian Charter of Rights and Freedoms.*

5. *Economic Disparities, Equalization and Regional Development*

Section 36 of the *Constitution Act, 1982* currently commits Parliament and the Government of Canada and the governments and legislatures of the provinces to promote equal opportunities and economic development throughout the country and to provide reasonably comparable levels of public services to all Canadians. Subsection 36(2) currently commits the federal government to the principle of equalization payments. This section should be amended to read as follows:

> "Parliament and the Government of Canada are committed to making equalization payments so that provincial governments have sufficient revenues to provide reasonably comparable levels of public services at reasonably comparable levels of taxation."

Subsection 36(1) should be expanded to include the territories.

Subsection 36(1) should be amended to add a commitment to ensure the provision of reasonably comparable economic infrastructures of a national nature in each province and territory.

The Constitution should commit the federal government to meaningful consultation with the provinces before introducing legislation relating to equalization payments.

A new Subsection 36(3) should be added to entrench the commitment of governments to the promotion of regional economic development to reduce economic disparities.

Regional development is also discussed in item 36 of this document.

6. *The Common Market*

Section 121 of the *Constitution Act, 1867* would remain unchanged.

Detailed principles and commitments related to the Canadian Common Market are included in the political accord of August 28, 1992. First Ministers will decide on the best approach to implement these principles and commitments at a future First Ministers' Conference on the economy. First Ministers would have the authority to create an independent dispute resolution agency and decide on its role, mandate and composition.(*)

II: INSTITUTIONS

A. The Senate

7. *An Elected Senate*

The Constitution should be amended to provide that Senators are elected, either by the population of the provinces and territories of Canada or by the members of their provincial or territorial legislative assemblies.

Federal legislation should govern Senate elections, subject to the constitutional provision above and constitutional provisions requiring that elections take place at the same time as elections to the House of Commons and provisions respecting eligibility and mandate of Senators. Federal legislation would be sufficiently flexible to allow provinces and territories to provide for gender equality in the composition of the Senate.

Matters should be expedited in order that Senate elections be held as soon as possible, and, if feasible, at the same time as the next federal general election for the House of Commons.

8. *An Equal Senate*

The Senate should initially total 62 Senators and should be composed of six Senators from each province and one Senator from each territory.

9. *Aboriginal Peoples' Representation in the Senate*

Aboriginal representation in the Senate should be guaranteed in the Constitution. Aboriginal Senate seats should be additional to provincial and territorial seats, rather than drawn from any province or territory's allocation of Senate seats.

Aboriginal Senators should have the same role and powers as other Senators, plus a possible double majority power in relation to certain matters materially affecting Aboriginal people. These issues and other details relating to Aboriginal representation in the Senate (numbers, distribution, method of selection) will be discussed further by governments and the representatives of the Aboriginal peoples in the early autumn of 1992.(*)

10. *Relationship to the House of Commons*

The Senate should not be a confidence chamber. In other words, the defeat of government-sponsored legislation by the Senate would not require the government's resignation.

11. *Categories of Legislation*

There should be four categories of legislation:

1) Revenue and expenditure bills ("supply bills");
2) Legislation materially affecting French language or French culture;
3) Bills involving fundamental tax policy changes directly related to natural resources;
4) Ordinary legislation (any bill not falling into one of the first three categories).

Initial classification of bills should be by the originator of the bill. With the exception of legislation affecting French language or French culture (see item 14), appeals should be determined by the Speaker of the House of Commons, following consultation with the Speaker of the Senate.

12. *Approval of Legislation*

The Constitution should oblige the Senate to dispose of any bills approved by the House of Commons, within thirty sitting days of the House of Commons, with the exception of revenue and expenditure bills.

Revenue and expenditure bills would be subject to a 30 calendar-day suspensive veto. If a bill is defeated or amended by the Senate within this period, it could be repassed by a majority vote in the House of Commons on a resolution.

Bills that materially affect French language or French culture would require approval by a majority of Senators voting and by a majority of the Francophone Senators voting. The House of Commons would not be able to override the defeat of a bill in this category by the Senate.

Bills that involve fundamental tax policy changes directly related to natural resources would be defeated if a majority of Senators voting cast their votes against the bill. The House of Commons would not be able to override the Senate's veto. The precise definition of this category of legislation remains to be determined.

Defeat or amendment of ordinary legislation by the Senate would trigger a joint sitting process with the House of Commons. A simple majority vote at the joint sitting would determine the outcome of the bill.

The Senate should have the powers set out in this Consensus Report. There would be no change to the Senate's current role in approving constitutional amendments. Subject to the Consensus Report, Senate powers and procedures should be parallel to those in the House of Commons.

The Senate should continue to have the capacity to initiate bills, except for money bills.

If any bill initiated and passed by the Senate is amended or rejected by the House of Commons, a joint sitting process should be triggered automatically.

The House of Commons should be obliged to dispose of legislation approved by the Senate within a reasonable time limit.

13. *Revenue and Expenditure Bills*

In order to preserve Canada's parliamentary traditions, the Senate should not be able to block the routine flow of legislation relating to taxation, borrowing and appropriation.

Revenue and expenditure bills ("supply bills") should be defined as only those matters involving borrowing, the raising of revenue and appropriation as well as matters subordinate to these issues. This definition should exclude fundamental policy changes to the tax system (such as the Goods and Services Tax and the National Energy Program).

14. *Double Majority*

The originator of a bill should be responsible for designating whether it materially affects French language or French culture. Each designation should be subject to appeal to the Speaker of the Senate under rules to be established by the Senate. These rules should be designed to provide adequate protection to Francophones.

On entering the Senate, Senators should be required to declare whether they are Francophones for the purpose of the double majority voting rule. Any process for challenging these declarations should be left to the rules of the Senate.

15. *Ratification of Appointments*

The Constitution should specify that the Senate ratify the appointment of the Governor of the Bank of Canada.

The Constitution should also be amended to provide the Senate with a new power to ratify other key appointments made by the federal government.

The Senate should be obliged to deal with any proposed appointments within thirty sitting-days of the House of Commons.

The appointments that would be subject to Senate ratification, including the heads of the national cultural institutions and the heads of federal regulatory boards and agencies, should be set out in specific federal legislation rather than the Constitution. The federal government's commitment to table such legislation should be recorded in a political accord.(*)

An appointment submitted for ratification would be rejected if a majority of Senators voting cast their votes against it.

16. *Eligibility for Cabinet*

Senators should not be eligible for Cabinet posts.

B. The Supreme Court

17. *Entrenchment in the Constitution*

The Supreme Court should be entrenched in the Constitution as the general court of appeal for Canada.

18. *Composition*

The Constitution should entrench the current provision of the *Supreme Court Act*, which specified that the Supreme Court is to be composed of nine members, of whom three must have been admitted to the bar of Quebec (civil law bar).

19. *Nominations and Appointments*

The Constitution should require the federal government to name judges from lists submitted by the governments of the provinces and territories. A provision should be made in the Constitution for the appointment of interim judges if a list is not submitted on a timely basis or no candidate is acceptable.

20. *Aboriginal Peoples' Role*

The structure of the Supreme Court should not be modified in this round of constitutional discussions. The role of Aboriginal peoples in relation to the Supreme Court should be recorded in a political accord and should be on the agenda of a future First Ministers' Conference on Aboriginal issues.(*)

Provincial and territorial governments should develop a reasonable process for consulting representatives of the Aboriginal peoples of

Canada in the preparation of lists of candidates to fill vacancies on the Supreme Court.(*)

Aboriginal groups should retain the right to make representations to the federal government respecting candidates to fill vacancies on the Supreme Court.(*)

The federal government should examine, in consultation with Aboriginal groups, the proposal that an Aboriginal Council of Elders be entitled to make submissions to the Supreme Court when the court considers Aboriginal issues.(*)

C. House of Commons

21. *Composition of the House of Commons*

The composition of the House of Commons should be adjusted to better reflect the principle of representation by population. The adjustment should include an initial increase in the size of the House of Commons to 337 seats, to be made at the time Senate reform comes into effect. Ontario and Quebec would each be assigned eighteen additional seats, British Columbia four additional seats, and Alberta two additional seats, with boundaries to be developed using the 1991 census.

An additional special Canada-wide redistribution of seats should be conducted following the 1996 census, aimed at ensuring that, in the first subsequent general election, no province will have fewer than 95 per cent of the House of Commons seats it would receive under strict representation-by-population. Consequently, British Columbia and Ontario would each be assigned three additional seats and Alberta two additional seats. As a result of this special adjustment, no province or territory will lose seats, nor will a province or territory which has achieved full representation-by-population have a smaller share of House of Commons seats than its share of the total population in the 1996 census.

The redistribution based on the 1996 census and all future redistributions should be governed by the following constitutional provisions:

(a)   A guarantee that Quebec would be assigned no fewer than 25 per cent of the seats in the House of Commons;
(b)   The current Section 41(b) of the *Constitution Act, 1982*, the "fixed floor", would be retained;
(c)   Section 51A of the *Constitution Act, 1867*, the "rising floor", would be repealed;
(d)   A new provision that would ensure that no province could have

fewer Commons seats than another province with a smaller population, subject to the provision in item (a) above;
(e) The current provision that allocates two seats to the Northwest Territories and one seat to Yukon would be retained.

A permanent formula should be developed and Section 51 of the *Constitution Act, 1867,* should be adjusted to accommodate demographic change, taking into consideration the principles suggested by the Royal Commission on Electoral Reform and Party Financing.

22. *Aboriginal Peoples' Representation*

The issue of Aboriginal representation in the House of Commons should be pursued by Parliament, in consultation with representatives of the Aboriginal peoples of Canada, after it has received the final report of the House of Commons Committee studying the recommendations of the Royal Commission on Electoral Reform and Party Financing.(*)

D. First Ministers' Conferences

23. *Entrenchment*

A provision should be added to the Constitution requiring the Prime Minister to convene a First Ministers' Conference at least once a year. The agendas for these conferences should not be specified in the Constitution.

The leaders of the territorial governments should be invited to participate in any First Ministers' Conference convened pursuant to this constitutional provision. Representatives of the Aboriginal peoples of Canada should be invited to participate in discussions on any item on the agenda of a First Ministers' Conference that directly affects the Aboriginal peoples. This should be embodied in a political accord.(*)

The role and responsibilities of First Ministers with respect to the federal spending power are outlined at item 25 of this document.

E. The Bank of Canada

24. *Bank of Canada*

The Bank of Canada was discussed and the consensus was that this issue should not be pursued in this round, except for the consensus that the Senate should have a role in ratifying the appointment of its Governor.

III: ROLES AND RESPONSIBILITIES

25. *Federal Spending Power*

A provision should be added to the Constitution stipulating that the Government of Canada must provide reasonable compensation to the government of a province that chooses not to participate in a new Canada-wide shared-cost program that is established by the federal government in an area of exclusive provincial jurisdiction, if that province carries on a program or initiative that is compatible with the national objectives.

A framework should be developed to guide the use of the federal spending power in all areas of exclusive provincial jurisdiction. Once developed, the framework could become a multilateral agreement that would receive constitutional protection using the mechanism described in item 26 of this report. The framework should ensure that when the federal spending power is used in areas of exclusive provincial jurisdiction, it should:

(a)   contribute to the pursuit of national objectives:
(b)   reduce overlap and duplication;
(c)   not distort and should respect provincial priorities; and
(d)   ensure equality of treatment of the provinces, while recognizing their different needs and circumstances.

The Constitution should commit First Ministers to establishing such a framework at a future conference of First Ministers. Once it is established, First Ministers would assume a role in annually reviewing progress in meeting the objectives set out in the framework.

A provision should be added (as Section 106A(3)) that would ensure that nothing in the section that limits the federal spending power affects the commitments of Parliament and the Government of Canada that are set out in Section 36 of the *Constitution Act, 1982.*

26. *Protection of Intergovernmental Agreements*

The Constitution should be amended to provide a mechanism to ensure that designated agreements between governments are protected from unilateral change. This would occur when Parliament and the legislature(s) enact laws approving the agreement.

Each application of the mechanism should cease to have effect after a maximum of five years but could be renewed by a vote of Parliament and the legislature(s) readopting similar legislation. Governments of Aboriginal peoples should have access to this mechanism. The provision should be available to protect both bilateral and multilateral agreements among federal, provincial and territorial governments, and the governments of Aboriginal peoples. A government negotiating an agreement should be accorded equality of treatment in relation to any government which has already concluded an agreement, taking into account different needs and circumstances.

It is the intention of governments to apply this mechanism to future agreements related to the Canada Assistance Plan.(*)

27. *Immigration*

A new provision should be added to the Constitution committing the Government of Canada to negotiate agreements with the provinces relating to immigration.

The Constitution should oblige the federal government to negotiate and conclude within a reasonable time an immigration agreement at the request of any province. A government negotiating an agreement should be accorded equality of treatment in relation to any government which has already concluded an agreement, taking into account different needs and circumstances.

28. *Labour Market Development and Training*

Exclusive federal jurisdiction for unemployment insurance, as set out in Section 91(2A) of the *Constitution Act, 1867,* should not be altered. The federal government should retain exclusive jurisdiction for income support and its related services delivered through the Unemployment Insurance system. Federal spending on job creation programs should be protected through a constitutional provision or a political accord.(*)

Labour market development and training should be identified in Section 92 of the Constitution as a matter of exclusive provincial jurisdiction. Provincial legislatures should have the authority to constrain federal spending that is directly related to labour market development and training. This should be accomplished through justiciable intergovernmental agreements designed to meet the circumstances of each province.

At the request of a province, the federal government would be obligated to withdraw from any or all training activities and from any or all labour market development activities, except Unemployment Insurance. The federal government should be required to negotiate and conclude agreements to provide reasonable compensation to provinces requesting that the federal government withdraw.

The Government of Canada and the government of the province that requested the federal government to withdraw should conclude agreements within a reasonable time.

Provinces negotiating agreements should be accorded equality of treatment with respect to terms and conditions of agreements in relation to any other province that has already concluded an agreement, taking into account the different needs and circumstances of the provinces.

The federal, provincial and territorial governments should commit themselves in a political accord to enter into administrative arrangements to improve efficiency and client service and ensure effective coordination of federal Unemployment Insurance and provincial employment functions.(*)

As a safeguard, the federal government should be required to negotiate and conclude an agreement within a reasonable time, at the request of any province not requesting the federal government to withdraw, to maintain its labour market development and training programs and activities in that province. A similar safeguard should be available to the territories.

There should be a constitutional provision for an ongoing federal role in the establishment of national policy objectives for the national aspects of labour market development. National labour market policy objectives would be established through a process which could be set out in the Constitution including the obligation for presentation to Parliament for debate. Factors to be considered in the establishment of national policy objectives could include items such as national economic conditions, national labour market requirements, international labour market trends and changes in international economic conditions. In establishing national policy objectives, the federal government would take into account the different needs and circumstances of the provinces; and there would be a provision, in the Constitution or in a political accord, committing the federal, provincial and territorial governments to support the development of common occupational standards, in consultation with employer and employee groups.(*)

Provinces that negotiated agreements to constrain the federal spending power should be obliged to ensure that their labour market development programs are compatible with the national policy objectives, in the context of different needs and circumstances.

Considerations of service to the public in both official languages should be included in a political accord and be discussed as part of the negotiation of bilateral agreements.(*)

The concerns of Aboriginal peoples in this field will be dealt with through the mechanisms set out in item 40 below.

29. *Culture*

Provinces should have exclusive jurisdiction over cultural matters within the provinces. This should be recognized through an explicit constitutional amendment that also recognizes the continuing responsibility of the federal government in Canadian cultural matters. The federal government should retain responsibility for national cultural institutions, including grants and contributions delivered by these institutions. The Government of Canada commits to negotiate cultural agreements with provinces and to ensure that the federal governments and the province work in harmony. These changes should not alter the federal fiduciary responsibility for Aboriginal people. The non-derogation provisions for Aboriginal peoples set out in item 40 of this document will apply to culture.

30. *Forestry*

Exclusive provincial jurisdiction over forestry should be recognized and clarified through an explicit constitutional amendment.

Provincial legislatures should have the authority to constrain federal spending that is directly related to forestry.

This should be accomplished through justiciable intergovernmental agreements, designed to meet the specific circumstances of each province. The mechanism used would be the one set out in item 26 of this document, including a provision for equality of treatment with respect to terms and conditions. Considerations of service to the public in both official languages should be considered a possible part of such agreements.(*)

Such an agreement should set the terms for federal withdrawal, including the level and form of financial resources to be transferred. In addition, a political accord could specify the form the compensation would take (i.e. cash transfers, tax points, or others).(*) Alternatively, such an agreement could require the federal government to maintain its spending in that province. A similar safeguard should be available to the territories. The federal government should be obliged to negotiate and conclude such an agreement within a reasonable time.

These changes and the ones set out in items 31, 32, 33, 34 and 35 should not alter the federal fiduciary responsibility for Aboriginal people. The provisions set out in item 40 would apply.

31. *Mining*

Exclusive provincial jurisdiction over mining should be recognized and clarified through an explicit constitutional amendment and the negotiation of federal-provincial agreements. This should be done in the same manner as set out above with respect to forestry.(*)

32. *Tourism*

Exclusive provincial jurisdiction over tourism should be recognized and clarified through an explicit constitutional amendment and the negotiation of federal-provincial agreements. This should be done in the same manner as set out above with respect to forestry.(*)

33. *Housing*

Exclusive provincial jurisdiction over housing should be recognized and clarified through an explicit constitutional amendment and the negotiation of federal-provincial agreements. This should be done in the same manner as set out above with respect to forestry.(*)

34. *Recreation*

Exclusive provincial jurisdiction over recreation should be recognized and clarified through an explicit constitutional amendment and the negotiation of federal-provincial agreements. This should be done in the same manner as set out above with respect to forestry.(*)

35. *Municipal and Urban Affairs*

Exclusive provincial jurisdiction over municipal and urban affairs should be recognized and clarified through an explicit constitutional amendment and the negotiation of federal-provincial agreements. This should be done in the same manner as set out above with respect to forestry.(*)

36. *Regional Development*

In addition to the commitment to regional development to be added to Section 36 of the *Constitution Act, 1982* (described in item 5 of this document), a provision should be added to the Constitution that would oblige the federal government to negotiate an agreement at the request of any province with respect to regional development. Such agreements could be protected under the provision set out in item 26 ("Protection of Intergovernmental Agreements"). Regional development should not become a separate head of power in the Constitution.

37. *Telecommunications*

The federal government should be committed to negotiate agreements with the provincial governments to coordinate and harmonize the procedures of their respective regulatory agencies in this field. Such agreements could be protected under the provision set out in item 26 ("Protection of Intergovernmental Agreements").

38. *Federal Power of Disallowance and Reservation*

This provision of the Constitution should be repealed. Repeal requires unanimity.

39. *Federal Declaratory Power*

Section 92(10)(c) of the *Constitution Act, 1867* permits the federal government to declare a "work" to be for the general advantage of Canada and bring it under the legislative jurisdiction of Parliament. This provision should be amended to ensure that the declaratory power can only be applied to new works or rescinded with respect to past declarations with the explicit consent of the province(s) in which the work is situated. Existing declarations should be left undisturbed unless all of the legislatures affected wish to take action.

40. *Aboriginal Peoples' Protection Mechanism*

There should be a general non-derogation clause to ensure that division of powers amendments will not affect the rights of the Aboriginal peoples and the jurisdictions and powers of governments of Aboriginal peoples.

IV: FIRST PEOPLES

Note: References to the territories will be added to the legal text with respect to this section, except where clearly inappropriate. Nothing in the amendments would extend the powers of the territorial legislatures.

A. The Inherent Right of Self-Government

41. *The Inherent Right of Self-Government*

The Constitution should be amended to recognize that the Aboriginal peoples of Canada have the inherent right of self-government within Canada. This right should be placed in a new section of the *Constitution Act, 1982,* Section 35.1(1).

The recognition of the inherent right of self-government should be interpreted in light of the recognition of Aboriginal governments as one of three orders of government in Canada.

A contextual statement should be inserted in the Constitution, as follows:

"The exercise of the right of self-government includes the authority of the duly constituted legislative bodies of Aboriginal peoples, each within its own jurisdiction:

(a)   to safeguard and develop their languages, cultures, economies, identities, institutions and traditions; and,

(b)   to develop, maintain and strengthen their relationship with their lands, waters and environment

so as to determine and control their development as peoples according to their own values and priorities and ensure the integrity of their societies."

Before making any final determination of an issue arising from the inherent right of self-government, a court or tribunal should take into account the contextual statement referred to above, should enquire into the efforts that have been made to resolve the issue through negotiations and should be empowered to order the parties to take such steps as are appropriate in the circumstances to effect a negotiated resolution.

42. *Delayed Justiciability*

The inherent right of self-government should be entrenched in the Constitution. However, its justiciability should be delayed for a five-year period through constitutional language and a political accord.(*)

Delaying the justiciability of the right should be coupled with a constitutional provision which would shield Aboriginal rights.

Delaying the justiciability of the right will not make the right contingent and will not affect existing Aboriginal and treaty rights.

The issue of special courts or tribunals should be on the agenda of the first First Ministers' Conference on Aboriginal Constitutional matters referred to in item 53.(*)

43. *Charter Issues*

The *Canadian Charter of Rights and Freedoms* should apply immediately to governments of Aboriginal peoples.

A technical change should be made to the English text of sections 3, 4 and 5 of the *Canadian Charter of Rights and Freedoms* to ensure that it corresponds to the French text.

The legislative bodies of Aboriginal peoples should have access to Section 33 of the *Constitution Act, 1982* (the notwithstanding clause) under conditions that are similar to those applying to Parliament and the provincial legislatures but which are appropriate to the circumstances of Aboriginal peoples and their legislative bodies.

44. *Land*

The specific constitutional provision on the inherent right and the specific constitutional provision on the commitment to negotiate land should not create new Aboriginal rights to land or derogate from existing Aboriginal or treaty rights to land, except as provided for in self-government agreements.

B. Method of Exercise of the Right

45. *Commitment to Negotiate*

There should be a constitutional commitment by the federal and provincial governments and the Indian, Inuit and Métis peoples in the various regions and communities of Canada to negotiate in good faith with the objective of concluding agreements elaborating the relationship between Aboriginal governments and the other orders of government. The negotiations would focus on the implementation of the right of self-government including issues of jurisdiction, lands and resources, and economic and fiscal arrangements.

46. *The Process of Negotiation*

Political Accord on Negotiation and Implementation
– A political accord should be developed to guide the process of self-government negotiations.(*)

Equity of Access
- All Aboriginal peoples of Canada should have equitable access to the process of negotiation.

Trigger for Negotiations
- Self-government negotiations should be initiated by the representatives of Aboriginal peoples when they are prepared to do so.

Provision for Non-Ethnic Governments
- Self-government agreements may provide for self-government institutions which are open to the participation of all residents in a region covered by the agreement.

Provision for Different Circumstances
- Self-government negotiations should take into consideration the different circumstances of the various Aboriginal peoples.

Provision for Agreements
- Self-government agreements should be set out in future treaties, including land claims agreements or amendments to existing treaties, including land claims agreements. In addition, self-government agreements could be set out in other agreements which may contain a declaration that the rights of the Aboriginal peoples are treaty rights, within the meaning of Section 35(1) of the *Constitution Act, 1982.*

Ratification of Agreements
- There should be an approval process for governments and Aboriginal peoples for self-government agreements, involving Parliament, the legislative assemblies of the relevant provinces and/or territories and the legislative bodies of the Aboriginal peoples. This principle should be expressed in the ratification procedures set out in the specific self-government agreements.

Non-Derogation Clause
- There should be an explicit statement in the Constitution that the commitment to negotiate does not make the right of self-government contingent on negotiations or in any way affect the justiciability of the right of self-government.

Dispute Resolution Mechanism
- To assist the negotiation process, a dispute resolution mechanism involving mediation and arbitration should be established. Details of this mechanism should be set out in a political accord.(*)

47. *Legal Transition and Consistency of Laws*

A constitutional provision should ensure that federal and provincial laws
will continue to apply until they are displaced by laws passed by governments of Aboriginal peoples pursuant to their authority.

A constitutional provision should ensure that a law passed by a government of Aboriginal peoples, or an assertion of its authority based on the
inherent right provision may not be inconsistent with those laws which
are essential to the preservation of peace, order and good government in
Canada. However, this provision would not extend the legislative authority of Parliament or of the legislatures of the provinces.

48. *Treaties*

With respect to treaties with Aboriginal peoples, the Constitution should
be amended as follows:

– treaty rights should be interpreted in a just, broad and liberal manner
  taking into account the spirit and intent of the treaties and the context
  in which the specific treaties were negotiated;
– the Government of Canada should be committed to establishing and
  participating in good faith in a joint process to clarify or implement
  treaty rights, or to rectify terms of treaties when agreed to by the
  parties. The governments of the provinces should also be committed,
  to the extent that they have jurisdiction, to participation in the above
  treaty process when invited by the government of Canada and the
  Aboriginal peoples concerned or where specified in a treaty;
– participants in this process should have regard, among other things
  and where appropriate, to the spirit and intent of the treaties as understood by Aboriginal peoples. It should be confirmed that all Aboriginal
  peoples that possess treaty rights shall have equitable access to this
  treaty process;
– it should be provided that these treaty amendments shall not extend
  the authority of any government or legislature, or affect the rights of
  Aboriginal peoples not party to the treaty concerned.

C. Issues Related to the Exercise of the Right

49. *Equity of Access to Section 35 Rights*

The Constitution should provide that all of the Aboriginal peoples of
Canada have access to those Aboriginal and treaty rights recognized

and affirmed in Section 35 of the *Constitution Act, 1982* that pertain to them.

50. *Financing*

Matters relating to the financing of governments of Aboriginal peoples should be dealt with in a political accord. The accord would commit the governments of Aboriginal peoples to:

- promoting equal opportunities for the well-being of all Aboriginal peoples;
- furthering economic, social and cultural development and employment opportunities to reduce disparities in opportunities among Aboriginal peoples and between Aboriginal peoples and other Canadians; and
- providing essential public services at levels reasonably comparable to those available to other Canadians in the vicinity.

It would also commit federal and provincial governments to the principle of providing the governments of Aboriginal peoples with fiscal or other resources, such as land, to assist those governments to govern their own affairs and to meet the commitments listed above, taking into account the levels of services provided to other Canadians in the vicinity and the fiscal capacity of governments of Aboriginal peoples to raise revenues from their own sources.

The issues of financing and its possible inclusion in the Constitution should be on the agenda of the first First Ministers' Conference on Aboriginal Constitutional matters referred to in item 53.(*)

51. *Affirmative Action Programs*

The Constitution should include a provision which authorizes governments of Aboriginal peoples to undertake affirmative action programs for socially and economically disadvantaged individuals or groups and programs for the advancement of Aboriginal languages and cultures.

52. *Gender Equality*

Section 35(4) of the *Constitution Act, 1982*, which guarantees existing Aboriginal and treaty rights equally to male and female persons, should be retained. The issue of gender equality should be on the agenda of the first First Ministers' Conference on Aboriginal Constitutional matters referred to under item 53.(*)

53. *Future Aboriginal Constitutional Process*

The Constitution should be amended to provide for four future First Ministers' Conferences on Aboriginal constitutional matters beginning no later than 1996, and following every two years thereafter. These conferences would be in addition to any other First Ministers' Conferences required by the Constitution. The agendas of these conferences would include items identified in this report and items requested by Aboriginal peoples.

54. *Section 91(24)*

For greater certainty, a new provision should be added to the *Constitution Act, 1867* to ensure that Section 91(24) applies to all Aboriginal peoples.

The new provision would not result in a reduction of existing expenditures by governments on Indians and Inuit or alter the fiduciary and treaty obligations of the federal government for Aboriginal peoples. This would be reflected in a political accord.(*)

55. *Métis in Alberta/Section 91(24)*

The Constitution should be amended to safeguard the legislative authority of the Government of Alberta for Métis and Métis Settlements lands. There was agreement to a proposed amendment to the *Alberta Act* that would constitutionally protect the status of the land held in fee simple by the Métis Settlements General Council under letters patent from Alberta.

56. *Métis Nation Accord(*)*

The federal government, the provinces of Ontario, Manitoba, Saskatchewan, Alberta, British Columbia and the Métis National Council have agreed to enter into a legally binding, justiciable and enforceable accord on Métis Nation issues. Technical drafting of the Accord is being completed. The Accord sets out the obligations of the federal and provincial governments and the Métis Nation.

The Accord commits governments to negotiate: self-government agreements, lands and resources; the transfer of the portion of Aboriginal programs and services available to Métis; and cost-sharing arrangements relating Métis institutions, programs and services.

Provinces and the federal government agree not to reduce existing expenditures on Métis and other Aboriginal people as a result of the Accord or as a result of an amendment to Section 91(24). The Accord defines the Métis for the purposes of the Métis Nation Accord and commits governments to enumerate and register the Métis Nation.

V: THE AMENDING FORMULA

Note: All of the following changes to the amending formula require the unanimous agreement of Parliament and the provincial legislatures.

57. *Changes to National Institutions*

Amendments to provisions of the Constitution related to the Senate should require unanimous agreement of Parliament and the provincial legislatures, once the current set of amendments related to Senate reform has come into effect. Future amendments affecting the House of Commons, including Quebec's guarantee of at least 25 per cent of the seats in the House of Commons, and amendments which can now be made under Section 42 should also require unanimity.

Section 41 and 42 of the *Constitution Act, 1982* should be amended so that the nomination and appointment process of Supreme Court judges would remain subject to the general (7/50) amending procedure. All other matters related to the Supreme Court, including its entrenchment, its role as the general court of appeal and its composition, would be matters requiring unanimity.

58. *Establishment of New Provinces*

The current provisions of the amending formula governing the creation of new provinces should be rescinded. They should be replaced by the pre-1982 provisions allowing the creation of new provinces through an Act of Parliament, following consultation with all of the existing provinces at a First Ministers' Conference. New provinces should not have a role in the amending formula without the unanimous consent of all of the provinces and the federal government, with the exception of purely bilateral or unilateral matters described in sections 38(3), 40, 43, 45 and 46 as it relates to 43, of the *Constitution Act, 1982*. Any increase in the representation for new provinces in the Senate should also require the unanimous consent of all provinces and the federal government. Territories that become provinces could not lose Senators or members of the House of Commons.

The provision now contained in Section 42(1) (e) of the *Constitution Act, 1982* with respect to the extension of provincial boundaries into the

Territories should be repealed and replaced by the *Constitution Act, 1871,* modified in order to require the consent of the Territories.

59. *Compensation for Amendments that Transfer Jurisdiction*

Where an amendment is made under the general amending formula that transfers legislative powers from provincial legislatures to Parliament, Canada should provide reasonable compensation to any province that opts out of the amendment.

60. *Aboriginal Consent*

There should be Aboriginal consent to future constitutional amendments that directly refer to the Aboriginal peoples. Discussions are continuing on the mechanism by which this consent would be expressed with a view to agreeing on a mechanism prior to the introduction in Parliament of formal resolutions amending the Constitution.

VI: OTHER ISSUES

Other constitutional issues were discussed during the multilateral meetings.

The consensus was to not pursue the following issues:

- personal bankruptcy and insolvency;
- intellectual property;
- interjurisdictional immunity;
- inland fisheries;
- marriage and divorce;
- residual power;
- legislative interdelegation;
- changes to the "notwithstanding clause";
- Section 96 (appointment of judges);
- Section 125 (taxation of federal and provincial governments);
- Section 92A (export of natural resources);
- requiring notice for changes to federal legislation respecting equalization payments;
- property rights;
- implementation of international treaties.

Other issues were discussed but were not finally resolved, among which were:

- requiring notice for changes to federal legislation respecting Established Programs Financing;
- establishing in a political accord a formal federal-provincial consultation process with regard to the negotiation of international treaties and agreements;
- Aboriginal participation in intergovernmental agreements respecting the division of powers;
- establishing a framework for compensation issues with respect to labour market development and training;
- consequential amendments related to Senate reform, including by-elections;
- any other consequential amendments required by changes recommended in this report.

Notes

Chapter 1 The Question of Our Time

1 Quoted in O.D. Skelton, *Life and Times of Sir Alexander Tilloch Galt* (Toronto: McClelland and Stewart 1966), 97
2 Letter from Premier Clyde Wells to J.W. Pickersgill and R.L. Stanfield, 15 Jan. 1990, 5
3 This principle was adopted by the Beaudoin-Dobbie Committee in its 1992 report, *A Renewed Canada*. See *Report of the Special Joint Committee of the Senate and the House of Commons* (Ottawa: Supply and Services Canada 1992), 32.
4 Alan C. Cairns, *Disruptions: Constitutional Struggles from the Charter to Meech Lake*, ed. Douglas E. Williams (Toronto: McClelland and Stewart 1991). See especially chap. 4.
5 For the most recent example of the traditional stereotyping of Canadians see Seymour Martin Lipset, *Continental Divide: The Values and Institutions of the United States and Canada* (New York: Routledge 1990).
6 John Locke, *The Second Treatise of Government* (New York: Liberal Arts Press 1952) 55
7 For an elaboration of this concept see Kenneth McRae, ed., *Consociational Democracy: Political Accommodation in Segmented Societies* (Toronto: McClelland and Stewart 1974).
8 'The Forum: A Report to the People from the Citizens' Forum on Canada's Future,' Toronto *Globe and Mail*, 29 June 1991

Chapter 2 The Sovereignty of the People

1 For an analysis of the different aspects of sovereignty see W.J. Rees,

'The Theory of Sovereignty Restated,' in Peter Laslett, ed., *Philosophy, Politics and Society: A Collection* (Oxford: Basil Black-well 1956).

2 Edmund S. Morgan, *Inventing the People: The Rise of Popular Sovereignty in England and America* (New York: W.W. Norton 1988), 169

3 Louis Henkin, 'Constitutionalism and Human Rights,' in Louis Henkin and Albert Rosenthal, eds., *Constitutionalism and Rights: The Influence of the United States Constitution Abroad* (New York: Columbia University Press 1990), 385

4 For an overview of its influence see Henkin and Rosenthal, eds., *Constitutionalism and Rights.*

5 On the founding of Australia see J.A. La Nauze, *The Making of the Australian Constitution* (Melbourne: Melbourne University Press 1972).

6 Quoted in Charles Howard McIlwain, *Constitutionalism, Ancient and Modern* (Ithaca: Cornell University Press 1947), 2

7 Ibid., 3

8 Daniel J. Elazar, 'Constitution-making: The Pre-eminently Political Act,' in Keith G. Banting and Richard Simeon, eds., *Redesigning the State: The Politics of Constitutional Change in Industrial Nations* (Toronto: University of Toronto Press 1985), 244

9 Quoted in Russell Kirk, *The Conservative Mind: From Burke to Santayana* (Chicago: Henry Regnery 1953) 33

10 Donald Creighton, *The Road to Confederation: The Emergence of Canada, 1863–1867* (Toronto: Macmillan 1964), 142–3

Chapter 3 Confederation

1 For the political theory of the French-Canadian rebels see Denis Monière, *Ideologies in Quebec: The Historical Development,* trans. Richard Howard (Toronto: University of Toronto Press 1981), chap. 3. For the constitutional ideas of the Upper Canadian rebels see W.P.M. Kennedy, *The Constitution of Canada, 1534-1937: An Introduction to Its Development, Law and Custom,* 2nd ed. (London: Oxford University Press 1938), chap. 11.

2 George F.G. Stanley, *A Short History of the Canadian Constitution* (Toronto: Ryerson 1969), 26

3 Ibid.

4 Kennedy, *Constitution of Canada*, 39

5 The phrase is from Christian Dufour, *A Canadian Challenge / Le Défi québécois* (Halifax: Institute for Research on Public Policy; Lantzville, BC: Oolichan Books 1990), 42.

6 See Stanley, *Short History*, 29.

7 Quoted in R. Douglas Francis, Richard Jones, and Donald B. Smith, *Origins: Canadian History to Confederation* (Toronto: Holt, Rinehart & Winston 1988), 190

8 Stanley, *Short History*, 47

9 Quoted ibid., 49

10 For a good account of the establishment of responsible government see Phillip Buckner, *The Transition to Responsible Government: British Policy in British North America, 1815–1850* (Westport, Conn.: Greenwood Press 1985).

11 For an account of conventions in the Canadian constitution see Andrew Heard, *Canadian Constitutional Conventions: The Marriage of Law and Politics* (Oxford: Oxford University Press 1991).

12 This quotation is from Macdonald's speech on the Quebec Resolutions and is quoted in Stanley, *Short History*, 75–6.

13 For a discussion of the compact theory and its current relevance see Robert C. Vipond, 'Whatever Became of the Compact Theory? Meech Lake and the New Politics of Constitutional Amendment in Canada,' *Queen's Quarterly*, 96 (1989): 793.

14 For a detailed account of the events leading to Confederation see Creighton, *Road to Confederation.*

15 See chapter 10 below.

16 The words are from the newspaper, *Le Pays*, and are quoted in A.I. Silver, *The French-Canadian Idea of Confederation, 1864–1900* (Toronto: University of Toronto Press 1982), 38.

17 Creighton, *Road to Confederation*, 32

18 Ibid., 35

19 Ibid., 20

20 For an account of newspaper coverage of Confederation see P.B. Waite, *The Life and Times of Confederation, 1864–1867: Politics, Newspapers, and the Union of British North America*, 2nd ed. (Toronto: University of Toronto Press 1962).

21 Creighton, *Road to Confederation*, 98

22 Waite, *Life and Times of Confederation*, 139

23 Creighton, *Road to Confederation*, 188
24 R. MacGregor Dawson, *The Government of Canada*, 4th ed., revised by Norman Ward (Toronto: University of Toronto Press 1966), 105
25 Creighton, *Road to Confederation*, 152
26 Section 133 of the BNA Act
27 Section 93 of the BNA Act
28 Section 94 of the BNA Act
29 Sections 98 and 22 of the BNA Act
30 Section 119 of the BNA Act. That section is now spent.
31 Section 9 of the Constitution Act, 1867 (the new title of the BNA Act) states that 'the Executive Government and Authority of and over Canada is hereby declared to continue and be vested in the Queen.'
32 Besides responsible government, the other principle incorporated in this phrase is the independence of the judiciary.
33 P.B. Waite, ed., *The Confederation Debates in the Province of Canada, 1865* (Toronto: McClelland and Stewart 1963), 44
34 Creighton, *Road to Confederation*, 187
35 Waite, *Life and Times of Confederation*, 122
36 Creighton, *Road to Confederation*, 189–90
37 Waite, ed., *Confederation Debates*
38 For an analysis of the vote see ibid., xviii.
39 His older brother, W.H. Pope, had attended the Quebec Conference, but in the legislature went no further than proposing that the Island put off its decision until the terms of union had been submitted to the people in a general election.
40 Waite, *Life and Times of Confederation*, 173
41 For an analysis see 'The Opposition to Confederation in Nova Scotia, 1864–1868,' in Ged Martin, *The Causes of Confederation* (Fredericton: Acadiensis Press 1990), 114–29.
42 Creighton, *Road to Confederation*, 366
43 Ibid., 381
44 The original section 26 provided that the Queen, on the advice of the governor general, could appoint three or six senators (representing equally the three Senate divisions, Ontario, Quebec, and the Maritimes). This was amended in 1915 to provide for four or eight extra senators to accommodate a fourth Senate division consisting of the four western provinces. The Mulroney government

used the provision, for the first time ever, in 1990 to ensure passage of its Goods and Services Tax Bill.

45 Creighton, *Road to Confederation*, 424
46 The first federal election following Confederation was based on the provincial election laws. It is estimated that, on average, about 15 per cent of the population of the four original provinces was eligible to vote. See Reginald Whitaker, 'Democracy and the Canadian Constitution,' in Keith Banting and Richard Simeon, eds., *And No One Cheered: Federalism, Democracy and the Constitution Act* (Toronto: Methuen 1983), 245.
47 Ralph C. Nelson, Walter C. Soderlund, Ronald H. Wagenberg, and E. Donald Briggs, 'Canadian Confederation as a Case Study in Community Formation,' in Ged Martin, ed., *Causes of Confederation*, 85
48 For an account of the Proclamation and its continuing relevancy in Canada's constitutional system see Bruce Clark, *Native Liberty, Crown Sovereignty: The Existing Aboriginal Right to Self-Government in Canada* (Montreal and Kingston: McGill-Queen's University Press 1990).
49 Section 91(24) of the BNA Act
50 See, especially, Eugene Forsey, *A Life on the Fringe: The Memoirs of Eugene Forsey* (Toronto: Oxford University Press 1990), chap. 11.
51 Section 146 of the BNA Act
52 These words are from his contribution to the Confederation Debates. Waite, ed., *Confederation Debates*, 50–1
53 J.M.S. Careless, *Brown of the Globe* (Toronto: Macmillan 1963), vol. 2, 171

Chapter 4 Provincial Rights

1 For an account see Kennedy, *Constitution of Canada*, 318–20.
2 Silver, *French-Canadian Idea of Confederation*, 111
3 Ibid., 121
4 Christopher Armstrong, *The Politics of Federalism: Ontario's Relations with the Federal Government, 1867–1942* (Toronto: University of Toronto Press 1981), 14
5 A. Margaret Evans, *Sir Oliver Mowat* (Toronto: University of Toronto Press for The Ontario Historical Studies Series 1992)
6 For a succinct account of the National Policy see Craig Brown,

'The Nationalism of the National Policy,' in Peter H. Russell, ed., *Nationalism in Canada* (Toronto: McGraw-Hill 1966), 155–63.

7 Whitaker, 'Democracy and the Canadian Constitution,' 250

8 For a full account see Paul Romney, *Mr. Attorney: The Attorney General for Ontario in Court, Cabinet and Legislature, 1791–1899* (Toronto: University of Toronto Press 1986), chap. 6.

9 Sections 55–7

10 Dawson, *Government of Canada,* 142

11 For a contemporary statement on this point see Peter W. Hogg, *Constitutional Law of Canada,* 2nd ed. (Toronto: Carswell 1985), 38.

12 For a full account of the use of these powers see Gerard V. LaForest, *Disallowance and Reservation of Provincial Legislation* (Ottawa: Department of Justice 1965).

13 For a detailed account see Romney, *Mr. Attorney,* 255–6.

14 Armstrong, *Politics of Federalism,* 29

15 See Paul Gérin-Lajoie, *Constitutional Amendment in Canada* (Toronto: University of Toronto Press 1950), 142–3.

16 For a full account see Frank MacKinnon, 'The Establishment of the Supreme Court of Canada,' *Canadian Historical Review* 27 (1946): 258–74.

17 [1878] 2 S.C.R. 70. For a compendium of Supreme Court and Judicial Committee decisions on the constitution see Peter H. Russell, Rainer Knopff, and Ted Morton, *Federalism and the Charter: Leading Constitutional Decisions* (Ottawa: Carleton University Press 1989).

18 [1979] 3 S.C.R. 575

19 [1881] 7 App. Cas. 96

20 F. Murray Greenwood, 'Lord Watson, Institutional Self-Interest and the Decentralization of Canadian Federalism in the 1890's,' *University of British Columbia Law Review* 9 (1974): 267

21 Russell v. The Queen (1882), 7 App. Cas. 829

22 Hodge v. The Queen (1883), 9 App. Cas. 177 (upholding provincial power), and the McCarthy Act Reference (not reported). For a discussion see Russell et al., *Federalism and the Charter,* 53.

23 Attorney General for Ontario v. Attorney General for Canada, [1896] A.C. 348

24 Liquidators of the Maritime Bank of Canada v. Receiver General of New Brunswick [1992] A.C. 437

25 Waite, ed., *Confederation Debates,* 156

26 For a classical statement of the theory see K.C. Wheare, *Federal Government*, 4th ed. (London: Oxford University Press 1963). On the basis of the centralizing elements in the constitutional text, Wheare concluded that Canada was not a true federation but a 'quasi-federation.'

27 On the absence of a theoretical understanding or agreement on federalism at the time of Confederation see Waite, *Life and Times of Confederation*, chap. 8.

28 The saying is attributed to Charles Evans Hughes, later chief justice of the United States. See A.T. Mason and W.M. Beaney, *American Constitutional Law* (Englewood Cliffs, NJ: Prentice-Hall 1959), 3.

29 For a discussion of the views of the Fathers of Confederation on this subject see Jennifer Smith, 'The Origins of Judicial Review in Canada,' *Canadian Journal of Political Science* 16 (1983): 115–34.

30 Section 93(4)

31 For the evidence see Peter H. Russell, *The Supreme Court of Canada as a Bilingual and Bicultural Institution* (Ottawa: Queen's Printer 1969), chap. 1.

32 See Alexander Hamilton, 'The Federalist No. 78,' *The Federalist Papers* (New York: Modern Library 1937).

33 For an account see W.L. Morton, *The Kingdom of Canada: A General History from Earliest Times*, 2nd ed. (Toronto: McClelland and Stewart 1969), chap. 19.

34 On the demographic changes see Janice Staples, 'Consociationalism at Provincial Level: The Erosion of Dualism in Manitoba, 1870–1890,' in McRae, ed., *Consociational Democracy*, 288–99.

35 Section 23 of the Manitoba Act, 1870

36 Attorney General for Manitoba v. Forest [1979] 2 s.c.r. 1032. Earlier challenges that were successful in the local courts were simply ignored.

37 Section 22 of the Manitoba Act, 1870

38 City of Winnipeg v. Barrett [1892] A.C. 445

39 Brophy v. Attorney General for Manitoba [1895] A.C. 445

40 Morton, *Kingdom of Canada*, 379

41 After the election, Laurier worked out a compromise with Manitoba premier Greenway that allowed periods of minority language and religious instruction where numbers warranted.

42 Silver, *French-Canadian Idea of Confederation*, 243

43 D.V. Smiley, *Canada in Question: Federalism in the Eighties*, 3rd ed. (Toronto: McGraw-Hill Ryerson 1980), 1

44 See Edwin Black, *Divided Loyalties: Canadian Concepts of Federalism* (Montreal and London: McGill-Queen's University Press 1975), 132–5.

45 For a fuller elaboration see Whittaker, 'Democracy and the Canadian Constitution.'

46 Quoted in Robert Vipond, *Liberty and Community: Canadian Federalism and the Failure of the Constitution* (Albany: State University of New York Press 1991), 79

47 Ibid., especially chap. 3

48 For a full account of the theory see Ramsay Cook, *Provincial Autonomy, Minority Rights and the Compact Theory, 1867–1921* (Ottawa: Queen's Printer 1969).

49 Black, *Divided Loyalties*, 154

50 This is the definition of myth given by R.M. MacIver in *The Web of Government* (New York: Macmillan 1947), 4. For the application of this sense of myth to the compact theory see Donald V. Smiley, *The Canadian Political Nationality* (Toronto: Methuen 1967), 30.

51 Arthur R.M. Lower, *Colony to Nation: A History of Canada*, 4th ed. (Toronto: Longmans 1964), 432

52 The British North America Act of 1871 and the British North America Act of 1886. The third, the Parliament of Canada Act, 1875, concerned the privileges and immunities of the House of Commons. For a brief account of all constitutional amendments up until 1964 and how they were obtained see the Honourable Guy Favreau, *The Amendment of the Constitution of Canada* (Ottawa: Queen's Printer 1965).

53 The British North America Act of 1907

54 The British North America Act of 1915

55 Cook, *Provincial Autonomy*, 44

56 For an analysis of the relationship between the two compact theories see Filippo Sabetti, 'The Historical Context of Constitutional Change in Canada,' *Law and Contemporary Problems* 45 (1982): 11–32.

57 Quoted ibid., 21

58 For an analysis of this tendency for French-speaking Canadians to view the Constitution as a compact between two peoples while the

English-speaking population view the Constitution as an organic development see Elazar, 'Constitution-making,' 245–6.

59 Sabetti, 'Historical Context of Constitutional Changes in Canada,' 20

60 Dawson, *Government of Canada*, 63

Chapter 5 An Autonomous Community

1 Dawson, *Government of Canada*, 53

2 For an account of the whole process of acquiring dominion autonomy see Stanley, *Short History*, chap. 7, and R. MacGregor Dawson, *The Development of Dominion Status, 1900–1936* (London: Oxford University Press 1937).

3 See Carl Berger, ed., *Imperialism and Nationalism, 1884–1914: A Conflict in Canadian Thought* (Toronto: Copp Clark 1969).

4 Favreau, *Amendment of the Constitution of Canada*, 18

5 Gérin-Lajoie, *Constitutional Amendment in Canada*, 229

6 Some of these amendments will be discussed later in the chapter. During the same period there were three amendments of the Australian Constitution and five amendments of the American Constitution.

7 For a discussion of autochthony and how it has been achieved in other parts of the Commonwealth see K.C. Wheare, *The Constitutional Structure of the Commonwealth* (Oxford: Clarendon Press 1960), chap. 4.

8 Gérin-Lajoie, *Constitutional Amendment in Canada*, 234

9 For an overview of the developing role of women in Canadian politics see Janine Brodie, *Women and Politics in Canada* (Toronto: McGraw-Hill Ryerson 1985).

10 Henrietta Muir Edwards v. Attorney-General Canada [1930] A.C. 124

11 See Walter S. Tarnopolsky, *Discrimination and the Law in Canada* (Toronto: Richard DeBoo 1982).

12 J.R. Miller, *Skyscrapers Hide the Heavens: A History of Indian-White Relations in Canada* (Toronto: University of Toronto Press 1989), 206

13 For an account of the convention and subsequent referendums see Peter Neary, *Newfoundland in the North Atlantic World, 1929–1949* (Kingston and Montreal: McGill-Queen's University Press 1988), chaps. 10 and 11.

14 Gérin-Lajoie, *Constitutional Amendment in Canada*, 245–6

15 Ibid., 242. Scott, incidentally, argued that the majority vote should be by a joint session of both Houses.

16 Favreau, *Amendment of the Constitution of Canada*, 19

17 For an analysis of these events see Glendon A. Schubert, *Constitutional Politics: The Political Behaviour of Supreme Court Justices and the Constitution* (New York: Holt Rinehart & Winston 1960), 155–72.

18 For an account of the legislation and its review by the courts see W.H. McConnell, 'The Judicial Review of Prime Minister Bennett's "New Deal,"' *Osgoode Hall Law Review* 6 (1968): 39.

19 This section is based on the brief summary of how amendments were obtained in Favreau, *Amendment of the Constitution of Canada*, 10–15, and the account of the 1940 amendment in Gérin-Lajoie, *Constitutional Amendment in Canada*, 104–9.

20 Section 146 sets out a similar procedure for the union of British Columbia and Prince Edward Island with Canada.

21 Reference re Legislative Authority of Parliament to Alter or Replace the Senate [1980] 1 S.C.R. 54

22 Favreau, *Amendment of the Constitution of Canada*, 24

23 See Alan C. Cairns, "The Judicial Committee and Its Critics,' *Canadian Journal of Political Science* 3 (1971): 301.

24 For a discussion of the debate over the abolition of Privy Council appeals and the adverse reaction in Quebec in particular, see Russell, *Supreme Court of Canada.*

25 J.A. Corry, 'Constitutional Trends and Federalism,' in A.R.M. Lower, F.R. Scott, et al., *Evolving Canadian Federalism* (Durham, NC: Duke University Press 1958), 103

26 There have been few judicial decisions on the limits of the federal spending power. It is generally held that the federal government can spend or lend its funds to any government, institution, or individual and attach conditions to its grant or loan so long as its legislation does not directly regulate conduct in a field of provincial jurisdiction. For a discussion see Hogg, *Constitutional Law of Canada*, 123–6.

27 For a summary and analysis of these programs see Black, *Divided Loyalties*, chap. 3.

28 David Kwavnick, ed., *The Tremblay Report* (Toronto: McClelland and Stewart 1973), 50

29 Favreau, *Amendment of the Constitution of Canada*, 30

Chapter 6 Mega Constitutional Politics, Round One: Fulton–Favreau to Victoria

1 The Fulton–Favreau formula was named after the two federal justice ministers, Davie Fulton and Guy Favreau, who presided over the meetings of attorneys-general that developed the formula. Fulton, minister of justice in John Diefenbaker's Conservative government, presided at the meetings in 1960–1. When the Liberals under Lester Pearson formed a minority government in 1963, Guy Favreau became minister of justice and presided at the 1964 meeting. For an account of the formula and the meetings that produced it see Favreau, *Amendment of the Constitution*, 26–53.
2 Legislative power could be delegated from Parliament to provinces only if four provinces were involved.
3 Of the many accounts there are two that are highly acclaimed: Léon Dion, *Quebec: The Unfinished Revolution*, trans. Hugh Thorburn (Montreal and London: McGill-Queen's University Press 1976), and Kenneth McRoberts, *Quebec: Social Change and Political Crisis*, 3rd ed. (Toronto: McClelland and Stewart 1988).
4 For a classic account of this phenomenon see Rupert Emerson, *From Empire to Nation: The Rise to Self-Assertion of Asian and African Peoples* (Boston: Beacon Press 1960).
5 For a discussion of the changing nature of Quebec nationalism see Ramsay Cook, *Canada, Quebec, and the Uses of Nationalism* (Toronto: McClelland and Stewart 1986).
6 Quoted in D.V. Smiley, *Canada in Question: Federalism in the Seventies* (Toronto: McGraw-Hill Ryerson 1972), 10
7 Daniel Johnson, *Egalité ou indépendance* (Montréal: Les Editions de l'Homme 1965)
8 In some earlier writings I have used the term 'macro constitutional politics' to depict efforts at broad constitutional renewal as compared with piecemeal constitutional reform. See Peter H. Russell, 'The Politics of Frustration: The Pursuit of Formal Constitutional Change in Australia and Canada,' in Bruce W. Hodgins, John Eddy, Shelagh D. Grant, and James Struthers, eds., *Federalism in Canada and Australia: Historical Perspectives 1920–88* (Peterborough: Broad-

view 1989), 59, and Peter H. Russell, 'Can the Canadians Be a Sovereign People?' *Canadian Journal of Political Science* 24 (1991): 691. I now think that the more ominous sounding 'mega' is the appropriate term for Canadian efforts at large-scale constitutional change because it captures the serious, crisis-like nature of the cleavage in the political community that generates these efforts. I am grateful to my colleague Stefan Dupré for this suggestion.

9 For a good discussion see Stephen L. Schechter, 'Amending the United States Constitution: A New Generation on Trial,' in Banting and Simeon, eds., *Redesigning the State*, 160–202.

10 Note 8 above

11 Banting and Simeon, eds., *Redesigning the State*, 25

12 Quoted in Cook, *Canada, Quebec, and the Uses of Nationalism*, 65

13 For Trudeau's critique of ethnic nationalism see his 'Federalism, Nationalism and Reason,' in Pierre Elliott Trudeau, *Federalism and the French Canadians* (Toronto: Macmillan 1968). See also Stephen Clarkson and Christina McCall, *Trudeau and Our Times, I: The Magnificent Obsession* (Toronto: McClelland and Stewart 1990), chap. 4.

14 Trudeau, *Federalism and the French Canadians*, 43

15 For an account of this conference see Richard Simeon, *Federal-Provincial Diplomacy: The Making of Recent Policy in Canada* (Toronto: University of Toronto Press 1972), chap. 5.

16 For a critical account of that perspective see Garth Stevenson, *Unfulfilled Union: Canadian Federalism and National Unity*, 3rd ed. (Toronto: Gage 1989), 241–9.

17 Simeon, *Federal-Provincial Diplomacy*, 94

18 Royal Commission on Bilingualism and Biculturalism, *A Preliminary Report* (Ottawa: Queen's Printer 1965), 13

19 Ibid., 119

20 Trudeau, *Federalism and the French Canadians*, 54

21 Peter H. Russell, 'The Political Purposes of the Canadian Charter of Rights and Freedoms,' *Canadian Bar Review* 61 (1983): 33

22 Prime Minister's Office, *Federalism for the Future: A Statement of Policy by the Government of Canada* (Ottawa: Queen's Printer 1968)

23 Trudeau, *Federalism and the French Canadians*, 193

24 Kenneth McRoberts, *English Canada and Quebec: Avoiding the Issue* (North York: Robarts Centre for Canadian Studies, York University

1991). My own analysis of the implications of the 'Trudeau vision' owes much to McRoberts's insights. A full-length treatment of his analysis, *Separate Agendas: English Canada and Quebec*, is soon to be published by McClelland and Stewart.

25 For a penetrating analysis of this limitation of Trudeau's brand of liberalism see Will Kymlicka, *Liberalism, Community and Culture* (Oxford: Clarendon Press 1989).

26 Simeon, *Federal-Provincial Diplomacy*

27 For a discussion of this phenomenon see Smiley, *Canada in Question: Federalism in the Seventies*, chap. 3.

28 Simeon, *Federal-Provincial Diplomacy*, 122

29 Quoted ibid., 98

30 In Jones v. Attorney-General Canada [1975] 2 S.C.R. 182, the Supreme Court ruled that Parliament could validly enact this legislation under its general power to make laws for the peace, order, and good government of Canada.

31 Edward McWhinney, *Quebec and the Constitution, 1960–1978* (Toronto: University of Toronto Press 1979), 48

32 *Shaping Canada's Future Together: Proposals* (Ottawa: Supply and Services Canada 1991), 39–41

33 The federal proposal was set out in Prime Minister's Office, *Federal-Provincial Grants and the Spending Power of Parliament: Government of Canada Working Paper on the Constitution* (Ottawa: Queen's Printer 1969).

34 Quoted in Simeon, *Federal-Provincial Diplomacy*, 112

35 Claude Morin, *Quebec versus Ottawa: The Struggle for Self-Government 1960–72*, translated from *Le Pouvoir québécois ... en négotiation* and from *Le Combat québécois* by Richard Howard (Toronto: University of Toronto Press 1976), 61

36 For a shrewd analysis of bargaining in this forum see Michael B. Stein, *Canadian Constitutional Renewal, 1968–1981: A Case Study in Integrative Bargaining* (Kingston: Queen's University, Institute of Intergovernmental Relations 1989).

37 *Globe and Mail*, 18 June 1971

38 The full text of the Victoria Charter is printed in Paul Fox, ed., *Politics: Canada*, 4th ed. (Toronto: McGraw-Hill Ryerson 1977), 22–32.

39 Russell, Knopff, and Morton, eds., *Federalism and the Charter*, 145–7

40 For an analysis of the English-speaking, common-law dominance of the court up to that time see Russell, *Supreme Court of Canada.*

41 Most recently it was proposed in the report of the Special Joint Committee of the Senate and the House of Commons (Beaudoin-Edwards Committee), *The Process for Amending the Constitution of Canada,* 20 June 1991 (Ottawa: Supply and Services Canada 1991).

42 Toronto *Daily Star,* 23 June 1971

43 *Globe and Mail,* 23 June 1971

44 Simeon, *Federal-Provincial Diplomacy,* 121

Chapter 7 Round Two: New Constitutionalism

1 Special Joint Committee of the Senate and the House of Commons on the Constitution of Canada, *Final Report* (Ottawa: Queen's Printer 1972), 7

2 Ibid., 13

3 Ibid., 13

4 For a penetrating discussion of the principle of self-determination in the Canadian context see David Cameron, *Nationalism, Self-Determination and the Quebec Question* (Toronto: Macmillan 1974).

5 Note 1 above, 13

6 Department of Indian Affairs and Northern Development, *Statement of the Government of Canada on Indian Policy, 1969* (Ottawa: Queen's Printer 1969). For an analysis of this paper and reactions to it see Sally M. Weaver, *Making Canadian Indian Policy: The Hidden Agenda 1968–1970* (Toronto: University of Toronto Press 1981).

7 Note 1 above, 15

8 Calder v. Attorney-General of British Columbia [1973] S.C.R. 313

9 Justice Pigeon, the seventh member of the panel that heard the case, based his decision entirely on procedural grounds and did not deal with the merits of the Nishgas' claim. For a discussion of the case and its long-term significance see Thomas R. Berger, *Fragile Freedoms: Human Rights and Dissent in Canada* (Toronto: Clarke, Irwin 1981), chap. 8.

10 Ibid., 243

11 Task Force to Review Comprehensive Claims Policy, *Living Treaties: Lasting Agreements* (Ottawa: Department of Indian Affairs and Northern Development 1986), 12

12 Quoted in Simeon, *Federal-Provincial Diplomacy*, 93

13 For a discussion see Merv Leitch, 'The Constitutional Position of Natural Resources,' in J. Peter Meekison, *Canadian Federalism: Myth or Reality*, 3rd ed. (Toronto: Methuen 1977), 170–9.

14 C.I.G.O.L. Ltd. v. Saskatchewan [1978] 2 S.C.R. 545; Central Canada Potash Co. Ltd. v. Saskatchewan [1979] 1 S.C.R. 42

15 David Elton and Roger Gibbons, 'Western Alienation and Political Culture,' in Richard Schultz, Orest M. Kruhlak, and John C. Terry, eds., *The Canadian Political Process*, 3rd ed. (Toronto: Holt, Rinehart & Winston 1979), 83

16 For the first application of this term see E.R. Black and A.C. Cairns, 'A Different Perspective on Canadian Federalism,' *Canadian Public Administration* 9 (1966): 27–45.

17 Fox, ed., *Politics: Canada*, 69

18 See Peter H. Russell, 'The Supreme Court and Federal-Provincial Relations: The Political Use of Legal Resources,' *Canadian Public Policy* 11 (1985): 161–70.

19 Alan C. Cairns, 'The Governments and Societies of Canadian Federalism,' *Canadian Journal of Political Science*, 10 (1977): 695–726

20 David Elkins and Richard Simeon, *Small Worlds: Provinces and Parties in Canadian Political Life* (Toronto: Methuen 1980)

21 For an analysis of this movement see Sylvia Bashevkin, *True Patriot Love: The Politics of Canadian Nationalism* (Toronto: Oxford University Press 1991).

22 Quoted in Smiley, *Canada in Question: Federalism in the Eighties*, 80

23 Ibid., 81

24 See McWhinney, *Quebec and the Constitution*, chap. 6.

25 Alan C. Cairns, 'The Politics of Constitutional Renewal in Canada,' in Banting and Simeon, eds., *Redesigning the State*, 102

26 *Options Canada* (Toronto: University of Toronto 1977), iii

27 Task Force on Canadian Unity, *A Future Together: Observations and Recommendations* (Ottawa: Supply and Services Canada 1979), 3

28 Prime Minister's Office, *A Time for Action: Toward the Renewal of the Canadian Federation* (Ottawa: Government of Canada 1978)

29 See chapter 4, above.

30 *The Constitutional Amendment Bill: Text and Explanatory Notes* (Ottawa: Government of Canada 1978)

31 Ibid., 2–4

32 *A Time for Action,* 25
33 Canadian Bar Association, Committee on the Constitution, *Towards a New Canada* (Ottawa 1978)
34 Roy Romanow, John Whyte, and Howard Leeson, *Canada ... Notwithstanding: The Making of the Constitution 1976–1982* (Toronto: Carswell/Methuen 1984), 33
35 See, in particular, Government of British Columbia, *Constitutional Proposals: Reform of the Senate,* paper 3 (Victoria: Queen's Printer for British Columbia 1978).
36 See Cairns, 'Politics of Constitutional Renewal,' 102–4.
37 Gouvernement du Québec, *Quebec–Canada: A New Deal: The Quebec Government Proposal for a New Partnership between Quebec and Canada* (Québec: Conseil Executif 1979)
38 Ibid., 62
39 Constitutional Committee of the Quebec Liberal Party, *A New Canadian Federation* (Montreal: Quebec Liberal Party 1980)
40 Ibid., 22
41 Constitutional Committee of the Quebec Liberal Party, *A Quebec Free To Choose* (Quebec: Quebec Liberal Party 1991)
42 Ibid., iii
43 Task Force on Canadian Unity, *A Future Together,* 141
44 Constitution Act, 1867, s.92(10)(c)
45 Romanow, Whyte, and Leeson, *Canada ... Notwithstanding,* 53
46 Ibid., 52
47 Reference Re Legislative Authority of Parliament To Alter or Replace the Senate (1980) 1 S.C.R. 54
48 See Clarkson and McCall, *Trudeau and Our Times,* chap. 7.

Chapter 8 Round Three: Patriation

1 Clarkson and McCall, *Trudeau and Our Times,* 179
2 Dufour, *A Canadian Challenge,* 85
3 Quoted in Meekison, *Canadian Federalism: Myth or Reality,* 493
4 Ibid., 496
5 McRoberts, *Quebec: Social Change and Political Crisis,* 327
6 Robert Sheppard and Michael Valpy, *The National Deal: The Fight for a Canadian Constitution* (Toronto: Fleet Books 1982), 33
7 Romanow, Whyte, and Leeson, *Canada ... Notwithstanding,* 84

8 Ibid., 85

9 *Globe and Mail*, 28 Nov. 1991

10 Quoted in Stein, *Canadian Constitutional Renewal*, 27

11 Ibid.

12 Quoted in David Milne, *The New Canadian Constitution* (Toronto: James Lorimer 1982), 83

13 The quoted words in this paragraph are contained in section 36 of the Constitution Act, 1982. For a discussion of equalization payments and their results see Smiley, *Canada in Question: Federalism in the Eighties*, 163–78.

14 For a discussion of this element of the package see Sheppard and Valpy, *National Deal*, 74–7.

15 This amendment would partially reverse Supreme Court decisions rendered in the 1970s (see above, 95–6). It added section 92A to the list of provincial powers, giving the provinces concurrent power to regulate natural resources in interprovincial trade and to levy indirect taxes on natural resources. But it denied the provinces any regulatory power over international trade in natural resources.

16 See Sheppard and Valpy, *National Deal*, chap. 6.

17 Ibid., 137

18 This clause became section 28 of the charter.

19 This clause was eventually amended by adding the word 'existing' before aboriginal rights. It was not made part of the Charter, but became section 35 of the Constitution Act, 1982.

20 This became section 27 of the Charter.

21 Subsections covering New Brunswick were added to sections 16 to 20 of the Charter, the sections making English and French 'the official languages of Canada' and establishing the right to use both languages in federal institutions and in communications with the federal government.

22 The other prohibited grounds of discrimination in section 15 of the Charter are race, national or ethnic origin, colour, religion, sex, and age.

23 This became section 24(2) of the Charter. Evidence obtained in violation of Charter rights is to be excluded if its admission 'would bring the administration of justice into disrepute.'

24 The Charter's original section 1 stated that the rights and freedoms

in the Charter were subject 'only to such reasonable limits as are generally accepted in a free and democratic society with a parliamentary system of government.' This was changed to 'only to such reasonable limits prescribed by law as can be demonstrably justified in a free and democratic society.'

25 Sheppard and Valpy, *National Deal*, 151

26 See especially Alan C. Cairns, 'Constitutional Minoritarianism in Canada,' in Ronald L. Watts and Douglas M. Brown, eds., *Canada: The State of the Federation, 1990* (Kingston: Queen's University, Institute of Intergovernmental Relations 1990).

27 See, for instance, Donald V. Smiley, *The Canadian Charter of Rights and Freedoms, 1981* (Toronto: Ontario Economic Council 1981), and the author's testimony to the special parliamentary committee.

28 For information on public opinion on the Charter at this time see Sheppard and Valpy, *National Deal*, especially chap. 7. Data on public ignorance about the contents of the Charter were collected as part of a larger study on Canadians' attitudes to civil liberties carried out by Paul Sniderman, Joseph Fletcher, Philip Tetlock, and the author. For an early report of key findings see Peter H. Russell, 'Canada's Charter: A Political Report,' *Public Law* (1988): 385.

29 Sheppard and Valpy, *National Deal*, 184

30 See ibid., chap. 9.

31 On the use of symbols in political combat see Raymond Breton, 'The Production and Allocation of Symbolic Resources: An Analysis of the Linguistic and Ethnocultural Fields in Canada,' *Canadian Review of Sociology and Anthropology* 21 (1984): 123.

32 For an account of this effort see Douglas Sanders, 'The Indian Lobby,' in Banting and Simeon, eds., *And No One Cheered*, 301–32.

33 House of Commons (UK), *British North America Acts: The Role of Parliament* (London: Her Majesty's Stationary Office 1981)

34 Ibid., para. 114

35 Canada, Department of Justice, *The Role of the United Kingdom in the Amendment of the Canadian Constitution* (Ottawa: Publications Canada 1981)

36 Milne, *New Canadian Constitution*, 97

37 Russell, Knopff, and Morton, *Federalism and the Charter*, 707

38 Peter H. Russell, 'The Supreme Court Decision: Bold Statescraft

Based on Questionable Jurisprudence,' in Peter Russell et al., *The Court and the Constitution: Comments on the Supreme Court Reference on Constitutional Amendment, 1982* (Kingston: Queen's University, Institute of Intergovernmental Relations 1982), 1

39 On the role of conventions in the Canadian constitutional system see Heard, *Canadian Constitution Conventions.*

40 Text of his 'Convocation Speech at Opening of Bora Laskin Law Library, University of Toronto, March 21, 1991.' Brian Dickson, the recently retired chief justice of the Supreme Court, who as an ordinary justice was one of the authors of the opinion Trudeau attacked, was in the front row of the audience to which Trudeau delivered his diatribe. This speech has now been published as Pierre Elliott Trudeau, *Fatal Tilt: Speaking Out About Sovereignty* (Toronto: HarperCollins 1991).

41 *Globe and Mail,* 29 Sept. 1981

42 For blow-by-blow accounts of this conference see Romanow, Whyte, and Leeson, *Canada ... Notwithstanding,* chap. 7, and Sheppard and Valpy, *National Deal,* chap. 13.

43 Trudeau proposed that the outcome of such a referendum be determined by majorities within the four regions defined by the Victoria Charter.

44 Romanow, Whyte, and Leeson, *Canada ... Notwithstanding,* 208

45 The other items requiring unanimity are Canada-wide English and French language rights and the guarantee that no province's representation in the House of Commons should be less than in the Senate. As with previous amending formula proposals, this one, which as sections 37 to 49 of the Constitution Act, 1982, was written into Canada's constitutional law, was extraordinarily complex. In addition to the key elements discussed in the text, other clauses authorize the amendment of provisions applying to one or more but not all the provinces by the federal Parliament and the provinces concerned, and, on a very restricted basis, unilateral amendments by the federal Parliament and each of the provinces to their own constitutions and institutions.

46 For reasons that are obscure, the wording adopted in this revision of the Charter's section 6 applies the qualification, where 'the rate of employment' in the province 'is below the rate of employment in Canada.'

322 Notes to pages 121–8

47 See John D. Whyte, 'On Not Standing for Notwithstanding,' *Alberta Law Review* 28 (1990): 347.

48 See Paul C. Weiler, 'Rights and Judges in a Democracy: A New Canadian Version,' *University of Michigan Journal of Law Reform* 18 (1984): 51, and Peter H. Russell, 'Standing Up for Notwithstanding,' *Alberta Law Review* 29 (1991): 293.

49 This is the language now in section 40 of the Constitution Act, 1982.

50 This provision is still in the Constitution as section 59 of the Constitution Act, 1982.

51 See Milne, *New Canadian Constitution*, 156–7.

52 For an account of the campaign and its significance see Penny Kome, *The Taking of Twenty-Eight: Women Challenge the Constitution* (Toronto: Women's Press 1983).

53 This now appears in section 35(1) of the Constitution Act, 1982, which reads as follows: 'The existing aboriginal and treaty rights of the aboriginal peoples of Canada are hereby recognized and affirmed.'

54 See Sanders, 'The Indian Lobby,' 321.

55 *Globe and Mail*, 20 Jan. 1982

56 For a discussion of this ruling see Sanders, 'Indian Lobby,' 322–3.

57 See chap. 5.

58 Special Joint Committee of the Senate and the House of Commons on the Constitution of Canada, *Final Report*, 8. For a discussion of this issue see Melvin Smith, 'Patriation: A Myth or Reality?' *Policy Options*, Dec. 1981.

59 *Globe and Mail*, 26 Nov. 1981

60 For a discussion of the distinction between autonomy and autochthony see Hogg, *Constitutional Law of Canada*, 44–9.

Chapter 9 Round Four: Meech Lake

1 Trudeau used this phrase in his May 1987 newspaper article attacking the Meech Lake Accord. See Andrew Cohen, *A Deal Undone: The Making and Breaking of the Meech Lake Accord* (Vancouver: Douglas & McIntyre 1990), 165.

2 Re Objection to a Resolution to Amend the Constitution [1983] S.C.R. 793

3 Re Resolution to Amend the Constitution [1981] 1 S.C.R. 753, at 888
4 For an appraisal of the court's opinion see Marc Gold, 'The Mask of Objectivity: Politics and Rhetoric in the Supreme Court of Canada,' *Supreme Court Law Review* 7 (1985): 455.
5 See note 3 above, at 883
6 Trudeau, *Fatal Tilt*, 15
7 Section 37 of the Constitution Act, 1982
8 Ibid.
9 Section 35(3) of the Constitution Act, 1982
10 For a discussion of these agreements see Task Force to Review Comprehensive Claims Policy, *Living Treaties; Lasting Agreements*, chap. 1.
11 There is exclusive federal jurisdiction over 'Indians, and Lands reserved for the Indians' in section 91(24) and section 25 of the Charter of Rights, which protect aboriginal rights from being abrogated by other provisions of the Charter, and sections 35 and 35(1) of the Constitution Act, 1982.
12 Section 35(1) of the Constitution Act, 1982
13 Section 35(4) of the Constitution Act, 1982
14 The main discrimination was a section denying Indian status (including the right to live on reserves) to Indian women who married non-Indians while Indian men marrying non-Indians retained their status. In Attorney General Canada v. Lavell and Bedard [1974] S.C.R. 1349, the Supreme Court of Canada held that this section did not violate the right to equality before the law in the Canadian Bill of Rights. This particular form of discrimination was removed by amendments to the Indian Act in 1985.
15 Section 37(1) of the Constitution Act, 1982
16 For a review of these conferences see David C. Hawkes, *Aboriginal Peoples and Constitutional Reform: What Have We Learned?* (Kingston: Queen's University, Institute of Intergovernmental Relations 1989).
17 For a collection of aboriginal views on self-government see Leroy Little Bear, Menno Boldt, and J. Anthony Long, eds., *Pathways to Self-Determination: Canadian Indians and the Canadian State* (Toronto: University of Toronto Press 1984).
18 For an insightful discussion see Michael Asch and Patrick Macklem, 'Aboriginal Rights and Canadian Sovereignty,' *Alberta Law Review* 29 (1991): 498.

19 *Globe and Mail,* 7 Aug. 1984

20 Ibid., 13 Dec. 1985

21 There are two full accounts of the Quebec round: one which is critical and written from the vantage point of a journalist observing the events is Cohen, *A Deal Undone*; the other, which is supportive and written from the vantage point of an inside participant is Patrick Monahan, *Meech Lake: The Inside Story* (Toronto: University of Toronto Press 1991).

22 Cohen, *Deal Undone,* 74

23 The Parti Québécois government's constitutional proposals released on 17 May 1985, a few months before its fall from power, included proposals for expanding Quebec's powers in the economic sphere and in international relations and for giving Quebec's Charter of Rights primacy with respect to rights and freedoms. See Government of Quebec, *Draft Agreement on the Constitution* (Quebec, May 1985).

24 Monahan, *Meech Lake,* 61

25 Cohen, *Deal Undone,* 18

26 R.A. Vineberg, 'Federal-Provincial Relations in Canadian Immigration,' *Canadian Public Administration* 20 (1987): 299

27 In a political protocol attached to the Meech Lake Accord the federal government pledged that Quebec should receive a number of immigrants equal to its proportion of the population and be able to exceed that number by 5 per cent.

28 For discussions of different aspects of the Meech Lake Accord see *Canadian Public Policy,* special issue, Sept. 1987; Michael D. Behiels, ed., *The Meech Lake Primer: Conflicting Views of the 1987 Constitutional Accord* (Ottawa: University of Ottawa Press 1989); K.E. Swinton and C.J. Rogerson, eds., *Competing Constitutional Visions: The Meech Lake Accord* (Toronto: Carswell 1988).

29 Monahan, *Meech Lake,* 86

30 Section 2 of the Constitution Act, 1867 (the BNA Act). Section 1 was the title of the act.

31 Léon Dion argued that recognition of Quebec's English minority in the distinct society clause might mean that Quebec could not use the override clause in the Charter to protect a law requiring unilingual French signs. *Globe and Mail,* 15 May 1987

32 Monahan, *Meech Lake,* 109

33 For a full statement of the final accord and analysis of its terms see Peter W. Hogg, *Meech Lake Constitutional Accord Annotated* (Toronto: Carswell 1988).

34 The non-derogation clause put to rest Quebec's concern that the original version might have undermined its freedom to use the override clause in the Charter of Rights.

35 Monahan, *Meech Lake*, 137

36 Ibid., 133

37 William (Binx) Remnant, clerk of the Manitoba Legislative Assembly, 'Comments to the Commonwealth Parliamentary Association, Ontario Branch,' Toronto, 25 Nov. 1987

38 *Globe and Mail*, 24 June 1987

39 The three-year deadline does not apply to amendments subject to the unanimity rule.

40 Richard Simeon, 'Why Did the Meech Lake Accord Fail?' in Watts and Brown, eds., *Canada*, 28

41 J. Stefan Dupré, 'Canada's Political and Constitutional Future: Reflections on the Bélanger-Campeau Report and Bill 150,' in J.L. Granatstein and Kenneth McNaught, eds., *'English Canada' Speaks Out* (Toronto: Doubleday 1991), 67–8

42 Until 1982, new provinces could be created by the federal Parliament alone using authority granted it by the Constitution Act, 1871.

43 A.W. Johnson, 'The Meech Lake Accord and the Bonds of Nationhood,' in Swinton and Rogerson, eds., *Competing Constitutional Visions*, 146. For arguments that the spending-power proposal was well balanced and that it was dangerously centralizing, see the contributions of J. Stefan Dupré and Andrée Lajoie, respectively, to the same volume.

44 For an expression of this viewpoint see Philip Resnick, *Letters to a Québécois Friend* (Montreal and Kingston: McGill-Queen's University Press 1990).

45 Quebec v. Ford et al. [1988] 2 S.C.R. 712

46 Monahan, *Meech Lake*, 164

47 See, for instance, Ramsay Cook, 'Manitoba, Quebec Premiers Have Done Canada a Big Favour,' *Toronto Star*, 22 Jan. 1989.

48 Paul M. Sniderman, Joseph F. Fletcher, Peter H. Russell, and Philip E. Tetlock, 'Political Culture and the Problem of Double Standards: Mass and Elite Attitudes toward Language Rights in the Canadian

Charter of Rights and Freedoms,' *Canadian Journal of Political Science* 22 (1989): 259

49 Monahan, *Meech Lake*, 170

50 *Report of the Manitoba Task Force on Meech Lake*, Summary of Recommendations, 72–9, 21 Oct. 1989

51 *Globe and Mail*, 25 Oct. 1989

52 Letter from Clyde Wells to Brian Mulroney, 18 Oct. 1989

53 The Newfoundland legislature had approved the accord in July 1988. Section 46(2) of the Constitution Act, 1982, permits a legislature to revoke a resolution assenting to a constitutional amendment any time before an amendment is fully ratified and proclaimed.

54 *Globe and Mail*, 16 May 1990

55 Ibid., 18 May 1990

56 Cohen, *Deal Undone*, 251

57 For a copy of the communiqué see Monahan, *Meech Lake*, app. 4, 306–9.

58 Ibid., 306

59 *Globe and Mail*, 23 June 1990

60 Toronto *Star*, 8 April 1990

61 *Globe and Mail*, 22 March 1990

Chapter 10 Round Five: The Canada Round I

1 For a summary of constitutional events during this period see Darrel R. Reid, 'Chronology of Events July 1990–June 1991,' in Douglas M. Brown, ed., *Canada: The State of the Federation, 1991* (Kingston: Queen's University, Institute of Intergovernmental Relations 1991).

2 *Globe and Mail*, 26 June 1990

3 Ibid., 29 June 1990

4 Léon Dion has referred to the proposed referendum on sovereignty as 'a knife at the throat of English Canada'; David Olive, 'The Mischievous Léon Dion Seeks Autonomy and Prosperity for Quebec,' ibid., 14 Dec. 1991.

5 For expressions of this aroused sense of English-Canadian nationalism see Granatstein and McNaught, eds., *'English Canada' Speaks Out*.

6 See chapter 1.

7 Peter H. Russell, 'Towards a New Constitutional Process,' in Ronald L. Watts and Douglas M. Brown, eds., *Options for a New Canada* (Toronto: University of Toronto Press 1991), 142

8 For an English translation of a wide range of submissions see Richard Fidler, *Canada, Adieu? Quebec Debates Its Future* (Lantzville, BC: Oolichan Books 1991).

9 Constitutional Committee of the Quebec Liberal Party, *A Quebec Free To Choose*, 1

10 An Act To Establish the Commission on the Political and Constitutional Future of Quebec (Bill 90), s.2

11 Michel Bélanger was president of the Quebec-based National Bank of Canada and Jean Campeau was chairman of the Caisse de Dépot et de Placement du Québec.

12 Pierre Fortin, 'How Economics Is Shaping the Constitutional Debate in Quebec,' in Robert Young, ed., *Confederation in Crisis* (Toronto: James Lorimer 1991), 36

13 *A Quebec Free To Choose*, 18

14 Ibid., 38

15 Even this demand was later modified when Quebec's manpower minister, André Bourbeau, stated a preference for administrative rather than constitutional control over unemployment insurance. *Globe and Mail*, 12 Dec. 1991

16 Ibid., 28

17 Ibid., 32

18 Ibid.

19 For a discussion of these problems see Peter M. Leslie, *The European Community: A Political Model for Canada?* (Ottawa: Supply and Services Canada 1991).

20 *Montreal Gazette*, 10 March 1991

21 *Cahier des Amendements au Rapport du Comité Constitutionnel*, 8 March 1991, amendment no. 37 and no. 40

22 Ibid., amendment no. 56

23 *Report of the Commission on the Political and Constitutional Future of Quebec*, Quebec, March 1991, 15

24 An Act Respecting the Process for Determining the Political and Constitutional Future of Quebec, s.1

25 Ibid., s.5

26 Ibid., s.6

27 Ibid., preamble
28 Office of the Prime Minister, Press Release, 1 Nov. 1990
29 *Globe and Mail*, 2 Nov. 1990
30 Ibid., 10 Nov. 1990
31 Graham Fraser, 'Slouching towards Canada,' in Brown, ed., *Canada: The State of the Federation 1991*, 96
32 *Citizens' Forum on Canada's Future* (Ottawa: Minister of Supply and Services 1991), 16. In addition, 300,000 participated in a special Students Forum.
33 Ibid., 29
34 Ibid., 53
35 Ibid., 47
36 *Report of the Special Joint Committee of the Senate and the House of Commons on the Process for Amending the Constitution of Canada* (Ottawa: Queen's Printer, 20 June 1991), 26
37 Ibid., 42
38 Bill 81 – 1991. The results of a constitutional referendum are not binding on the government. For a discussion see Melvin H. Smith, *The Renewal of the Federation: A British Columbia Perspective* (Victoria: Queen's Printer for British Columbia 1991), 84.
39 Ibid., 47
40 Ibid., 50–1
41 Ibid., 47
42 Ibid., 73–6
43 Such a proposal was put forward to Beaudoin-Edwards by the author and is outlined in 'Towards a New Constitutional Process.'
44 For a review of constituent assemblies in history see Patrick Fafard and Darrel R. Reid, *Constituent Assemblies: A Comparative Survey* (Kingston: Queen's University, Institute of Intergovernmental Relations 1991). For an analysis of their possible use in Canada see Patrick Monahan, Lynda Covello, and Jonathan Batty, *Constituent Assemblies: The Canadian Debate in Comparative and Historical Perspective* (North York: York University Centre for Public Law and Public Policy 1992).
45 Toronto *Star*, 14 May 1991
46 Ibid.
47 Ibid.
48 For a discussion of these initiatives up to June 1991 see Kathy L.

Brock, 'The Politics of Process,' in Brown, ed., *Canada*, 67–8. I am indebted to my research assistant, Stephen Johnson, for assembling information on developments since the failure of the Meech Lake Accord in June 1990. For an ongoing account of all these initiatives see *Network* (newsletter of the Network on the Constitution, University of Ottawa).

49 Manitoba's committee was chaired by a professor who did not sit in the legislature, and Ontario's committee excluded cabinet ministers.

50 The first of these studies, by Melvin H. Smith, is cited in note 38.

51 See Alan C. Cairns, 'Constitutional Change and the Three Equalities,' in Watts and Brown, eds., *Canada: The State of the Federation 1991*, 93.

52 *Globe and Mail*, 6 July 1991

53 For an account of the native parallel process see *Network*, Jan. 1992, 9.

54 The commission's terms of reference are set out in its first report, *The Right of Aboriginal Self-Government and the Constitution, a Commentary*, Ottawa, 13 Feb. 1992.

55 See chapter 7.

56 See, for instance, David J. Bercuson and Barry Cooper, *Deconfederation: Canada without Quebec* (Toronto: Key Porter 1991).

57 *Shaping Canada's Future Together* (Ottawa: Minister of Supply and Services 1991). At the same time and in the same format the government published background documents on *Aboriginal Peoples, Self-Government and Constitutional Reform, Canadian Federalism and the Economic Union, Shared Values and The European Community*.

58 The proposal differs from Meech in one respect: the creation of new provinces would not require unanimity but would remain under the seven-province/half-the-population rule.

59 Bordering on the insignificant are proposals to remove the federal Parliament's declaratory power to bring local works under federal jurisdiction, a power that has not been used for many years, and its power over residual matters not of national importance. Under s.92(16) of the Constitution, the provinces already have exclusive jurisdiction over 'all Matters of a purely local or private Nature in the Province.'

60 For an analysis of the economic union aspect of the proposal see

Robert Howse, *Economic Union, Social Justice, and Constitutional Reform: Towards a High but Level Playing Field* (North York: York University Centre for Public Law and Public Policy 1992).

61 The commitment would take the form of an expansion of section 36 of the Constitution Act, 1982, which contains a commitment to promote equal opportunities for 'well-being' and maintain fiscal equalization across the federation. See Select Committee on Ontario in Confederation, *Final Report*, Feb. 1992, recommendation 21.

62 The legislative committee proposes that these standards be 'monitored' by a joint committee of the House of Commons and a reformed Senate. A statement issued by Premier Rae on 14 February 1992 suggests that the monitoring be done by a commission appointed jointly by the federal and provincial governments.

63 Quebec's intergovernmental affairs minister, Gil Rémillard, indicated that federal proposals might be considered by the National Assembly's committee on 'binding offers' before they were fully ratified in the rest of Canada. See *Globe and Mail*, 29 Aug. 1991.

64 The federal commitment is qualified by requiring that such an amendment not mean a right to separate from Canada or the uniliteral determination of powers. See *The Right of Aboriginal Self-Government*, 7.

65 For a summary of provincial positions see Graham Fraser and Susan Delacourt, 'Looking at the Constitutional Gambits,' *Globe and Mail*, 18 Jan. 1992.

66 For a discussion of the extent and forms of asymmetry in Canada's constitutional arrangements see David Milne, 'Equality or Asymmetry: Why Choose?' in Watts and Brown, eds., *Options for a New Canada*, 285.

67 See chapter 5.

68 Atlantic Provinces Economic Council, *Renewal of Canada: Division of Powers Conference Report*, Halifax, 22 Jan. 1992, 21

69 Toronto *Star*, 27 Jan. 1992

70 Ibid., 3 Feb. 1992

71 See, for instance, the summary statement of Raymond Brisson, an Acadian leader, in Graham Fraser, 'Harmony Emerges among Delegates,' *Globe and Mail*, 10 Feb. 1992.

72 Ibid., 17 Feb. 1992

73 Report of the Special Joint Committee of the Senate and the House of Commons, *A Renewed Canada* (Ottawa: Supply and Services Canada, 28 Feb. 1992)
74 Ibid.
75 Ibid., 105. Note that alternative preambles and Canada clause are provided in appendix B of the report.
76 Ibid., 22
77 Ibid., 106
78 *Renewal of Canada Conferences Compendium of Reports* (Ottawa: Privy Council Office 1992), 15
79 *A Renewed Canada,* 108
80 Ibid., 32
81 Ibid., 46
82 Ibid., 54
83 Ibid., 118
84 Ibid., 100

Chapter 11 The Canada Round II

1 If the Charlottetown Accord had been adopted, all references in the Constitution to 'aboriginal' would have been changed to the upper case, 'Aboriginal.' This would have been more than a cosmetic change in that it would reflect the view of Aboriginal peoples that fundamentally they are political communities, not racial or ethnic groups. In this chapter I will respect this Aboriginal view.
2 For an account of the process see Ronald L. Watts, 'The Process of Canadian Constitutional Reform 1990–92,' paper presented at International Seminar on Canada in Transition, National Autonomous University of Mexico, 25–27 November 1992.
3 *Globe and Mail,* 19 Oct. 1992
4 Ibid, 28 Oct. 1992
5 Native Women's Association of Canada v. Canada (1992), 95 DLR (4th), 106. This decision may not be the last word on the issue as the Supreme Court of Canada, on 11 March 1993, announced that it had granted the federal government leave to appeal the Federal Court of Appeal's ruling.
6 *Globe and Mail,* 2 April 1992
7 See chapter 10, 185

8 The Aboriginal delegations may be an exception.
9 *Status Report of the Multilateral Meetings on the Constitution,* 11 June 1992, section 26
10 Ibid., sections 27 and 28
11 See above, 25.
12 This was prompted by the federal government's unilateral capping of its fiscal transfers to the provinces to support the Canada Assistance Plan. In 1991 the Supreme Court of Canada rejected a provincial challenge to this unilateral change (Reference Re: Canada Assistance Plan, 1991 2 SCR 525).
13 See above, 159–60. The principal transfers called for in the Allaire Report were unemployment insurance, agriculture, industry and commerce, communications, energy, environment, regional development, and health.
14 Ontario spoke of a 'social charter' and the Beaudoin-Dobbie Report of a 'social covenant.' In the multilateral process the proposal was turned into a statement on 'The Social and Economic Union.'
15 *Status Report,* 11 June 1992, section 5
16 Ibid., section 47
17 Ibid., section 49
18 Ibid., section 52
19 Ibid., section 59
20 Ibid., section 46
21 Frank Cassidy and Robert L. Bish, *Indian Government: Its Meaning in Practice* (Lantzville, BC: Oolichan Books 1989)
22 Constitution Amendment Proclamation 1983
23 *Status Report,* 11 June 1992, section 55
24 Ibid., section 64. This provision goes further than the provision already in section 35(1)(b) that requires the prime minister to invite the Aboriginal peoples to participate in discussions concerning amendments affecting their constitutional rights.
25 Toronto Star, 9 June 1992
26 *Status Report,* 11 June 1992, section 2
27 Some of these provinces, for instance Manitoba and Nova Scotia, stood firm despite the fact that public consultations produced reports that took a more flexible position on Senate reform.
28 *Status Report,* 11 June 1992, section 7
29 Ibid., section 12

30 Graham Fraser, 'Fumbling on Both Fronts,' *Globe and Mail*, 8 June 1992

31 *Status Report of the Multilateral Meetings on the Constitution*, 16 July 1992, section 21

32 Ibid., section 12

33 Ibid., section 7

34 The single transferable vote system was devised by Thomas Hare in 1859. It was John Stuart Mill's favourite solution to the problem of minority representation. See Mill's *On Representative Government*, chap. 7. For a contemporary analysis of how it works see Douglas Rae, *The Political Consequences of Electoral Laws* (New Haven: Yale University Press 1971), 36–8.

35 *Status Report*, 16 July 1992, section 6

36 *Globe and Mail*, 9 July 1992

37 Ibid., 5 Aug. 1992

38 *Consensus Report on the Constitution*, Charlottetown, 28 August 1992

39 A permanent formula for redistribution would be worked out subject to preserving the 'fixed floor' whereby a province cannot have fewer seats in the House than it has places in the *existing* Senate, Quebec's 25 per cent guarantee, and a guarantee that a province never have fewer seats than a province with a smaller population. Charlottetown Accord, section 21

40 Ibid., section 41

41 Ibid., section 47

42 Ibid., section 1(2)

43 Ibid., section 1(d)

44 Ibid., section 25

45 *Globe and Mail*, 24 Aug. 1992

46 Ibid., 31 Aug. 1992

47 For a summary of the act and a discussion of Canada's previous experience with referendums, see Patrick Boyer, *Direct Democracy in Canada: The History and Future of Referendums* (Toronto: Dundurn 1992).

48 Statutes of Quebec, 1978, chap. 6

49 In Alberta's case that required amending its law. See Alberta's Constitutional Referendum Act, chap. C-22.25, s12.

50 *Proclamation Directing a Referendum*, S1/92–180, 7 Oct. 1992

51 The twelve who were opposed included the eight members of the

Bloc Québécois, two Independents, the one Reform party MP, and one Conservative MP.

52 Referendum Act, s.15

53 For the committee membership see *Globe and Mail*, 23 Sept. 1992. The retired politicians included former leaders of two national parties, Ed Broadbent of the NDP and Robert Stanfield of the Conservatives, and three former premiers, William Davis of Ontario, Peter Lougheed of Alberta, and Gerald Regan of Nova Scotia.

54 *Globe and Mail*, 9 Oct. 1992

55 Ibid., 29 Sept. 1992

56 In addition to the changes noted in the text, other significant modifications were the insertion of a reconciliation process as the first step to be taken when the Senate and the House of Commons disagreed on legislation, and a stipulation that provincial nomination lists for Supreme Court appointments include at least five names.

57 Section 4 of the Legal Text provides for a wholesale replacement of sections 21 to 36 in the Constitution Act 1867. These are the sections on the Senate in Canada's original Constitution.

58 Legal Text, section 29

59 *Globe and Mail*, 7 Oct. 1992

60 Richard Johnson, 'An Inverted Logroll: The Charlottetown Accord and the Referendum,' *PS: Political Science & Politics* 26 (1993): 43

61 Ms Wilhelmy obtained a ten-day injunction on publication in the Quebec media, but this did not prevent Toronto's *Globe and Mail* from publishing excerpts. *Globe and Mail*, 16 Sept. 1992

62 See Johnston, 'An Inverted Logroll.' The Quebec campaign, legally, was shorter than the federal campaign. Quebec's referendum law sets a twenty-eight-day minimum which cannot begin until 20 days after the National Assembly debate on the referendum question. Officially, the Quebec campaign did not begin until nearly the end of September.

63 Complete results for all voting districts were printed in the Toronto Star on 27 October 1992.

Chapter 12   Canada Returns to Constitutional Normalcy

1 John Gray, 'Johnson Wants Fast Referendum,' *Globe and Mail*, 14 Sept. 1994

2 The text was reproduced in the *Globe and Mail* on 7 Dec. 1994.

3 Ibid.

4 Rhéal Séguin, 'Sovereignty Hearings Launched,' *Globe and Mail*, 4 Feb. 1995

5 'Bouchard Loses Leg to Blood Infection,' *Globe and Mail*, 2 Dec. 1994

6 Rhéal Séguin, 'Delay of Vote Puts Parizeau Between Rock and Hard Place,' *Globe and Mail*, 7 Apr. 1995

7 Rhéal Séguin, 'Parizeau Bends on Political Ties,' *Globe and Mail*, 12 Apr. 1995

8 Tu Thanh Ha, 'Bloc Urges New Sovereignty Stance,' *Globe and Mail*, 8 Apr. 1995

9 For details see Andrew C. Tzembelicos, 'Chronology of Events,' in Douglas M. Brown and Johnathan W. Rose, eds., *Canada: The State of the Federation 1995* (Kingston: Institute of Intergovernmental Relations, Queen's University, 1995), 249–50.

10 The text was printed in the *Globe and Mail* on 8 Sept. under the headline 'Quebec's Bill of Divorcement.'

11 Ibid.., section 26

12 Ibid., section 8

13 'The Question,' *Globe and Mail*, 8 Sept. 1995

14 Rhéal Séguin, 'Quebec Secession Ruled Unconstitutional,' *Globe and Mail*, 9 Sept. 1995

15 See Lawrence Martin, *Iron Man: The Defiant Reign of Jean Chrétien* (Toronto: Viking Canada 2003), 122.

16 Rhéal Séguin, 'Pariseau Saw That He was the Enemy,' *Globe and Mail*, 9 Oct. 1995

17 Eddie Goldenberg, Chrétien's chief political adviser, is quoted by Lawrence Martin as recalling that the 'no' side was 'fifteen to twenty points ahead' up to two or three weeks before the referendum. See Lawrence, *Iron Man*, 123. Political scientist Edouard Cloutier's analysis of polls taken throughout the referendum campaign shows a smaller 'no' side lead in the early weeks of the campaign and the 'yes' side moving ahead in early October. See Edouard Cloutier, 'The Quebec Referendum: From Polls to Ballots,' *Canada Watch* 4(2) (1995): 37, 39.

18 Martin, *Iron Man*, 128

19 See Robert Everett, 'Parliament and Politics,' in David Leyton-Brown,

ed., *Canadian Annual Review of Politics and Public Affairs 1995*
(Toronto: University of Toronto Press 2002), 15.

20 Edouard Cloutier's analysis (note 17 above) of polling data supports
this suggestion.

21 André Picard, 'Parizeau Promises to "Exact Revenge" for Sovereignist
Loss,' *Globe and Mail*, 31 Oct. 1995

22 Everett, 'Parliament and Politics,' 16

23 Edward Greenspon and Jeff Sallot, 'PM Pledges Reconciliation with
Quebec,' *Globe and Mail*, 31 Oct. 1995

24 For the Crees' position, see Grand Council of the Crees, *Sovereign
Injustice: Forcible Inclusion of the James Bay Crees and the Cree Territory into
a Sovereign Quebec* (Nemaska: Grand Council of the Cree 1995).

25 Martin, *Iron Man*, 134

26 For a fuller exposition of this point, see Peter H. Russell, 'Can Quebeckers Be a Sovereign People?' *Canada Watch* 4(2) (1995): 38–9.

27 For a detailed analysis of the referendum vote, see Pierre Drouilly,
'An Exemplary Referendum,' *Canada Watch* 4(2) (1955): 25–7.

28 Susan Delacourt, 'PM Offers Quebec Distinct Status,' *Globe and Mail*,
28 Nov. 1995

29 See chapter 6, 90.

30 In Chrétien's distinct society resolution, it is the House of Commons,
not the courts, that would 'undertake to be guided' by the reality that
'Quebec is a distinct society within Canada.'

31 Brian Lagh and Graham Fraser, 'Premiers Develop Unity Plan,' *Globe
and Mail*, 15 Sept. 1997

32 Rhéal Séguin, 'Bouchard Reviles Unity Proposal,' *Globe and Mail*,
17 Sept. 1997

33 Miro Cernetig, 'Chrétien's Distinct Society Backfires in West,' *Globe
and Mail*, 29 Nov. 1995

34 Susan Delacourt and Miro Cernetig, 'BC Wins Constitutional Veto,'
Globe and Mail, 8 Dec. 1995

35 *Statutes of Canada*, 1996, chap. 1

36 Boyer, *Direct Democracy in Canada*, chap. 5

37 See Herman Bakvis, 'Federalism, New Public Management and
Labour-Market Development,' in Patrick C. Fafard and Douglas M.
Brown, eds., *Canada: The State of the Federation, 1996* (Kingston:
Institute of Intergovernmental Relations, Queen's University 1996),
135–65.

38 See Peter H. Russell, 'Preserving the Canadian Federation: A Two-Track Approach,' in James M. Pitsula, ed., *New Perspectives on the Canadian Constitutional Debate* (Regina: Canadian Plains Research Centre, University of Regina 1997), 1–18, and Patrick J. Monahan and Michael J. Bryant with Nancy C. Côté, 'Coming to Terms with Plan B: Ten Principles Governing Secession,' in David R. Cameron, ed., *The Referendum Paper: Essays on Secession and National Unity* (Toronto: University of Toronto Press 1999), 245.

39 On the Trudeau/Dion comparison, see Peter H. Russell, 'Preface' in Stéphane Dion, ed., *Straight Talk: Speeches and Writings on Canadian Unity* (Montreal and Kingston: McGill-Queen's University Press 1999).

40 Stéphane Dion, 'Letter to Mr. Lucien Bouchard, September 11, 1997,' in ibid., 189

41 Rhéal Séguin, 'Quebec, Ottawa Head for Showdown,' *Globe and Mail,* 11 May 1996

42 For an account of the events leading up to the Quebec Secession reference, the questions, the Court's decision, and comments on the case, see David Schneiderman, ed., *The Quebec Decision: Perspective on the Supreme Court Ruling on Secession* (Toronto: James Lorimer 1999).

43 Canada, House of Commons, Debates, 6 Sept. 1996, 4707

44 David Schneiderman, 'Introduction,' in Schniederman, ed., *The Quebec Decision*

45 Reference re the Secession of Quebec [1998] 2 s.c.r. 217

46 The Court declined to explain how the constitutional amending formula applies to a negotiated agreement on Quebec secession. For an analysis of how it might apply, see Peter H. Russell and Bruce Ryder, 'Ratifying a Postreferendum Agreement on Quebec Sovereignty,' in Cameron, ed., *The Referendum Papers,* ch. 8.

47 Reference re the Secession of Quebec, para. 125

48 Ibid. para. 138.

49 Ibid. para. 93

50 Ibid. para. 96.

51 Ibid. para. 88.

52 This is also the conclusion of a special study for the Royal Commission on Aboriginal Peoples. See Renée Dupuis and Kent McNeil, *Canada's Fiduciary Obligation to Aboriginal Peoples in the Context of Accession to Sovereignty by Quebec* (Ottawa: Canada Communication Group 1995).

53 See Annis May Timpson, 'The Challenges of Intergovernmental Relations for Nunavut,' forthcoming in Michael Murphy, ed., *The State of the Federation 2002 – Reconfiguring Aboriginal-State Relations* (Kingston: Institute of Intergovernmental Relations, Queen's University).

54 Reference re Secession of Quebec, para. 103

55 See chapter 8, 118–19.

56 Edward Greenspan and Anne McIlroy, 'Bouchard and PM Square Off,' *Globe and Mail*, 22 August 1998

57 Ibid.

58 Reference re Secession of Quebec, para. 100

59 (2000) Statutes of Canada, chap. 26, section 1(1)

60 Ibid., section 1(6)

61 Ibid., section 2(1)

62 Ibid., section 3(2)

63 'An Act Respecting the Exercise of the Fundamental Rights of the Quebec People and the Quebec State, (2001) Statutes of Quebec, chap. 46, section 2

64 Ibid., section 14

65 Robert McKenzie, 'Bouchard Quits Today as Quebec Premier,' Toronto *Star*, 11 Jan. 2001

66 Rhéal Séguin, 'Charest Sweeps PQ Aside,' *Globe and Mail*, 15 Apr. 2003

67 See, for instance, Charles Blattberg, *Shall We Dance? A Patriotic Politics for Canada* (Montreal and Kingston: McGill-Queen's University Press 2003).

68 See chapter 2.

69 See above, p. 10.

70 For details on this and the other section 43 amendments, see Peter W. Hogg, *Constitutional Law of Canada*, 4th ed. (Scarborough, ON: Carswell 1999), section 1.4, note 28, pp. 1–7.

71 For an account of this amendment and the Newfoundland schools amendment, see Dion, *Straight Talk*, 80–92.

72 Nelson Wiseman, 'Clarifying Provincial Constitutions,' *National Journal of Constitutional Law* 6 (1994–5): 269–94 at 270.

73 Section 45 of the Constitution Act gives provincial legislatures exclusive jurisdiction over amendments to provincial constitutions that do not involve the terms of their becoming part of Canada.

74 Harvey Lazar, 'Non-Constitutional Renewal: Toward a New Equilibrium in the Federation,' in Harvey Lazar, ed., *Canada: The State of the*

Federation 1997: Non-Constitutional Renewal (Montreal and Kingston: McGill-Queen's University Press 1998), at 9.

75 For an account of the negotiations leading to the AIT, see G. Bruce Doern and Mark MacDonald, *Free-Trade Federalism: Negotiating the Canadian Agreement on Internal Trade* (Toronto: University of Toronto Press 1999).

76 For an account and analysis of these developments, see Douglas M. Brown, *Market Rules: Economic Union Reform and Intergovernmental Policy-Making in Australia and Canada* (Montreal and Kingston: McGill-Queen's University Press 2002).

77 For two appraisals, see Robert H. Knox, 'Economic Integration in Canada through the Agreement on Internal Trade,' and Daniel Schwanen, 'Canadian Regardless of Origin: Negative Integration and the Agreement on Internal Trade,' in Lazar, ed., *Canada: The State of the Federation 1997.*

78 Note that these developments are referred to as 'non-constitutional' in Lazar, *Canada: The State of the Federation 1997.*

79 Roger Gibbins and Katherine Harmsworth, 'Time Out: Assessing Incremental Strategies for Enhancing the Canadian Political Union,' in Cameron, ed., *The Referendum Papers*, 49–83 at 79.

80 For an account of these reforms of the federation, see Dion, *Straight Talk*, 93–102.

81 Gordon Di Giacomo, 'Who Should Train the Canadian Labour Force?' Federations: *What's New in Federalism Worldwide* 3(4) (Nov. 1993): 9–10

82 Heather Schoffield, 'Ottawa Creates Learning Body,' *Globe and Mail*, 9 Dec. 2003

83 Di Giacomo, 'Who Should Train the Canadian Labour Force?'

84 Canada. *A Framework to Improve the Social Union for Canadians* (Ottawa: 1999)

85 Anne McIlroy and Brian Laghi, 'PM Gets Social-Union Deal but Quebec Won't Sign,' *Globe and Mail*, 5 Feb. 1999

86 Harvey Lazar, 'Managing Interdependencies in the Canadian Federation: Lessons from the Social Union Framework Agreement,' in Douglas Brown and France St Hilaire, eds, *Constructive and Co-operative Federalism: A Series of Commentaries on the Council of the Federation*, no. 5 (Kingston: Institute of Intergovernmental Relations, Queen's University; Institute for Research on Public Policy, Montreal, 2003)

87 Canada, Commission on The Future of Health Care in Canada, *Final Report*, November 2002, 52–9. Romanow recommended that the Council's fourteen members be appointed by 'a consensus' of the federal, provincial, and territorial health ministers.

88 Caroline Mallan, 'Federal Health Council Launched,' *Toronto Star*, 10 Dec. 2003

89 The provincial and territorial leaders agreed to create the Council in July 2003. The Council had its first meeting in Quebec City in October 2003, and detailed plans for the Council were agreed to at Charlottetown in December 2003. See Robert Benzie, 'Premiers Meet to Create New Council of the Federation,' *Toronto Star*, 5 Dec. 2003.

90 Alain Noel, 'The End of a Model? Quebec and the Council of the Federation,' in Brown, ed., *Constructive and Co-operative Federalism?*, no. 10

91 See chapter 2, 40.

92 For some positive possibilities, see Douglas Brown, 'Getting Things Done in the Federation: Do We Need New Rules for an Old Game?' in Brown, ed., *Constructive and Co-operative Federalism?*, no. 1.

93 See Gordon Robertson, *Northern Provinces: A Mistaken Goal* (Montreal: Institute for Research on Public Policy 1985).

94 See International Work Group for Indigenous Affairs, *The Indigenous World, 2002–2003* (Copenhagen: IWGIA 2003).

95 Canada, Royal Commission on Aboriginal Peoples, *People to People, Nation to Nation: Highlights from the Royal Commission Report* (Ottawa: Minister of Supply and Services Canada 1996)

96 Minister of Indian Affairs and Northern Development, *Aboriginal Self-Government: The Government of Canada's Approach to Implementation of the Inherent Right and the Negotiation of Aboriginal Self-Government* (Ottawa: Minister of Public Works and Government Services 1995)

97 Minister of Indian Affairs and Northern Development, *Gathering Strength: Canada's Aboriginal Action Plan* (Ottawa: Minister of Public Works and Government Services 1997), 13

98 Canada, Royal Commission on Aborginal People, *Report* (Ottawa: Minister of Supply and Services 1996), vol. 2, part 1, chap. 3

99 For an influential critique of the federal government's approach by an Iroquoian scholar, see Taiaiake Alfred, *Peace, Power, Righteousness: An Indigenous Manifesto* (Toronto: Oxford University Press 1999).

100 For a full account, see Jens Dahl, Jack Hicks, and Peter Jull, eds., *Nunavut: Inuit Regain Control of Their Lands and Their Lives* (Copenhagen: International Work Group for Indigenous Affairs 2000).

101 In 1997, by a vote of 57 to 43 per cent the people of Nunavut rejected a proposal that each constituency elect one male and one female member of the legislature. See ibid, 68–75.

102 For details on land provisions of modern treaties up to 1995, see Royal Commission on Aboriginal Peoples, *Report*, vol. 2, part 2, chap. 4, app. 4A.

103 Department of Indian Affairs and Northern Development, 'Working Group Report Confirms Success of Claims Implementation in Yukon,' Media Release 1-01156, 6 June 2001

104 See Royal Commision on Aboriginal Peoples, *Report*, vol. 2, part 2, 729–32.

105 Nathan Vanderklippe, 'Deal Gives Tlicho Self-Government,' *National Post*, 26 Aug. 2003

106 Canada, Department of Indian Affairs and Northern Development, *Deh Cho First Nations Framework Agreement* (Ottawa: Minister of Supply and Services 2001). For an account, see 'Agreements, Treaties and Settlements,' *Australian Aboriginal Law Reporter* 6(3) (2001): 109–27.

107 *Nisga'a Final Agreement* (Ottawa: Federal Treaty Negotiation Office 1998)

108 See Hamar Foster, 'Honouring the Queen's Flag: A Legal and Historical Perspective on the Nisga'a Treaty,' *BC Studies* 120 (1998–9): 11–35.

109 See Christopher McKee, *Treaty Talks in British Columbia* (Vancouver: UBC Press 1996).

110 *Nisga'a Final Agreement*, chap. 11, section 20

111 For a detailed account of the negotiations, see Tom Molloy, *The World Is Our Witness: The Historic Journey of the Nisga'a Into Canada* (Toronto: Fifth House 2000).

112 *Nisga'a Final Agreement*, chap. 2, section 22

113 Molloy, *The World Is Our Witness*, 154

114 Campbell et al. v. British Columbia (1997) 153 D.L.R. (4th) 193

115 See chapter 8, 122–5.

116 R. v. Sparrow [1990] 1 S.C.R. 1075 at 1106

117 R. v. Van der Peet [1996] 2 s.c.r. 507; R. v. Gladstone [1996] 2 s.c.r. 723; R. v. Pamejewan [1996] 2 s.c.r. 821

118 On the history and nature of this obligation, see Leonard Ian Rotman, *Parallel Paths: Fiduciary Doctrine and the Crown-Native Relationship in Canada* (Toronto: University of Toronto Press 1996)

119 R. v. Badger [1996] 2 s.c.r. 771

120 Delgamuukw v. British Columbia [1997] 3 s.c.r. 1010 at 1052

121 See Peter H. Russell, 'My People's Courts as Agents of Indigenous Decolonization,' *Law in Context* 18(2) (2000): 50–61.

122 Delgamuukw v. British Columbia, paras. 263–4

123 R. v. Marshall (Marshall No. 1) [1999] 3 s.c.r. 456. For a discussion of the Marshall cases, see Thomas Issac, *Aboriginal and Treaty Rights in the Maritimes: The Marshall Decision and Beyond* (Saskatoon: Purich 2001).

124 R. v. Marshall (Marshall No. 2) [1999] 3 s.c.r. 533

125 Bill C-7, section 3(a)

126 John Borrows, *Recovering Canada: The Resurgence of Indigenous Law* (Toronto: University of Toronto Press 2002)

127 See, for instance, two books by Donald J. Savoie, *Governing from the Centre: The Concentration of Power in Canadian Politics* (Toronto: University of Toronto Press 1999), and *Breaking the Bargain: Public Servants, Ministers and Parliament* (Toronto: University of Toronto Press 2003); Jeffrey Simpson, *The Friendly Dictatorship* (Toronto: McClelland and Stewart 2001); and Luc Bernier, Keith Brownsey, and Michael Howlett, eds., *Executives Styles in Canada: Cabinet Decision-Making Structures and Practices at the Federal and Provincial Levels* (Toronto: University of Toronto Press, forthcoming).

128 See Richard Johnston, 'A Conservative Case for Electoral Reform,' *Policy Options* (July–August 2001): 7–14.

129 Ian Urquhart, 'PM, Premier Talk the Reform Talk,' Toronto *Star*, 13 Dec. 2003

130 Constitution Act, 1982, section 44

131 Canadian Charter of Rights and Freedoms, section 4(1)

132 See Eugene Forsey, *The Royal Power of Dissolution of Parliament in the British Commonwealth* (Toronto: Oxford University Press 1943).

133 Robert Ivan Martin, *The Most Dangerous Branch: How the Supreme Court of Canada Has Undermined Our Law and Our Democracy* (Montreal and Kingston: McGill-Queen's University Press 2003), at 41

134 For a balanced account and appraisal, see Kent Roach, *The Supreme*

Court on Trial: Judicial Activism or Democratic Dialogue (Toronto: Irwin Law 2001).

135 Canadian Charter of Rights and Freedoms, section 33

136 On the value of the Charter's override clause for parliamentary democracy, see Peter H. Russell, 'Standing Up for Notwithstanding,' *Alberta Law Review* 29(2) (1991): 293–309.

137 On the role of Parliament in interpreting the Charter, see Janet Hiebert, *Charter Conflicts: What Is Parliament's Role?* (Montreal and Kingston: McGill-Queen's University Press 2002).

138 See Jacob S. Ziegel, 'Merit Selection and Democratization of Appointments to the Supreme Court of Canada,' in Paul Howe and Peter Russell, eds., *Judicial Power and Canadian Democracy* (Montreal and Kingston: McGill-Queen's University Press, 2001), 131–64.

139 For a summary of these developments see 'Six Breakthroughs in Six Months!', the October 2003 newsletter of Doris Anderson, President of Fair Vote Canada, *www.fairvotecanada.org.*

140 *Renewing Democracy: Debating Electoral Reform in Canada* (Ottawa: Law Commission of Canada) 2002

141 See Carolyn Bennett, 'Three Lenses for Judging Electoral Reform,' *Policy Options* (July–August 2001): 61–5.

142 See articles by James Bolger, former New Zealand Prime Minister, and Paul Harris, executive director of New Zealand's Electoral Commission in *Policy Options* (July–August 2001), 25–36.

143 Patrick Dunleavy, Helen Margetts and Stuart Weir, *The Politics of Electoral Reform in Britain* (London: Politico's Publishing & Artillery Row 1998)

144 David Beatty, 'Making Democracy Constitutional,' *Policy Options* (July–August 2001): 50–4

145 No bill introduced in the Parliament of Canada can become law without the consent of the Senate. Money bills cannot be introduced in the Senate, and the Senate cannot veto but only delay a proposed constitutional amendment for six months.

146 David E. Smith, *The Canadian Senate in Bicameral Perspective* (Toronto: University of Toronto Press 2003)

147 Under section 24 of the Constitution Act, 1867, the Governor General is authorized to 'summon qualified Persons to the Senate.'

148 John Ibbitson, 'Abolish, rebalance or ignore the Red Chamber?' *Globe and Mail*, 23 Dec. 2003

149 For a discussion of these developments, see F.L. Morton, ed., *Law,*

Politics and the Judicial Process in Canada, 3rd ed. (Calgary: University of Calgary Press 2002), chap. 4.

150 For a recent statement of western aspirations, see Roger Gibbons and Loleen Berdahl, *Western Visions, Western Futures* (Peterborough, ON: Broadview Press 2003).

151 David M. Thomas, *Whistling Past the Graveyard: Constitutional Abeyance, Quebec and the Future of Canada* (Toronto: Oxford University Press 1997)

152 On the notion of constitutional patriotism, see Jürgen Habermas, *The Inclusion of the Other* (Cambridge: MIT Press 1996).

153 On this modification of Habermas's idea, see Omid A. Payrow Shabani, *Democracy, Power, and Legitimacy: The Critical Theory of Jürgen Habermas* (Toronto: University of Toronto Press 2003), 170.

Index

Abella, Rosalie, 180

Aboriginal peoples: alluded to, 134, 167–8, 175, 188, 242–4, 256–65, 272; attitude to Europeans toward, 4, 32, 59; Calder case, 94, 260, 316n.8; Charlottetown Accord and, 192–8, 201–4, 208–9, 211, 215–16, 224, 226, 257, 288, 292–8, 331n.1, 332n.8; Charter of Rights and, 202, 240, 256, 323n.11; Constitution Act and, 124, 130–1, 183, 262–3, 300, 322n.53, 323n.11, 332n.24; Cree, 130; de-colonization, 257–65, 272; distinct society, 147, 160, 179; 'existing' rights, 124, 131, 182, 322n.53; female, 131, 194–5, 202, 224, 297, 323n.14; House of Commons representation, 233–4, 248; Indian Act, 131, 264–5, 323n.14; inherent right to self-government, 131–2, 156, 169–70, 172, 174, 177, 180, 182–3, 194, 201–2, 211, 215–16, 224, 257–8, 288–97; Inuit, 130, 169, 192–4, 201, 258, 265; Inuvialuit, 164, 259; land claims, 94, 130, 215, 258–61, 294; Meech Lake and, 138, 140, 143, 147, 150–2; Métis, 37, 122, 169, 192–3, 201, 265, 298–9; Mohawks, 154–5; Molgat-MacGuigan reference to, 93–4; Nisga'a, 94, 260–2, 316n.8; political organization, 95, 122, 126, 169, 264–5; public support of, 123, 131, 165, 180, 182; Quebec and, 6, 51, 160, 170, 179, 232, 242–4, 332n.8; role in provincial succession, 244; Senate seats for, 179, 281; sovereignty, 257; Supreme Court and, 262–4, 284–5; treaties, 32, 114, 117, 123, 130–1, 201, 233, 258–63, 296, 322n.53; Trudeau policy change regarding, 94

Aboriginal Peoples, Royal Commission on (1991). *See* Erasmus-Dussault Commission

Acadiens, 249

Act of Union (1840), 14–16

Agreement on Internal Trade (AIT), 251, 256

Akaitcho people, 259

An Act Respecting the Future of Quebec, 232

An Act Respecting the Process for Determining the Political and Constitutional Future of Quebec, 289n.24

An Act to Establish the Commission on